UNDERSTANDING LIFE IN THE BORDERLANDS

STUDIES IN SECURITY AND INTERNATIONAL AFFAIRS

SERIES EDITORS

Gary K. Bertsch
University Professor of Public and International Affairs and Director of the Center for International Trade and Security, University of Georgia

Howard J. Wiarda
Dean Rusk Professor of International Relations and Head of the Department of International Affairs, University of Georgia

SERIES ADVISORY BOARD

Pauline H. Baker
The Fund for Peace

Eliot Cohen
Paul H. Nitze School of Advanced International Studies, Johns Hopkins University

Eric Einhorn
Center for Public Policy and Administration, University of Massachusetts, Amherst

John J. Hamre
The Center for Strategic and International Studies

Josef Joffe
Hoover Institution, Institute for International Studies, Stanford University

Lawrence J. Korb
Center for American Progress

William J. Long
Sam Nunn School of International Affairs, Georgia Institute of Technology

Jessica Tuchman Mathews
Carnegie Endowment for International Peace

Scott D. Sagan
Center for International Security and Cooperation, Stanford University

Lawrence Scheinman
Monterey Institute of International Studies, CNS-WDC

David Shambaugh
The Elliott School of International Affairs, George Washington University

Jessica Stern
John F. Kennedy School of Government, Harvard University

UNDERSTANDING LIFE IN THE BORDERLANDS

Boundaries in Depth and in Motion

EDITED BY
I. WILLIAM ZARTMAN

The University of Georgia Press
Athens and London

© 2010 by the University of Georgia Press
Athens, Georgia 30602
www.ugapress.org
All rights reserved
Designed by Walton Harris
Set in 10/14 Minion Pro by Graphic Composition, Inc.
Printed digitally in the United States of America

Library of Congress Cataloging-in-Publication Data

Zartman, I. William.
Understanding life in the borderlands : boundaries in depth and in motion / edited by I. William Zartman.
     p.   cm. — (Studies in security and international affairs)
Includes bibliographical references and index.
ISBN-13: 978-0-8203-3385-4 (hardcover : alk. paper)
ISBN-10: 0-8203-3385-9 (hardcover : alk. paper)
ISBN-13: 978-0-8203-3407-3 (pbk. : alk. paper)
ISBN-10: 0-8203-3407-3 (pbk. : alk. paper)
1. Boundaries—Social aspects. 2. Borderlands—Social aspects. I. Zartman, I. William. II. Title.
JC323.Z37 2010
306.2—dc22
2009022657

British Library Cataloging-in-Publication Data available

To CAORC and all its AORCs
For their great contribution to interdisciplinary knowledge
And intercultural understanding

CONTENTS

Acknowledgments *xi*

INTRODUCTION. Identity, Movement, and Response *1*
I. William Zartman, The Johns Hopkins University

Part I. Structures in Evolution

CHAPTER ONE. Borderland Dynamics in the Era of the Pyramid Builders in Egypt *21*
Miroslav Bárta, Charles University

CHAPTER TWO. Conflict and Control on the Ottoman-Greek Border *40*
George Gavrilis, University of Texas at Austin

CHAPTER THREE. Illicit Trade and the Emergence of Albania and Yemen *58*
Isa Blumi, Georgia State University

CHAPTER FOUR. On the Margin of Statehood? State-Society Relations in African Borderlands *85*
Judith Vorrath, Center for Security Studies, ETH Zurich

CHAPTER FIVE. Change and Non-change in the U.S.-Mexican Borderlands after NAFTA *105*
David Stea, Jamie Zech, and Melissa Gray, Texas State University–San Marcos

Part II. Identities in Transition

CHAPTER SIX. Colonialism or Conviviencia in Frankish Cyprus? *133*
James G. Schryver, University of Minnesota, Morris

CHAPTER SEVEN. Constructing National Identity in Ottoman Macedonia *160*
İpek K. Yosmaoğlu, University of Wisconsin–Madison

CHAPTER EIGHT. Pioneers and Refugees: Arabs and Jews in the Jordan River Valley   189
Rachel S. Havrelock, *University of Illinois at Chicago*

CHAPTER NINE. Who's Who across the U.S.-Mexico Border: Identities in Transition   217
Harriett Romo and Raquel R. Márquez, *University of Texas at San Antonio*

CHAPTER TEN. Looking across the Horizon   235
Shelley Feldman, *Cornell University*

CONCLUSION. Borderland Policy: Keeping Up with Change   245
I. William Zartman, *The Johns Hopkins University*

References   251

Contributors   279

Index   283

ACKNOWLEDGMENTS

CAORC is the federation of twenty-three American Overseas Research Centers located in five continents. The centers, structured as consortia of American universities, colleges, and museums, sponsor advanced research by American and host-country scholars, primarily through fellowships for pre- and postdoctoral scholars focusing on projects in the humanities and social sciences, and their work in the field is gratefully acknowledged as a basis for this project

The Borderlands Interdisciplinary Project (BLIP) began with a discussion in the Board of Directors' meeting of the Council of American Overseas Research Centers (CAORC) concerning converging research interests of scholars funded by CAORC member institutions. CAORC vice-chairman I. William Zartman, a political scientist representing "modern" studies, and CAORC Executive Committee member-at-large Kenneth Sams, a classical archaeologist, examined the list of scholars and their topics for the previous three-year period and identified three prevailing themes: gender studies, identity, and borderland studies, selecting the third as the theme of the first Interdisciplinary Project. Of the fifteen scholars originally identified in the CAORC fellowship database, seven are represented in this volume: Miroslav Bárta, Associate Professor, Charles University, Prague, funded by CAORC's Andrew W. Mellon East-Central European Fellows Program to carry out research at the Albright Institute of Archaeological Research; Isa Blumi, doctoral candidate, CAORC Multi-country Fellowship Program funded by the U.S. Department of State for residence at American Research Institute in Turkey; James G. Schryver, doctoral candidate, at the Cyprus American Archaeological Research Institute, funded by the Fulbright Program; İpek Yosmaoğlu, doctoral candidate, Princeton University, at the American School of Classical Studies at Athens, funded by the Frantz Fellowship; and Shelley Feldman, Professor, Cornell University, at the American Institute of Bangladesh Studies; George Gavrilis, doctoral candidate, Columbia University, at the American Research Institute in Turkey; and Rachel S. Havrelock, doctoral candidate, University of California, Berkeley, at the American Center of Oriental Research, Amman, the last three funded by the Department of State.

Melissa Gray, Raquel R. Márquez, Harriett Romo, David Stea, and Jamie Zech joined the project through the Mexico-North Research Network. Judith Vorrath was funded by the Swiss National Science Foundation. Their various sources of support are gratefully acknowledged by the recipients and by CAORC.

    We are all most grateful to the Council of American Overseas Research Centers, under the dynamic leadership of Dr. Mary Ellen Lane, for its broad and farsighted support for this project, the first of a series of Interdisciplinary and Inter-Center Studies. We are also deeply grateful for the skilled assistance of Isabelle Talpain-Long for her meticulous editorial work and liaison with the authors. Cecily Brewer also carefully compiled the bibliography and Joshua Scharff the index.

UNDERSTANDING LIFE IN THE BORDERLANDS

INTRODUCTION
Identity, Movement, and Response

I. William Zartman

Borders run across land but through people. On maps they appear as fine one-dimensional lines, whereas on the ground they have many dimensions. Borderlands are boundaries in depth, space around a line, the place where state meets society, and "where no one ever feels at home" (Simon 1997). They are a *terra de pas* (footlands or steplands) to Catalonians and "the third country" to Mexican Americans. In human terms, it is impossible to understand borders, and indeed the peripheral relations between the states and societies they contain—without understanding how it is to live along them. The core of that understanding, as this work shows, is found in a recognition of the distinct identity and dynamics of borderland communities and the realization that any measures to deal with specific current dynamics contain within themselves the seeds of new dynamic problems.

The various academic definitions (since academics rarely stick to one definition) all stress the effect that borders have on our lives. Borderlands are "subnational areas whose economic and social life is directly and significantly affected by proximity to an international boundary" (Hansen 1981) or, more extensively, "zones of varying widths, in which people have recognizable configurations of relationships to people inside that zone, on both sides of the borderline but within the cultural landscape of the borderlands, and, as people of the border, special relationships with other people and institutions in their respective nations and states" (Donnan and Wilson 1994, 8). This collection of case studies is an attempt to begin to understand both these areas and the interactions that occur within and across them. It is an attempt to understand *how* borders affect the groups living near them.

Borderlands are inhabited territories located on the margins of a power center, or between power centers, with *power* understood in the civilizational as well as the politico-economic sense. But like the sea at the edge of the land (and the reverse), they are continually in movement, both fast and slow, and any static depiction of the moment contains within it the elements of its change—Kokoschka in motion, to build on the image of Ernest Gellner (1983, 140). It is that dynamic quality that is the message of this collective interdisciplinary study. Borderlands need to be understood, not as places or even events, but as social processes.

There is an enormous literature on interstate boundaries as lines, and much literature on secessional territories bounded by lines. But until relatively recently there was little attempt to understand the nature of the land and people abutting on and divided by the boundary—the boundary in depth or borderlands. The collective work edited by Frederick Barth (1969) on ethnic groups and boundaries launched the field of study and led scholars to investigate the human condition in regions split by state sovereignty. The focus was above all on ways of maintaining identity under challenge from other identity groups or changing situations (Barth 1969, 127, 132). Whereas previous studies in the social sciences tended to focus on communities within states, so as to hold one variable constant, or on comparisons of different communities in different states, so as to analyze the differences, the new field of inquiry concerned transborder communities affected by a political line imposed on them. In most cases, these studies (such as the larger studies behind the individual chapters in this volume) concentrated on one locale, exploring and developing concepts on the basis of a single community; edited works (such as the present study) brought together a number of such studies to compare cases and construct concepts. But as Thomas Wilson and Hastings Donnan (1998, 5) point out, "Regardless of theoretical orientation or locale, however, most of these studies have focused on how social relations, defined in part by the state, transcend the physical limits of the state and, in so doing, transform the structure of the state at home and its relations with its neighbours."

The presence of borderlands is not dependent on the existence of a particular type of power center or state. Borderlands have existed during all times. Whenever there have been political communities so large that distinctions could be made between the power center and a periphery far enough away from it to be able to enjoy some degree of difference and autonomy, relations between center and periphery tended to be counterbalanced by relations between neighboring peripheries or by relations within the autonomous periphery. Empires both ancient and modern, cultural blocs and civilizational areas, and evolving states even from the pre-Westphalian era all have had their borderlands. The phenomenon is sharpened by the territorial state, a Western invention, established by the Romans and revived after 1648 in the Westphalian system. In the territorial state, the political boundary is imposed on the population regardless of its social structure—in a process sometimes termed "territoriality" (Winichakul 1994, 14)—and has an important influence on that structure as a result. But borderlands can also be found on the edges of a communitarian state, whose writ runs wherever its people are, not where its territorial limits end, but whose people mingle with other communitarian states' people as minorities. In the communitarian state, the social and political boundaries coincide, at least in theory, although even the purest community can contain subcommunities within it or give rise to forces that seek to define the pure community in a way offensive to another part of the same community.

The phenomenon is further heightened by the nation-state. The broadest sociopolitical structure or community is called a nation, marked most strongly by a sense of identity and more loosely by other structural and cultural characteristics. Since the rise of nationalism at the end of the eighteenth century, there is a presumed coincidence between the state and its nation, but this coincidence can run in either of two directions. Originally the presumption has been one of a nation-state, in which the pre-existence of the identitarian community defines the existence, legitimacy, and limits of the political institution. However, more recently new states have been created, usually as a result of anticolonial nationalist movements, with the need to unite a number of component traditional nations into a state nation, a new identity community that coincides with the political unit. In both directions, however, the coincidence of state and nation is a best approximate, and nowhere more approximate than at their edges, where the official presumption is quite the opposite—one of sharp distinctions with neighboring nations and states.

Borders, even political borders, have a social aspect. Social communities can exist in relation to the political border in other forms than as coterminous nation and state—as majoritarian communities that spill over as majorities into a neighboring state, as majoritarian communities that spill over as minorities into a neighboring state, as communities that exist as minorities on both sides of a border, and as minority communities that do not hang over across a political border (cf. Wilson and Donnan 1998, 14). The political border may or may not contain or correspond to a *social boundary*, defined as a "criteri[on] for determining . . . and. . . . signaling membership and exclusion, . . . for judg[ing] value and performance, . . . [and for] mark[ing] difference in behavior" (Barth 1969, 15) or a "zone of contrasting identity, rapid transition, or separation" (Tilly 2004, 3; Abbott 1995).

But not all border and transborder activities are performed by ethnic groups or other social units, whether as local minorities or as the dominant community within their state. Transborder activities and the general dynamics that they produce can be performed by socioeconomic categories, such as professions, occupations, or classes, with little sense of identity and membership in diverse communities or identity groups. Indeed, some of these activities, such as smuggling, taking refuge, or guarding borders, create their own agents and would not exist were it not for the border. Although studies may focus on one sort of group or another for analytical purposes, full reality can be a jumble of actors, understandable only as a mesh. All social life is, of course, such a mesh, but such a mixture of levels, actors, activities, and identities may be most pronounced when activated by the intrusion of the division constituted by a state boundary line. In sum, borders are not simply passive agents but can act on groups, encouraging the development of separate identities.

As a result, the rising study of borderlands has been undertaken by several disciplines. The most active has been anthropology, which claims Barth as its scoutmaster, orienting its analysis on social and cultural borders and on the bounded units' efforts to maintain their identity. Much of the anthropological work showed borderlands to be areas where the sharpness of ethnic and other cultural limits and differentiations clashed with the groups' need to interact with other groups on the other side of the dividing lines. As a result, walls and moats tend to dissolve into hills and marshes, with their own syncretic characteristics. Such understanding has come to replace the initial study of boundaries, in line or in depth, as conducted by geographers, whose focus was on the moats and walls themselves (Boggs 1940). Human geographers supplemented the work of physical geographers by broadening the notions of natural and artificial boundaries to relate to social criteria as well as topographical criteria. Political scientists have added a concern with the state as the defining agent of boundaries and of relations of authority, identity, transaction, and organization behind them; lawyers have sought to relate the line to the law (Brownlie 1979). The state, however, is not a featureless terrain, but rather a set of relationships between center and periphery, where the functional features of the latter often coincide with the physical location of borderlands. On the other hand, some borderlands are conceived by their inhabitants as proto-states, peripheries seeking to break off from the center to form their own center (with its own peripheries). All of these features have been woven through borderlands' analytical chronologies supplied by historians of specific areas, bringing to light the diachronic characteristics of world events on the fringes of states, empires, and civilizations.

The purpose of the Borderlands Interdisciplinary Project (BLIP) of the Council of American Overseas Research Centers (CAORC) is to draw out conceptual characteristics of the human condition in borderlands across enormous variations in time, in development, and in history. These characteristics involve such dimensions of life as identity, socioeconomic relations, power exercise and relations, security, and culture. While the technology of the times has its effects, it is not likely to affect the basics of these dimensions, which are at least relevantly comparable across time. Such multidimensionality of the human condition in borderlands, however, demands an equally multifaceted analytical approach, an interdisciplinarity that sets this collective enterprise apart from most other borderland studies. While the individual studies presented here have often originated in a particular discipline, the whole is broader than its parts and thereby richer, since the parts are obliged to take into account elements that are prominent in other chapters in the work. Anthropology, history, political science, religious studies, and archaeology join together in their particular contributions to the subject, and in addition several of the authors have multi- or interdisciplinary identities and points of view. The result, then, is not undisciplined but truly multidisciplinary, with different analytical approaches enriching the combined understanding by building on each other.

BORDERS AND BORDERLANDS

The nature and conditions of the borderland is affected by the nature of the border itself. The border is an artificial—that is, man-made, political—line running through the region. Borders can be sharp, clear, deep lines where the political line is reinforced by "natural" distinctions in terms of physical and human geography, that is, where populations are clearly different on either side of the line and where they are thinned out by clearly marked, less inhabitable distinctions such as natural walls and moats, mountain ridges, or water bodies. Or they can be indistinguishable on the ground, corresponding to no natural features, penetrable, uncontrolled; indeed, in the extreme, the border can be the region itself, a buffer state or neutral zone controlled by neither side and tolerated by both. Borders, according to Strassoldo, "divide and unite, bind the interior and link with the exterior, [as] barriers and junctions, walls and doors, organs of defense and attack. Frontier areas (borderlands) can be managed as to maximize either of such functions. They can be militarized, as bulwarks against neighbors, or made into areas of peaceful interchange" (Strassoldo 1989, 393). Two characteristics of the border are salient, its political nature and its depth. *Political* means its relation to the power center, the strength of the force and authority behind it, the degree of enforcement that sustains it, the will and capacity to maintain the artificial division running through a populated area. Borders can be backed by weak states, undemarcated and unadministered, or can be forcibly asserted and maintained by a strong central authority running its writ to the ends of its earth, or some condition in between these two extremes.

Depth refers to the degree of difference occurring in that area between the two sides of the border. Again, the line can be merely a political imposition, resting lightly on an undifferentiated population that largely ignores the attempt to separate their sameness, or it can correspond to pre-existing or rapidly adopted distinctions of identity, based on language, religion, culture, ethnicity, history, race, and other things that make people think themselves different from the Other. The U.S.-Canada border is not very deep; it does not divide much except customs officials and tax forms, whereas the Iron Curtain was much, much deeper, and where it was not naturally deep, as between East and West Germany, it made itself so by creating new distinctions between people on either side. Interestingly, even borders that purport to be very deep, such as the Israeli or Cypriot Green Lines, the Korean DMZ or the Kashmiri LOC, the U.S.-Mexico border, or the border between apartheid South Africa and the Front Line States, turn out to be more disruptive than separative for the borderlands and less deep than authorities might wish. The deepest boundaries are places where civilizations meet, clash, and then draw a truce, between historical, religiously backed empires.

People in borderlands are living on the edge, meeting people living on the edge on the other side of the border, in constantly—if gradually—changing relationships. These three conditions comprise the defining characteristics of borderlands—a population on the margins of power centers, traversed by a formal political boundary, living dynamic relations internally and externally (with the power center).

Introduction   [7]

But change is within something, from something to something, not unidentifiable chaos, and it is the further task of this study to identify some of these patterns. The situations that frame the dynamics of change can be expressed in three possible spatial models for social relations in borderlands: black-and-white, grey, and some intermediate types—spotty, buffered, and layered, as well as mixtures of the three (cf. Barth 1969, 19–20; Strassoldo 1989; Martinez 1994).

1. The *black-and-white* model pictures a sharp distinction between two different peoples along a clear borderline running through the borderlands, the closed border with alienated borderlands in Martinez's (1994) terms. The "different" people are self-defining; whether they are "really" (objectively) different is less important than their feeling different, although there is likely to be some objective fact on which subject feelings are based. The separation in the situation requires some sort of border, although it can be formal or informal, externally or internally drawn. In this model, borderland populations are cohesive outposts of the respective power center, inherently hostile in their transborder relations, lacking cross-border interaction, knowledge, and communication, and protected in their security and self-image by the hostility between the two power centers. The situation in contemporary Cyprus is a good example of this model, as were relations along the Iron Curtain. Images and in some periods reality along the nineteenth-century Ottoman Balkan border are also examples.

2. The *grey* model is quite opposite, with the different populations fully intermingled, whether they feel "different" or not. This is a model of integration, producing an intermediate population and culture composed of a combination of traits and people from the two sides. Borders may still exist but they are permeable, making cultures permeated too. The Tex-Mex border, Schleswig-Holstein between Germany and Denmark, and Alsace, where German and French cultures overlap, are examples marked by hybrid cultures. Balkan reality in periods of the nineteenth century and African reality in the twentieth century often took a grey form in reaction to the official black-and-white policy.

3a. The other three models fall between the two extremes. The *buffered* model is an extreme form of the grey model: a different culture is located between the two main cultures/populations to insulate them from one another, distinct in its characteristics and established for the internal or external purpose of keeping the two populations separate. Hybrid cultures have evolved, or third groups are strategically placed separating opposing power centers. Serbs placed in the Krajina by the Austrians to separate the Croats from the Ottoman Muslim populations constitute one example among many.

3b. The *spotty* model has islands of one culture/population within the other, separated by internal boundaries and living in ghettos or enclaves, but still with diverse contacts and influence across the borders. Doubtless, the surrounding culture will rub off on the islands, but they try to maintain their own integrity. Jewish ghettos in Europe and the Arab world (e.g., Morocco) and African-American populations living in segregated America are examples, although not borderland cases; Jewish settlements in Palestine are "reverse" examples, in which the "ghettos" or enclaves are implanted to displace and control the majority. The nobility of Lusignan Cyprus in the first half of the second millennium provides a softer example.

3c. Finally, the *layered* model espouses horizontal rather than vertical separations, imposing a dominant population from one culture over another of a different culture. Colonizations, especially settler colonies, are examples, as in the Maghrib between the European and the Arab world; Apartheid South Africa is a fine example, but only a borderland in the extremely symbolic sense, since it did not lie geographically between two power centers but was itself such a center. The Palestinian West Bank combines the last two into a spotty-layered model, and many other realities are in fact messy combinations of the neat types identified above.

However, despite the particular markings of the object, one characteristic overshadows and contains all of the models—the fact that borderlanders constitute an identifiable unit unto themselves, distinct from the populations further back from the line by their experiences and their identity. *This idea of a distinct population is the first message of this wide collection, and it informs all the subsequent analysis, extending to the policy implications in the final chapter.*

DYNAMICS AND REACTIONS

These models—Weber's ideal types or Barth's (1964; 1969, 20) gross simplifications—are only snapshots of a doubly dynamic reality that never stays still. At best, they refer to a side of the border or assume a symmetry that is not likely to exist. Even in the strictest approximations of the models to reality, the fit is never tight and the components never impermeable, hermetically sealed from each other, unproductive of crossings and interactions. Nor is the situation static, as the snapshot tempts us to believe. Borderlands are always in movement from here to there and within the here and there of the moment. *The second part of the thesis and novelty of this work is the identification of movement rather than any particular model as the characteristic of borderlands.* Borderland reality is a moving machine at any moment, and it changes its movements as it moves through time, in motion both synchronically and diachronically. Because of the complexity of the machine, it is tempting to revert to a picture of incomprehensible chaos, a seemingly endless number of factors locked together, describable but unordered. Instead, that movement has to be captured in identification and description by particular terms of analysis. Three dimensions need to be handled in the analysis—time, space, and activity.

Time, first. The picture of a borderland over a five-hundred-year time period will naturally be different in its detail from a picture of a decade, and the depiction of a span of time will vary from a comparative analysis of two time periods at either end of the span, just as the examination of a machine will differ from the study of a mill and that from the analysis of an industry.

Space is the second aspect in the dimensions of analysis. Borderlands involve local interactions as a primary focus, but they in turn are affected by relations with and between the power centers (generally, states) that purport to govern them, and these in their turn are affected by the larger regional or global order, often reaching directly into the local interactions. Indeed, no standard dimensions identify a borderland; they are self-defining and can even be multiply defined for portrayal or analysis, containing themselves in larger or smaller regions like Russian Matrushka dolls. Perhaps confusingly, the lessons of the analysis can vary with the focus within the same region. Is the best subject for understanding the Cerdanya valley in Catalonia (Sahlins 1989) or Catalonia itself (Douglass 1998), a neighborhood in Cyprus or Cyprus itself (Schryver 2006a), Transnistria or Moldova (Dawisha and Parrott 1997; Hopmann 2001), (Trans-)Jordan or Cis-Jordan (West Bank)? In fact, any borderland will embody characteristics of all three conditions, displaying component integrity, internal separation, and external differentiation, at the same time. While the levels of analysis in time and in focus should complement each other, they may also reveal tensions that are part of their dynamic. Since it is not only the nature but the source of the dynamics of borderlands that is sought, these analytical relationships will be important and elucidating.

A third type of variable concerns the nature of the interaction that is the focus of the analysis. While social science contains a vigorous rivalry over competing claims for decisive terms of analysis, a number of facets of life in the borderlands stand out as particularly important. On the local level, these involve various dimensions of participation such as economic production and exchange (trade), land ownership, social ownership (identity), rule, geographic location (fixed and migratory), communications (language), and security. On the national level, they involve, particularly, pressures to "modernize" (in the meaning of the times) and to centralize power; the first involves relations between the external/global level and the regional level, whereas the second is internal to the regional power centers. Hanging over all is the mythological level, the way borderlands are perceived from either side of the dividing line. While different apperceptions of the dynamics of borderland life may emphasize different terms of analysis from this list, the others need to be kept in sight to keep single factor analysis under control. However important a single term of analysis may be and how ever necessary it may be to emphasize its role to restore an analytical balance or introduce a new perspective, it is the balance and interaction among variables that provides a full understanding of the borderland dynamics. The broad range of studies in this collection represents an attempt to incorporate as many of these variables as possible.

The epistemological result of these sets of components of borderland life and analysis is a Rubic cube of interactions, complex but limited, spinning its own planes and traveling through time (there are limitations to any analogy). A number of salient variables as identified interact internally, among themselves, and between levels, to constitute a dynamic that characterizes the historic subject. However, this fluid structure only sets up the possibility of identifying some salient interactions that stand out in determining the dynamics of borderland life. *The third part of this work's thesis is that in their characteristic mobility, borderlands always prepare for the next move at the same time as they respond to the last one—not just movement, but movement in response to a particular situation, producing pressures for a future situation.* The studies collected here offer a step toward understanding these interactions. No claim can be made for universality, but only for windows that permit better-informed observation and understanding of the dynamics of life in borderlands. There are doubtless examples and perhaps universes beyond the cases presented here. But the examples, ranging over four millennia from the twentieth century BC to the twentieth century AD, show at least that the three defining characteristics—a population on the margins of power, traversed by a political boundary, living internally and externally dynamic relations—encompass an area of human activity and scientific analysis that continues across history and is therefore relevant to understanding events yet to come.

One major source of dynamics in the borderlands derives from the *evolution of power centers* controlling the borders. When a power center (state) seeks to grow, consolidate its authority, or modernize (in the understanding of the times), it is likely to harden its borders, centralize economic supplies and exchanges, inhibit local border control mechanisms and transborder cooperation, and introduce conflict between the two sides of the borderland. The result on either side is a heightened sense of differentiation and identity, an increase in migration and relocation, and a growth of nostalgia for the territorial expression of identity.

A strong power center bent on controlling its side of the borderlands is bound to send "foreign" populations to occupy its (often already populated) territory and confirm its consolidation, as the colonizers and newly formed United States did in North America and the Ottomans did in the Balkans. These populations can be military and border guards, administrators, and settlers, whose authority depends on their ability to resist assimilation (in either direction) with the local population. But the effect of such foreign implantations often works in two opposite directions—to create the very opposite of the separation and control that they were sent to achieve, and to provoke violence and resistance to imposed internal changes, as seen in late nineteenth-century Balkans and Yemen in Isa Blumi's chapter. Both violent resistance and the creation of new social categories create the seeds for heightened local identities and eventual separatism.

However, if this physical, economic, and identitarian separation is not achieved completely, as is likely, the old habits of transborder communication, the need for economic exchanges, differentiation within the unhomogenized population, and reactions against the efforts to create a black-and-white borderland are likely to produce new groups working to tie the two halves of the borderland together. These include dayworkers, smugglers and bandits, traders, indigenous minorities, and tax collectors, among others. Their activities will prompt further conflicts within the borderlands and will either be reduced if the power center is effectively consolidated or create a new type of relations within the borderlands, further weakening the state. As African states attempt to bring their writ to their borders and control permeability and profitable smuggling, they risk riling up separatist identities and troubling current acceptance of the borders, as Judith Vorrath's chapter indicates.

A weak power center will tend either to leave its borderlands alone on their own or to make compensating efforts to assert what little power is left to secure its borderlands. It may delegate security and other functions to local authorities, as along the nineteenth-century AD Ottoman borderlands, or make preemptive raids along the border to keep potential adversaries off balance, as in nineteenth-century BC Egypt, or "leap the local" and invest in international norms, symbols, and lore to tighten their weak control, as in the African continent and the Jordan valley in the twentieth century, as discussed in Rachel S. Havrelock's chapter. The Berlin Congresses of 1878—discussed by Blumi—and 1895 and the Dayton Conference of 1993, and the maps that followed them, discussed by İpek K. Yosmaoğlu, gave international legitimacy to dubious boundaries. If the opposing power center is weak too, the internal characteristics of the borderland, whether harmonious or conflictual, become dominant, local groups become salient, and functional specialization gives rise to local purveyors of products and activities that the power centers still require. If the opposing power center is strong, local autonomy in the borderland and indeed the border itself may be in danger; security means either bandwagoning with the stronger neighbor or finding a balancer from outside. A grey area between two weak power centers such as contemporary Eastern Congo or mid-nineteenth-century Texas is a vacuum that requires that the region either rise to the challenge of handling its own internal coherence and external security or call in assistance from an external protector, not too close but not too distant. A grey area between two strong power centers such as eighteenth-century Andorra or nineteenth-century Belgium is either the result of a protective pact or the preparation for an impending battlefield. The first contributes to the internal coherence of the area; the second tears it apart into union and rebel sympathizers in the border state.

Stepping down from the level of power centers, a second dynamic is triggered by sudden *attempts to impose a new boundary* on an old borderland, in the form of a ceasefire line, green line, or line of control. Typically, such a line attempts to arbitrate between competing claims from rival centers and overlapping loyalties within the borderland population and is often accompanied by a physical or virtual "national cleansing," in which populations homogenize either by taking on the newly imposed loyalties or by moving. The Israelo-Palestinian and Cyprus Green Lines, the Kashmir Line of Control, the Korean 38th Parallel corrected to the Ceasefire Line, the German Iron Curtain, the various Ottoman Balkan borders, and many others are diverse examples. The cases immediately recall that the imposed homogeneity is not only artificial but also incomplete and unstable in its attempt to construct identity and meaning. Competing with the state efforts to create new identities and their supporting social structures are the borderland peoples' efforts to overcome the line, and this competition is the basis of the new dynamic.

"Green lines" create physical and social mobilities, quite the opposite of their intent. New refugees transport their territorial identity on their backs, and refugee camps become little homelands on the wrong side of the border. Leftover islands from either side reach back in space and memory across the new line. New professions, such as middlemen for commerce and communications and smugglers of goods and people, poke holes in the border that other new professions, such as guards and administrators, try to close. The authorities seek to overcome the new artificiality of the border by giving it civilizational meaning as the end of the world, with nothing on the other side, loading it with significance that would not be necessary if the border were more natural. Pressures to soften the border only became reasons to harden it.

Against these tensions, artificially imposed borders tend to be dismantled as dramatically as they were imposed, rather than gradually eroding. The flood released when the wall is torn down, however, does not wash away its traces; just as the field of the previous borderland was hard to fence definitively, so the imprint of the wall and the differences they created are difficult to erase. The Iron Curtain is gone, but there are still Östlis from the recovered territories, just as there were Östlanders from the lost territories after World War II.

A third source of dynamics and change is found in *shifts in and interactions among horizontal divisions of class* and other stratifications that arise in the borderlands and interact across the frontier. Most writing about borderlands, beginning with the anthropological tradition and the idea of social boundaries, has been a two-dimensional analysis emphasizing the vertical or ethnic divisions and relations within society. Much less attention has been paid to a three-dimensional analysis of horizontal or class divisions within the borderlands and then to their interaction with the vertical divisions and relations; Barth (1969, 27–28) treats "stratification" as a given, like geography. But all cannot be subsumed within vertical relations; to the contrary, it is often the horizontal position that gives role and meaning to the vertical divisions. Borderlands have their own social stratification, one that typically incorporates some ethno-national elements in particular places in the strata. A three-dimension analysis is needed to comprehend change and dynamics.

Local relations in the borderlands frequently replicate in the small Barrington Moore's classic dynamic between central authority (monarchy), landowners (barons), and commercial forces, adding a fourth force of labor to replace peasantry in modern times. An additional element to complete the array of players is the military, who are particularly important actors in borderlands; regime overthrow by dissatisfied military forces stationed in the borderlands is a frequent phenomenon, as experiences from Caesar in Rome to Franco in Spain illustrate. In this schema, it is the particular alliances among forces that determine the social evolution and create particular reactions in the next round of history. Local dynamics can be quite independent of the larger national dynamics but can also be the tail that wags the national dog.

There are a number of possibilities for these dynamics. If the borderland elites or upper strata do well in relation to the power center, they can invade the capital, either to take over or to be assimilated. These were the outcomes for the Oranais in independent Algeria and the Phanariots in nineteenth-century Wallachia, respectively. Or they can stay at home, raising rivalries with the power center and eventually notions of autonomy and secession, usually because they feel they are not getting their due from the center and want to keep their own resources for themselves. This is what happened in recent times in Kurdistan, Biafra and Katanga, Slovenia and Croatia, and the Baltic States. Horizontal relations can also determine the ways in which the borderlands will swing in relation to competing—bordering—power centers. The civil war in Northern Ireland is as much a class conflict as an ethnic or religious conflict, ultimately pitting demographic against economic power to decide whose borderland the territory will be. Socioeconomic changes through development raise the power of the workers; vertical consolidation through nationalism or ethnic solidarity comes as a natural reaction to the introduction of class consciousness and warfare, although lower-class ideological leaders may then seek support from excluded ethnicities. This is what happened in Catalonia at the end of the nineteenth century (Douglass 2002, 68–73). In another aspect of the modernization process, the classical struggle between the herders and the farmers, reinforced by social boundaries separating ethnic groups dominating each occupation, can escalate into genocide in the borderlands, as in the American West, Darfur (Haaland 1969), and Kivu, among many others. In all these cases, among others, it is the interaction between vertical and horizontal divisions that provided the dynamic of sociopolitical relations within the borderland, a process of movement that could not be accounted for by one dimension of divisions alone.

CASES AND LESSONS

In an age of globalization, borderlands may seem to have gone the way of all borders, overwhelmed by the penetrating effects of transnational actions. Yet the following chapters convey two important lessons to the contrary. They tell us first that borderlands maintain their own dynamics and identities against some of both the most robust and most dissolving situations, and if these events drawn from the distant or current past are not exact replicas of the new challenges and conditions of the near or distant future, they certainly cover the gamut of possibilities in similarity to those in times to come. Then too, the following chapters show, in visions ranging from telescopic to microscopic, that seemingly stable solutions drawn up in response to a past challenge bear within them the elements of new challenges calling for new solutions—the theme of this collective effort.

The collection of analyses in the first part focuses on borderlands as the fringes of structures of power in evolution. The first moving picture, rather broad in its range, comes from the second millennium before our era, along the borders of the great—if not super—power of its time, Pharaonic Egypt. Miroslav Bárta of Charles University in Prague examines "Borderland Dynamics in the Era of the Pyramid Builders in Egypt," showing how efforts to shore up a declining power were played out on the large swath of borderlands. The borderland was part of Egyptian mythology, used physically and mythologically by the great state to define itself, much as the Ottoman state or the Soviet Union would later define themselves by their borders. Originally an interaction zone, its permeability required a fortified line when the Asiatic influx appeared. But as the state weakened, it first used a policy of preventive strike to discourage neighbors from taking advantage of its weakness. When the power center then collapsed, its structured borderlands collapsed with it, but economic, cultural, and commercial traits began to develop within the prevailing anarchy that were to define the upcoming centralized state and its borderlands in its new incarnation.

Nearly twenty centuries later, George Gavrilis of the University of Texas at Austin and Isa Blumi of Georgia State University examine borderland structures on the edges of the Ottoman Empire, another great power sliding from consolidation to decline. Gavrilis analyses "Conflict and Control on the Ottoman-Greek Border," as a new border delineation creates elements of change that undermine its own stability that it was created to maintain. Blumi compares two borderlands of the Ottoman Empire where "Illicit Trade and the Emergence of Albania and Yemen" turns measures at consolidation into causes of fractionalization. In both cases, economic activities within and across the borderlands proved untamable elements that refused to stay within their assigned bottles and so built up presses to break their containers, much as trade found its way across the Pharaonic borderlands and created its own supporting populations.

Judith Vorrath of the Center for Security Studies at ETH Zurich presents a comparative picture of African borderlands in "On the Margin of Statehood? State-Society Relations in African Borderlands," drawn from thirteen different studies of twenty-one different countries. She shows that the border location provides locals with economic opportunities, mainly associated with contraband trade as in the Ottoman borderlands but constituting a legitimate survival strategy under the conditions of weak statehood. There is a complete lack of interest on the side of borderland communities in redrawing African borders. Instead, they blunt border policing through informal arrangements with state actors that integrate them into local power structures. National identity is reinforced at the border, not despite but because of transborder interaction. Yet permeability can have negative effects on security in borderlands, which become entrance points for conflict-generating factors, generating new problems requiring new policy responses.

David Stea, Jamie Zech, and Melissa Gray of Texas State University–San Marcos evaluate the sources and impact of the North Atlantic Free Trade Agreement on the southern U.S. and northern Mexican borderland. Identity is built around the border and within the borderlands—the *chorizo*—in ways that are sovereign over the attempts of the legally sovereign states to control. Incomplete efforts to open the border more liberally while controlling the undesirable aspects of openness provide a multiplicity of contrary characteristics of "Change and Non-change along the Border after NAFTA," as the Stea, Zech, and Gray chapter illustrates.

The second part of the collection deals with identities in transition as the structures attempt to stabilize. James G. Schryver of Cornell University dissects "Colonialism or Conviviencia in Frankish Cyprus" in the fourteenth century to find a complex interweaving of cultures washing around some very deliberate attempts to assert identities within them, defying a single black-and-white or grey understanding of the island borderland. The selective porosity (or selective hermetism) of the horizontal and vertical divisions within the island were not only coincident but dynamic, shifting according to the discomforts they produced. İpek K. Yosmaoğlu of Princeton University returns to the Ottoman Balkans to throw an equally focused light on the methods of "Constructing National Identity in Ottoman Macedonia," revealing the power of totally foreign artifices such as mapmaking to freeze fluidity in identity. Again, efforts to consolidate territorial authority sharpened identities that they sought to amalgamate and separate, preparing for the next—but then unforeseen—stage of disintegration. Rachel S. Havrelock of the University of Illinois at Chicago portrays the way in which populations combined fixed geographic and fluctuating political components of their border and its hinterlands, as "Pioneers and Refugees: Arabs and Jews in the Jordan Valley." Each side has its images of the other side of both the borderland population and the area in which it lives, in both human and geographic terms, so that the borderlands overlap and differ in each other's reality and identity. As if images were territory, a shared symbol proved more contentious than separate symbols for the same object.

Harriett Romo and Raquel Márquez at University of Texas at San Antonio focus on the multiple notions of identity that borderland inhabitants carry along with them in movement, in their analysis of "Who's Who across the U.S.-Mexico Border: Identities in Transition." Black-and-white and grey models vie to present a clear picture of identitarian confusion that clearly marks an undefined borderland and carries new pressures for change and transition to an unclear next stage. Multiple identities, including borderland identity itself, express themselves through the vertical and horizontal categories.

Each chapter, in its way and across great distances of space and time, illustrates the dynamic quality of borderlands and their successively responsive nature. Shelley Feldman of Cornell University, in "Looking across the Horizon," emphasizes the importance of seeing a social process such as borderlands in its historical context and across history at the same time as lessons from the past and enlightenment of the present. Only by looking diachronically, at times rather than moments, can we see where the moments come from and go. This change is a constant feature of the globalized context in which borderlands persist. It calls for wise policy measures to avoid exacerbated problems and unprepared responses to evolving borderlands. No single policy response fits all borderland situations, as the conclusion, "Borderland Policy: Keeping Up with Change," by I. William Zartman of the Johns Hopkins University School of Advanced International Studies, emphasizes. The point is not to provide a borderlands policy, but to offer lessons from historical and contemporary experience that will help policymakers deal with the characteristically dynamic nature of the subject. The overarching lesson is that there is no model picture or "solution," but rather that the response to each situation carries with it new situations requiring new responses.

PART I

Structures in Evolution

CHAPTER ONE

Borderland Dynamics in the Era of the Pyramid Builders in Egypt

Miroslav Bárta

I set out on the road again, going northwards,
I reached the Walls of the Ruler
which were built to ward off the Asiatics and trample the Bedouin.
I crouched behind a bush out of fear
that the watch of the day standing on the battlements would see me.
I set out at night time
and when dawn came, I reached Peten.
When I raised up my heart and pulled together my limbs,
(B, 25) I heard the sound of cattle and caught sight of Asiatics.
One of their chiefs, who had been in Egypt, recognised me.
 —Sinuhe, on his crossing of the eastern border of Egypt,
 twentieth century BCE.

One may wonder what research on extinct societies can actually contribute to our current knowledge and society. The means of interaction, the seizing of prestigious goods, the performance of power, strategies of order and legitimacy, the rise and decline of the state, and the state's responses to inner crises and outer pressure, as reflected in contemporary Egyptological evidence, find many parallels in our modern world. The position and character of Egyptology has traditionally been mainly a philological one for objective historical reasons. Only over the recent two decades or so has Egyptology gained its proper place among anthropological disciplines (for an introduction see Bard 2008). Yet the reasons for contemporary relevance are obvious: the nature of the data acquired by Egyptologists has significant bearings on current, much debated issues such as the origins of premonetary economics, state formation and development, the formation of different social segments, the anatomy of afterlife conceptions, or the creation and formation of administrative and governmental structures. Last but not least, ancient Egyptians devised a genuine system of order legitimacy and status display (Baines and Yoffee 1998). For many aspects connected to the enumerated issues (and there are many more, to be sure), interaction or exploitation of neighboring lands and territories was essential.

A specific case may be made for early Egyptian state development and its attitudes toward the outside world. In this contribution I attempt to show the mechanism of mutual contacts between the ancient Egyptian state and the Levant during the third millennium BC across the borderlands between the two. The emphasis is on the transition between the third and second millennia BC when a consolidation of the second "phase" of a centralized Egyptian state took place (the so-called Middle Kingdom) (Brink and Levy 2002).[1]

We entirely lack written sources that would embrace any concept indicating that there was a notion of "border" in Egypt at that time. Yet it may have existed. In trying to understand this issue, all we have to use is contemporary archaeological evidence combined with titles of high officials of the Egyptian state and written sources. The third millennium BC undoubtedly counts as one of the most obscure periods with regard to mutual contacts between Egypt and the Levant; this study reviews the current state of research and publication from the Egyptological point of view. As shown, archaeological evidence amply demonstrates that direct or indirect interactions between Egypt and the Levant almost never ceased entirely (see Brink and Levy 2002 for an overview). A case is made that our standard concept of border and borderlands is not always suitable to describe earlier phases—or modes, if you wish—of interaction between two neighboring entities.

As for the current theme of "borders, frontiers, and borderlands," the impressions at the beginning of the chapter illustrate best the contemporary concept and, in fact, one of the earliest concepts of *border* held by the ancient Egyptians dating to the twentieth century BC. In this specific case, Sinuhe refers to the border as a single point in space, an artificial wall behind which starts foreign land and live foreign populations speaking different languages and living in a different culture (as he details later in his story). Thus the border was set as a clear-cut borderline regulating, controlling, and above all determining the modes of interaction of populations living on both sides of the barrier. Here we have a more developed understanding of a border as a political boundary identical with a social boundary. Such a strict formulation was the result of a long development starting deep in the fourth millennium BC.

The limited discussion of the issue for the period under examination makes it clear that a notion of borders must have existed. Even in the latest literature covering various aspects of ancient Egypt, this issue has been largely neglected (Helck 1977, cols. 896–97; see Redford 2001, which does not include this subject matter). The word used for *border* in ancient Egyptian language was ⟨hieroglyphs⟩ reading *taš* and determined by ⟨hieroglyph⟩, hieroglyphic sign for a stele or a boundary stone. Its earliest attestations may be found in the Old Kingdom Egypt, but never used in a clear context meaning a frontier between two neighboring countries (Hannig 2003, 1405). In most cases the word was used to express notions of field limits, limits of settlements, and delineation of administration units. In specific cases the term occurs in connection with the royal dogma, as it was the king's task to protect the borders of Egypt against evil forces of the "Chaos" and enemies that would threaten to touch the limits of the country and thus endanger its integrity. Along the same lines may be interpreted the ancient Egyptian distinction between *ta-kemet* "Black Land" and *ta-desheret* "Red Land," between the Nile valley populated by the ancient Egyptians and the surrounding deserts, empty and evil space constantly representing a threat to their civilization and symbolized by the god Seth.

Before imperial politics of the New Kingdom period that resulted in a very precise formulation of borders, the term for *border* was rather vague and not necessarily of primary importance (see Galán 1995). Our current evidence seems to support the idea that at this time the border was in most cases represented by a somewhat fuzzy stretch of territory with meager occupation controlled at different times by one or another party, depending on their actual power and temporarily limited dominance—in other words, borderlands.

Probably due to the geomorphology of the Nile valley, the ancient Egyptians did not elaborate on the proper concept of the border during the given period. The ancient Egyptian state developed within the narrow borders of the Nile valley, bordered on the east by the mountains of the Eastern Desert and the desert plateau of the Western Desert on the west. To the north was the Mediterranean Sea and to the south the First Cataract region (Baines and Málek 1980). The ancient Egyptians were well protected in all four directions, so it is no wonder that at the beginning they did not bother to set their borders precisely. Only when venturing behind these natural limits of the state did the Egyptian king leave behind inscriptions accompanied by his figure showing him smiting an enemy such as in Wadi Maghara in Sinai (Gardiner, Peet, and Černý 1952). These markings were typical for the Egyptian areas of interest, such as mining places. During most of the third millennium BC there were no impelling reasons to set precise borders. We may think of these areas as *overlapping* spaces dominated temporarily by one or another party.

In order to come closer to the issue of *border* and *frontier*, we focus on the eastern Delta in Egypt, Sinai with the so-called Ways of Horus, and the area of southern Canaan.[2] Already during the Early Bronze Age I period (EB I, 3,300–3,050 BCE) at the end of the fourth and the beginning of the third millennium BCE, a significant degree of contacts between Egypt and Canaan was attained (Ben-Tor 1992, 82, 161). The publication of cemeteries at Maadi and Wadi Digla and the settlement at Maadi located in the contemporary southern suburbs of Cairo shows that there existed a "Levantine" trade colony, an envoy of the Negev Beersheva culture in this part of Egypt. Its primary task was to facilitate mutual exchange of rare and valued products (Hoffman 1979, 200–201; Rizkana and Seeher 1989).

The exploration of Sinai in the 1980s of the twentieth century has shown clearly that local populations there, mainly transhumant tribes, maintained trade contacts with Egypt already by the end of the fourth millennium. The earliest contacts, however, are dated, according to finds of the Naqada Decorated Ware pottery, to Naqada II c-d. The cemetery sites of Nawamis such as Gebel Gunna provided sufficient evidence for this phenomenon—in several tombs faience beads, most probably from Egypt, were discovered as a part of the funerary equipment (Bar-Yossef et al. 1986, 136–37). The sites with Nawamis tombs are probably contemporary with EB I and EB II (3500–2700 BCE) sites (Oren and Gilead 1981, with a find of a Naqada II palette on p. 41, fig. 13).

It is interesting to observe that the Maadi colony disappears as soon as the unification of Upper and Lower Egypt takes place. Instead, reverse policy evolves: the first Egyptian rulers establish Egyptian trading outposts close to the Egyptian territory in Asia.

The study of the material culture of settlements in southwestern Canaan has shown that at the beginning of the third millennium there were at least seven sites with an explicitly attested Egyptian presence. In at least three places—Tel Arad, En Besor, and Tel Sakan—there existed Egyptian settlements, though they lasted no longer than one hundred years. The archaeological evidence supports the conclusion that at least some of the settlements were built on previously destroyed sites. This would lend additional credibility to the Egyptian commemorative palettes showing the subjugation of foreign cities with typical square-shaped bastion fortification walls, nonexistent in Egypt. If we look, for example, at the "city palette," we can see that seven cities or fortifications are being destroyed by the personified forces of the Egyptian king, although this and similar monuments can only be interpreted symbolically at best (Schulz and Seidel 1998, 28, fig. 35).

One of the most prominent of these sites seems to be En Besor, where remains of an Egyptian settlement were identified in Layer III. Probably the most important finds are the lumps of clay with Egyptian-style seal impressions. Originally these were thought to be seal impressions originating directly from Egypt, sealing items that were imported here from Egypt to provide for the Egyptian colony. Petrographic analysis of these bullae has shown, however, that these were made locally. In addition to this, the inferior quality of the imprints of the seals indicates that the seals were also made locally. All this and the close association with the central, Egyptian-style administrative building seems to indicate that the seals were used for the registration and storage of local items that were supposed to be further distributed to local centers (Brandl 1992). In the meantime, similar sealings also have been found in Gezer and quite recently in Nahal Tillah.

The case study by B. Brandl provides additional support to the above conclusion. He identified about a thousand vessels of Egyptian provenience that were distributed in nine levels of EB I strata in En Besor. The petrographic analysis of the pottery has made it possible to discern three assemblages of pottery: local Canaanite pottery, imported Egyptian pottery, and Egyptian-style pottery that seems to have been made locally by the Egyptian potters there. The same tripartite division was noted with regard to the flint industry (Ben-Tor 1991, 5–6).

From the above evidence it seems clear that during the EB I period there are indications of several, relatively independent Egyptian settlements in south Canaan, concentrated in the southern Shephelal and the western Negev. The locally based Egyptian population equaled several hundred inhabitants, and its subsistence was based on agricultural products such as honey, wine, bitumen, oil, and various resins. These products, de facto, also represent the chief components of the Egyptian imports. The Canaanite imports in Egypt during this period are concentrated mainly in the Delta sites. Nevertheless, a large concentration of luxury vessels was also found in a predynastic cemetery at Abydos located in Upper Egypt, where, for instance, in tomb Uj about seven hundred vessels were found with wine residues (Hartung, Exner, Porat, and Goren 2001).

During the First Dynasty, it is primarily the so-called Abydos Ware that became popular as tomb equipment, as attested from the cemeteries in Saqqara, Tarkhan, Lahun, and Abydos. This pottery, produced in the area to the west of the Dead Sea, is represented mainly by small jugs and juglets covered with a burnished red slip and some with a painted decoration limited to the upper part of the vessels and composed mainly of triangles, dots, arches, and semicircles painted red. Originally the pottery contained scented oils, medicines, and cosmetics. It seems to have left the Egyptian scene during the reign of the last pharaoh of the First Dynasty, Qaa.

The settlement evidence comprising elements of Egyptian culture was expanded in 1994 by the discovery of a purely Egyptian-style tomb of the stairway type in Nahal Tillah dated to the EB IB period. It contained an adult female burial, lying on her left side, facing southeast (Levy et al. 1997, 14–16, figs. 12–14). This would be the first attestation of the Egyptian burial practices outside, at least from our view, the borders of what constituted the territory of the Egyptian state at that period. The best explanation, however, is that the local elite emulated Egyptian burial practice of the day to gain power and status within their own local community.

The reasons for the disappearance of Egyptian elements in settlements in the area of southern Canaan during the second half of the First Dynasty seem to be unclear. However, we can make some guesses based on indirect evidence. The first reason would be the appearance of intensive urbanism in Canaan and the fact that the area settled by the Egyptians became a zone of interest for the newly emerging city states that could use their power to rule over these territories. In fact, the analysis of the geographical expansion of the EB I and EB II settlements shows clearly that during the EB I the majority of settlements concentrated in the northern part of Israel's coastal plain, whereas during the EB II the center of the settlement pattern moves southward (Gophna and Portugali 1988, 11–28, esp. 2–3 and figs. 2–3). Additional evidence supporting this hypothesis is dated to the reign of Den. This monument shows Den smiting an Asiatic enemy. The caption reads "first time of smiting the East." This may be another indication of tensions between Egypt and Canaan.

Another reason for the disappearance of Egyptian elements might have been the internal political crisis of the Egyptian state, starting from the latter half of the First Dynasty onward. It is probably not by chance that the first explicit attestations of the Egyptian interest and presence in Sinai, in Wadi Maghara, date to the early Third Dynasty, to the reigns of Djoser and Sekhemkhet. The Egyptian interest and exploitation of Sinai lasted for most of the Old Kingdom period (Mumford and Parcak 2004, 83–116). At exactly the same time in Egypt, we witness the emergence of monumental royal architecture, funeral monuments in stone as exemplified by the first step pyramid of Egypt built by Djoser, a clear mark of the increasing power and wealth of the Egyptian ruler.

The borderland between Egypt and Levant existed during this period in the zone between modern cities of El-Arish and Gaza. According to recent investigations by Y. Yekutieli, it is probable that approximately halfway between the Delta and southwestern Canaan there was an Egyptian-fortified site of a military nature, given the extremely high concentration of transversal stone arrow points. We can be quite sure that there were no other significantly large settlement centers, since the carrying capacity of this strip of land, as calculated by Yekutieli, would have enabled it to support only about 5,500 people, 38,000 sheep, 2,450 donkeys, and 2,450 heads of cattle at maximum, or their equivalents. This site indicates that already at this time there was not only lively trade connecting Egypt, Sinai, and southern Canaan but also a need to protect this land (Yekutieli 1998). Based on later models in the same area, we may presume that this was a typical borderland where a centrally located Egyptian garrison shared the space and resources with local transhumant Bedouin communities, occupying the region together and interacting in such a manner that control was not usurped by one party and that mutual cooperation was common (Oren 1987).

Simultaneously, there is clear evidence for an apparent intensification of trade relations with the Lebanese coastal city of Byblos from the Fourth Dynasty onward (Marcus 1998, 53). Contacts between Egypt and Byblos existed from the predynastic period on; nevertheless, it is only from the beginning of the Fourth Dynasty that the marine trade between Egypt and Byblos assumes bolder contours and gains in intensity. The main advantage of these maritime contacts was that they enabled easy and quick transportation of bulk commodities and items in large quantities—above all, very valuable cedar wood to Egypt. On the other side, it is rather unconvincing, given the present evidence, to suppose that the Egyptian settlements in Canaan disappeared at the time when it was possible to sail directly from the Delta to Byblos. The firm connection between Egypt and Byblos began much later (Brandl 1992, 448). This was probably one of the reasons why the zone between Egypt and the Levant, being of secondary importance, did not develop more fully, as was the case later, at the beginning of the second millennium BCE.

Another zone of interaction between Egypt and the Levant is the Sinai Peninsula. For the EB II (3050–2700 BC) period, the major body of our evidence about the situation in the southern Sinai Peninsula is represented by approximately forty connected seasonal Arad settlements, concentrated in two areas: the oasis of Wadi Feiran and the Watyia Pass. Six of these sites have been excavated so far, and there may be some evidence in archaeological records that connect them in terms of economy and trade. For instance, it is the discovery of lumps of bitumen that connects Arad, levels III and II, and the Dead Sea with these sites in Sinai (Beith Arieh 1974, 1981). Given the context of the finds including copper implements, probably produced locally, smelting molds, and copper pellets, it is probable that a significant number of these communities were engaged in the copper industry, if not directly in copper ore procurement from the sites at Wadi Riqita. These sites were closely related to Arad in terms of pottery, flint industry, seashell jewelry, the internal structure of the houses, and so forth. Even the arkose sand, used as a temper for the pottery found both in Arad and in South Sinai sites, is attested to in the area of Eilat and was apparently transported up to Arad to be used in the pottery matrix there (Amiran, Beit Arieh, and Glass 1973, 193–97). Egyptian sites such as Tell el-Farain (Buto) and Tell Ibrahim el-Awad in the eastern Delta would undoubtedly have been terminal sites in Egypt for caravans trading copper from the Sinai Peninsula. Needless to say, so far there is no indication that these caravans were crossing any officially established and maintained border line.

Despite intensive commercial traffic between Egypt and Byblos via sea, some authors, such as E. Marcus, suppose that trade contacts between Egypt and Canaan continued during the Old Kingdom (ca. 2,700–2,200 BCE). This trade was mediated by Palestinian coastal cities that have not been excavated yet. The main objection is obvious: there is no proof of this whatsoever. Based on the current evidence, one may say that the traditional contacts were maintained, if only in a limited extent. It seems that the prevalent attitude of most of the Old Kingdom rulers was to limit themselves to the protection of the eastern border and the Ways of Horus that provided one of the access routes for Sinai. In support of this argument, one can bring some epigraphic evidence from tombs in Giza and Abusir dated to the twenty-fifth and twenty-fourth centuries BCE showing that there were overseers of the Ways of Horus at this time, such as a Fifth Dynasty official Hekenkhenenu buried in Giza (Jones 2000, 83, no. 357). Another official Kaaper served at several garrisons as a military scribe at the beginning of the Fifth Dynasty. And it is very probable that these garrisons were stationed along the Ways of Horus. This seems to indicate that the area of southern Canaan became the sphere of dominance of local city states and that the Egyptians considered it necessary to fortify the eastern border to demarcate their own spheres of interest and to secure the entrance route leading to the resources of the southern Sinai exploited from the Third Dynasty onward. In addition, Kaaper was not only "Scribe of the army of the king in Wenet, Serer, Tepa, Ida," but also in the "Terraces of Turquoise and the Western and Eastern foreign lands" (Fischer 1959, 260–65; Fischer 1963, 50; Helck 1962, 16–17; Jones 2000, 854–55, nos. 3120–25; Bárta 2001).

The evidence for the sites at Wenet, Serer, Tepa, and Ida is extremely sparse during the given period, and it is probably of some importance that with only one exception the sites are not attested to in later periods (Ahituv 1984). This corroborates their supposed character: fortified military campsites with Egyptian troops situated on or behind the northeastern Egyptian border. Moreover, it seems that their existence did not last long enough to let them be called permanent stations. This assumption may be corroborated by the fact that all enumerated toponyms associated with Kaaper were mentioned in such a context that allows one to suppose these are names of sites located in "foreign" countries. It is equally possible that these sites were surrounded by camps of semi-nomadic local populations who provided some economic support for the Egyptian mining caravans to Sinai, as was the case with the New Kingdom forts on the Ways of Horus (Oren 1987, 69–119). The fact is that after the EB I period, there are no more Egyptian settlements or any other proof of Egyptian presence in southern Canaan (Brandl 1992, 441–77; Marcus 1998, 17–34). The only likely option is to seek the location of Wenet, Serer, Tepa, and Ida along the north Sinai coastal line connecting the Egyptian eastern Delta with western Asia. The fact that the Wadi Maghara quarries (Terraces of Turquoise) are referred to by Kaaper in this connection makes this reconstruction even more plausible (Mumford 1999, 875–78). Finally, one is tempted to conclude that given Kaaper's two more unusual titles—"herdsman of dappled cattle" and "scribe of the pasture land(s) of the dappled cattle," he was also involved with the administration of the pasture lands, probably located in the eastern Delta.

The upkeep of these "watch posts" was occasionally combined with preventive military encroachments into south Canaan such as detailed in a report of Weni and the fortress siege scenes in tombs at Saqqara and Deshasheh (McFarlane 2003, pl. 48; Kanawati and McFarlane 1993, pls. 26–27; for Weni's account see Strudwick 2005, 352–57).

It is not without interest that most of the reports of military campaigns and the scenes of destruction of towns are dated to the late Fifth and the early Sixth Dynasty, that is, the final stage of the Old Kingdom. It is generally held that already during this period Egypt was losing some of its power and dominance. These military campaigns may therefore paradoxically indicate the growing instability and political and economic weakness of the declining Egyptian state, as a "power display" converted into military attacks on the close neighbors.

Besides this sporadic evidence, we have no other indication of direct trade contacts between Egypt and south Canaan during the Old Kingdom period. During this period, the major role was undoubtedly played by the maritime trade with Byblos. If we therefore automatically posit that the raison d'être of the city states of southern Canaan was the demand by the Egyptian market, we have to suppose a mediator capable of realizing the transactions. This is probable mainly because of the fact there is no indication whatsoever of direct trade of any sort or communication between Egypt and Canaan. It seems that this mediator could have been Byblos. This would also explain the occurrence of Canaanite EB III metallic ware in Egyptian tombs of the Fourth and Fifth Dynasty officials (Helck 1962). These vessels were suitable for ship transport but would pose problems if transported on donkeys.

What continued were expeditions to Sinai with the task of bringing rough copper ore and turquoise. The recent investigations of G. Mumford and S. Parchak into the western coast of Sinai have shed new light on this issue. The excavation of a previously known building has shown that it was a fortress built by the Egyptian army. Its purpose was simple: to provide protection for Egyptian mining expeditions. It is also feasible that this was the last outreach of what the Egyptians considered to be their territory (Mumford 2006).

Following the collapse of the Old Kingdom during the twenty-second century BCE we are faced with correspondingly significant changes in the settlement area of southern Canaan (Dever 1985b). During this period we can observe the virtually complete disappearance of cities and large settled areas in northern and central Palestine and the appearance of small settlements in Transjordan, the Jordan valley, and Negev and the Sinai with a preference for herding, dry farming, and stock breeding. This subsistence economy is also confirmed by the animal offerings in EB IV tombs, consisting mainly of goats and sheep (Greenhut 1995, 29). This shift in the economy was probably the result of a combination of factors such as the warming and drying of the climate and the disappearance of what was perhaps a too tight trade relationship with the vanishing Old Kingdom period in Egypt and thus the disappearance of rich market opportunities (Esse 1989).

Regardless, there is no indication whatsoever that a change in the subsistence pattern would have been a response to some natural calamity such as an epidemic. It has been estimated that the EB III population consisted of about 100,000–150,000 inhabitants, and the density of EB IV sites throughout the region seems to correspond with this number. What has changed basically, however, was the borderland region. In contrast to the Old Kingdom period when there existed an interaction zone situated between modern El Arish and Gaza, now the eastern borderland of Egypt disappeared and could be easily penetrated and trespassed upon by the Bedouin tribes from the southern Levant.

There are several settlements that attest to the nature of the period. One of the principal ones is the site of Beer Resisim in Negev. This was a one-period occupation site consisting of several dozen circular sleeping huts made of stone, measuring two to four meters in diameter, roofed with timber and chalk slabs and plaster construction usually resting on a central pillar. The finds attest to some dry farming of wheat or barley, whereas copper ingots may indicate long-distance trade, as was the case with the EB I and II sites. Each cluster of circular huts of both sleeping and other character was grouped around an open court. It seems that each cluster might have been assigned to a single family unit consisting of one male, one to three females, and two to six children. The whole population residing in Beer Resisim may be estimated as being about forty to eighty persons (Dever 1985a).

The sites excavated in Gebel Qaaqir in Hebron Hills and several sites in Transjordan such as Khaled Iskander and Bab ed-Dhra show clearly that there was no marked break or even discontinuity during the transition of EB III and EB IV. This was proved mainly by the unbroken pottery sequence. Another indication for a continuum in terms of the population and its cultural traits is represented by the EB IV cemeteries. The manifold typology of individual tomb types shows also some Syrian influence during this period (Greenhut 1995). Finally, there is a clearly discernible tumuli tradition in Sinai and Negev continuing, as mentioned already, in EB IV and probably following in the tradition of the EB I–II tumuli cemeteries (Greenhut 1995, 37). This shows that the political, economic, and administrative decline in Egypt was not a general tendency in the whole Levant.

We therefore have to ask about the nature of any contacts between Egypt and Canaan. The 1996 study by M. Haiman has indicated that there might have been a relatively intensive copper trade between Egypt and south Canaan undertaken by the Asiatic population precisely during this period. His conclusions were based on permanent and temporary sites discovered in the Negev. The distribution pattern of these sites shows that most of the temporary sites were connected with the permanent ones. Moreover, they were situated in a belt thirty kilometers wide to the south of the permanent sites. They densely covered the area extending from the southwest of the Dead Sea westward to the Nile Delta along the line of the northern Sinai seashore. More importantly, the whole area is characterized by the same uniform culture traits of the pottery S group. The lack of central authority in Egypt and absence of frontier guards made such an enterprise even more easy.

One of the most instructive sites was Har Yaroham. On this site, almost 30 percent of Stratum C was occupied by industrial activity. About thirty installations and magazines were found with a significantly large number of hammer stones, mortars, and grinding stones. Along with these features, the site contained many stone installations with ashes and other traces of intensive burning and a large number of copper chips and fragments of copper ingots everywhere on the site. Altogether nineteen ingots were found in area C. Much similar evidence was discovered at sites such as En Ziq, Har Zayyad, and Mashabbe Sade. This means that a significant number of permanent sites in Negev contained these traces of copper hammering and transportation activities. Since the temporary sites consisted mainly of single huts suitable only for sleeping, it is certainly possible that they were used by the caravan members during their travel to or from Egypt.

According to Heiman, it is possible that the EB IV fortified city of Khirbet Iskander (where remains of copper working were also found), Iktanu, Bab ed Dhra, Aroer, Tell el-Hayat, Ader, Tell Um Hammad, and other cities may have been organizing the whole copper caravan trade, and the copper may have originated from Wadi Faynan to the south (Richard 1987, 241–46). In this light, it is probably correct to speak of the EB IV period in terms of urban regression, rather than of a nomadic interlude. It seems that the center of development during the EB IV period was to the east of the Jordan River. The red slipped and burnished pottery of the EB III period—platters, bowls, jars, jugs—also demonstrates the same continuity. However, until now there has been no EB IV/FIP site in the eastern Delta that would confirm the supposed copper trade.

The Egyptians had a number of synonyms for the Bedouin that are also indicative of their concept of neighbors based on their different customs and subsistence. Ever since Middle Kingdom times, they had named the Asiatics after several of their characteristic features, such as "people with the knot on their shoulder," since they tied their clothes with a knot on the shoulder, "the pig-tailed ones," for those who tied their hair into a pigtail, or "kilt-wearers," for those who wore that type of garment. Often they were called the "bowmen" or "people of the bow," after their predominant weapon. Geographical classification perhaps also played its role, since the Bedouin living beyond the Sinai were referred to as "those who dwell on the sand." "The sand" in this case referred to the Sinai Peninsula, and in the third millennium BC, this name was frequently used for any population from Syria-Palestine. The nomads living immediately beyond the eastern border of Egypt were also called "Easterners."

The penetration of the Bedouin, that is, of Asiatics, into Egyptian territory is also mentioned by the Instructions for King Merikare, which dates from the Heracleopolitan period (twenty-first century BCE, rule of Kheti III). It is also one of the earliest unequivocal references to the borders of Egypt. The account directly describes the expelling of the Asiatics from Egypt and the constructions of strongholds to defend Egypt against the invasion form the east:

But while I lived and was here,
the bowmen were inside the fortress, which was open.
I drove them out of it
and I made the Northern land defeat them.
I captured their people,
I seized all their nourishment
and killed . . .
so that Asiatics detest Egypt now.
Do not worry about it:
the Asiatic is like a crocodile on the bank,
he attacks on a barren road,
but does not make assault on the place of a populous city.

Dig a ditch (in Wadi Tumilat) . . .
and fill one of its halves with water all the way to the Bitter Lakes:
it will be a defense against the bowmen.
The strongholds there are prepared for the fight, the soldiers are numerous
and the subjects know how to use weapons.

The presence of nomads in Egypt was not an uncommon phenomenon, and even Sinuhe mentions in his account that he met a sheikh who had visited Egypt, perhaps in the time of the reign of Amenmehat I. Starting with the twentieth century BCE the influx of the Bedouin is controlled and limited one more time. This form of contact between the two cultures is confirmed by the famous scene from the tomb of Khnumhotep II at Beni Hassan, which depicts the Bedouin chief Abishay with his family. This scene comes from the sixth year of Senusret II and shows the Bedouin chief together with his retinue, comprising eight men, four women, three children, and donkeys (the accompanying text states that altogether there should be thirty-seven persons in the caravan), as they pay homage to the tomb owner, bringing him powder for eye paint as a present. In no way does it depict wretched Bedouin pleading for permission to pasture their cattle on Egyptian territory. The possibility of a trade expedition is also unlikely, since the number of people is rather high for a trade caravan and would make its sustenance burdensome. The group includes women and children, who usually did not take part in trade expeditions. Furthermore, the commodity brought by the Asiatics is black cosmetic powder, which was commonly exploited in Egypt or in the Eastern Desert. These two facts exclude the interpretation of the scene as one depicting a trade caravan from Asia. The accompanying inscriptions over the scene state: "The arrival for the bringing of black powder" and "he [i.e., Abishay] brings thirty-six Asiatics." These labels are complemented by a document held in the hand of "the scribe of the royal documents" Neferhetep, who ushers the entire group led by Abishay into Khnumhotep II's presence. The text of the document runs as follows: "Year 6 under the Majesty of Horus Leader of the Two Lands, King Khakheperra: list of the Asiatics, whom the son of the monarch Khnumhotep brings because of black eye powder: Asiatics from Shu: 37" (Newberry 1893, pls. 31 and 32 for the scene and the hieroglyphic text).

Besides Neferhetep, the scene includes another royal official, the overseer of hunters, Kheti, who may have accompanied the Asiatics on their journey through Egypt all the way to Beni Hassan. The circumstances seem to indicate that the scene depicts Asiatics, who have come to Egypt in order to settle there and take part in the mining of black eye powder. The act of accepting the nomads takes place under the cautious supervision of royal deputies, the scribe of the royal documents and the overseer of hunters, Neferhetep and Kheti. This shows that an intensive penetration of Egypt from the east continued in a limited and controlled way during the Middle Kingdom (see also below).

The evidence from the early Twelfth Dynasty suggests that southern Canaan was considered only as a potential enemy with some fortresses that were necessary to subjugate and as a source of manpower. Egypt's number one economic connection remained Byblos. It is interesting to note that whereas during the reign of Senusret I Canaan is described as a land of the Bedouin, Amenemhat II considers it important in his Annals to mention that he subjugated two fortresses in Canaan (given the booty listed, quite small ones) and that the last military campaign dates to the reign of Senusret III, probably against Sekhem. As urbanism developed during the latter half of MB IIA and reached its peak in the seventeenth century BC in southern Canaan in a power formation centering on Sharuhen (Oren 1997), one gets the impression that as soon as there were numerous city states the Egyptians were no longer willing to take their chances venturing into Canaan. It seems likely that they preferred to renew and re-establish borders in Nubia as Senusret III did or to intensify trade with Byblos and focus on expeditions to Sinai—from the reign of Amenemhat III at least forty-nine inscriptions are known from Serabit el-Khadim. Indeed, it is striking that from the reigns of the wealthiest pharaohs, no true military campaigns against the Asiatics are known. Thus from the diachronic perusal of the Middle Kingdom written sources a picture emerges with different priorities during different periods.

Simultaneously, there is more evidence for the presence of the Asiatics in Egypt than the Beni Hassan painting would suggest. It is above all the stratigraphy of Tell el-Dabba that provides a cornerstone for any attempt to classify the available evidence diachronically. The recent study by E. Czerny shows that the early Middle Kingdom "Asiatic" artifacts are limited to layer F/1, Str. e. In this layer, together with Egyptian pottery, also discovered were handmade and coarsely fired cooking pots of Palestinian MB I, attesting to the behavioral interface with a probable tradelike pattern with the Canaanite and Sinai nomads during this time. Even the petrographic composition of several sherds has shown that some of the clays are non-Egyptian and supposedly originate from south Sinai or the area of Arad (Czerny 1999, 110–12). It is possible that these sherds were left behind by nomads grazing their herds in the Delta, a possibility alluded to also in the story of Sinuhet.

Moreover, it has convincingly been shown by Czerny that during the Middle Kingdom it was probably the Pelusiac branch of the Nile that represented the eastern border of Egypt (Czerny 1999, 14–15). Tell el-Dabba at this time played a vital role as one of the important sites on the Ways of Horus from Palestine to Egypt, and it may be even interpreted as one of the border sites. Generally speaking, we can observe that most of the MB II sites in the Delta are concentrated along the eastern bank of the Pelusiac branch of the Nile or along the two principal communication routes: Wadi Tumilat and the Ways of Horus. The MB IIA sites are concentrated in the northern half of the eastern Delta whereas MB IIB sites extend further to the south, such as to Tell el-Yahudia and Inshas.

The initial settlement (Stratum F/1) of the Canaanites in Tell el-Dabba goes back to the late Twelfth Dynasty, to the reign of Senusret III, who seems to be the first ruler to pay more attention to this settlement. The settlement exemplifies architecture that is foreign in Egypt—the "Mittelsaal-" and "Breitraumhäuser." This settlement also included cemeteries attached to the houses. The tombs are constructed in a purely Egyptian manner. It is interesting that about half of the male burials contained weapons, a clear indication that these settlers were soldiers in the military service of the Egyptian king. Clearly, they were also engaged in other activities, such as participation in expeditions to Sinai, organized presumably from Tell el-Dabba. The inscriptions from Wadi Maghara clearly attest to this fact, and most of them are dated to the reign of Amenemhat III. They clearly show that Asiatic soldiers were accompanying these expeditions. Some of the expeditions were even headed by an Asiatic, as in the case of Imeni. Moreover, it seems that their camps in the Sinai were supplied by Asiatic tribes—for example, Khebded, who was the brother of the prince of Retjenu.

The magisterial work of Do. Arnold on the Middle Kingdom pottery from the pyramid necropolis at Lisht has shown clearly that imports of Canaanite pottery in Egypt first occur only during the second half of the Middle Kingdom, starting with the reigns of Senusret III and Amenemhat III. The same result was reached by the EES excavation at Kom el-Rabia at Memphis (Arnold, Arnold, and Allen 1995, 13–32; Bourriau 1990, 19).

Another vital source of our information about Canaan during the Middle Kingdom are several groups of Egyptian Execration texts dated from 1,850–1,750 BC designed to defeat on a magical level the forces hostile to the pharaoh and Egypt. These are coming from the Nubian site of Mirgissa (dated as 1,900–1,850 BC), Berlin group (Senusret III or early Amenemhat III) and Saqqara/Brussels group (about twenty to forty years later than the Berlin group). Even though these texts were purely magical, and their structure and composition were to a high degree a matter of formalism, we can discern vital differences and shifts in their factual information. In the earlier texts, the Mirgissa and Berlin groups, several chiefs are connected with one toponym, in six cases no less than three. In the Brussels group, each place is connected just with one ruler. In the Mirgissa texts four toponyms refer to coastal sites: Byblos, Ulazza, and probably Anaki and Mugar, one in Transjordan and none in central Palestine. The Berlin group refers to coastal toponyms—Arkata, Ashkelon, Ulazza, and Byblos, in three cases to maritime sites—Anaki, Mugar, and Sapa. The picture that emerges is that of a rural country with several city states along the coast. The Brussels group, on the other hand, being about two generations later, seems to be much more logically structured, and in principle, the listing of sites follows the main communication roads. This group quotes about four times more sites than the Berlin group, is well organized, and seems to reflect a change in the geopolitical situation in the region, with much settlement inland and intensive reurbanization of the territory. How are we to explain this phenomenon? Is it just by chance that the texts look as they do? Despite their much disputed historical significance or irrelevance, given the progress in chronology, we may claim, based on archaeological evidence, that they reflect the actual development in Canaan.

We can see that during the Middle Kingdom the concept of border as a clear-cut line developed, mainly because of political reasons and out of the historical experience of the Old Kingdom period. The need to stop the influx of pastoral communities and to codify the result of reunification of the state that was penetrated by the foreign elements (Merikare says: "the borders are firm, the garrisons valiant") led to a new concept of the border. This new de facto approach established frontiers of the territory permanently occupied and exploited by an Egyptian population.

CONCLUSION

During the existence and evolution of ancient Egyptian state(s), the concept of a *border* and *borderlands* underwent substantial development. At the beginning the border was a zone of interaction dominated temporarily by one or another party; later on it became an area with a clear-cut political delineation separating two entirely different populations. At the beginning there was a concept of a political border not identical with ethnic/population boundaries; later on it became a boundary that clearly separated different populations and cultures. The reasons for this development may be seen in the history of the First Intermediate Period when Egypt was invaded by Asiatic nomadic tribes on the northeast. This historical experience became part of the state formation ideology at the beginning of the Middle Kingdom (twentieth century BCE), and part of the state's policy materialized in the creation of an artificial border—"Wall of the Ruler" started by Kheti III. Apparently, the new concept of border also led to the creation of a specific type of construction, fortresses, with permanent semimilitary units, otherwise not attested to in the Nile valley. Quite clearly, these complexes develop from the Middle Kingdom onward and not only on the northeastern border but also in Nubia (Vogel 2004). This shows a marked contrast with the previous development during the third millennium BCE when only small fortified posts were built as witnessed by inscriptions of Kaaper and Hekenhenenu and later on by Mumford's discovery in Sinai. Their function was also different—in most cases to provide temporarily limited protection to short-term Egyptian expeditions pursuing economic interests of the state.

In response to the introductory essay in this book, I would like to emphasize another important issue: namely the way the borderlands are being reflected in the official ideology and the contrast arising from the comparison with our everyday record. In the specific case of Old Kingdom Egypt what seems to emerge is a picture of a strong primary state reflected in the official record on one hand and a society losing the wealth of its privileges as they are being taken over, for the lack of agency, by their borderland partners.

What we actually have here are the black-and-white model and the grey model in full swing, interacting according to the temporary location of the power base. In a diachronic perspective, however, we see that there is something deeper underlying both models. It is a commonly shared necessity to account for the basic needs resulting from the different political organization of the mutually dependent entities, be it a grazing-herding activity of the nomads in the Egyptian Delta (archaeologically and historically almost invisible during the Old Kingdom and apparent during the First Intermediate Period) or copper trade organized by the Egyptian state, taken over during the First Intermediate Period by the Bedouin from Palestine.

Was there any clear-cut frontier concept during the period under discussion? Given the present evidence, it is fair to say no—at least prior to the twentieth century BC. So far there is no archaeological evidence that would support this notion. Perhaps even more important is that this situation is likely to change in the future. Surely, the ancient Egyptian state had to define its limits rather clearly. This situation was made easier by the existence of clear geographic limits on the east and west (Eastern and Western Desert) and the north (the Mediterranean). To the northeast, the clear end of its territory probably marked the easternmost Pelusiac branch of the Nile. The stretch of land to the east provided the only overland bridge to the Middle East and was mainly part of the political existence under its control as well. Yet further to the east, in southern Canaan, there was a political "vacuum" filled with temporarily limited city states (as indicated by the execration texts). This fact may be self-explanatory: it was technically almost impossible to define a proper frontier of the Egyptian state against a borderland of intermittent city states. Only in the twentieth century BC do we find evidence for a creation of Egyptian border concept for the protection of the country's integrity against the Bedouin. Despite this "technical" difference, the ways of the ancient Egyptian state's interaction with its neighbors and that interactive effect on the existence and nature of the borderlands may be worth further exploration.

Notes

I am indebted to Professor William Zartman and the director of the ASOR office in Washington, D.C., Mary Ellen Lane, for inviting me to take part in the project launched in 2004. The principal research for this article was carried out during my fellowship at the Albright Institute, Jerusalem, in 2001, kindly granted by the A. W. Mellon Foundation.

Note to epigraph: Sinuhe's remarks were made on his crossing of the eastern border of Egypt in the twentieth century BCE (Bárta 2003, 14).

1. For a reliable and up-to-date introduction to the history of ancient Egypt see Shaw (2000). For the sake of convenience, absolute dates used in the Shaw book are also used in this contribution.

2. Canaan is the region including the modern political entities of Israel, the Palestinian Territories, Lebanon, and adjoining coastal lands and parts of Jordan, Egypt, and Syria.

CHAPTER TWO

Conflict and Control on the Ottoman-Greek Border

George Gavrilis

The introduction to this volume urges us to think of borderlands as evolving and mobile. This idea may seem counterintuitive, as most borders are characterized by a persistent fixity. However, the conceptualization is sound, reminding us that borders are dynamic institutions that determine both political control over territory and restrict access to that territory. To treat borders and borderlands as dynamic processes is to heed Newman's cogent reminder that "it is the process of bordering, rather than the course of the line per se, which is important to our understanding of how boundaries affect the nature of interaction, cooperation, and/or conflict between peoples" (2006, 101).

The process of bordering, or creating and maintaining an interstate boundary, is worthy of our attention not just as an academic venture; it bears substantive implications. Boundaries are not just lines around sovereign states, but essential structures of rule where states make and enforce political claims. These structures of rule involve critical decisions on who to deploy to guard the boundaries, how much to invest in policing borders, how much revenue to extract from people and goods crossing, and who to allow access across the border. In *The Dynamics of Interstate Boundaries* (2008), I explain why border control institutions vary so widely and why some borders deter insurgents, smugglers, bandits, and militants while most suffer from infiltration and crisis. Border control strategies emanate from core policies of state formation and the local design of border guard institutions. Secure and open borders depend on institutional design, not on military power.

In this essay, I investigate the relationship between core state policies and border control officials along a late Ottoman imperial frontier that no longer exists. Tracing the institutional history of the first Ottoman-Greek land boundary from its inception in the 1830s to its extinction in the 1880s, I examine the pinnacles of the Ottoman and Greek states and the evolving relationship of each to its local border authorities. Readers who are not historians or Ottomanists may wonder what is to be gained from an essay about a long-gone border. I suggest that there are at least three points of interest: First, in examining the life course of an entire border, it is possible to document the effects of different border control policies on territorial security. Second, present-day borders and the problems of smuggling, banditry, and extremism that affect them bear a striking resemblance to those problems historical borders faced, even alongside the purported effects of globalization (Kahler and Walter 2006). Third, political elites' management and mismanagement of the late Ottoman boundary serves as a warning to policymakers today on how to think about designing border control organizations that provide both security and openness.

In addition to these substantive concerns, there is much to gain conceptually and theoretically in this case. The Ottoman boundary is a case study of institutional evolution and conflict that demonstrates movement across three of the six borderland types Zartman outlines in the introduction: "grey" to "layered" to "black-and-white." I divide my case study into three sections, each corresponding to a category in Zartman's typology. The first section discusses the birth and initial years of the boundary, which fits the grey model. While Zartman and other scholars of borderlands normally measure integration in terms of the intermingling of cultures and populations (Martinez 1994), the Ottoman-Greek boundary regime considered here qualifies as part of the grey model because officials and organizations along both sides were fused and jointly dependent. The border was managed as a broad institutional zone by Ottoman and Greek border guards acting in concert for the initial decades of its existence.

That border control should fit such an integrated model is surprising given that the land boundary was born out of a protracted ethnic and civil conflict that devastated the Ottoman Empire's southern Balkan provinces during the 1820s. The Great Powers saw the conflict as an unlimited war of extermination between Muslim and Christian populations and decided to create an independent Greek state with a remote boundary cutting across mountain ranges that would ensure tranquility through a complete partition of the area's ethnic and religious groups. Yet the partition was far from clean, leaving religious and ethnic minorities stranded on both sides of an area known for its poverty, remoteness, rebellion, and endemic banditry. Worse, both states alarmed their Great

Power brokers by deploying a group of former bandits, mercenaries, and domestic police units to take up positions along the boundary rather than well-armed army regulars (Strong 1842, 263). Despite these conditions that primed the boundary for unrest, within several years it became a site of cooperation between Ottoman and Greek border guards who innovated procedures to administer the boundary jointly and with minimal escalation of incidents.

In the 1840s, the two states were quick to devolve administration to local authorities and expected their border guards to jointly manage the boundary. Both Greece and the Ottoman Empire demonstrated an unwillingness to escalate border incidents, even those that involved disputes over the location of the boundary. Border guards along both sides of the boundary cooperated in policing the border to suppress banditry, smuggling, and irredentist movement. Border authorities learned how to defuse crises and patrol the boundary locally, without escalating incidents. This cooperation included innovative policing tactics. Border authorities coordinated patrols and met regularly to discuss common concerns and implementation of joint procedure. Eventually Ottoman and Greek border guards extended to one another the right to cross the border in pursuit of fleeing suspects and border jumpers. The stabilization of the border and the unwillingness of state elites in the two capitals to directly intervene in matters of border control are puzzling given the otherwise conflict-prone quality of Greek-Ottoman relations.

Yet by the 1870s, two states began to militarize their boundary, intervene in the day-to-day administrative tasks of border authorities, and restrict the activities of their own border guards in ways that made it increasingly difficult to effectively police and protect the line against bandits and smugglers. Why did the Ottoman and Greek states replace successful joint management practices with a unilateral and inefficient border regime that led to escalation and crisis? In other words, why did the grey border of local cooperation and stability evolve into a black-and-white border where both Ottoman and Greek authorities micro-managed their border guards, precluded cooperation with the other side, and engaged in destructive escalation of border incidents that had previously been locally and quietly resolved?

I show that the boundary's evolution from grey to black-and-white was the result of a series of attempts by both states to reform, streamline, and improve their domestic institutions of rule. These domestic changes moved the border from a grey model to a layered one. The reforms and institutional changes each state undertook layered more and more contradictions and restrictions on local authorities, making it increasingly difficult for the guards to cooperate with their foreign counterparts and to deal with local conflicts without involving high-level officials. The more restrictions and monitoring the Greek and Ottoman states layered on their respective border officials, the more they unwittingly undermined the functioning of their border authorities. The remainder of this essay is, therefore, divided into three sections that correspond to the evolution of the boundary from a grey autonomous, bilateral zone of security to a layered institution, and, finally, a black-and-white line of hostility.

THE BIRTH OF A GREY BORDER

As diplomatic officials sat down in London in 1832 to sign a peace treaty that would create an independent Greek Kingdom, British officials brokering the conference expressed great anxiety about how to carve out a boundary between the two sides. They awarded the island of Evia to Greece in order to secure the spine of the Greek mainland, and gave the peninsula of Punta to the Ottoman Empire in order to secure shipping in the Gulf of Arta. A British diplomatic memorandum in circulation prior to the delimitation of the boundary argued that the overriding aim ought to be the complete separation of the populations through a boundary capable of restricting contact between the two sides.[1] In attempting to engineer an efficient and restrictive boundary, the British were hoping to pass on to the Greek and Ottoman states a view of the border as an instrument of sovereign power. The two states would enhance their sovereignty and lower the costs of territorial control by a) monitoring and restricting contact along the boundary; b) defending the boundary against a military threat from the other side; and c) extracting a set of customs duties from goods and people passing through the boundary. In short, the two states were to take careful and deliberate measures to mark their territories as exclusive and seal them off from challenges coming from the other side.

Yet Greece and the Ottoman Empire precisely did the opposite of what was expected. Instead of actively monitoring events at the boundary, they demanded that local boundary authorities solve administrative and positional disputes locally without requesting assistance from high state ministries. Flooded by a large number of complaints, claims, and requests from local boundary authorities, the Greek secretary of state made an exasperated (and apparently often repeated) request that the minister of interior prevent local boundary authorities from harassing Athens about border events and disputes.[2] The Ottomans simultaneously made similar demands down their administrative hierarchies and demanded that their border guards cooperate with their Greek counterparts instead of asking for high state intervention.[3]

As border guards and engineers took positions along the boundary in 1836, a series of disputes occurred regarding the construction of blockhouses and their proximity to the boundary. These disputes are instructive insofar as they were treated as non-events by the states. Border guard reports that reached the capitals were forwarded to diplomatic agencies with little to no urgency, despite the fact that some blockhouses violated territory and were to house large numbers of armed guards. In 1842/1843 such a dispute took place between border authorities in the area of Molocha. Border authorities reported that after a water source on their side dried up, the Ottomans began the construction of a new blockhouse a quarter-hour within Greek territory at a source of potable water called Armatolobryse.[4] Instead of accusing the Ottoman state of provocation and territorial violations, Greek high state officials noted that the construction of the blockhouse could potentially harm relations among border guards and affect public health (as it would violate quarantine laws). The Ottoman foreign minister's response was to order an end to the construction, before confirming whether or not the territory in question actually belonged to Greece.[5]

It is telling to note that the language of exclusive territoriality in disputes such as this one originates with local authorities. Border guards, captains, and municipal authorities along the border initially accused the other side of territorial violations and spoke in the name of defending national territory. High state agencies, on the other hand, did not act according to such a territorial imperative and either ignored or downplayed local reports on violations of the boundary. If the Ottoman-Greek boundary was to mark the end of one sovereign territory and the beginning of the exclusive jurisdiction of another, Istanbul and Athens were seemingly acting with an alternative understanding.

Although the boundary separating the Ottoman Empire and Greece was new, both states implemented existing institutional practices to administer the boundary. The derbent institution of the Ottoman Empire traditionally served as the primary provincial police force. Derbents were armed guards who were chosen from the local populations—both Muslim and Christian—and stationed in strategic points such as caravan roads, bridges, and important passes linking towns and provinces (Orhonlu 1990, 61). The derbents were the best candidates for the new border guard positions since their former duties had included the protection of roads and strategic passes from criminals, restriction of access to bridges and caravan roads, and the collection of tolls. Their experience meant that they would require little training for the tasks required. While Greek high state officials discussed sending regular armed forces to guard the border, by the time the boundary was diplomatically recognized in 1837, local chieftains and their clients had already taken their posts. Although an 1838 decree incorporated the border guard to the army with higher pay, in actuality the derbents were in full control of boundary administration (Strong 1842, 263). The derbent institution was contained to the provincial level, tied to local mayors and their clients, and, as long as they received their pay, performed its functions with little need for the high states to intervene. Furthermore, derbent posts were geographically fluid; villages and derbents could switch duties among themselves as well as their positions (Orhonlu 1990, 61–64). The mobility required as well as the revolving nature of many positions gave the system a zonal quality. Although many derbent zones were well defined and guards did not interfere in each other's affairs, they were expected to cooperate when necessary. They were also held legally and financially responsible for crimes committed in their area, which meant that they monitored locals and other derbents alike to ensure that criminal and bandit activity did not spill over into their borderland zones of jurisdiction.[6]

By the 1840s the Greek state was attempting to extend its newly designed institutions into the Greek countryside and into matters of the economy, while the Ottoman Empire was investing huge efforts in the ambitious Tanzimat reforms of 1839 to 1876.[7] This section examines the impact of the simultaneous state-building efforts on the Ottoman-Greek boundary. Although the high states were reluctant initially to intervene too much in boundary management, in times of crisis they displayed an understanding that the overall security of the boundary was a mutual task. And while governors and government ministers were likely to pass on to diplomatic agencies complaints from local border authorities regarding the indolence of one side, they were just as likely to hand down decrees and commands demanding their border authorities take measures to suppress populations along their side of the boundary.

In the early years of the boundary, the Greek state attempted to expand state control in the borderlands by implementing draconian measures to settle nomads along the boundary, destroy the huts of mountaineers, and relocate villages suspected of causing unrest along the border (Koliopoulos 1987, 107). These policies are comparable with those described in much of the state-building literature on the projection of state power (Migdal 2001; Scott 1998;

Wilson and Donnan 1998; Tilly 1992, 1999). By settling populations and expanding the realm of state control, the Greek state was attempting to stabilize residence as grounds for obligation and service to the state. The state was well aware that such measures would meet fierce resistance, but implemented them anyway.

Tight border controls can enhance the coercive capacities of states by removing the exit option for those who refuse to submit to the obligations and extractive policies demanded (Sahlins 1991; Hirschman 1978). However, the Greek state did not have to directly or vigilantly monitor its border since it was aware that its Ottoman neighbor was taking similar measures to settle nomadic populations, eradicate banditry, and expand control over the countryside via expansive structural and fiscal reorganization of its provincial administrative apparatus.

An example from archival documents is instructive. A relatively large number of Greek mercenary captains found themselves in the Ottoman city of Tırhala (Trikkala), near the boundary. The number of captains and their entourage totaled 168, and most had committed crimes of banditry throughout Greek and Ottoman territories. Local authorities had housed and fed the captains and wrote to the Porte requesting that salaried posts be given to the captains along the boundary. The Porte responded with an interesting decision: the captains were to be transported and settled in the Anatolian city of İzmir (on the other side of the Aegean). They were not to be settled anywhere near the land boundary as this would upset the security of the area and give the Greek side license to make similar appointments in the future. Despite having committed crimes in Greece, they were to be returned to Greece only in the event that settlement in the İzmir area failed.[8]

This decision represents an emerging obligation between the two states to cooperate diffusely to secure the boundary zone. In the same year that this event took place, Hacı Hüseyin Paşa, head of the Ottoman derbents in Tırhala, reported to İstanbul that domestic security in Greece was in shambles and unlikely to recover any time soon: "Bandits are everywhere and there is no security to speak of. The Greek people don't know what to do and are too scared to even stick their heads out of their houses."[9] The Ottoman state monitored the insecurity in Greece. In settling the captains in its own internal territory, it was assisting the overall security of the border zone at the expense of its other provinces.

Borders are potentially important sites for extraction of resources for states.

Customs posts collect duties, excise, and value added taxes (Gavrilis 2008). These modes of extraction can assist the fiscal solvency of governments, especially those that have weak internal surveillance capacities and are not in a position to monitor income and prevent tax evasion (Tilly 1992). Yet high extraction rates at borders can trigger interstate disputes on customs policy, strangle outbound trade and hurt the importing economy, and create incentives for evasion, smuggling, and crime.

Despite the fact that the Greek state and (less so) the Ottoman state had weak extractive capacities compared with their European counterparts, the border did not become a site of competitive customs extraction. Disputes over customs policy seem to have largely been localized and not escalated. The borderland's remoteness and sparse population might explain the lack of emphasis on customs collection: too many costs would be required to collect too few duties. Few passports were issued for travelers heading out of borderlands in Greece in comparison to the number of passports issued for port arrivals.[10] Indeed, compared to duties and customs levied at port cities in various parts of the Empire and the Kingdom, both states seem to have paid little attention to the implementation of customs functions along the boundary. The heavy volume that ships carried in and out of port cities near the boundary region gave the states more concentrated and easier sites for levying duties and generating revenue.

The expenditures of the Ottoman and Greek states along the boundary far outstripped any customs duties they collected from passage of goods and people. Both the Ottoman and Greek states commissioned a larger than necessary force of military captains and their clients to watch over the boundary and the borderlands.[11] It was argued that those appointed to the boundary were part of the region's traditional security forces. However, they also included a large number of former bandits along both sides who both pillaged and fought in the recent war as rebels.

In extending amnesty to many of the bandits and offering employment along the boundary, the high states were attempting to pacify the area. The policy was a rather smart one, tried and proven before in Ottoman state-building. It co-opted bandit elements, amnestying and employing some, while suppressing and punishing the rest via coercive practices (Barkey 1994; Koliopoulos 1987). It also maximized border security relative to state input. Hiring bandits effectively removed a substantial number of individuals from the pursuit of criminal acts (levying unofficial taxes, establishing protection rackets, etc.) by giving them a stable and decent salary in an otherwise impoverished region. Furthermore, these former bandits knew the tricks of the bandit trade and were adept at taking measures leading to the effective suppression and capture of those that remained on the margins of state authority.

In short, in the early period the two states saw the security of their boundary zones as mutual and reciprocal tasks—an integration of administration and border management that fits with Zartman's grey model of an integrated, zonal borderland. In their exchanges and interactions on the boundary, the Ottoman and Greek states demonstrated a) an understanding of the borderlands as an interdependent security zone; b) an obligation to absorb certain costs domestically to assist the security of the other side; and c) an indication that such interaction would continue. Border guards from both sides intermingled and cooperated, treating the border as an integrated administrative zone in order to solve positional disputes and to suppress border jumping and banditry along the boundary. As a result, the boundary was insulated from the frequent ups and downs that characterized Ottoman-Greek relations. While the Ottoman Empire and Greece repeatedly came to the brink of war on issues such as commercial relations, the treatment of diplomats, and the sponsorship of irredentism in Ottoman territories, the boundary remained a jointly, locally managed institution.

A LAYERED BORDER

By 1853, the Ottoman Empire was engaged in open conflict with Russia in the Crimea. Sentiment in Athens was highly pro-Russian, and the Greek government soon began to make public claims on Ottoman territories where Greek-speaking Christians constituted a large part of the population (Veremis 1990). In 1854, a large rebellion swept through the Ottoman provinces of Epirus and Thessaly (the sancaks of Yanya and Tırhala). Greek forces took part in this rebellion, besieging Ottoman border cities such as Narda (Arta) and Tırhala (Trikkala). The rebellion resulted in the severing of diplomatic relations between the Empire and Greece. Ottoman forces later swept through the area to suppress disorder. Meanwhile, the Great Powers, led by the British, launched a punitive expedition against Greece and occupied its main port city, Pireaus (Driault and Lheritier 1925, 2:393).

Despite the massive disorder and violence, the Ottoman and Greek high states initially did not attempt to implement a more direct form of control over boundary matters. Under British diplomatic pressure, the two states restored diplomatic ties and signed into force the Convention on the Suppression of Brigandage in 1856. The convention essentially codified practices that already existed at the local level, including cross-territorial pursuit, information exchange, and extradition of suspects. Following the signing of the convention, the two states fell back upon their previous views of the boundary as a local zone of employment and mutual security. Border guards again cooperated with one another as if the events of 1854 had not occurred.

However, the Convention of 1856 represented a turning point. It certified the existing border regime at the same time that the boundary came to the forefront of Greek political discussions. Moreover, the codification of the border regime contained one clause stipulating that only regulars could be stationed along the border. This clause would become a point of contention, despite the continued practice of amnestying bandits and captains and commissioning them as frontier guards.

Following the signing of the convention, both the Ottoman and Greek states began to invest increasingly larger pieces of the budget to the boundary. The Ottoman state, in particular, announced its intent to renovate radically its border infrastructure. More and bigger stone blockhouses were to be built along the length of the boundary, replacing the crude wooden shacks or local villagers' room and board used traditionally.[12] This would enable the guards to carry on their duties more properly, and it would also solve the issue of housing. The new blockhouses were built just behind the boundary line, allowing border guards to continue to cooperate, communicate, and monitor one another.

However, in order to build the blockhouses, engineers descended on the boundary with newer and more precise maps in hand. These maps presented the boundary line in more specific detail and revealed mistakes in demarcation as well as disputed spaces that border guards had managed quietly and cooperatively without reporting to their respective states. Detailed maps and topographical surveys were the result of advances of cartography in European capitals (Biggs 1999; Black 1997). Greece, for instance, had contracted French military officials to carry out a huge geographical survey. The survey was published in 1850 in the form of a massive book itemizing villages and other manmade features and containing a huge multi-foil map that showed Greece and the borderland in unprecedented detail.[13] At the same time, the Porte was busy at work with the French in setting up courses on mapmaking at the military academy. By 1860, as more blockhouses were being put up, the academy was turning out map officers and sending state officials to France for advanced studies in cartography (Ülkekul 1998).

The infrastructure projects along the boundary and advances in mapmaking meant that both states now had a more precise image of the boundary. The maps inventoried resources along the boundary and clarified the nationality of many border villages that were previously unmapped. This precision did not create territorial claims or positional disputes.[14] It also did not automatically generate a more precise awareness of national geography; newspapers in Athens regularly misplaced Ottoman towns in Greece when reporting events.[15] However, these new maps, deposited in state agencies, gradually began to contradict the zonal image of the boundary.

A second factor that affected high state views on the boundary was a series of political claims originating from the local level. Residents living near the land boundary began to demand a share of state investment, either in the form of salaried positions along the boundary or building contracts. Such claims began in 1856 and persisted throughout the 1860s. Borderland residents in the Ottoman Empire were particularly ingenious in manipulating petitions in an attempt to secure jobs, subsidies, and contracts pertaining to boundary administration. One village, for example, requested that it be declared regional headquarters for border security and that surrounding villages be tied to its jurisdiction.[16] It noted that the sizable budget required for this task would be well worth the increase in security, given the threat across the boundary. Elsewhere, residents asked for tax relief in light of the frequent bandit disasters visited upon their villages because of their proximity to Greece.[17]

Such petitions from Muslim and Christian villages alike consistently share two themes: they underscore their strategic value given proximity to the Greek boundary; and they demand a slice of the budget to implement territorial defense against a perceived Greek threat. Villages along the boundary competed with one another for limited funds. They outdid each other in describing their strategic value and in casting the specter of invasion over the boundary. So tight was the competition for funds that one cluster of villages sent a plan to the Porte underbidding surrounding settlements. They described in detail their plan to protect a stretch of the boundary and informed the state that theirs was the cheapest per-man bid in the region.[18]

A third factor making the high states more actively regulate their borderland administration was the politics of citizenship. Since its inception, the Greek state had made a habit of extending passports to Greek-speaking Ottoman Christians upon completion of a brief residency requirement while denying passports to its Muslim minorities. Through this process the Greek state was able to both shape citizenship to include only Orthodox Christians while extending nationality and protection to Ottoman Christians outside its territory.

The Greek state was confronted with two facts that were in direct contradiction with its citizenship policy. First, a substantial number of its border guards were (and had long been) holders of solely Ottoman passports. Certain members of the 9th regiment, which had been stationed along the more remote stretches of the border and had demonstrated excellent ability to cooperate with Ottoman guards, did not meet criteria for Greek citizenship in light of their Muslim background (Koliopoulos 1987, 156). Second, in the 1856 Convention (and its renewed version in 1865), the Greek state had certified the long-standing practice of extraditing Ottoman army deserters, now including Christian army deserters (not just bandits) who otherwise would have qualified for protection and a Greek passport.[19]

By the late 1860s, a major contradiction had arisen concerning the boundary. While local boundary authorities continued to cooperate with one another to administer the boundary as a common institutional zone, the Greek and Ottoman states had shifted to an understanding of their boundary as a sovereign line that deserved more monitoring and intervention than had previously been the case. Detailed maps and surveys made it easier for the central states to view their boundary as an exclusive line and to follow developments with specific reference to place and territory. Local political claims had likewise territorialized the boundary and contradicted local reports that enumerated cross-border cooperation. The citizenship debates revealed the divergence between theory and practice. For the first time, the Greek high state was confronted with the fact that its border guard looked little like the nation it purported to defend.

What thus emerged in this period was a "layered" border control model. While Ottoman and Greek border guards continued to cooperate across the border, high state authorities began to impose policies from above that undermined and contradicted the autonomy of local authorities. The high states began to monitor the boundary more vigilantly and to restrict its administrative autonomy. Boundary authorities found themselves trying to sustain cooperation against both the hostility of local populations and growing interference from their respective states. The border became characterized by a series of vertical and horizontal institutions that in all their layers could not coexist indefinitely.

The shift from a grey to a layered border is highlighted by one seemingly minor event that took place in 1867 along the central region of the boundary. The Greek prime minister received a report of a serious violation of Greek territory; Ottoman guards had penetrated one hour into Greek territory, entering villages around Karitza, killing a woman and carrying off seventy oxen, and had threatened to come back and punish the district more severely.[20] A Greek border guard captain answered the inquiry, stating that the reports had been greatly exaggerated and that, facing a similar situation, he would have acted no differently than the Ottoman guards.[21] The exchange demonstrates that the content of interactions between the state and its border authorities had changed: the high state had become suspicious of local cooperation and uncomfortable with its territorially loose boundary administration, while the border guards had become uncomfortable at being called to justify long-standing administrative practices. The contradiction between the local and top-down dynamics of the borderland would soon be resolved to the advantage of the latter.

A BLACK-AND-WHITE BORDER TAKES SHAPE

Historians describe the 1870s as a period of rapprochement in Greek-Ottoman relations. Diplomatic relations had been restored, public and joint efforts to stamp out brigandage in the border zones had been declared, and the two states were both campaigning (albeit for different reasons) against Russian interference in Ottoman affairs (Tatsios 1984; Dakin 1972; Sergeant 1897). But despite the rapprochement, both states moved to exert direct and unilateral management over their border. Both states increasingly restricted the form and content of local cross-border cooperation and enforced border control policies that proved counterproductive in producing public security. In this period, the vestiges of cross-border cooperation were wiped out, resulting in a black-and-white border control model where the two sides' border authorities were alienated from their foreign counterparts and micro-managed by high state authorities. In this period, the border authorities became cohesive outposts of their respective capitals, hostile to their colleagues on the other side, and lacked channels of cross-border communication to prevent escalation and conflict.

2. *Conflict on the Ottoman-Greek Border* [53]

In the early 1870s, both states announced their intent to cooperate and stamp out banditry once and for all following the highly publicized bandit kidnappings of British officials (Koliopoulos 1987, 179–90). The kidnapping, known as the Dilessi incident, had attracted unfavorable foreign attention to the domestic situation in Greece and the Ottoman Empire, and both the Porte and Athens were determined to suppress public disorder and bandit activity. Moreover, Russia's influence over the Ottoman Empire was in ascendance. Russia made public its sweeping plans for autonomy and independence of Ottoman territories with Slavic populations. Many of these territories were populated by Greek speakers or Christians tied to the Patriarchate, and this created panic among Greek leaders and diplomats (Kofos 1975). These events prompted a period of rapprochement and virtual alliance between the Ottoman and Greek high states.

Cooperative relations on the surface seemed to have extended to border administration. A series of high-level meetings took place along the border to discuss security and administration, and governors along both sides of the boundary offered joint rewards for the capture of border jumpers, deserters, and fugitives. Finally, high state officials discussed and implemented the use of mixed regiments of Ottoman and Greek border guards along the boundary.[22]

Despite the rapprochement and seemingly cooperative nature of boundary administration, the locally embedded boundary regime was gone. The high states had adopted an understanding of the frontier that was linear rather than zonal. Substantive meetings along the boundary, which formerly had taken place between local border officials, were replaced by spectacles of pomp and circumstance lacking in content. High-level officials were given twenty-one gun salutes as they crossed the border.[23] The fanfare served as an indication that the act of leaving and entering the boundary had now become a formal act.

More importantly, during these meetings the states demonstrated a willingness to restrict border crossing by the other side's border guards even as they recertified the practice of cross-territorial pursuit. In May of 1871 military and government officials discussed the implementation of mixed companies along the frontier. Ottoman and Greek border guards were to fight brigands using a coordinated strategy under a single captain.[24] While the right of cross-territorial pursuit was affirmed, a set of restrictions was placed on the companies. They could only meet, communicate, and cross over at two selected points along the entire border.[25] High state officials agreed that the companies should act in nightfall to surprise border jumpers and bandits, but they also demanded that the companies first request permission from governors in whose territorial jurisdiction the ambush was to take place.[26]

The results were disastrous for the boundary regime. The mixed regiments were a failure. The companies could not operate under the conditions the high states attached to the execution of their duties. Border jumpers and bandits seem to have been aware of the procedural limitations placed on the companies and eluded the regiments by cropping the frontier along points where passage was not certified.[27] The mixed companies found their activities frustrated in other ways. The quarantine houses and officials, which multiplied along the boundary, routinely detained mixed regiments in hot pursuit as they entered Greece, citing sanitary regulations.[28] The regiments looked on helplessly as bandits escaped.

As a result, border guards were working unilaterally and more furiously to combat banditry and crime along the boundary. Events that otherwise would have been solved jointly and without escalation were now rushed up administrative hierarchies. Boundary authorities also became more willing to blame disorder and crime occurring on their side as a consequence of the negligence of their foreign counterparts. Before the major crises of irredentism (1896 and 1912), the Russo-Turkish War (1877), and any obvious decline in their relations, the Greek and Ottoman states militarized their boundaries and declared martial law in most of their frontier provinces.

In 1881 the Ottoman sancak of Tırhala (Thessaly) and the region of Arta were incorporated into the Greek state by the Congress of Berlin following the Russo-Turkish War of 1877. The Greek state had diplomatically agitated for the annexation, fearing one-sided gains by Russia and their Slavic client states to the north, and the Congress agreed (Davison 1983, 1999; Macfie 1996; Yasamee 1996; M. S. Anderson 1966). The British brokered the terms of the handover. Ottoman forces were to evacuate Tırhala piecemeal by the spring of 1882 and cede control to Greek authorities town by town, garrison by garrison (Sfeka-Theodosiou 1989; Paganele 1882). Following the handover of Thessaly to Greece and the establishment of a more northern boundary line, relations among the border authorities remained adversarial and hostile. Skirmishes erupted along multiple posts, and Athens refused to renew the Convention of 1856, arguing that cross-border pursuit was anachronistic, unnecessary, and bound to be abused by Ottoman authorities.[29] Both sides militarized and micro-managed the border as a black-and-white defense line. Traces of the grey model of the early years had all but been wiped out.

CONCLUSIONS

This chapter has shown that institutions of border control are evolving and highly dynamic. Indeed, the institutional shifts and dynamics along the Ottoman-Greek boundary were substantial; during its relatively short lifespan, the boundary demonstrated a trajectory that fits three of Zartman's six borderland types. In addition to verifying and demonstrating Zartman's model, the case in this chapter yields substantive lessons for scholars and policymakers who wish to better understand boundaries and institutions of border control. First, the case showed that boundary security may be determined by domestic processes rather than the anarchic dynamics of the international system (also see Gavrilis 2008; Tilly 2005; Andreas 2000; Tronvoll 1999; Chandler 1998; Sahlins 1991; Kratochwil 1986; Luhman 1982). This runs counter to claims in security studies and international relations scholarship that see modern interstate boundaries as lines of defense that states use aggressively and unilaterally to guarantee their sovereignty against neighboring states (Mearsheimer 2001; Vasquez 1993). Second, top-down micro-management does not necessarily create a stable, well-patrolled border. As the theme of this collective work emphasizes, the attempt to deal with one problem in the borderlands lays the grounds for another. In the case of the Ottoman-Greek boundary, the attempt to streamline and unilaterally micro-manage the border was inefficient from a security standpoint; it prevented border authorities from pooling their resources, innovating policing tactics, and locally resolving incidents. The design of a stable and secure border is a process that might best have been left to the border officials themselves.

Finally, the findings of the nineteenth century speak to the twenty-first. Many states in Africa and Central Asia possess borders that run through security-scarce areas blighted by banditry, cross-border rebellion, and contraband. Such problems are similar to those seen along the Ottoman-Greek boundary. The Ottoman and Greek states, precisely because of their weakness and inability to penetrate their peripheral provinces, created autonomous border agencies and allowed these agencies to pool their efforts in policing matters—much as the Early Kingdom in Egypt did four millennia earlier, as Bárta's chapter shows.

Locally embedded boundary regimes are both effective at providing security and cheap to maintain and may benefit states in the developing world that are both insecure and poor. Yet, foreign policy makers and international organizations tend not to promote such boundary regimes. They more often than not provide monetary and military aid encouraging states to militarize and unilaterally police their borders. In a seminal study of the U.S.-Mexican border, Peter Andreas (2000) showed how such high-cost, high-profile policies are prone to failure. Instead, a viable policy option is for the international community to promote the creation of autonomous and bilateral border control agencies in places where states face mutual threats. While establishing local boundary regimes requires trial-and-error processes, such boundary regimes may hold the key to borderlands that are both open and secure.

Notes

The author is grateful for the support of the American Research Institute in Turkey (ARIT) and the Institute of Turkish Studies. This essay benefited from comments and feedback from Val Bunce and Sid Tarrow and other participants at the Conference on "Colonial Experiences and Colonial Legacies" at Cornell University. Thanks are also due to Bill Zartman, Mary Ellen Lane, and all other members of the BLIP group whose work appears in this volume.

1. Başbakanlık Arşivi (Archives of the Prime Ministry, Istanbul; henceforth BBA), HR.SYS, 1677/2, 1827-7-6.

2. Historical Archive of the Greek Foreign Ministry, Athens (henceforth AYE), 1836, 4/1b, 30 July 1836.

3. AYE, 1840, 4/1, 3/15 March 1840; and AYE, 1842, 4/1; n.d.; order of the Greek minister of war to the troops and gendarme in Lamia; and AYE, 1843, 4/1d; letter of Tayyar Mehmet Paşa, Kaymakam of the Sancak of Tırhala to the Greek consul in Salonika. Also see, BBA, Cevdet Hariciye, 8995.

4. AYE, 1843, 4/1b, 3 March 1843 and 1 March 1843.

5. AYE, 1843, 4/1b, 23 November/5 December 1843.

6. See, BBA, Hatt-ı Hümayun, 1256.M.5.

7. The Tanzimat reforms involved a massive reorganization of state bureaucracy involving both elements of centralization and devolution. On the general scope of reorganization and reform, see Barkey (2008), Köksal (2002), Rogan (1999), Cadırcı (1997, 1988), Yıldız (1992), Kasaba (1989), Ortaylı (1985), and İnalcık (1973). On studies of other Ottoman borderlands set before and during the reforms, see the edited volume by Karpat and Zens (2003).

8. BBA, İrade Yunanistan, 129, 1264.M.6.

9. BBA, Cevdet Zaptiye 2372, 1264.S.29; Hacı Hüseyin was also the Ottoman representative to the delimitation commission.

10. AYE, 1841, 54/1, on sanitary and quarantine regulations involving major points of entry; also, see Georges (1996, 116).

11. FO 169/19, 7 March 1842; here, the British also express concern with the large number of security forces dispatched by Greece to the border.

12. BBA, İrade Dahiliye, 26785, 1274.S.24; and 28670, 1275.H.3; also, FO 195/494, 22 October 1855; description of new plan as reported to British consular agents.

13. This commissioned project is described in AYE, 3/1, 11 May 1850; "Peri katartiseos geografikou chartou tou basileiou tes Hellados."

14. The maps, however, were silent on ethnicity, unlike late nineteenth- and early twentieth-century maps. On maps and ethnic identity, see Yosmaoğlu's contribution to this volume and Peckham (2001).

15. See complaint about poor geographical knowledge in *Faros tes Othryos,* Letter to the editor, 12 May 1856.

16. BBA, A.MKT.NZD, 1272.N.18.

17. İrade Dahiliye, 30255, 1276.S.15.

18. FO 195/801, 18 May 1864; this was reported by the British vice consul stationed in the Ottoman provincial city of Yanya (Ioannina).

19. AYE, 1866, 4/2a, 14/26 December 1865, on discussion of extradition and composition of the army. On conceptual issues of extraterritoriality, see Kayaoğlu (2007).

20. FO 195/868, From Greece 1866–67; 14 February 1867.

21. FO 195/868, From Greece 1866–67; 23 February 1867.

22. AYE, 1840, 4/2b, 19 May 1870.

23. See "He eleusis tou Mechmet Ali Pasa eis Lamia," *Faros tes Othryos,* 18 May 1874.

24. See discussion on boundary between government officials: AYE, 1871, 4/1e, 19 April 1871.

25. AYE, 1871, 4/1e, 25 June 1871; Minister of Foreign Affairs reports to consulates in London, St. Petersburg, Paris, etc.

26. AYE, 1871, 4/1e, 4/16 February and 17 February/1 March 1871.

27. FO 195/980, 16 December 1871.

28. FO 195/980, 26 December 1871.

29. See, FO 32/541, 31 August 1882.

CHAPTER THREE

Illicit Trade and the Emergence of Albania and Yemen

Isa Blumi

Over the last forty years of Ottoman rule in the Balkans and southern Arabia, the borderland constituted a central arena of political, economic, and cultural transformation. For much of the empire's history, the regions in question—roughly along present-day borders separating Albania, Kosova, and Montenegro and, until 1990's reunification, North and South Yemen—were not frontiers at all. It was during the course of the nineteenth century that military defeat and economic vulnerability resulted in the retraction of Ottoman territorial possessions in the Balkans and Arabia, leading to the creation of a borderland phenomenon in Albania and Yemen respectively. It is in this critical period of territorial reconfiguration—1872 to 1908—when new aspects of the borderland experience are highlighted in hitherto unstudied ways.

As borderlands begin to receive attention in the larger academic world, what actually transpired in the Ottoman frontier zones from 1872 to 1908 seems to be especially important, both as a reinforcement to some of the basic themes addressed in the literature and as an important corrective. For one, the frontier regions of the Ottoman Empire highlight the precarious nature of political order as state management of territorial resources is forced to account for local political and social factors. In turn, the attempts to manage the assortment of human and natural resources along borderlands seems to intensify with new methods of resource management and its associated expansion of direct state rule that mirrors modern developments throughout the world.

In the case of the Ottoman Empire, it was the era of administrative reform, known as the Tanzimat (reformation) period that lasted between 1839 to 1876 that most often accounts for the dramatic changes in methods of governance.

What is largely lost in current historiography is that the imperial state's transformation was largely reflective of socioeconomic and political conditions that were not representative of those experienced by communities straddling newly contested borderland areas, such as northern Albania and Southern Yemen covered here. For example, issues of fiscal discipline, commercial regulation, and expansion of state control over social and cultural resources would prove impossible to implement in the areas of territorial dispute well into the post-Tanzimat era (1876–1909) that is largely associated with the tyrannical reign of Sultan Abdülhamid II. It is thus an entirely new set of conditions that one finds along the recently established (and still contested) frontiers of the Ottoman Empire as it faces considerable expansionist threats from rival imperial enterprises, including Russia, Austria-Hungary, Italy, and Britain. Indeed, it is over the course of the post-Tanzimat era of Ottoman rule that one can observe the fluctuations of state capacity to manage the territories and the infringement of Ottoman sovereignty along borderlands that increasingly became zones of imperial contestation. These measures of often chaotic modification intensified a new form of interaction between states as well as between those states and the borderland inhabitants that will ultimately need to be studied outside the framework of previous research into modern imperialism and the rise of the modern state.

Fluctuating between strategy and liability, the borders of the Ottoman Empire seem to be the most ideal set of cases to flesh out just how scholars attempt to theorize borderlands while at the same time highlighting the necessity of focusing on the specifics of each case. This point is highlighted when comparing northern Albania and southern Yemen, as these regions' histories expose a range of activities both locals and state administrators adopt when these regions become an arena of domestic and international power struggles. Not only will it become clear that ethno-national, sectarian, and ideological concerns informing much of the scholarship on these two regions is inadequate—both regions are inhabited by populations who comfortably fused multiple associations that blur any lines of distinction used by historians or theorists of identity—but the process of transforming regions into borderlands immediately undermines our normative models of statecraft, state/society dualities, and ultimately, the very notion that agents of history necessarily need to be fixed to a limited set of interests and motivations.

To make the larger point, this chapter initiates a detailed study of types of commercial and political alliance making that are impossible to generalize. By exploring the fluidity of action/interaction between the inhabitants of two distinctly complex regions of changing imperial borderlands, it will be possible to understand the phenomenon of the border's immediate impact on state capacities to rule spaces that are constantly transformed as a result of numerous factors. Among these factors are the imposition of new frontiers meant to separate newly created states from the former Ottoman polity and the resulting bureaucratic adjustments states on both sides of the border need to adopt in order first to understand the subsequent political economy of the new borderland and ultimately to manage it for political, military, and ideological reasons. As noted in the introduction of the volume, the state apparatus necessarily adopts a policy toward the borderland, be it a black-and-white model, soft zone/grey model, or a mixture, the state's adjustments and the ensuing dynamics determine whether the border "works" or not. This chapter explores in detail the consequences of such exchanges at a threshold period of Ottoman relations with its Balkan and Arabian subjects in order to illuminate new angles of interpretation. Not only are the areas of study intensely disputed zones of competing imperial projects, but they subsequently transform into incubators of social, cultural, and political reanimation that produce temporary polities, alliances, and associations. Put differently, as Zartman explains in the introduction, "horizontal divisions of class and other stratifications" created by borderland policies do not easily fit into our modern categories of identity and political affiliation.

CONTEXTUALIZING THE BORDER

The crucial animating factor leading to the creation of new borderlands was Ottoman military defeat, economic subordination, and diplomatic marginalization. The Berlin Congress of 1878, perhaps the watershed in the diplomatic history of Europe and its interactions with the Islamic world, marks the moment in which Ottoman weakness translates into territorial reconfiguration. Among other things, it served as a diplomatic template from which European imperialism in Africa and Asia would later be developed. Likewise, the underlying principles of European diplomacy vis-à-vis the Ottoman Empire in the future were shaped by the way events in 1878 translated into the newly established states of Montenegro and Serbia, the expansion of Greece northward, and Austro-Hungarian occupation of Bosnia and Herzegovina (Blumi 2007).

Perhaps the most important factor introduced by the treaty was the imposition of territorial frontiers separating the Ottoman Empire from many of its former provinces. To better appreciate how the frontiers drawn by the Great Powers impacted the way imperial subjects and states interacted, I explore events taking place in the Malësia e Madhe region that separates Montenegrin and Ottoman territories in the Balkans, today enclosing parts of Kosova, Albania, and Montenegro (Blumi 2008). To provide further insight into how local factors can contribute differently to the ultimate contours of imperial frontiers, the second half of this chapter explores how similar processes in Yemen helped define the way both the British and Ottoman empires administered their respective borderlands in 1905 and beyond. In the case of Southern Yemen, the Berlin Congress model of 1878 seems to have at once been an invaluable template as well as a barrier to fully laying out a rational justification for the drawing of a frontier through communities that proved equal to the task when the time came to resist these foreign impositions of borders (Blumi 2004).

Both cases represent acts of arbitrary use of state power designed to resolve the problems of governing restive populations in the defeated empire. The measures of imposing new borders, however, had the unanticipated consequence of dividing vibrant cultural and economic districts into competing zones of political and economic interests. The resulting reactions by locals and the subsequent reactions by the two imperial administrations reveal how key aspects of the emerging modern world were not enforceable under all circumstances and created new problems under the guise of resolving the old. As Zartman suggests in the introduction, with Sahlins (1991), Douglass (1998), and Schryver (this volume) as his foundation, the effects of borders on borderlands prove theoretically crucial to adopting a new approach to studying how the modern state emerges in the nineteenth century as space becomes multidimensional and standard dimensions of state power become inadequate.

At the heart of the formal claims of the modern state are territorial transactions in the Balkans in 1878 and southern Arabia in 1905 that took place within a new order of international law. What this enforcement of power in its modern coloration failed to address, however, was the concerns of the inhabitants of the regions. In response, locals openly challenged and eventually disrupted smooth transactions between states negotiating their territorial redefinition. In the course of disruptions caused by what was called local insubordination in the archival material, an imperial ontological fact—the "frontier" that was to separate different peoples, nations, and states—was transformed into a precarious object of negotiation that opened new opportunities for state borderland subjects to become agents of change.

Understanding how locals directly influenced a faulty process of negotiating and delineating territorial boundaries offers us a series of potentially complex angles to reinterpret the phenomenon of borderlands. For example, the range of opportunities to confront the process of "modernization" becomes vast the moment the limitations of the enforceability of, for instance, realized "facts" on maps becomes clear, as Yosmaoğlu's chapter also brings out. The question, therefore, immediately becomes one of feasibility. As the cases in the Malësia e Madhe and Yemen prove, the imperial state, be it Ottoman, Russian, Austrian, or British, only had limited means of enforcing new forms of social, economic, and political order. This altered the attitudes among all the states involved in the transformations of the period and inspired new kinds of administrative reforms that were designed to correct obvious shortcomings to earlier policies.

In time, the reforming state tried to mobilize the principal generators of change in the period—the inhabitants themselves—by incorporating local communities into a scheme of differentiation and political empowerment. Ostensibly, the state's subject became a strategic consideration and an object of patronage to send out to perform the duties of making the modern world. Borderland populations, in other words, were a central part to the process of change we identify here as one of the many consequences of empire.

NORTHERN ALBANIA

The Berlin Congress of 1878 may be characterized as the Great Powers' attempt to impose a particular reading of space in the Balkans in order to establish an order to the larger world based on some basic guiding principles. Locals resisted this. The Malësorë (the inhabitants of the northern alpine region today straddling the Montenegrin, Albanian, and Kosovar borders) in particular became participants in the performance of empire because they resisted. The areas in which they lived in a matter of months became "known" as contested areas that needed to be renegotiated between agents of empire and its inhabitants. This assured a place for the Malësorë in history as the authorities began to write about the Malësorë and ultimately engaged them. Such a transformation forces us to understand the relationship people have with territories in ways that assure a reading of history as a process by which interaction rather than abstraction is crucial. The dots with names on maps suddenly become "places" that have meaning to people who live there and thus have been ascribed value (Yi-Fu Tuan 1977, 31–129; Gregory 1994, 23–41; Carter 1987, 31–106). This ultimately resurrects Edward Said's important assertion that some people do make their own history by way of their understanding of geography (Said 1979, 49–71). Where one could differ from Said is the focus of who partakes in the process. As discussed throughout, it is a fluid movement of opportunities presented to objects of state control along the borderlands that end up shaping the dynamics of the frontier. In other words, it is the marginal Albanian or Yemeni objects who actually draw the lines of state, community, and history.

OBJECT OF STATE BECOMES SUBJECT IN BALKAN HISTORY

In order to politically assure that the "sick man of Europe" survived Russia's efforts to tear it apart after the 1877–1878 war, new mechanisms were introduced by Istanbul to streamline the political and administrative operation of the Ottoman state. On the back of an already long tradition of state centralization reforms during the Tanzimat period, the tools mobilized by the Abdülhamid II regime were supposed to establish a cartographic order to its territories as demanded by the Berlin Treaty of 1878. The most striking manifestation of this was the attempt to establish a stable method of naming land within the confines of an ethno-national state. In order to effectively accomplish this, certain bureaucratic routines—surveying, place-naming and mapmaking—were adopted and normalized. This is Zartman's "evolution of power" par excellence.

Although there was a long history of such activities in the Ottoman Empire, a new set of operational demands caused by military defeat transformed the way the state monitored and conceived its territories. Texts in the form of maps, titles, deeds, and geographic descriptions found in the Ottoman archives reveal a process in which bureaucrats and speculators strove to produce new conceptual spaces in order to grasp an objective reality that carried analytical, ideological, or monetary value. Basically, the Berlin Congress of 1878 established the importance of cartographic order in maintaining a global system dependent on a state system centered in Europe. In time, Ottoman modifications of how it conceived the state in maps, thereby marking state frontiers with named "spaces" like the provinces of Kosova, Işkodra, Serbia, or Montenegro, created a sense of stability essential for the performance of government. The process of realizing this stability, however, quickly produced material facts of their own that ultimately contradicted that sense of order. Solutions to the existing problems created new problems demanding new solutions. This observation fits perfectly with the third organizing theme of this volume, nicely laid out in Zartman's introduction as a "fluid structure [that] only sets up the possibility of identifying some salient interactions that stand out in determining the dynamics of borderland life.... [B]orderlands always prepare for the next move at the same time as they respond to the last one—not just movement, but movement in response to a particular situation, producing pressures for a future situation."

Associated with this process of responsive movement was the reworking of those categorical objectifications of the state subject that justified an otherwise arbitrary procedure. The Berlin Congress of 1878 and the first set of frontiers drawn on maps ignored key components of local life, and yet they were drawn as if they represented territorial definitions on the map in human terms. Human ethnography, for example, as a discipline that had a long history in the Ottoman and European world, served as an extension of the territorial frontiers that became a legal centerpiece to the European order. The problem was local objects of such Foucault-like methods of power could not neatly fit within the state's tools.

By June 1878, signatory powers at Berlin would use statistical surveys about "the people of European Turkey" to draw their version of the new frontiers in the Balkans that would assure a "fair" and "just" solution to the crisis. In fact, all the powers involved redefined the Ottoman Balkans along racial, sectarian, and ethno-linguistic lines, often using quite different categories to create a factual representation of the inhabitants of a selected space on the map. Despite the subtle differences in the categories used by each interested party (Greece, Bulgaria, France, Austria, Britain, Russia, and the Ottomans), the assumed ethnicity and religious association of the populations in question defined the frontiers of the state. The act of defining and then enforcing frontiers by linking them to ethno-national populations became the axis on which all state relations would gravitate. These frontiers would also become a defining mechanism for widespread communal change that will help more accurately explain the transformations discussed below.

The 1878–1909 period in the Balkans is therefore especially important because it marks a conjuncture of disciplinary and operational developments that attributed new significance to territorial and cultural borders by way of defining people in certain ways. Among other things, boundaries began to serve as tools for states to make sovereign claims over geographical, historical, and, more importantly, sociological spaces defined by ethnicity and faith. What made this change possible was in part the growing capacity of the state to assume and then project power in all aspects of its relationship with subject populations (Pyenson 1993; Vincent 1990, 23–33). As a consequence, the redefinition of communal identities became a product of central administrative policy, resulting in an exchange of at times conflicting readings of the world and local reality. Importantly, these contradictory interpretations of the "frontiers" (both territorial and cultural) calibrated by the imperial state created over time a context for exchange that did not fully confine itself to parameters set by the state.

Tragically, the exchanges between subjects and the state over where local readings of territory and space end and the state's readings begin evolved into governmental policies (and their organized local reactions) that sought to correct the "inconsistencies and anomalies" within newly conceived borders. In other words, both the state and their subjects, many of whom objected to and resisted the changes to their lives caused by new cartographic realities, adopted similar methods of redefining their respective communities. As a result, imperial rivalries along the frontiers translated into the systemic use of modern technology (guns, maps, bureaucracies) to realize self-fulfilling prophecies of "recaptured" ethnic heartlands, while locals adopted what I call strategic identities that required the use of violence in order to protect new interpersonal boundaries. This permanently destroyed the Balkans' heterogeneous past and quickly pitted state allies against resistant "rebels." One of the consequences was ethnic cleansing, which became a tool of state that ultimately created the modern world's image of itself and its Other in the Balkans.

The Berlin Congress of 1878 is therefore a perfect case to study a process in which the modern state quickly identified and then aggressively sought to dismantle the heterogeneous nature of world civilization. For one, the Berlin Congress served as a watershed for the procedural components of the kind of diplomacy that inscribed "Otherness" to human beings; the Berlin Congress along with European intervention in Lebanon may have been the birth child of a long progression in liberal theory as practiced in Britain and France during the first half of the nineteenth century. The Austrian consul in Işkodra, Fredlich Lippich, for example, took part in the exercise of cataloging the Balkans in order that it might be better divided. His 1877 "Denkschrift über Albanien" served as a comprehensive ethnographic survey of the inhabitants of future border areas.[1] Importantly, in the process of collecting "vital intelligence" on those who lived within contested regions, he realized that these ethnographies and statistical surveys ultimately limited his understanding of local concerns. Not only were the populations living in the Malësia e Madhe prone to marry outside their religious group, their "ethnicity" was also ambiguous. Orthodox Christian

"Montenegrins" may in fact have been people who adopted Slavic family names but still related to Catholic or Muslim "Albanians" living in the same region.[2]

Lippich's documented skepticism, in particular, helps highlight the range of factors involved in pushing the territorial and operational limits of empire at the time and why such measures ultimately caused so much turmoil. The maps Lippich produced to guide and ultimately determine the outcome of the Berlin Congress of 1878, with their color-coded boundaries differentiating arbitrarily defined ethnic, religious, or racial groups, actually failed to accommodate the contingencies that would make it impossible for local Malësorë to accept borders that the Great Powers sought to impose. That many of those so-called experts were in fact skeptical of the justifications for these frontiers highlights the transitional and still highly malleable nature of the world order at the end of the nineteenth century.

The use of ethnicity and religious affiliation supposedly helped delegates at the Berlin Congress draw the borders "judiciously" in order to separate communities presumably engaged in an ancient struggle for regional ascendancy (Medlicott 1938, 162, 192, 221; Jelavich and Jelavich 1993, 360–71). Paradoxically, as proven within months after the various parties signed the treaty, an attempt to conduct an "orderly" transfer of sovereignty from a multicultural empire to a homogeneous nation-state created the conditions for more violence, not less. In 1878 Kosova, for instance, Belgrade was able to recruit local Slavs to create a "self-defense" committee in the heart of a society that was intermixed and largely harmonious. The *Drustvo Svetoga Save* quickly became notorious for its aggressive engagement with neighbors, using the influence of newly created diplomatic corps in Istanbul, Pristina, and Mitrovica to pressure Ottoman officials into granting greater concessions to "Serbs."

Much as Consuls Green of Britain and Lippich of Austria expressed their concerns that the original boundaries drawn by the Berlin Congress would instigate destabilizing violence, some Ottoman state officials also felt uncomfortable about the new tools of government being used. Some clearly labored from the beginning of negotiations to assure an orderly process of territorial exchange in the face of clear violations of so many fundamental local needs.[3] Other Ottoman officials, however, were more eager to secure British or German favor and adopted the exclusionary policies of these two European powers striving to organize what they saw as a chaotic world. In the end, the concerns of those with local experience were cast aside at the most crucial stages.

The disconnect between officials concerned with local reactions and those who were not ultimately came down to strategic interests. The "larger" concern was limiting Russian expansion while securing a viable Ottoman state in the Balkans to serve as a buffer between competing powers. The frontiers of Montenegro, therefore, were drawn to address this dynamic rather than the principles of ethno-linguistic integrity, the very operational logic used to justify the creation of independent Slav states in the first place. A close inspection of the proceedings of the Berlin Congress and the events that immediately followed clearly show that conflicting territorial claims had little to do with the settlement of these lands by different "ethnic" groups. The end result was the creation of countries with large "minority" populations who were to face years of violence as the state tried to homogenize its territories.

The key obstacle to enforcing the Berlin Congress's cartographic reality was local borderland populations' resistance to the lines drawn on a map. The extent of the resistance and the inability of the Ottoman state to strenuously enforce them ultimately forced the European powers to once again change the frontiers they had twice before declared "just and fair." Here lays the first of many important lessons to draw from the Berlin Congress. Local borderland resistance could ultimately force the Great Powers to modify their diplomatic decrees. In response to Malësorë resistance, the Great Powers introduced a dangerous series of new measures that would ultimately sanction the use of force in order to assert Montenegro's territorial claims as well as Ottoman stability. In place of the Malësia, Montenegro was awarded the port of Ulqin (Dulcino), a source of yet another round of confrontation between local Albanians and the outside world.[4]

GUARDING THE FRONTIER AND TAXING THE MERCHANT

The series of events that reshaped the territorial frontiers of the Ottoman period makes the period 1872–1908 exceptionally well suited for observing and comparing change from a local perspective. The process of adjusting to new territorial realities became a multilayered one that pitted abstract administrative goals against changing local perceptions of where and what constituted a community's interests. Over time, the administrator's job in Albania, just as in Yemen discussed below, was made more difficult by the effort to impose "progress" and "modernity" by circles of power that were fragmented and largely untested in these areas. A history of the "illegal" trade in commodities such as salt in northern Albania helps further illustrate the complex nature of economic and imperial relations. More important is the role of neighboring Montenegro, which, much like the Italian, French, and British authorities in the Red Sea, harbored and cultivated economic networks that helped undermine Ottoman regulatory policies. By creating attractive conditions for key merchant interests inside Montenegro, Prince Nikola was able to dictate how events on the other side of his state's borders would satisfy long-term territorial and economic ambitions for much of the forty years studied here.

Much as will be seen in the Red Sea, influential family-based networks of traders/transporters—Çoba, Bianki, Isa Boletini, and Haci Zeynel—have left traces of their economic activities in the archives. In northern Albania, Albanian-speaking families maintained long-distance trade links connecting the Adriatic port cities of Işkodra and Ulqin with Egypt, Malta, Sicily, Tunisia, and the Aegean Islands (Papajani 2001, 19–28). By studying how these commercial agents were all involved in smuggling, a key manifestation of local adaptation, it is possible to demonstrate more fully how "movement" in the borderlands enabled actors to operate within spaces often seen as exclusionary. Likewise, monitoring smugglers can help us better appreciate the resiliency of borderland economies and those who operated within them to highlight the underlying concern this volume has with suggesting that "[b]orderland reality is a moving machine at any moment and changes its movements as it moves through time, in motion both synchronically and diachronically."

The creation of independent Slav states by the Berlin Congress of 1878 introduced a new set of conditions in the Balkans that completely changed the way people conducted their commercial affairs. While the process of installing and ultimately regulating the internationally recognized boundaries separating what remained of the Ottoman Empire's territories in Albanian-speaking lands and Montenegro and Serbia is crucial, it is equally important to recognize that because of these frontiers, often drawn right across centuries-old trade routes, areas of production, and individual and collective properties, much of what the Ottoman Empire aspired to do with its economic policies would be challenged in unexpected ways. That included leveling tariffs on traded goods, a project in part imposed on the Ottoman administration because of its financial subordination to Western banks.

One of the results of this heightened effort to tax trade in the newly created borderland economies was a transformation of local trading strategies. At the heart of these changes were local efforts that gravitated toward circumventing state regulation, including setting up smuggling channels. Researching the account books of merchants shows that trade between local Albanians (and even Slavs) geographically shifted, both in terms of the larger region as well as within the urban context. Trade did not take place exclusively in the market. Indeed, the heavy duties placed on imported salt, a commodity bought for centuries from Malta, Sicily, and the Aegean Islands, proved a disincentive for merchants to buy it in the central bazaar (Blumi 2003, 262). In response to heavy taxation, merchants discovered ways of supplying their long-term customers without paying the Ottoman customs duty charged in markets. Instead of passing through official customs' checkpoints found along the Bojana River and in Işkodra itself, traders began to unload their goods in Ulqin (in Montenegrin hands since 1879) and then transport their goods over land to buyers waiting inside Ottoman territory. It appears that these smuggled goods were pre-purchased by regional traders who came to Işkodra and then redistributed to other markets. The actual goods apparently never reached the city itself. Regional buyers seemed to have picked up their purchases at previously arranged areas outside the market (or even beyond the city's limits as customs officials guarded access roads). According to the records available, goods like salt sold at rates considerably (*ma shume ygjyz*) below those available in that market.[5]

The territory in which these Albanian merchants traditionally traded was since divided, and in many cases virtually eliminated from the map by the creation of an independent Montenegro. Many communities dependent on trade nevertheless adapted and actually developed a new market niche for their products. By clever manipulation of conditions on the ground, giving Ottoman officials little authority to monitor activities outside Ottoman borders, and a guaranteed demand for "below" market prices driven up by Ottoman taxation, the Işkodra trading families helped create a thriving smuggling network. What is particularly interesting here is that it appears the Montenegrin state actively encouraged this activity while at the same time seeking to cleanse its territories of the very Albanians who conducted this trade.

Clearly, the Montenegrin government saw an opportunity and assured that conditions in Ulqin and all along its frontiers would facilitate this smuggling. In fact, large amounts of state funds went into investing in road and bridge construction all along these routes.[6] There were even plans to build a rail line to link the Montenegrin ports of Antivari/Bar to the Ottoman border, potentially helping smugglers deliver goods into the Ottoman Empire.[7] In a matter of years, therefore, Montenegrin officials working with Albanian merchants successfully shifted large amounts of trade revenue away from Ottoman coffers. As shrewd economic policy, Prince Nikola's alliance with Işkodra Albanian merchants denied Istanbul much needed money to help develop the empire and strengthened his political leverage over many communities living inside Ottoman territory.[8]

Since the creation of an independent Montenegro and the transfer of Ulqin to that country, internationally enforced boundaries cut through long-used trade routes, leaving many traders isolated from their historical zones of activity. To address this and assure that much of the lucrative trade flowing into northern Albania would continue to go through the Ottoman ports of Shkodër/Scutari, Medua, or Draç further south, Ottoman authorities devised a number of strategies. The first was to encourage the "legal" importation of goods through Ottoman-controlled ports by heavily taxing goods that crossed from what was now a foreign country, Montenegro.[9] Realizing that a great deal of disruption had taken place to regional trade and that many alternative routes, including the one through Ulqin, were attracting traders away from Işkodra, Istanbul initiated projects to modernize its ports all along the coast.[10] In particular, there appears to have been a great deal of activity to make the city of Işkodra itself more accessible to the large cargo steamers now calling regularly at Ulqin. The problem for Ottoman officials was that the route through Ulqin proved far cheaper because larger ships could not sail up the shallow Bojana River that connects the Adriatic with Lake Işkodra. As only medium-sized cargos actually reached Işkodra, transport costs were much higher for products unloaded in Işkodra as opposed to those shipped in high-volume steamers docking at Ulqin. Clearly, the combination of cheaper transport costs and high volume made it economically possible to simply skirt Ottoman ports altogether and smuggle salt into Ottoman territory from Ulqin. The ultimate problem for Ottoman officials, just as in Yemen, was that they needed neighboring states to respect trade agreements and not support, as Montenegro and Italy did, smuggling activities.[11]

ADAPTATION IN SMUGGLING

What happened in northern Albania was not a process of subordination, in which locals were co-opted by Europeans (either as smugglers or legitimate partners) to fit their imperial designs.[12] Likewise, it was not a case of succumbing to Ottoman reforms. Rather, a dynamic of local empowerment was evident, giving the big merchant families of Işkodra and the small-scale traders the opportunity to adjust to the new conditions.

General discontent among borderland populations arose when the economic consequences of the new international boundaries drawn right through northern Albania became apparent. In addition, inflationary pressures were levied on these communities with the creation of an independent Montenegro in 1878. Officials noted that rising prices and shortages of staples exacerbated the tensions brought by an occupying army and its bureaucracy on both sides of the now militarized frontier; as the new boundaries imposed artificial limits on where shepherds could lead their flocks or suppliers of basic goods could reach their customers, political tensions rose.

The tensions were heightened by various events the state had little capacity to control. Climatic disasters played a particularly conspicuous role in northern Albania at the time. After the Berlin Congress, shepherds were restricted to survive in artificially designated spaces that were occasionally impacted by drought. In the past, the impact of drought could be mediated by taking flocks to other pasture areas, areas that since Berlin were awarded to Serbia and Montenegro. This made winter pasture [mer'asi] harder to find for inhabitants.[13] Soon the overuse of grazing lands put greater pressure on herders to push the limits of state boundaries. Meanwhile, crop production also dropped dramatically in the drought of 1895–1898. With greater economic hardship, "traditional" practices such as raiding increased to compensate for depleting flocks and lost revenue. The Albanian-speaking populations on either side of the militarized boundaries began to accuse each other of stealing herds of sheep, provoking armed clashes that drew in both the Montenegrin and Ottoman armies.[14] It is in this context that the droughts of the mid-1890s are especially important and created the kinds of local adjustments that not only disrupted old patterns of interaction but also broadened the range of actors with interests in skirting the state. Nutritional safety would be a regular problem in the highlands. Another famine led to widespread unrest that helped create the events in 1906. As the Kosova governor's office reports at the end of the year, events involving land use issues, shortages of grains to feed sheep, and the drought provided conditions for the emergence of regional leaders who confronted the state to address the impending famine.[15]

Beyond respecting the local perspective when writing regional economic history, it is important to return to how much state taxation schemes undermined Ottoman authority in places like northern Albania. Ottoman tax policies depended on the assumptions that the borders could be policed and that officials would be loyal in their enforcement. That much of the revenue extracted from local trade went directly into the pockets of those enforcement officials who clearly abused their powers forced traders to find and use an alternative route the next time they went to trade in Işkodra. Such new patterns of trade reflected adjustments to the state's taxation efforts, which, in turn, denied the Ottoman state (and its corrupt officials) the opportunity to realize its long-term state-building ambitions for raising much needed revenue.

Technological deficiencies aside, there is another important factor in the early years of the state-building project that explains the success of smuggling. Regarding both Yemen and Northern Albania, the Ottoman Empire's immediate neighbors—Britain, Italy, and Montenegro—actively encouraged smugglers to pass through their territories.[16] The reason why so little trade eventually went on in Ottoman-monitored markets in Işkodra is that the regional economy and its participants adjusted to the conditions and found alternative means. One of the important new factors was, again, the existence of a new Montenegrin state willing to assist in the creation of new trade routes that favored the passage of vital goods through their territory.[17] Consequently, by the mid-1880s, most of the mule and foot traffic between Işkodra and Kosova passed through Montenegrin territory, signaling larger ramifications of such strategies throughout the region. The border area around Tuz northeast of Lake Shkodër, in particular, became a key economic center for the Hoti, Gruda, and Kelmendi hinterland area.[18] Importantly, the main merchant families of Işkodra were not active in this smuggling boomtown. Rather, much of the products traditionally sold exclusively at port towns controlled by Işkodra-based merchant elite were being sold by a new class of regional elite emerging along the inland boundary of Montenegro.[19] This had long-term consequences for the region as a new rivalry over regional power, centered on who controlled the smuggling trade, would emerge.

While smuggling often receives little attention among historians, it nevertheless has an important impact on how communities organize and indeed how the state operates its institutions. Profits earned from smuggling are significant for both coastal and inland communities connected to markets that offer a potential pool of customers for their goods and services. Indeed, a merchant's profits in Kosova from smuggling could be upward of 10 percent for most of the post-1878 period as Prenkaj discovered by calculating the profit margin located in the accounts of known smugglers of salt in the city of Prizren (Prenkaj 1998, 100–101). Obviously this gives a considerable advantage to those merchants who could secure a reliable channel of exchange, an advantage that translates into political influence as communities vie for access to these channels of profit and reward patrons who can assure safe passage for goods.

The concern states had with unmonitored traffic between frontiers inspired administrative innovations and even cross-boundary cooperation to address issues of economic sovereignty and control of commercial flows. Such interactive, cooperative measures are the foundation of present-day protocols for shared policing responsibilities and international law.[20] In other words, much of the legal structure discussed here emerged out of trial-and-error interactions with local communities adamantly resisting efforts by centralizing states to streamline the taxation of commerce across arbitrarily drawn frontiers. These modifications, in turn, created new economic spaces and opportunities for those who could make the necessary counter-adjustments, transforming the region's political and social dynamic and influencing the very process of nation-building in the twentieth century. It is perhaps in this sense that the borderland "movement" can best be appreciated comparatively as events in Yemen would prove at once distinctly local as well as offering an intriguing set of parallels to processes just discussed in regard to northern Albania.

(RE)CREATING EMPIRE ALONG AN UNMARKED FRONTIER IN ARABIA

For the Ottoman state, geography proved its biggest adversary to harnessing this trade. The range of alternate points of exchange for local communities was immense, making any monitoring of such trade ultimately futile. Trails, bridges, forests, and mountain passes, as well as bodies of water such as seas, rivers, and lakes with their coastlines, were all potential routes for illicit trade. How the state reacted to this reality would ultimately serve as a key generative force for the kinds of changes associated today with modernization. The Ottoman government's concern with smuggling became especially acute in the newly incorporated territories of Yemen.

Almost immediately after entering in the highlands in 1872, officials were facing local contingencies that frustrated initial administrative goals. Among the many responses to these local dynamics was the establishment of greater military control of the territory in order to better tax productivity. Already in

1865, a series of commissioned reports written by the Russian Konstantin Zahorov started a process in which the Ottoman state attempted to tax traded goods along its coastal possessions in Yemen and 'Asir.[21] Immediately upon visiting the region, Zahorov identified a weakness in how the Ottomans coordinated their institutions throughout the Hijaz/Red Sea and chastised authorities for a far too porous internal network of roads that after 1872 extended into the highlands of Yemen. These unmonitored roads served as ideal routes for merchants from all over the Arabian Peninsula to circumvent heavily regulated ports and trade in the Red Sea. To address this issue, Zahorov suggested that a greater police presence on the internal roads, even setting up customs posts manned by military personal, would ensure that agents could monitor untaxed goods.[22]

The Sublime Porte responded by creating a corridor through which all commerce between the Hijaz and 'Asir (and soon highland Yemen) would have to pass.[23] Such a scheme, in theory, extended to the border areas marking off British-controlled zones around Aden. In a short period of time, such attempts to tax adversely affected commerce between the Hijaz and Yemen. As Yemeni merchants explored new trade routes to avoid Ottoman taxes, the actual shift in how trade was conducted in the region empowered certain communities that could assure safe passage of the caravans that smuggled goods. At the same time, of course, those communities whose villages lost out as trade flowed through new regions were severely affected. Such shifts in wealth literally disrupted the way communities conducted their daily affairs, perhaps accounting for the periodic outbursts of popular Islamic movements or revolts led by previously unheard of community leaders. The widespread famine and subsequent migration that is evident in the period's history can also be connected to the disruption in patterns of trade caused by new forms of borderland regulation, smuggling, and counter-regulation.[24]

Such dramatic events give us a taste of what was at stake for borderland communities. Paradoxically, the precarious nature of Ottoman-ruled Yemen sometimes helped government officials. For the administrator, the authority to redistribute funds, offer protection, or selectively arrest rivals gave him considerable power that could be used to both co-opt locals who would assist in regulating the imperial economy as well as coerce less compliant members of the subject population. This leverage was used to great effect in Ta'izz, even at the expense of the British in Yemen, who witnessed growing Ottoman influence over many of the communities that straddled a still undetermined frontier between Aden and Ottoman Yemen.

In much of the loosely defined "imperial" territories of Yemen in the 1870s, a reconfigured matrix of regional possibilities for local actors as well as innovative Ottoman officials led to a momentary adjustment in local power distribution. I focus below on two key regions in Yemen that underwent these lumpy interactions. The first region is the unmarked highland that divides the administrative centers of Ottoman Ta'izz and British Aden. The other is the coastal region known today as 'Asir and Tihama, which had direct links to the larger Red Sea world. In these areas, a new set of opportunities corresponded with the arrival of the Ottoman state after 1872. As the Ottoman state sought to harness local commercial activities and also balance off Italian, French, and British influence with its own, the sociology of the "borderland" surfaces. As already demonstrated, it is the local who proves key to the transactions of empire that ultimately result in the complete modification of the way the Ottomans, British and Italians understood the role of their state in the region.

In the eyes of the British Empire's agents, Ottoman "incursions" were examples of imperial overreach that needed to be contained (Jacob 1915, 213–25). Unfortunately for the British authorities, Ottoman successes highlighted more the weaknesses of the British and their allies in the region than inappropriate behavior on the part of a fellow imperial state. Britain's failure to effectively read the situation convinced the Aden authorities that they needed to be better informed about events in the highlands. In time, the question of better local intelligence would transform the way the British administered Aden and dramatically raise the stakes for local potentates.

In all, the British, like their Ottoman (and Italian and French) counterparts, would engage in a new era of interaction with subject populations, a transformation in a relationship that had manifested itself after the Berlin Congress of 1878. Unlike the blind arrogance of imperial bureaucrats instrumentalizing subjects, however, the borderlands of southern Arabia would become a territory in which the imperial agent conceded that he would have to actually negotiate with locals.[25]

LOCALS IDENTIFYING NEW OPPORTUNITIES AND THE CHANGING POLITICS OF EMPIRE

Yemen was in the throes of a commercial and political transformation that had long-term consequences for both empires. Since the 1870s, new revenue flows created by an increasingly effective administration and the sudden spike in demand for local goods enriched the anointed surrogates of both empires. Accompanying the growing revenues earned from increased trade was greater local investment in cash-producing activities like harvesting tobacco and qat, along with produce meant to feed Ottoman and British soldiers (Bury 1911, 9).

Such activities placed greater "developmental value" on land, leading to the kinds of conflicts between locals discussed throughout. This can be observed in Ottoman Yemen as an elaborate survey conducted in early 1876 demonstrated the extent of economic activity taking place throughout the area.[26] The detailed study of the various trade routes noted that specific trade patterns connecting Mukha (an Ottoman port) and its hinterland enriched surrogates of Ottoman power in and around the Hawshabi region that eventually fell under the jurisdiction of a local ally of the Ottoman state, Muhammad Nasir Muqbil, discussed elsewhere (Blumi 2000, 117–45). Importantly, the Hawshabi was believed at that time to be under treaty with the British. As made clear with the Muqbil case below, elements of this extended community did not subscribe to that treaty and actively pursued new commercial opportunities through the Ottomans (Blumi 2004, 107–18). The shifting value of these lands intensified, thereby creating unanticipated factions as claims of ownership diverged. This all forced the hand of imperial administrators who were dragged into internecine struggles for local power.

The profits earned from land appropriations and extracting duty from caravan trade led to competition between rival land holders and imperial agents as each one strived to secure the patronage of the many imperial powers in the area. In their search for a greater portion of regional wealth, many newly emerging players in Yemen proved willing to go to great lengths to undermine the credibility and power base of those who stood in their way, including those who were charged with maintaining imperial order by the British. As a result, a new kind of political entrepreneurialism emerged, eventually undermining established family networks and weakening the coalitions on which Ottoman and British polices depended. In the early 1870s, for example, the recognized Sultan of Lahj, Fadl b. Muhsin, an important ally to the British, was forced to distribute large amounts of revenue earned off his lands to rivals such as ʿAbdallah b. Muhsin, who was threatening open conflict. This can be easily interpreted as a serious breach in the British capacity to securely operate using its old system of alliances, perhaps explaining why new measures were slowly being introduced in Yemen to bring these locals more closer to Aden (Gavin 1975, 117–18). British policies were showing signs of breaking down by as early as 1874. Men like

Shaykh Abdallah Bey Sabil, son of the Shaykh of Lahj, actually aligned with the Ottoman state as it consolidated control of the region south of Ta'izz.[27] In return for their pledges of allegiance, such actors in Lahj were given land in much the same way Albanian refugees were given land in 1878 (Atif 1908, 15–25, 39; Raşid 1874, 19–23, 79–82).

Authorities in Aden (and the British media in London), within weeks of the first Ottoman incursions into the 'Abdali/Lahj area, voiced fears that the Ottomans had gained an upper hand in the region. According to the London press, Ottoman "interferences" in Yemen undermined the ability of local "sovereigns" previously allied with British Aden to control their subordinates, thereby threatening lucrative commercial relations.[28] This Ottoman interference took many forms, including outright patronage of rivals to British allies in the region.

One of the more revealing cases had to do with a family dispute over local authority, pitting the so-called Sultan of Lahj, whom the British authorities in Aden recognized as sovereign in the region, and his younger brother 'Abdallah, who had openly challenged his authority (Ingrams 1938, 634–39). Aden's immediate response, therefore, was to secure its "traditional" areas of influence. Aden, under the behest of the Sultan of Lahj, arrested 'Abdallah in the hope that by removing him from the scene, the potentially dangerous set of conflicts in the Lahj could be resolved. The problem was that the British authorities at the time could do little to stop Ottomans from cultivating a relationship with 'Abdallah. Instead, with active Ottoman involvement (and much local cultivation of the authorities in Ta'izz), the Ottomans organized 'Abdallah's release and set in motion a struggle in the entire 'Abdali region for power.[29]

In a gesture that was meant to be registered far and wide, the governor of Ta'izz promptly rewarded 'Abdallah with a public commendation and a position in the Ottoman administration. In no time, he became a valuable ally for the Ottomans and adeptly subverted British influence in and around Lahj. By mid-1874, a daily exchange between British Foreign Ministry officials and the Ottoman embassy revealed how London tried in vain to convince the Ottomans that they had no legal right to challenge the "rightful" sovereign leader of Lahj.[30] Unfortunately for the British, Ottoman ascendancy to the north completely changed the local dynamics in and around Lahj. The real issue behind Aden's panic was not formality and diplomatic protocol but the fact that the popular support among the Lahj communities in the borderland was for 'Abdallah and his new Ottoman patron.

The question to ask about this challenge to British presumptions of hegemony was, what attracted borderlanders to the Ottoman administration? The answers lay not only in the capacity of the Ottomans to project power, conjure up sentiments of religious solidarity, or offer more than the British in terms of stipends. The issue was the stratification of local power and the opportunity for those otherwise trapped by bottlenecks in regional power networks to find an alternative resource to challenge local patriarchs like the Sultan of Lahj. This immediately had a crossover effect in trade, as the Ottoman state utilized its capacity to reward pliant locals seeking opportunities to circumvent trade networks dominated by established regional leaders. Not only did new trade possibilities arise with the arrival of Ottoman authorities—garrisons needed to be fed, roads protected, taxes collected—but an alliance with the Ottoman administration demonstrated to many locals sitting on the sidelines that previously subordinate elements of Yemen's hierarchical society could find new political or economic niches in the region.[31]

THE ITALIAN FACTOR AND THE "REGULATION" OF TRADE

The consequences of these borderland dynamics extended beyond just relations between the Ottomans and their British neighbors. Italy became an increasingly effective regional power that manipulated Ottoman vulnerabilities in Yemen as concerns grew that Red Sea trade was under threat due to the lack of security. As more and more competition over fewer and fewer legal trade options put pressure on coastal communities throughout the region, some local entrepreneurs entered into the business of robbing local commercial vessels. The problem of "piracy" hence became an issue of transregional and diplomatic significance. Ironically, the "pirates" that so exercised Italian and French authorities were often allies of one or the other regional powers who helped enforce commercial order.[32]

In an attempt to assure that enough revenue-producing trade reached Italian-controlled ports, Italian officials in Massawa were particularly aggressive in protecting their merchants, many of whom also robbed local traders, in order to secure territorial claims throughout the western coast of the Red Sea. Part of the process of securing the interests of local allies was to encourage them to explore the most lucrative trading niches in the region. Italy, as well as France, used their increasing influence over Red Sea merchants to help protect smugglers who began to tap into the growing demand for modern rifles. Over time, these weapons would find their way to Yemen, satisfying a demand among local Yemenis facing increasing Ottoman and British pressure. This development threatened both the British and Ottoman monopoly of modern weapons in the region and would prove to have dramatic consequences to how these two administrations operated in Yemen.[33]

The infiltration of weapons into the Arabian Peninsula was particularly alarming for the British and their control over the so-called nine borderland districts surrounding Aden. British "indirect rule" in the nine districts of Aden's hinterland relied on the administration's capacity to offer exclusive assistance to communities who were otherwise vulnerable to Ottoman incursions. The weapons trade emerging after 1885 threatened this balance of power. As non-aligned communities got their hands on increasingly modern rifles—erasing any advantage British allies had over their rivals—efforts to maintain stability in its districts became increasingly tenuous.[34]

It is here that Italian and French manipulation of the smuggling/piracy industry helped create new kinds of forces on the ground by the late 1890s that would result in the changes discussed below.[35] The Ottomans and British both invested more energy to suppress the flow of traffic into their territorial waters. The increased use of force to police the coast eventually undermined any hope of winning over most of the people living there. In time, this gave the French and Italians the window of opportunity to become major players in Arabia for most of the period leading to World War I.[36]

CONCLUSION

Efforts to police the frontiers come to the surface here with grave consequences for all parties involved. The establishment of customs posts, border patrols, and toll stations introduced new kinds of restrictions on trade that cut profit margins in already squeezed markets. As noted above, the at times illogical measures taken to tax economic activity in and around Yemen's most productive regions enhanced the ability of Italy and Britain to secure allies who were willing to challenge Ottoman legitimacy in Yemen.[37] Not only did the British enclave in Aden or the Italians in Assab and Massawa on the African side of the Red Sea benefit by drawing more of Yemen's trade to their ports, but officials based in Hudaydah and Mukha also found themselves at odds with Istanbul as the local administration failed to meet unspecified expectations for revenue.[38]

The kinds of transactions that the Ottoman state wanted to regulate and from which ultimately draw revenue highlight the paradox of empire in these distant provinces: the more effort put into one aspect of asserting greater imperial control over "primitive" economies and peoples, the more complicated the relationship with these subject communities became, a striking example of one of this work's major themes.[39] In the end, these measures disrupted a relational balance as violence became the only means of interaction between key local stakeholders and state officials.[40] Any disruption in local patterns of trade had potentially grave consequences to the stability of the provinces.

The empire's documents disguised realities as best they could, so historians should be very cautious when using them. Trade data always projected an image of precision and order. In addition, Ottoman officials often were not familiar with the areas they were administering and thus were excluded from the business of the street by their officially sanctioned sense of social order. Ottoman state records may therefore not be the best source for economic historians eager to study local economic life and may be misleading for those seeking more micro-causalities to the devaluation of the Ottoman Empire.

Yemen, too, suffered, never to realize a *potential* of geographic and political unity, largely because of the way the Ottoman administrators and indigenous components of the state/society matrix actually coexisted. Yemen continued to be fragmented not so much because of the "disruptive" influences of modern cartographic interventions but because of the incalculable number of opportunities for local and outsider alike to interact in meaningful ways. As intimated earlier, the social matrix in the empire's Yemeni and Albanian borderlands was able to do so in part as a result of shifting patterns of regional trade that was often marginal to the activities of international regulatory bodies. Whether acts of smuggling were forms of resistance or simply a bureaucratic category with its own economic logic, it is clear that the "illegal" transportation, distribution, and sale of commodities throughout the Red Sea, as in the Adriatic, helped create new hierarchies in both these social environments. This observation goes a long way to reinforce the general themes of this volume and may be identified in the other chapters. In the end, the perspective taken here helps us see how societies on the edge of empires developed a capacity to create local economic networks to respond to difficult situations, stressing the need for a more localized understanding of the processes at work within any multidimensional imperial state and the imposition of borderlands. It also reveals that a fluid and ever-changing set of dynamics often unique in the larger imperial context has contributed to the blurring of neatly defined ethnic, sectarian, and ideological identities that remains the central issue for many post-imperial states in the world today.

Notes

1. Text of the report may be found in Haus, Hauf und Staatsarchiv (henceforth HHStA) PA, XII/256, dated Scutari, 20 June 1877, 1r-25r. Since the 1860s, British consuls also sought to establish a system of marking divides within the heterodox population of the Balkans. See, for instance, early reports on "relations between Christians and Muslims" in Kosova found in the Public Records Office (henceforth PRO) FO 881/909, Sir H. Bulwer to Lord J. Russell, dated Therapia, 31 July 1860.

2. The British consul in Işkodra also voiced concerns about these idiosyncrasies in the region. PRO FO, 78/2628, no. 15, Consul Green to Foreign Office, dated Scutari, 3 March 1877. Part of the problem for both Lippich and Green was that Albanians did not easily fit into a category. A large number of Albanian speakers who still today are living in Montenegro and whose families have taken on names of Slavic origin, such as Sokol, have become a source of great debate about the ethnic "purity" of people in these regions. Unfortunately, the environment in which such ethnically ambiguous "borrowings" were commonplace has been forgotten.

3. Recognizing the dangers of these frontiers, Kamil Pasha, chief representative in the implementation of the treaty, suggested trading Kuçi Kraina (located in Hoti) for the Gosine and Plava areas. See HHStA PA, XVII/35, Memorandum, 20 September 1879, document 31r.

4. For details of how another series of "compromises" were reached by the great powers as they faced diplomatic failure in Malësia see, among others, War Ministry report and summary of troops being sent under Riza Paşa to Işkodra to enforce the transfer of new Albanian-populated lands in return for the northern highland towns of Plave and Gosine to remain in Ottoman control; Başbakanlık Arşivi (henceforth BBA) YA. RES 7/7, report 801, 29 Cemaziyelahir 1297 [9 June 1880].

5. Details of this particular kind of transaction may be found in the diary of the Saraçi company, located in the Albanian state archives, Arkivi Qendror Shtetëror (henceforth, AQSH) F.143.D.915.f.44 and AQSH F.88.D.8.f.315.

6. Russian money helped build up the infrastructure of the frontier regions, improving roads and building bridges to cut travel time between the highlands and the coasts by days. See an example of such construction at Irjanica near Plava, BBA Y.MTV 70/174, copy of telegraph from Vali Farik Edhem Paşa, 28 Rebiyülahir 1310 [20 June 1892].

7. This desire to draw Ottoman trade to Montenegrin-controlled ports was manifested in the proposed plan to construct a rail line connecting Montenegro's other port, Antivari/Bar to Lake Işkodra. Such plans designed by an Italian firm clearly had Ottoman officials worried, BBA YA.RES 132/30, Ministry of Trade report no. 99, 15 Cemaziyelahir 1323 [18 August 1905].

8. For a history of the port in Ulqin/Dulcigno and its growing significance in regional trade, see a number of protocols written between Montenegrin and Ottoman of-

ficials outlining the borderlines. BBA HR.SYS 861/1, communiqué number 131, Radoviç to Djavid Paşa, 17 February 1886.

9. For thorough discussions on how Northern Albania was to be integrated politically with the empire, see report from locally organized "committee of unity" pledging its allegiance to the Sultan. BBA Y.PRK.MYD 2/1, 5 Rebiyülahir 1298 [8 March 1881] and BBA Y.PRK.MYD 2/15, 26 Zilhicce 1298 [21 November 1881].

10. ASMAE Serie P Politica (1891–1916), Busta 666, no. 19863/29, MAE a Consul Leoni in Scutari, dated Roma, 3 March 1904, outlines the projects underway in building the Medua port, a project meant to replace Ulqin. See also ibid., no. 36103/108, MAE a Consul Leoni in Scutari, dated Roma, 23 July 1904, on plans to build a railroad between Alessio in Mirdita and Medua. In addition, see ibid., no. 339/155, Consul Leoni to MAE, dated Scutari, 28 July 1904 on the efforts of Haydar Pasha, vali of Işkodra, in seeking funds to build a road to Medua. Finally, see ibid., no. 249/90, Consul a MAE, dated Uskub, 10 October 1904, on discussions over a concession for the construction of a rail line connecting Draç on the Adriatic coast to Prizren, deep in Kosova.

11. ASMAE Serie P Politica (1891–1916) Busta 666, no. 90/36, Consul a MAE, dated Scutari, 9 March 1905. It is reported that the vali sent a delegation to Tuz to pay one thousand Italian liras to the Castrati (Kastrati) communities in order to persuade them not to accept further money from Montenegro. Ottoman officials were clearly concerned about Montenegro influencing the four communities in the area, Kastrati, Kelmendi (Clementi) Hoti, and Gruda. For reports of smuggling along the Gosine and Plava border areas see BBA Y.PRK.MYD 6/14, 4 Cemaziyelahir 1304 [1 March 1887].

12. At times, Italians were thwarted, as noted in the Italian foreign ministry archives Archivio Storico del Ministero degli Affari Esteri (henceforth ASMAE), AiT, B. 107 F. 1.f.3 "Ostruzionismo del Vali di Medua Verso gli interessi Italiani 1901–2." In this case, the vali and locals would not permit an Italian vessel to enter the Drin River.

13. BBA MV 81/42, 4 Rebiyülahir 1312 [6 October 1892].

14. BBA Irade i Dahiliye 2/N.1316, 1 Ramazan 1316 [13 January 1899].

15. BBA TFR.1.KV 148/14736, Kosova Vilayet to the Rumeli Commissioner's office, document 748, dated 17 Şevval 1324 [5 December 1906].

16. Much of this illicit trade skirted state customhouses by using maritime routes and virtually inaccessible points of entry that constantly changed. See BBA YA.HUS 501/46, 6 Safer 1324 [3 April 1906].

17. BBA MV 56/54, 4 Muharrem 1308 [21 August 1890] reveals Istanbul's concern over Nikolla's payoffs to local Malësore leaders.

18. It also became the main distribution point for the Ottoman state's meager efforts to send assistance to famine-stricken areas around Hoti and Gruda. In one case, 40,000 kıyye [okka: approx. 1300 grams] of corn had been arranged for delivery. Judging from later reports, this was not nearly sufficient. BBA MV 87/63, 7 Zilhicce 1313 [21 May 1896].

19. See AQSH F.887.D.31 for an important survey of incidents that took place between 1888 and 1903 among Malësorë communities competing over smuggling routes that ran through the border area of Tuz. Kelmendi and Cali emerged as regional trade barons with a great deal of political power. Elsewhere, Zeynel Effendi and Ahmet Aga would be involved in the smuggling of wheat meal sent from Europe, suggesting they were able to tap into Montenegrin supplies of European aid to that country. BBA MV 57/2, 11 Muharrem 1308 [28 August 1890].

20. See BBA MV 22/58, 10 Zilkade 1304 [1 July 1887] on a discussion in Istanbul about recent cooperation with Serbia to stop cross-border raids.

21. BBA YEE 25/95, 19 March 1865.

22. These plans were adopted and later expanded throughout the Arabian Peninsula BBA MV 18/79, 16 Recep 1304 [11 April 1887] and BBA MV 80/33 18 Zilkade 1311 [24 May 1894] on similar plans drawn to maximize revenue collection in Arabia.

23. BBA MV 78/5, 18 Cemaziyelahir 1311 [28 December 1893].

24. See BBA MV 74/105, 23 Şevval 1310 [11 May 1893] for an outline of the Ministry of Finance's policies toward trade in Yemen. See BBA MV 78/18, 29 Cemaziyelahir 1311 [8 January 1894] for the kinds of products being smuggled into Yemen, which included salt, dried fish, cloth, and guns.

25. Mustapha Asim Pasha pursued a policy of using local leaders to secure regional order, especially in respect to the still unstable region of 'Asir in the north of Yemen. BBA Irade Dahiliye 50932, vali to Grand Vizier, 8 Cemaziyelevvel 1293 [1 June 1876]. In much the same manner, authorities had adopted an approach to raise local troops, which by 1885 became part of official state policy. See BBA Y.MTV 17/16, 7th army general state report to the Palace, 21 Rebiyülahir 1302 [7 February 1885].

26. BBA HR.SYS 90/10, Description of Survey by Major Stevens of Yafi'i and Fadhli area, dated 3 April 1876.

27. See BBA HR.SYS 87/47, Sublime Porte copy of letter sent to British FO, dated Istanbul, 30 July 1874, f. 71.

28. The Ottoman embassy in London provided Istanbul with detailed coverage of the British media, which was particularly paranoid about Ottoman advances in Yemen. BBA HR.SYS 90/2, report no. 5320/274, Embassy to Rshid Pasha, dated London, 4 December 1873.

29. BBA HR.SYS 90/3, correspondence no. 5516/166, Embassy to Sublime Porte, dated London, 13 June 1874. See also IOR R/20/A/418, no. 352, "Affairs of Yemen," FO to Earl of Granville, 19 November 1873.

30. A nuance to international protocol to which the Ottomans clearly refused to subscribe, as evidenced in a letter sent to the British Foreign Office. BBA HR.SYS 90/3, correspondence no. 5559/209, Ottoman Ambassador to Lord Derby, dated London, 29 July 1874.

31. BBA HR.SYS 90/3, correspondence no. 5516/166, Embassy to Sublime Porte, dated London, 13 June 1874. See also IOR R/20/A/418, no. 352, "Affairs of Yemen," FO to Earl of Granville, 19 November 1873.

32. See examples of how Ottoman officials were supposed to police its waters for such activity, BBA MV 106/89, 28 Rebiyülahir 1321 [25 July 1903]; for French involvement in the smuggling trade and how one French smuggler requests amnesty after being arrested in Yemen, BBA MV 106/91, 28 Rebiyülevvel 1321 [25 June 1903].

33. See report by Yemen's vali Ahmed Fevzi Paşa on the early stages of this trade in Ottoman Yemen, BBA Y.MTV 21/101, 20 Ramazan 1303 [23 July 1886].

34. On how the Ottomans often failed to make distinctions between "criminal" and normal local behavior in the context of lower Yemen and the issues surrounding the smuggling of weapons, see BBA Y.MTV 238/69, 12 Şevval 1320 [13 January 1903].

35. Events over the period of 1900 to 1911 hint at Italy's long-term strategy to gain influence in Mukha by supporting individuals like 'Umar Salim. BBA HR.SYS 1568/2. For a detailed report on the French connection in Yemen's weapons trade that clearly gave them political leverage there see BBA Y.MTV 238/82, 14 Şevval 1320 [15 January 1903].

36. A relatively late example of this suggests the scope of the smuggling enterprise as Ottoman officials captured 312 rifles, BBA MV 107/46, 16 Cemaziyelevvel 1321 [11 August 1903].

37. We can see in the period leading up to the new round of disturbances that trade from Yemen into and out of Aden-protected regions jumped from 278,921 rupees in 1892–1893 to 3,142,608 in 1897. PRO FO 78/4899, report n. 128 for 1897, "Imports to Aden in 1896–1897," dated Simla, 8 September 1897. Enclosed: Report no. 68, (confidential) C.A. Cuningham, PR, Aden to GOB, dated Aden, 3 June 1897.

38. Hudaydah's 1898 annual tally of 400,000 guruş apparently fell short of expectations, BBA MV 95/55, 10 Safer 1316 [1 July 1898]. Due to these shortfalls, Istanbul invested more in policing Yemen's territories, as reported by the Finance office as well as the military, BBA YA.HUS 274/28, 4 Zilkade 1310 [21 May 1893]. This increased investment in the policing of Yemen would last at least another six years, BBA YA. RES 93/66, 14 Safer 1316 [5 July 1898] and BBA YA. RES 102/37, 19 Rebiyülahir 1317 [28 August 1899].

39. Clashes between customs officials and Asi "tribesmen" in the 'Asir suggest such confrontations were frequent and debilitating as early as 1890. BBA MV 56/33, 27 Zilhicce 1307 [15 August 1890].

40. This became clear in how regulations imposed from the empire, for instance, in what was determined to be state lands that were to be taxed for revenue meant for the imperial coffers, antagonized those tilling the land. BBA YA. RES 87/29, 14 Muharrem 1315 [16 June 1897].

CHAPTER FOUR

On the Margin of Statehood?
State-Society Relations in African Borderlands

Judith Vorrath

A multitude of studies and research projects dealing with the state in Africa have led to a better understanding of the nature of statehood on the continent.[1] But many "construction sites" with regard to internal dynamics and state-society relations still remain in states labeled as weak or fragile according to Western standards. By analyzing borderland case studies, this chapter attempts to gain better insights into the center-periphery relations "on the margins" of the African state where concepts of space, identity, and social networking interact in a specific way. The reason to have a special interest in borderlands is that "borders are spatial and temporal records of relationships between local communities and between states" (Wilson and Donnan 1998, 5). While borderlands can be called "extreme" peripheries, state-society relations become visible in the relation of locals both to the border *and* to central power structures on the ground. Thus, one specific feature of borderlands is the "double triangle of power relations," with the state, regional elites, and local people as actors meeting at the international crossroads of two political entities (Baud and van Schendel 1997, 219).

This triangle has regularly been observed and analyzed in borderland case studies. However, the valuable insights from these studies on state-society relations have not been fully exploited. Though differences of location as well as different research rationales and disciplines limit the comparability of the studies, common patterns clearly emerge from a systematic analysis. These insights can help us to better understand borderland settings. It has also been pointed out that "[t]he study of borderlands invites us to look at states, concepts of social space, and local history from a different perspective. It helps us pose questions in a new form" (Baud and van Schendel 1997, 235). In this sense, it is important not only to examine and understand the borderland perspective but also to ask what we can learn from it about African states more generally. Therefore, the chapter introduces some theoretical approaches on African statehood after substantiating the research focus and some central definitions. The approaches are essentially state centered but imply certain assumptions on borders and state-society relations in peripheries. The relatively brief overview does not do justice to the rich and elaborated nature of the underlying works, but it is essential for framing the analysis and formulating some general expectations on what we might find in borderlands in terms of state-society relations. This part is followed by the actual case study analysis that contains sections on identity formation, cross-border economic activities, state-society interaction, and violent conflict in borderlands. The conclusions are far from final, but relate to the central messages of this collective project and summarize and interpret the results to provide new input for policy and further research.

THE FOCUS OF ANALYSIS

With the postmodern turn in social sciences, political geography increasingly focused on borders as socio-territorial constructs rather than as state boundaries. The chapters in this book from the beginning refer to state borders, meaning the political divides resulting from state-building (Baud and van Schendel 1997, 213–14). Borderlands are understood as "sub-national areas whose economic and social life is directly and significantly affected by proximity to an international boundary" (Hansen 1981). From this point of view, an exact definition of how close an area has to be to the border to be labeled borderland is not necessary since the impact of the border is the defining characteristic. In accordance with this definition, the analyzed case studies predominantly refer to what has also been called "the border landscape" or "border heartland"—areas whose social networks are shaped more or less directly by the border (Baud and van Schendel 1997, 221). As already indicated, the focus of the case studies and of this chapter is on peripheral borderlands, which means that borderlands very close to or even including a capital city as in either of the two Congos are excluded. Similarly, African borderlands using the sea as a natural border are excluded since this analysis is about intersections of two political entities.

Within the double triangle of power relations of borderlands, the main focus of this chapter is on the relation between the state and its borderlanders, seeking both to describe that relation and to explain the reasons for it. But how do state-society relations become manifest in borderlands? On the one hand, the border as such represents the state. Therefore, it is essential to examine the local view of and relation to the political dividing line. On the other hand, the state is often represented by agents on the ground. Border controls are the most common direct manifestation of the central state at borders. Thus, the encounter and interaction of borderland people with state officials, such as customs officers, border police, and soldiers, is also of great importance to find answers to the research question. Both aspects of state-society relations from a borderland view are analyzed against the background of different approaches to African statehood.

Though naturally the theoretical literature considered here takes a state-centered view and has not been written to explain the condition in the peripheries, its explanations contain hints as to what we should expect in areas far away from state capitals. This literature is used to get a better understanding of borderland views of the state by demonstrating the extent to which local settings conform to or contradict expectations derived from state-centered approaches. Surely, the outcome cannot challenge any approach, but it might shed light on aspects of African statehood that are commonly ignored or insufficiently taken into account. In order to find out more about the perception and meaning of the border for the communities living close to it, the specific aspects of identify formation in borderlands are analyzed in a first step. Before scrutinizing the direct relationship of these communities to state agents, it is also important to have a closer look at cross-border economic activities and what they tell us about the significance of the border for borderlanders. Since transborder movements and areas located close to international borders have commonly been associated with instability, the fourth section of the analysis tries to shed some light on the connection of borderlands and violent conflict. Overall, the analysis of case studies concentrates on the question whether borderland communities are really on the margin of statehood in Africa, out of reach and control while actively opposing or ignoring the state.

THE STATE AND BORDERS IN AFRICA

A look at the interactive world maps on the six governance indicators of the World Bank overall presents Africa as the continent in a most severe condition (with the usual exception of South Africa and, to some extent, Botswana and Namibia). This condition—often described as state failure—has commonly been related to peripheries that are portrayed as being opposed to the state or essentially out of control and thus further undermine the state (Zartman 1995; Rotberg 2003).

Many African states are not or are only very limitedly able to provide security and essential public goods to their citizens (Ottaway and Mair 2004, 1). There is no doubt that it would be desirable to see this performance improve in the future. But too many (international) responses to state failure have been formulated without any deeper knowledge of the internal dynamics of the countries under consideration. Ever since the mismatch of states and societies in Africa has come to the fore, studying "the local" and developing theories of interactive relations between state and society have been proposed (Migdal 1988, 260). Accordingly, this chapter takes on the views from the periphery to further explore the internal logic of African states. In the following paragraphs, different approaches to African statehood are reviewed concerning their potential explanatory power on the relation of borderlands to the boundary and the state it represents. In a first section, the literature on state-building and state failure in Africa is illustrated before the approach of neo-patrimonialism is introduced.

The most commonly stressed aspect of African borders is their artificiality, which is "in large part due to their haphazard demarcation by European colonialists who ignored locally existing societies" (Larémont 2005, 2). The division of unified cultural areas by boundaries drawn at the Berlin Conference in 1884–1885 has often been cited as the most important source of disintegration and instability in Africa (for a discussion of this point see Asiwaju 1996, 255). Beyond this argument and the reference to shortcomings of the colonial system, Herbst (2000, 15–17) stresses the process of state-building in Africa with a very different history of relations between capitals and their hinterlands, resulting in a strong center-periphery divide. Therefore, a contradiction has developed between the incomplete control over the peripheries and the full claims to sovereignty of the center. From this point of view, the fundamental problem with African boundaries is not that they are meaningless, but "that they are too integral to the broadcasting of power in Africa" (253). African leaders have successfully instrumentalized them for their own purposes, which prompts Herbst to propose the geographical redesign of at least some African states (Herbst 2000, 257–69).

Partly in contrast to this, important parts of the literature on state failure have regularly framed African borders as irrelevant, because of their permeability and the lack of state control. The focus here is not so much on the instrumentalization of borders or the division of groups by them. Rather, the deficiencies of African statehood when compared to the Western nation-state model and a downward dynamic between deteriorating state authority and uncontrolled transnational activities such as predatory operations by militias are underlined. The latter are seen as indicators of a decline in the relevance of borders and ultimately of state failure (Joseph 2003, 166; Rotberg 2003, 5–6). Transnational factors have become increasingly prominent in state failure and conflict research. For example, by analyzing crisis regions as "bad neighborhoods" (Weiner 1996), factors such as arms and refugee flows have been identified as potentially destabilizing. Against the background of structural weakness of (African) states, cross-border informal and criminal activities that ignore the existence of international borders are seen as further undermining statehood (Schneckener 2004, 7).

According to these arguments, one would expect borderlands to be especially "out of control." On the one hand, they belong to the territorial (and political) periphery where cultural groups live divided by the state border. On the other hand, the presence of informal networks in these "remote" areas seems to mirror their big (physical and mental) distance to the central state. Combining the two features of periphery and border location and looking at the theoretical approaches above, one would expect at best that local communities based along the border view it as irrelevant and at worst oppose it. While the mismatch of state and social boundaries and the instrumentalization of borders by African leaders rather hint at resistance toward the border in these communities, the failure of statehood implies that the uncontrolled movement of locals across borders is a sign of their irrelevance and further erosion.

The neo-patrimonial approach does not deny the endemic weakness of African states emphasized by the literature on state failure. But beyond the appraisal of shortcomings it primarily tries to detect and understand the reality of statehood on the continent. It aims at explaining how African states work and identifies a hybrid system in which patrimonialism coexists with rational-legal institutions (Bratton and van de Walle 1997, 62). Essentially this means that traditional and or static practices run parallel to modern or liberal ones (Brett 2006; Ohlson and Söderberg 2002).

According to this approach, the logic of the political system in Africa is focused on the local and the communal, and legitimacy is established by micro-networks of patronage and clientelism (Chabal and Daloz 1999; Bayart 1996). Beyond patrimonialism, Chabal and Daloz (1999, xix) have highlighted the political economy of disorder as a common feature of African states that not only indicates deterioration but also provides opportunities. Overall the state is characterized by "a high level of governmental and administrative inefficiency, a lack of institutionalization, a general disregard for the rules of the formal political and economic sectors, and a universal resort to personal(ized) and vertical solutions to societal problems" (xix). From this point of view, it seems reasonable to expect a reproduction of neo-patrimonialism in borderlands with micro-networks of patronage and informal procedures. The disorder and the permeability of borders could provide opportunities for borderland populations who would have every reason to use it to their advantage. Illicit cross-border activities, for example, would then not be interpreted as opposition to or disregard of the state, but as active use of the opportunities provided by its neo-patrimonial nature.

Whether this expectation or the ones formulated in the previous section can best grasp state-society relations in African borderlands is explored by the analysis of several case studies. The core question is what relation borderland communities have to the border and the state it represents and in how far the above outlined approaches can explain it.

CASES OF STATE-SOCIETY RELATIONS IN AFRICAN BORDERLANDS

The case studies that have been examined for the following analysis deal with thirteen different borderlands, normally connecting two, three, or more countries, as the table shows. The borderlands between twenty-one different countries have been analyzed in case studies conducted by thirteen different authors. Some studies focus mainly on one side of the border (e.g., one village or border market), and others view locations on more than one side (e.g., "twin towns"). Some have a rather narrow time frame, while most provide a historical background and general analysis on the whole border region before switching to the case of one specific zone. For obvious reasons, relatively few case studies investigate areas during ongoing violent conflict. Most researchers deal with borderlands where conflict took place at an earlier time, or where no serious uprisings or warfare have ever occurred. The thematic focus and thus the overall argument of the studies also vary. While some authors deal mainly with cross-border trade and smuggling, others concentrate on identity issues or migration. Because of these different research interests and the different disciplinary backgrounds, a controlled comparison is impossible. So are generalizations or falsification of the theoretical approaches on African statehood based on systematic testing. However, the extraction of information on the relation of borderlands to the border and the state can be used to identify common patterns and to call into question some assumptions on borders and borderlands in Africa by taking a view from the periphery.

This is possible because of the common ground in the case studies. All borderlands under examination include one or more ethnic groups separated by the boundary. Each one refers to transnational as well as local structures and actors. Basically all deal in one way or another with the phenomenon of clandestine or illicit trade, and nearly all broach the issue of borderland identity and the perception of the border by local people. Even where the overall research focus is different, these issues arise over the course of the study. What is especially illuminating is the variance among countries included in the case studies with regard to state failure. In the 2006 "failed states index" (Fund for Peace 2006), twelve countries are within the category "Alert," and nine have been assigned to the "Warning" category. Ranks differ even more—from 1 (Sudan) to 106 (Ghana). Though indices can be questioned, and obviously the case studies have not been conducted at the same time as this ranking was published, it hints that it is very unlikely that all borderlands referred to are located in countries with a very similar condition of statehood. This variance is important to prevent any of the theoretical approaches from having an outright advantage.

Four core thematic areas stand out as central to the case studies and important to providing first answers to the main focus of this chapter: identity formation, cross-border economic activity, state-society relations, and violent conflict in borderlands. The first point, borderland identity, is crucial because it can shed light on what references and affiliations are important for borderland communities. Depending on conditions, one could, for example, expect a strong connection to ethnic kin groups on the other side of the border associated with antiborder sentiments or an absence of relation of the identity to the border at all in cases where the border is essentially meaningless for locals. The second aspect, cross-border economic activity, mainly refers to transnational

Borderlands included in case study analysis

West Africa

Bénin-Nigeria
Ghana-Togo
Ghana–Côte d'Ivoire
Nigeria-Niger
Sierra Leone–Liberia

Central Africa

Nigeria-Cameroun-Chad*
Cameroun–Gabon–Equatorial Guinea
Cameroun-CAR†-Chad
Chad Basin* (Nigeria, Niger, Cameroun, Chad, and CAR†)

East Africa

Uganda-Sudan
Somalia-Kenya-Ethiopia
Zaire/DR Congo–Uganda*

Southern Africa

Mozambique-Zimbabwe

* These borderlands transcend one African region.
† Central African Republic

illicit trade that has regularly been interpreted as an indication of resistance to the border by local people or its irrelevance for their daily lives, since they can move back and forth without any real restrictions. The third point, state-society relations, directly deals with the interaction of local people with agents of the state at the border to see if the relationship is rather conflictive, if there is no real interaction, or if linkages and networks emerge. In a fourth section, the role and emergence of violence in borderlands are discussed. Since few case studies were conducted in the midst of violent conflict, this section can only explore whether borderlands are entry points of potentially destabilizing factors or if they also cause conflict outbreaks.

BORDERLAND IDENTITIES

According to a checklist of partitioned cultural groups in Africa, 103 international boundaries cut through a total of 131 culture areas, some of them partitioned by more than one boundary (Asiwaju 1985, 256; Griffiths 1996, 74). This division of groups by borders dating mainly from colonial regimes has often been related to resistance or violent conflict in borderlands. The different case studies, however, show that challenges to these demarcations and (successful) movements for unity of divided ethnic groups in borderlands are rare. There seem to be several reasons for this finding, but two are especially prominent: first, the development of a distinct borderland identity and, second, the affirmation of national identity at the border.

The first point, borderland identity, is mentioned in several case studies. Basically all who raise the issue of identity in partitioned ethnic groups recognize something like a sense of "shared borderlandness" (Miles 2005, 299). This deep rootedness in the border coexists with other identity layers; for example, the Niger-Nigerian border where Miles found that Hausa and Muslim identity are both undiminished in their relevance by the territorial identity that emerged at the boundary (299). Local and territorial identities can even be more salient than ethnic, national, and other identity layers (Merkx 2002, 113; Nugent 2002, 5). Most importantly, border identity is not simply a different local interpretation of ethnicity, where, for example, "membership" to groups that define themselves by their location at the border is not based on ethnicity or nationality, but by other criteria such as length of residency in the border area (Flynn 1997, 319). Generally, border identity transcends the demarcation line, is fueled by economic interests connected to transborder trade, and also provides refugees with the opportunity to settle in and integrate communities on the other side of a boundary (Flynn 1997, 312–13; Merkx 2002, 124). Whatever the exact configuration of territorial identity, borders seem to unite rather than divide local people (McDermott Hughes 1999, 536). Thus, while a border identity might or might not make ethnic identities less important, it reflects the relevance of the border for locals beyond mere economic considerations.

But alternative identity formation is often accompanied by another process that, on first sight, seems rather contradictory: the affirmation of national identity in borderlands. Nationalism is not only theoretically expressed at (or by) the border. The demarcation is also a real marker of separate national identities—not despite but because of transborder links (Bennafla 1999, 49; Miles 2005, 315). Border residents often distinguish themselves from people across the border by negative stereotypes of the other nation. Though they come from the same cultural group and share the same borderland, people normally do not want to change places with their ethnic kinsmen on the other side (Flynn 1997, 326; Nugent 2002, 266). In the case of Hausa at the Niger-Nigeria border, national identity has been found to be at least as important as ethnic identity (Nugent 1996, 60). In another example, nationality is the overriding criteria of land allocation in a borderland. At the Zimbabwe-Mozambique border, Zimbabwean headmen have allocated land favorably to fellow citizens migrating to the border zone compared to Mozambicans migrating to the same community from the other side of the border (McDermott Hughes 1999, 540–41). The author shows that national affiliation clearly outnumbers all other features of origin, identity, or status. Why national identity is reaffirmed in borderlands is beyond the focus of most studies. However, one frequently mentioned factor is that borders represent the demarcation between areas formerly governed by different colonial powers. Different languages as well as administrative practices such as the different role of traditional rulers in the British and French colonial systems in West Africa have left their mark in postcolonial societies (McDermott Hughes 1999, 537; Southall 1985, 100; Collins 1985, 198).

The development of a border identity combined with a peculiar sense of national identity in borderlands means that borders have not proved irrelevant to locals, nor has there been frequent opposition to borders. In borderland studies it has long been pointed out that "processes of 'bordering' . . . make distinct political communities possible" (Ackleson 2004, 324). As the first statement of this collective project indicates, African borderlands have their own identity as one of the layers of identity that they enjoy. In addition, aspirations to unite with ethnic kin groups on the other side have been surprisingly weak.[2] Overall, "far from being marginal, border communities have been active participants in the shaping of national cultures and indeed the contours of the state itself" (Nugent 2002, 5).

BORDERLANDS AS ECONOMIC ARENA

One common characteristic of borderlands is the prominence of transborder economic activities and networks. Especially under conditions of border permeability, underdevelopment, and declining or missing infrastructure in Africa, trade across borders is an important economic opportunity. Most often these transborder activities are informal or illegal; thus trade here normally means illicit or clandestine trade. Border residents can earn income as porters, guides, transporters, or guards or by the establishment of a trading enterprise (Nugent 1996, 56, 58–59; Roitman 2001, 245). Smuggling is dependent on the existence of the border since differences in prices, currencies, and the general commercial atmosphere between neighboring countries are naturally the incentives and driving forces of these activities (Collins 1985, 202; Nugent 1996, 56, 58–59; Richards 1996, 205; Southall 1985, 9; Stary 1999, 170). Though the state might be absent at a border, its policies still influence the direction, size, and kinds of goods of cross-border trade (Collins 1985, 202; Miles 2005, 303). Flows of goods and people across the border not only include agricultural products, natural resources such as diamonds, and labor migration, but also risky ventures such as arms trade (Roitman 2001, 243). The "new" forms of economic integration by transborder networks feature illegal trade and all forms of unauthorized transborder movement including such groups as criminals (Collins 1995, 196).

Most case studies demonstrate the importance of contraband trade as a significant source of income for numerous intermediaries along the border. Generally, those with cross-border links tend to be better off, and the boundary line works as a factor of urban growth (Merkx 2002, 122; Stary 1999, 171, 175). Cross-border trade brings together borderlanders from different sides of the border with each other and with nonlocals. During field studies at Ghanaian border markets, one author found that two-thirds to three-quarters of customers there were tradesmen from the Ivorian borderland (Stary 1999, 173). Flourishing marketplaces are a magnet for nonlocal traders, as in the case of producers and middlemen who came from as much as fifty kilometers away from the Nigeria-Niger border to bring their groundnuts to markets on the other side (Collins 1985, 201). The special role of borderland communities lies in the organized commercial networks behind cross-border economic activities (Stary 1999, 172). Sometimes these are rather separated from state structures and agents, as in the case of communities along the Benin-Nigeria border that tax goods and people passing their area parallel to official border posts (Flynn 1997, 321). But frequently commercial activities include the state in some form, as the section on state-society relations along the border shows in greater detail.

Independent of the factor of state presence, it can be concluded that borders are corridors of opportunity rather than dividing lines for locals (Merkx 2002,

116). Commonly, both smuggling and immigration have been interpreted as resistance to African boundaries. The African case studies show that this assumption has to be disputed. Illicit trade clearly is not an expression of antiborder sentiment, though it might be a response to or an indicator of the lack of an effective functioning of the state (MacGaffey and Bazenguissa-Ganga 1999, 179). As long as there is some freedom of movement across and around the borders for locals, the borderland can be seen as a corridor or theater of opportunity (Flynn 1997, 313; Nugent 2002, 273). The lack of interest of borderland communities in redrawing existing boundaries shows that this corresponds to their perception. However, this does not mean that the border is irrelevant for borderlanders, for the opportunities only arise out of the border's existence. For example, the failure of the Senegambian confederation in West Africa in the late 1980s has been attributed to the influence of transnational trade networks. A strong cross-border lobby resisted fiscal and customs tariff harmonization that would have deprived traders of income "from the border" (Stary 1999, 177). Incidences like this might be seen as resistance to the central state. However, it is not the nature of borders linked to African state-building that led to this opposition, but the expected change of this nature.

Generally, populations have been very well aware of how they profit from their location at the border; therefore, from a borderlander's point of view, contraband trade makes the border more legitimate, not less so. Such networks have a local character, because border markets are linked to centers of suppliers and consumers in other regions or countries. Thus, they do not constitute spaces detached from the national territory (Bennafla 1999, 39; Stary 1999, 173).

BORDERLANDS AS STATE-SOCIETY NETWORKS

While the preceding sections have shown that borders are neither opposed by locals nor seen as irrelevant concerning economic interests and identity, the direct involvement of state actors in borderlands has largely been ignored, which means the analysis has been undertaken as if there would be no state presence at the border. Indeed, on first sight there seems to be an amazing absence of state agents in African borderlands. An examination of the number of official crossing points in relation to the total length of boundary lines in Africa shows only one official road crossing point every 145 miles of boundary in 1996 (Griffiths 1996, 70). Though it certainly holds true that African borders tend to be permeable and that there was weak or no reinforcement of state authority in the decades after independence, there has been a process of thickening and hardening of the state at borders (Miles 2005, 312–13). Thus, there are borderlands among those analyzed here where the state and locals directly meet and interact. It is important to examine how borderland communities deal with these agents—if they tend to oppose or ignore their presence, or if they try to incorporate them and profit from informal arrangements.

Surely, states can indirectly influence commercial activities in borderlands by the provision of infrastructure, the creation of frontier markets, or price regulation, as already mentioned (Bennafla 1999, 43). But this paragraph confines itself to the direct intrusion of state actors into border zones. Where the state is present in borderlands, its role is ambivalent (48). From the point of view of local residents, state presence in the form of customs or immigration posts is initially a nuisance. The most evident reaction is to circumvent state order, especially when efforts to establish it go beyond the acceptable scope (Miles 2005, 298; Flynn 1997, 324). Most commonly, local residents try to avoid border posts by using their knowledge of alternative paths that they also "sell" to outsiders. For example, at the border of Ghana and Côte d'Ivoire groups of young, normally local people offer the service of crossing the border without administrative "procedures." These small cross-border networks are each controlled by few local people in town and specialize in certain types of products (Stary 1999, 174–75). This means that locals find ways to avoid state structures or to indirectly profit from them by using their knowledge of the border region.

According to the majority of case studies, however, most often traders try to engage state agents directly by "buying" them instead of circumventing border posts (Bennafla 1999, 44). Such taxes from cross-border activities seem to go largely unrecorded and often flow directly into guards' personal purses (Flynn 1997, 318). This might seem like a simple practice of corruption, but it also leads to the emergence of state-society networks that are worth looking at in greater detail. Often government agents are directly involved in the border traffic, and border trackers and smugglers have informal (and sometimes nearly formal) agreements with customs officials and government agents (Stary 1999, 176). After the initial opening of a post at the Benin-Nigeria border, local chiefs invited officials to discuss a working agreement. Negotiations took place between residents, traders, and custom guards, and a "free-trade pact" was indeed established (Flynn 1997, 320–23). At a Ghanaian border post the network between soldiers and smugglers was so tight that both very much disliked the "People's Militia" established to fight contraband trade, since it disturbed the local compact (Nugent 2002, 268). Specific borderline norms also developed along the Niger-Nigeria border between 1960 and 1980 ("frontier justice") from illegal cross-border trade. The giving and taking of bribes was not only accepted but was governed by informal rules (Miles 2005, 308).

The formalization of state-society relations in frontier zones has been found by other authors as well. Networks that define wealth and ways of appropriating it can include such diverse actors as rebel group members, local merchant and political elites, customs officials, and military officers looking for rents and can build what Roitman (2001, 249–50) calls "commercio-military alliances." In the Chad Basin, regional elites exercise regulatory authority by controlling access to networks of accumulation by protection fees, right-of-entry taxes, and so forth. Beyond cross-border trade, other factors can also create new networks of power including state and local nonstate actors, as periodic dispossessions in a district at the Zimbabwean border to Mozambique did. In the struggle over agricultural land in this border zone "a system of power and legitimacy" developed (McDermott Hughes 1999, 538). In all these cases, resistance to state presence was unnecessary because either the state could be bypassed, or established practices could continue because of informal arrangements and newly emerging networks.

It has been shown that the state regularly is an actor in cross-border trade. Generally, what can be observed is a reshaping of state structures to accommodate border populations, but border communities have also modified their networks and activities to incorporate state actors and to profit from their presence. Though antistate sentiment emerged or intensified as a reaction to the establishment of customs and immigration posts in some places, the local population also used the same post as another source of income. Shabe communities at the Benin-Nigeria border found a new occupation as mediators between guards and nonlocal traders at the border. Not only is this practice accepted by the state agents, but they will often prevent nonlocal people from passing without this procedure, and they pay their share of the fee for the mediator. In the process of negotiating the terms of passage for traders, local chiefs can be involved as well (Flynn 1997, 322). In a more indirect way, locals profit from the existence of border posts, because officials at army posts live well from their illegal earnings and also "reinvest" money in borderlands by using certain community services (Nugent 2002, 266–67). The fact that border communities can manipulate customs posts to their advantage explains why they prefer to have such a post in their area rather than in a neighboring village (Flynn 1997, 323).

Antistate sentiment is not absent from borderlands. Hindrance to engage in cross-border trade and movement can arouse communal resentment. The complete closure of Nigerian borders under the Buhari military regime between 1984 and 1986 was a time of particular hardship for borderlanders (Miles 2005, 310). If the state is perceived as the source of such economic hardship, antagonism toward it can increase as in Nigeria and Benin (Flynn 1997, 315–16). However, relatively few instances of antistate sentiments of borderland residents have been mentioned in the case studies, most likely because border infrastructure is seen as a further instance of development (Miles 2005, 314).

State structures and agents have frequently been included in local networks of accumulation—whether there was opposition to their imposition in the beginning or not. Border communities "have invoked state power when it has been to their advantage, and have successfully domesticated the local agents of state power when they have been placed in their midst" (Nugent 2002, 274). Such arrangements are basically part of the political logics of the neo-patrimonial state and contribute to its reproduction (Roitman 2001, 243). Ultimately, this state is dependent on regional economies for rents and means of redistribution. They serve the well-being of state administrators, contribute to the state's financial liquidity, and reinforce the rentier state (Bennafla 1999, 25; Roitman 2001, 241–42, 255).

BORDERLANDS AND VIOLENCE

As has been shown in the section above, there is little evidence or likelihood of irredentist sentiment in borderlands (Nugent 2002, 230; Bennafla 1999, 49; Southall 1985, 99). More generally speaking: "irredentism is conspicuous by its absence as a cause of dispute in Africa, except in the well-known case of Somalia" (Griffiths 1996, 76). Border disputes in present-day Africa are equally uncommon, and where they have taken place, few were caused by divided culture groups (Nugent 2002, 199; Merkx 2002, 116; Griffiths 1996, 76). However, borderlands as peripheries are often associated with violent conflict and instability.

Those few case studies that give insights into borderland conflicts mainly stress that these areas might be struck by violence because of terrain advantageous to guerrilla group operations, arms flows through border zones, and more generally the uncontrolled character of international borders in Africa (Richards 1996, 207; Schmidt 1996, 186). For all these reasons, rebel movements might decide to operate from hardly accessible or weakly controlled frontier zones (Merkx 2002, 124; Richards 1996, 207). Conflicts can also quite easily spill over from neighboring countries, because, on the one hand, their governments might support rebel groups on foreign territory as part of a strategy of proxy warfare, and because, on the other hand, most refugee crises are situated in borderlands like those between Uganda and Sudan, Zambia and Angola, and Liberia and Sierra Leone (Zartman 1992; Merkx 2002, 117). In all these instances, borderlands are mainly entry points for potentially destabilizing factors. Most authors do not ascribe the origin of violent conflict to borderlands. Indeed, it could be argued on the above stated evidence that borderland populations have less interest in violent conflict than other parts of the periphery. For example, it has been mentioned that warfare at the border can limit or stop transborder trade, as in the case of the Sierra Leone–Liberia border after the RUF intervention in 1991, thus depriving local residents of their income opportunities (Richards 1996, 205). It has also been found that cross-border political networks give borderland politicians more influence than their counterparts in the interior with regard to the state, and they also have access to political resources of two state units (Baud and van Schendel 1997, 226).

Conflict can spill over from abroad and take place in borderlands, but it might not be rooted in the communities on the "margins" of statehood. Certainly, local people can be involved in potentially destabilizing activities, such as arms trade, but they have little interest in causing the outbreak of violence. Once an armed conflict has started, however, they might again adapt to the situation and get involved in emerging "war economies." It would be desirable to conduct more detailed research to clarify if borders are mainly entrance points for destabilizing factors, or if violence also originates in borderlands, actively pursued by its inhabitants.

What seems quite clear is that the complete closure of borders by governments in response to conflict is an ambivalent procedure. In the case of the border of Somalia, Kenya, and Ethiopia, governments often chose this strategy in an attempt to control transfrontier traffic "on the mistaken assumption that this will minimize border friction" (Samatar 1985, 185). In any case, destabilizing cross-border effects and the occurrence of violent conflict in borderlands should be differentiated from the direct involvement of the local population.

CONCLUSION

In summary, the case study analysis indicates that the border location provides locals with economic opportunities mainly associated with contraband trade. The border becomes more legitimate in the eyes of local populations because of these and other cross-border activities. In this sense, the use of the opportunities of transnational (informal) trade by borderlanders is a "daily vote of confidence in favor of the status quo" (Nugent 2002, 232). One clear indication for this finding is the complete lack of interest on the side of borderland communities in redrawing African borders (Asiwaju 2000, 202). Partitioned ethnic groups in borderlands also do not oppose boundaries, as they develop a distinct territorial identity. In addition, national identity is reinforced at the border, not despite but because of transborder interaction (Wilson and Donnan 1998, 16). Concerning the direct interaction of locals and state agents, the installation of border posts is generally disliked by local residents. However, borderland people normally have two ways of blunting border policing: they bypass state structures by redirecting smuggling across the still permeable boundary or, more commonly, they find informal arrangements with state actors and integrate them into local power structures. In addition, the presence of border posts also provides new opportunities for the respective communities in the form of new occupations or money flowing back from state actors into local community services. The fourth section has argued rather than demonstrated that destabilization found in peripheries around borders might be due to intruding factors rather than originating in the local communities.

In focusing mainly on the insights from the first three sections, the explanatory power of the different state approaches for borderland settings needs further discussion. First, with regard to the relations of locals to the boundary, it has been demonstrated that the border influence on socioeconomic life is not perceived as negative. The analysis has clearly shown that borders are most often not opposed by those living along or near them; rather, "the once-colonial boundary has been fully internalized in the post-colonial era" (Miles 2005, 315). Thus, the deficiencies of state-building including the absence of demarcation can hardly explain the insights from borderlands. In addition, it has been shown that borders are also not perceived as irrelevant or meaningless by borderland communities, who even frequently develop a borderland identity and profit from the opportunities of their border location. Surely, it must be stressed that this is strongly linked to the opportunity to move relatively freely across borders in many African states, which might also explain the missing resistance to borders.

Here, however, it becomes important to look at the notion of the state to understand borderlands. In much of the literature on state failure borders are seen as relevant when they function as a protective barrier to secure territorial integrity. Since many African borders are permeable and do not live up to this standard, they can be labeled irrelevant from this point of view. However, this is at least misleading in the light of the findings from borderlands, because borders can take on other functions that are of relevance to locals and similarly to certain nonlocal actors. Ultimately, the flight of refugees or the "retreat" of armed groups to failing states would not make sense if borders were generally irrelevant.

At the least, how the border is perceived and used by locals can be better explained by the neo-patrimonial approach that stresses disorder as both decay and opportunity. The permeability of African borders and their location close to this line indeed provide borderland communities with specific opportunities. In the context of a neo-patrimonial system, informal borderland activities do not necessarily advance the process of state failure, and they even reproduce and sustain the state in its current condition.

Despite the findings on the relation and perception of the border by borderland people, one could argue that this setting can only exist as long as the state is not directly present on the scene and does not try to enforce its authority. State-society relations might display very different features when the permeability of the border is threatened, much as in the case of the Ottoman Balkans and Greece. Indeed, the intrusion of state agents into border zones has sometimes been seen as a nuisance but has rarely led to outright resistance. Instead, people try to bypass state structures on the ground or include them in their local settings. The bypassing could be interpreted as proof that the state—represented by its agents at the border—is irrelevant or resisted by locals, because people continue to pursue transborder activities largely uncontrolled and state authority is not enforced. One could, of course, argue that this was not the goal of state actors in the first place, but there is not sufficient information on the motives for opening new border posts to confirm or disprove this. Those interpreting the bypassing of border posts as resistance to the state cannot explain why in many places borderland communities have actually engaged directly with state officials and integrated them into the local setting. It can also not explain why people would prefer to have border posts set up in their own community and not in neighboring towns or villages. Therefore, this approach again has little explanatory power.

From the view of discourse on state failure, the border remains essentially irrelevant whether locals bypass it or engage in informal arrangements with state agents, for both are seen as further undermining state authority. In a normative sense, this is certainly true; the real problem with this argumentation, however, is that the neo-patrimonial state already exists and is fed and strengthened by networks at the border including state agents. Thus, the arrangements found in borderlands as such do not intensify state decay with destabilizing effects but rather help to maintain the state in its current form. While this conclusion is limited in its scope because it refers only to borderlands and not to peripheries in general, it might help shed light on why "state maintenance (in whatever weakened or decayed capacity) is still the norm, and state collapse the exception" (Milliken and Krause 2002, 765). However, the ultimate argument here is that local settings and state-society relations in borderlands can best be examined based on the neo-patrimonial concept of the state, as most often the particular power structures in borderlands seem to be an integral part of the (neo-patrimonial) African state.

This conclusion is more than a mere change of perspective since it impacts on the choice of strategies to deal with fragile statehood. First, redrawing Africa's borders, as has repeatedly been proposed (Herbst 2000; Englebert, Tarango, and Carter 2002, 1113), hardly seems a viable option because as much as borders are an instrument of state actors, they are also used by borderland communities to their own advantage. Redrawing may (or may not) solve the problem of split ethnic groups but will then create problems with other groups split as a result. Second, while violence near borders and the inflow of destabilizing external factors might be good reasons for strengthening the grip of the central state on borders, the consequences this has for local residents have to be taken into account. If people are not provided with alternative means to secure their survival, they might face severe economic hardship, and tensions will most likely arise. Depriving people of the opportunities connected to borders and questioning the legitimacy of their "border identity" may generally lead to a serious backlash. It is against this background that border(land) researchers have demanded as much flexibility and openness of African borders as possible to guarantee some freedom and opportunities for survival to subnational units (Southall 1985, 102). Third, informal networks at the border have been a way for borderland communities to accommodate state agents and thus secure the permeability of the border for them or open up new opportunities. It is essential to take these arrangements into account in devising policy. For example, a rapid change at the center (in regime or system) would probably cut out the core of a patchwork of state-society relations where the new core will not find its fit.

The statement that "[p]ressures to soften the border only became reasons to harden it" (Zartman, introduction to this volume) could be turned around for the African situation,[3] arguing that the permeability of borders and the reproduction of neo-patrimonial structures in borderlands have often made such pressure unnecessary—at least for local communities. Overall, borderlands are certainly on the margins of statehood in a spatial sense, but they contribute to the stability of the territorial frame and to the continuity of the (neo-patrimonial) African state.

Notes

The author gratefully acknowledges financial support by the Swiss National Science Foundation as part of the NCCR Democracy (National Centre of Competence in Research "Challenges to Democracy in the 21st Century").

1. In the following discussion, *Africa* refers to Sub-Saharan Africa.

2. Beyond borderlands, irredentism in Africa has been found to be confined to groups with a firm base in one particular nation-state that also have a common precolonial political and social history. Somalia is a case in point here (Southall 1985, 99).

3. This chapter certainly does not want to present neo-patrimonial structures as "natural" and therefore generally suitable to Sub-Saharan Africa; nor does it assume that all African states are functioning in exactly the same way. However, it argues that there are prevalent patterns—based on the theoretical approaches as well as the variety of countries included in the case study analysis.

CHAPTER FIVE

Change and Non-change in the U.S.-Mexican Borderlands after NAFTA

David Stea, Jamie Zech, and Melissa Gray

This chapter is a brief summary of the very complex contemporary situation along the U.S.-Mexico border, the nature of cross-border trade and interaction, and the impacts that the fifteen-year-old North America Free Trade Agreement (NAFTA) has had on the border and border life. We begin with a discussion of applicable border theory and modifications to such theory in the case of this particular border (for more detail, see Rosenau 1993), relating this to the introductory theme and continuing with the characteristics of this border and its major problems, the nature and nurture of NAFTA, and several topics specific to this border: land tenure, cultural identity, migration, *narcotrafico*, tourism, terrorism, and transborder perceptions. The chapter concludes with an assessment of the comparative impacts of NAFTA on the border region and the interior of Mexico, as well as with a discussion of measures proposed to further "harden" the border.

BORDERLINES AND BORDER REGIONS

International borders are never neutral. There seems to be something of a paradoxical "edge effect" operating that acts to both exaggerate and attenuate conflicts or contrasts. As indicated in the introduction to this volume, aspects of two nation-states that may be very different are, simultaneously, very closely related (of necessity) at a border. International borders are often places where contiguous landscapes or urbanscapes or populations have been "sawn" apart.

In some cases, both sides are similar, much like wood grains that are continuous from one side of a cut to another, but they may grow more disparate over time due to socioeconomic or political differences. Such joints may be "glued" together (however imperfectly) by cross-border commerce and social/familial relations, creating "seams," but those seams may be ruptured by "wedges" from the inside, as in increased socioeconomic differences, and from the outside, as in the case of recent fears of terrorism along U.S. borders. Nonetheless, seams can make borders "semi-permeable membranes," relatively more or less porous to people, depending upon their nationalities and stations in life, to economic exchange, to the passage of ideas, or to the diffusion of innovation. Borderland interactions ideally create mutually beneficial situations and opportunities for further development and advancement for both sides but also contain contrary pressures. In this chapter, the border ("semi-permeable membrane"), interactions ("seams"), and conflicts ("rips") along the U.S.-Mexico border region are explored in light of recent trends toward globalization and, in particular, the fifteen-year-old bonding agreement, whose acronym is NAFTA in the United States and TLCAN in Mexico. Of the four types of social communities posited in the introduction, the U.S.-Mexico border is clearly characterized by "majoritarian [Mexican] communities that spill over as minorities into a neighboring state [the United States]." Zartman's spatial model for social relations in borderland areas—black-and-white, grey, buffered, spotty, or layered—suggests that at least half of the U.S.-Mexico border (Texas and the three Mexican states it meets across the Rio Grande/Bravo) is "grey," in that different populations are fully intermingled. California–Baja California and Arizona-Sonora are "spotty" since the penetration of Mexican culture into the U.S. side is less continuous (Gerber 2007).

Considering that borders are never entirely "seamless," Martinez (1994) put forth another social typology and identified and discussed four levels of borderland interaction: alienated, coexistent, interdependent, and integrated. The U.S.-Mexico border remained very much on the margins of the two national power centers, with minimal proximal population for most of the nineteenth century. Not until after the Mexican Revolution did the two nations enter into the interdependent relationship that characterizes current interactions.

The hinterlands of borderlines are borderlands. The introductory chapter states that "borderlanders constitute an identifiable unit unto themselves, distinct from the populations further back from the line by their experiences and their identity." But what are the limits of such borderlands? How far "back from the line"? The U.S.-Mexican "official" borderland is defined as a *chorizo* 100 kilometers on either side of the political border, an arbitrary definition corresponding to no social, physical, economic, or linguistic reality. In a study conducted at Texas State University, located just over 200 miles north of the Texas-Mexico border, students were asked to draw boundaries of *border regions* on an outline map, using different criteria: one group was asked to delimit the *economic* border region, another the *linguistic* border region, still another the *cultural/ethnicity* border region, and so forth. When the results were aggregated, it appeared that the border regions, however defined, were seen as *very* different, that they were asymmetrical on the two sides of the border line, and that none resembled the official 200-kilometer-wide *chorizo*.

Borders both unite and divide. Mexicans in south Texas were effectively "stranded" when the border moved south in the mid-1800s as they were divided from their extended families south of the Rio Grande/Bravo. For a short time, the large region composing south Texas and northern Mexico declared itself an independent nation, the Republic of the Rio Grande (whose major remnant is a museum in Laredo, Texas), but this confederation lasted less than a year. Late in the nineteenth century, Mexicans, whose claim to their land was based on royal decrees of the Spanish Crown (rather than the fee-simple titles familiar to North Americans), were confronted by shrewd traders. The traders acted in much the same way as those who, after the General Allotment Act of the 1880s, broke apart Indian Reservations into individual land holdings and bought Indians' land at low prices. Those traders in the Rio Grande Valley, who were less than completely successful at this, then attempted to separate traditional owners from their land by invoking legislation that effectively challenged the validity of the royal decrees.

The once-porous U.S.-Mexico border has been "hardened" in recent years, assisted by the imposition of "foreign populations"—border guards and both military and paramilitary units—intent upon enforcing the separation represented by the borderline. Even more recently, an attempt to impose a new boundary on the old borderland has been initiated through construction of a Great Wall, ostensibly between U.S. border states and neighboring Mexican states, but actually several miles inland in the Texas case, separating Tejanos (Texans of Mexican ancestry) from parts of their own lands and even threatening to divide the University of Texas–Brownsville in half.

Other culture groups have been further separated by border-hardening. The Tohono O'Otam (Papago), for example, are Native American people who have lived in a large desert area that straddles southern Arizona and northern Sonora, Mexico. Over the years since the establishment of the Papago Reservation in Arizona, the Papago (more properly, the Tohono O'Otam) have crossed back and forth fairly freely to visit family and participate in culturally essential ceremonies. The communities on the two sides of the political border are completely intertwined and interrelated. Over the past decade, however, two factors have interfered with this pattern of intervisitation: the "war on drugs" and the "war on terror" in the aftermath of September 11, 2001. As a result, the border has been tightened, leaving the Tohono O'Otam to fight for the right to remain united. On Mexico's southern border, Mexican and Guatemalan Mayans exist in a similarly interdependent relationship (Stea, Elguea, and Perez Bustillo 1997) and are experiencing similar problems related to border crossing and border control.

IDENTITY ALONG THE BORDERLANDS

Border identity in the U.S.-Mexico border region is complex because it is influenced by so many factors: culture, communication (including language), ethnicity, trade, history, and economics. Though the *physical* border between Texas and Mexico (Rio Grande/Bravo) was politically established by 1853, emotional and psychological identity along the border has not been so easily demarcated (Vila 2003b; Warnock 1995). Borders, borderlands, and border regions are enigmatic places where people, ideas, and identities cross and recross or, alternatively, are forbidden from crossing, leading to a dynamic whereby certain amounts of transience and transmigration, as well as stasis, exist. Political borders tend to be places that in some ways maximize contrasts between neighbors; political forces foster and strengthen the concept of the *other* regarding ethnic and cultural practices as well as poverty and progress (Vila 2003a, 2003b), and may even *negate* the other: "authorities seek to overcome the new artificiality of the border by giving it civilizational meaning as the end of the world, with nothing on the other side" (Zartman, introduction). This is also true of the U.S.-Mexican borderlands, but it is marked by another, opposing phenomenon: *hybridization* of identity along the border (Anzaldúa 1987).

The border is made up mostly of Mexican and U.S. nationals, but the two groups may be further subdivided into, in popular parlance, Anglos, *indígenas, mestizos,* African Americans, Hispanics, Chicanos, Mexicans, and so on (Vila 2003b). These labels often overlap. Anzaldúa's hybrid-embracing border study explores the concept of *Chicana* as this identity has evolved on *la frontera*. Her prose and poetry explain identity through the eyes of a border woman—herself.

> *La Facultad* is the capacity to see in the surface phenomena the meaning of deeper realities, to see the deep structure below the surface.... Those who are pushed out of the tribe for being different are likely to become more sensitized (when not brutalized into insensitivity). Those who do not feel psychologically or physically safe in the world are more apt to develop this sense. Those who are pounced on the most have it the strongest—the females, the homosexuals of all races, the darkskinned [*sic*], the outcast, the persecuted, the marginalized, the foreign. (Anzaldúa 1987, 38)

Anzaldúa's hybridized "Chicana" identity is at odds with other border scholars who approach the border from an ethno-diversification perspective (Vila 2003a, 2003b; Wright 2003). Vila (2003b, 608) writes: "The main problem I have with those authors [scholars espousing hybrid border identity] is that they tend to homogenize the border, as if there were only one border identity, border culture, or process of hybridization." Nevertheless, an amalgamated "border culture," characterized by its own dialect and an integrated economy, characterizes the entire border region. On both sides, *la frontera* is still relatively isolated from centers of power. There is the question of the contribution of closeness across borders versus distance from the interior "central places" in the evolution of "border cultures," giving rise to inquiries about the possible emergence of nascent distinctive languages. As with *Franglais* in towns along the English Channel, *Portunol* on the Venezuela-Brazil frontier, *Joual* in the Quebec–New England border region, the use of *Spanglish*, or the more denigrative *Pocho*, has become prevalent in the U.S.-Mexican borderlands, particularly on the U.S. side (Stavans 2003).

While this debate is ever unfolding, there is yet another boundary, the economic boundary, which divides and develops border identity. In the years since the implementation of NAFTA, unemployment rates along much of the U.S.-Mexico border have been over 200 percent higher than those in the remainder of the United States, and heavy border industrialization has meant more people with less access to basic infrastructure services like water and sanitation (U.S.-Mexico Border Health Commission, 2009). *Colonias*, unincorporated rural communities that have appeared along the border and are largely populated by citizens of the United States, maintain living conditions similar to those in many third-world countries. Residents lack appropriate housing, sewage, electricity, and potable water. Living conditions experienced in these border communities deviate starkly from conditions experienced by most U.S. citizens, but they are remarkably similar to the conditions in which many Mexican citizens live. While some of the richest people in the world live in Mexico (fourth worldwide in the number of billionaires in the mid-1990s), a vastly larger percentage of the population is poor—some desperately poor. That fact has allowed wealthy Mexican and U.S. citizens alike to take advantage of populations and opportunities along the border.

The U.S.-Mexico border has been said to be among the most culturally, physically, and socioeconomically contrasting in the world. The kind and degree of contrast varies from point to point along the border (Arreola and Curtis 1993; Gerber 2007). The part of the border fronting on Texas (comprising almost 50 percent of the total border) is very different from the part dividing California from Baja California. In general, the border represents the cultural contrast between the legacies of British colonialism on one side of the line and longer Spanish colonialism on the other. The difference is apparent in the contrast between the near-absence of street life on the U.S. side and the vibrant street ballets on the Mexican side, and where the broad avenues and oceans of parking surrounding the "big box" architecture of the U.S. side are contrasted with the narrow streets and adobe-style zero lot-line architecture and urban layout typical of Mexico. Economic standards of living are also sharply different: for example, the minimum wage on the U.S. side is almost eight times the *salario minimo* on the Mexican side, though neither can be considered a living wage.

There is also an important cultural difference between the two major segments of the borderland: the Rio Grande/Bravo consists of half of the border where Texas faces Tamaulipas, Coahuila, and Chihuahua, while the other half is a land border of mainly straight-line segments where New Mexico, Arizona, and California face Chihuahua, Sonora, and Baja California Norte (Arreola and Curtis 1993; Gerber 2007). Mexican culture and language dominate both sides of the eastern half of the border region, penetrating for a considerable distance into Texas. Laredo, Eagle Pass, and other Texas border towns have retained much of their Mexican character. By contrast, such towns and cities as Deming, New Mexico, Bisbee, Arizona, and San Diego, California, all west of the Texas border region, represent predominantly "Anglo" culture. Tucson, Arizona, 65 miles north of the political border, is much less Mexican than San Antonio, Texas, 150 miles north of the border.

BORDER PRESSURES—POPULATION, ENVIRONMENT, AND NAFTA

From their final delineation in 1853, the borderlands were sparsely populated, and persons from both nations crossed interchangeably with minimal resistance. At that time, however, the city of El Paso del Norte was a node on a major thoroughfare between interior Mexico and the northern United States. At the turn of the twentieth century, and especially during and after the Mexican Revolution of 1910–1917, many Mexican families migrated to and crossed the border to escape the conflict. In the 1920s, El Paso experienced significant growth due to economic changes that encouraged the expansion of regional agricultural production, while the rest of post–World War I United States suffered severe declines in agricultural production. El Paso was able to expand its industrial and manufacturing capacities significantly, corresponding to and abetted by the expansion of rail transportation networks in the U.S. Southwest (Lorey 1999). As a result of sudden growth in the area, legal and illegal migration increased, and in 1924 the U.S. Border Patrol was officially installed to control illegal immigration.

Around the time of the Great Depression, El Paso became a focal point as the two nations were attempting to lower the rate of migration and unemployment and deter border-related crime. Instead of a wall or fence, towers were installed in order to spot illegal border crossers well before they arrived at the border. From the initial proposal of physical barriers to the construction of the towers, Mexican officials took offense at what they interpreted as impingement upon the stable and friendly relationship ostensibly assumed by both nations since the conclusion of the Mexican Revolution (Stoddard 2001). Since then, the border has been heavily monitored via towers, terrain vehicles, air patrol, and foot patrol, increasingly so in present-day efforts to impede the steadily rising flow of illegal migrants, including that of (hypothetical) potential terrorists.

NAFTA and Border Population

Significant population growth (with the exception of El Paso/Ciudad Juarez) was staved off until the mid- to late twentieth century, when U.S. agricultural production and harvesting needs steadily brought workers to the U.S. border area and beyond under the *Bracero* program until the 1960s. Then, as a result of enabling legislation, the number of industrial and manufacturing plants, or *maquiladoras*, mushroomed on the Mexican side of the border, and the number of these continues to increase even after the formalization of the NAFTA and its enactment at the beginning of 1994. In the decade between the inception of NAFTA and the new millennium, annual growth rates in U.S. border counties such as Yuma, Arizona, and Hidalgo, Texas, were as high as 4 percent; however, the *municipios* of Ocampo and Acuña in Mexico experienced growth rates well over 6 percent (Ocampo itself grew at a rate of 9.9 percent). These two Mexican *municipios*, in the state of Coahuila, are centered on the lineal array composing most of the Texas-Mexico *maquila* industry (Westerhoff 2000).

Mass migration of Mexican nationals from the interior of Mexico to the northern border region of Mexico has been prompted by the search for more financially rewarding employment and improved working conditions, such as those found in the industrial areas (Lorey 1999) whose growth was fueled first by the *maquiladora* program. Dramatic rates of both municipal expansion and population growth in the border region, along with spectacular industrial development in the Mexican state of Nuevo Leon, made the northernmost part of Mexico the wealthiest region of that country, while the southernmost "Valley" of Texas languished in relative poverty, remaining to this day the poorest region in the United States (Pick, Viswanathan, and Hettrick 2001; Stoddard 2001). Although NAFTA has had a major (not always positive) impact upon small-scale and peasant agriculture in Mexico (Calva 2003; Rubio 2003), agriculture is less important than other forms of economic activity on the Mexican side of the border, with the exception of the Rio Conchos and the extreme northwest of Baja California. There has been a concomitant increase in the number of *colonias* outside urban boundaries (Lorey 1999; Stoddard 2001; Ward 1999) on the U.S. side.

Population remains a major issue, particularly in urban areas. The border demographic growth that began with the Mexican Revolution when people came to escape violence on the Mexican side of the border and that continued with Prohibition on the U.S. side, followed by the start and conclusion of the *Bracero* Program and the *maquiladora* program that began shortly thereafter, was exacerbated by the enactment of NAFTA and the peso devaluation of the mid-1990s (Peach 2005). Mexicans have flocked to the border: of those not heading for the U.S. interior, some have remained south of the Rio Bravo, while others have sought employment in U.S. border cities.

NAFTA and Border Environment

The ecology of the environmentally defined U.S.-Mexico border region ranges climatologically from arid to semiarid to subtropical and is characterized by both coastal and mountainous regions that form backdrops for wetlands, deserts, forests, grasslands, and oceanic ecosystems. In the eastern border region, bounded by Texas's Colorado River and Rio Grande as well as thirteen lesser tributaries, a burgeoning population and associated environmental degradation threaten the border's biota. Environmentally, the border region cannot easily sustain the populations now attempting to thrive on the border. The increased legal and illegal migration to the southern part of Texas is said to have contributed to bringing "traffic congestion, environmental degradation, rise in crime, increased divorce rates, ethnic strife, and a rapid spread of disease" (Lorey 1999, 130) to the region. On both sides, increased population pressure has rendered the local infrastructure and environmental resources of the various border area communities incapable of supporting current and future populations. The most pressing issue at present is the availability of water in general and of potable water in particular; but air quality concerns, while perhaps secondary, are considerable (Quintero Nunez, and Forster 2005).

Water has been and, seemingly, will remain a significant environmental issue along the U.S.-Mexico border (Peña and Fuentes, 2005; Van Schoik 2004). Disputes regarding water allocation from the Rio Grande/Bravo to the two countries began arising during the nineteenth century when the frontier was pushed westward with the cry of "Manifest Destiny." By the turn of the twentieth century, Mexico and the United States had arrived at one of their first cooperative environmental agreements: the United States, in order to guarantee 60,000 acre-feet of Rio Grande/Bravo water annually to Mexico, constructed the Elephant Butte Dam (Turner 2000). In spite of that agreement, and in spite of the existence of an International Boundary and Water Commission (IBWC), jurisdictional confusions exacerbate the problems of cross-border pollution (Ganster 2000; IBWC 2003; Simon 1997; Westerhoff 2000).

South of Elephant Butte, the Rio Grande/Bravo's downstream course was girdled by levees, and once riparian eco-niches were replaced by irrigated agricultural land. By 1938, the U.S. states of Colorado, New Mexico, and Texas and Mexico's Chihuahua agreed to form the Rio Grande Compact Commission (after decades of accusations, violations, and political battles) in order to allocate water fairly to each state through which the river passes (Turner 2000). Those annual allocations are marked for agriculture, municipal services, and industrial use—with significant growth in both municipal and industrial uses.

Growing populations mean greater water consumption in a region with a fixed, and increasingly uncertain, supply. Water consumption is markedly dissimilar between both sides of the border, with Mexican border communities insufficiently served and abusive overdraft in bordering areas of Texas. The population of Ciudad Juarez, Mexico, is 50 percent greater than that of neighboring El Paso County, Texas, but water consumption in Juarez is only two-thirds that of El Paso (Westerhoff 2000). El Paso receives its water supply from a set of aquifers as well as from the Rio Grande, but the supply, upon which soils used for agriculture are also dependent, is not being naturally replenished. Formal and informal municipal infrastructure and accompanying water requirements are also growing.

Mounting population pressures on both sides of the border threaten to exacerbate already delicate wildlife habitat as well as water availability and municipal capacity. Environmental problems, like the physical landscape itself, straddle international borders. Political boundaries do not correspond to bioregions or eco-regions, and therefore twentieth-century "border wars" have created ecological disasters. Today, thirteen million people and highly diverse ecosystems are sustained by the Rio Grande/Bravo watershed as the river flows from its Rocky Mountain headwaters into the Gulf of Mexico. The Rio Grande/Bravo basin divides some of the least fertile lands in North America—with the exception of the lower Rio Grande Valley, on the Texas side. Still, the river's amenities are widely used to support growing permanent and transient populations in their agricultural, industrial, and even recreational uses.

A mere trickle after making its way around the Big Bend, the Rio Grande/Bravo is replenished by the Pecos River on the U.S. side and the Rio Conchos in Mexico. From Laredo and Nuevo Laredo to the southeast along the lower Rio Grande, the river is so depleted that it no longer reaches the Gulf of Mexico; without continuous dredging, it dies on the beach. Agricultural practices in the Rio Grande Valley currently comprise the largest category of water consumption. However, next to municipal use, *maquiladoras* also consume enormous quantities of water as factories, taking advantage of the lax enforcement of Mexico's otherwise stringent environmental laws, gulp river water and use the channel as a sewer for the disposal of toxic wastes (Johnston and Button 1994), seriously damaging the health of poor inhabitants, particularly children, on both sides of the river (Stea 2000). Due to the scarcity of aquatic resources, under this agreement growing cities must negotiate for the reallocation of water currently used for agriculture. Agriculture is by no means as important on the Mexico side of the border in its half of the *chorizo* as it is in the interior, where the impact of NAFTA upon corn production is currently being debated (Mendoza 2008). Thus, while the overwhelming proportion of water utilization in both Mexico and the United States as a whole is in agriculture, those currently increasing the border population are not agriculturists: "a shift in current water use [will be] from agricultural irrigation to domestic and industrial applications.... Water consumption is correlated with the standard of living, and as the standard of living increases in Mexico, water consumption will increase as well" (Westerhoff 2000, 5). It is clear that with more growth in border municipalities will come greater need for water.

While thus far the development gap between the United States and Mexico has widened over the past decade and a half—the number of undocumented workers in the United States has quadrupled since NAFTA's enactment (Payan 2006)—there is still the hope in certain quarters that NAFTA may someday actually increase Mexico's standard of living. Meanwhile, NAFTA-associated economic policy and the "environmental sidebars" will have to continue to address water as a central issue well into the foreseeable future.

TRANSBORDER PERCEPTIONS: THE CULTURAL ENVIRONMENT

Both opposition to and support of NAFTA prior to its enactment involved perceptions—particularly fears—as much as realities. In the United States it was fear of job loss, but, in fact, the border state of Texas alone added 166,000 jobs between 1987 and 1999, in part due to NAFTA (Gerber 2007). As to the north of Mexico—the border region—"northerners are generally more likely to have travelled to the U.S. or have relatives there . . . [residents] in the northern region [are] more likely to have a favorable view of the U.S. and the U.S. people, to exhibit more trust in the U.S. in business, and to be slightly more likely to support NAFTA" (Gerber 2007, 259). While the majority of Mexicans supported NAFTA just prior to and immediately after its enactment, there was considerable concern over potential impacts of possible U.S. economic and cultural imperialism upon Mexico.

Border perceptions vary depending on proximity to the border, nationality, and the respective lenses through which the border is viewed (Morris 2005). The most innocuous example involves perceived distance from the border, as detailed below, while other perceptions (realistic or not) may lead to governmental policy changes and action (i.e., terrorism reduction efforts). If we engage the adage *one's perception is one's reality*, what are the potential effects of collective perception on transboundary relations? Doolittle (1998) examined myths, stereotypes, and commonly accepted partial truths of culture, language, topography, climate, and so on concerning the northern part of La Republica Mexicana. His study attempted to dissect and correct the conventional wisdom of *uniformity* in all those aspects, of a hot, arid area stretching from Coahuila in the east through Sonora in the west, sparsely populated predominantly by light-skinned people. The reality, Doolittle indicated, is in fact much more varied.

The environment of the border region goes beyond the walls of the *maquiladora*, street, neighborhood, township, and country and encompasses every living organism in an ecosystem—including humans. In this view, the environment is cultural as well as physical and biological. For this reason, border identity becomes one channel through which to explore cultural and environmental perception in the border region.

From the standpoint of sociocultural, economic, and environmental perception, one may ask where, when, and how do things "feel" most different. For example, the presence of a border is likely to exaggerate perceived distances or, more particularly, time distances. In the case of the Texas-Mexico border region, the time distance between San Antonio and Cumbres de Monterrey may seem greater than the distance or time distance between San Antonio and Big Bend National Park, contrary to reality. The eastern part of the border, marked by the Rio Bravo/Grande, and the western part, largely arid and semiarid, have created sharp perceptual contrasts among border citizens.

Vila and Peterson (2003), with a focus toward environmental perception, conceptualize the U.S.-Mexico border through the experiences of individuals living and working on the border. They offer an example of residents dealing with a community landfill. Resident experiences on both sides of the border include skin irritation, property devaluation, stray garbage (some industrial), odor, wind-blown tailings, and (in the case of U.S. citizens) governmental discrimination (258-61). Little international solidarity, however, has resulted because Mexican citizens perceive a different environmental problem as more crucial to them—accessibility to potable water. Environmental degradation is seen as secondary, even where such degradation is truly hazardous, for basic human needs must be met first. In addition to basic human necessity, basic economic needs also function to overshadow environmental degradation (Vila and Peterson 2003). Poorly restricted effluent discharge on the Mexican side affects the potability of water. Having no piped water, workers living in *colonias* surrounding border cities must rely on delivery by truck, and the unending labor of sanitizing water vessels occupies much of their free time.

Another example of border perception comes from Elisabeth Kadel (2002), who spent several months working for the Center for Environmental Management (CERM) as a compost toilet technician in Juarez, Mexico. Her job was to install composting toilets in areas of Juarez lacking sewage infrastructure (she was forbidden by the U.S. government from installing the toilets in U.S. communities due to insufficient testing of their safety) and to periodically test the bacteria/pathogen content of the resulting compost. She used the project to gauge reactions of U.S. citizens in El Paso during her project ranging from disgust (of Kadel's daily proximity to *Mexican* fecal matter) to praise of her American "savior" technology (though none of the project's technology came from the United States).

Mexico has been fearful of its northern neighbor for over a century and a half, during the latter part of which the United States was also wary of its southern neighbor. Some of these fears had been imposed upon U.S. citizens and perpetuated by the negative images of Mexicans conveyed in the U.S. media, among which were popular magazines and motion pictures. The fears thus engendered or reinforced were perpetuated by the threat perceived and the subject of propaganda on the U.S. side of the border during the Revolutionary period and continued thereafter (Campbell 2005). This concern, underlying U.S. policy toward Mexico, was later enhanced through beliefs that U.S. jobs were about to be taken by undocumented "aliens" and, during the Reagan period, by the suggestion that Nicaraguan Sandinistas were on the verge of fomenting a mass Mexican incursion into the United States.

Propaganda calling for the protection of the southern U.S. border from foreign terrorist threats has increased significantly since September 11, 2001. Whereas previous border security focused on drug or economic concerns, the fear that fell upon the United States after the terrorist attacks of September 11 prompted security measures for threats unknown and uncontrollable. Stringent border controls were swiftly implemented at both the Canadian and Mexican borders. Fears at the Mexican border, compounded by existing beliefs that Mexican border security should keep out drugs and Mexicans as well as terrorists, resulted in security measures far beyond those implemented along the northern U.S. border (Andreas 2009). Canada has been historically considered more akin to the United States, with similar histories and cultures relative to Mexico. As Canada and Mexico work to relax their borders with the United States eight years later, there is still a sharp contrast in the way the two borders are perceived by the United States. In the case of Canada, "it's as though there's not a border at all" (Napolitano 2009). That sentiment may never be true for Mexico.

MIGRATION: PERMANENT, PERIODIC, AND REPEATED CROSSINGS OF THE BORDER

The U.S.-Mexico border is the most heavily trafficked in the world. Growth in U.S. border towns has been fueled by growth on the Mexican side in response to increased employment opportunities, and the *maquila* system, with its associated population explosion, has only compounded the congestion. The "short haul" traffic between border towns is in reality bidirectional: a tide of Mexicans crossing on a daily basis to work, shop, and visit relatives in the United States is matched by an equally large tide of U.S. tourists, shoppers, and businesspeople crossing into Mexico, some commuting to work as *maquiladora* managers.

Economically, persons crossing the U.S.-Mexico border contribute heavily to Mexico's gross national product (GNP). Two of the three major sources of Mexican GNP relate to the borderlands. Mexico depends heavily on revenue from tourist traffic, a substantial portion of which crosses the border daily, either stopping for a time in a border city or adjacent natural areas, or continuing on into the interior of the Republic. NAFTA has created a certain number of jobs south of the border but has redistributed income in such a way that rural areas in Mexico's interior have suffered greatly. Thus, there has been a substantial increase in the number of migrants crossing into the United States—both legal and undocumented. These migrants send billions of dollars a year back to their families ("remittances") and, occasionally, to their communities.

Before the enactment of NAFTA, and to some extent since, the "free trade" agreement was touted as the kind of impetus to economic growth in Mexico that would "trickle down" to ordinary citizens and reduce the number of undocumented immigrants crossing the border into the United States. While the treaty clearly was never intended to impact all three "border wars" described by Payan (2006), it has had no impact upon drug traffic, nor upon the much-later occurring "War on Terror" (none of the terrorists responsible for the World Trade Center destruction in 2001 crossed over from Mexico). But it was touted as a way to reduce cross-border undocumented migration. There is little evidence that this has happened (Payan 2006). Because of the current U.S. emphasis upon undocumented migration, especially from Mexico, it is worthwhile detailing some aspects of the issue, considering the migration phenomenon as a whole.

A 2004 study of out-migration from small towns in San Luis Potosi, Mexico, to points in the United States found not only that a large proportion of the male population migrated north across the border to work as undocumented laborers during at least part of their lives, but that this movement had become a "rite of passage." This practice became not only desired, but expected, and significantly increased a Mexican male's marriage-ability. Much of this cross-border binational immigration is viewed by the migrants themselves as temporary displacement from "home." Even when seen as a long-term or permanent move, migrants frequently return home, recrossing the border for important family events and the Christmas holidays. This has been rendered much more difficult since 2001.

BORDER TOURISM

Until quite recently the border region offered relatively easy access for nationals of both sides to explore pieces of the others' society and customs. For Mexican nationals, tourist trips across the border involve visits to friends and relatives, along with shopping and enjoyment of local tourism venues. U.S. citizens experiencing Mexican border communities are able to explore what they believe to be a microcosm of another country with different customs, architecture, foods, handicrafts, and entertainment locales. Inexpensive food, crafts, products, health care, and pharmaceuticals are major draws for many American tourists. Each side also offers at least a few museums, parks, shops, and galleries. The U.S. side caters to the retired U.S. tourist with golf courses and RV parks and provides numerous shopping opportunities for some U.S. and many Mexican patrons. Prior to the events of September 11, 2001, Mexican consumers came to the United States with forty-eight-hour visas in order to purchase items unavailable, or available only at greater cost, in Mexico. New passport requirements changed that. Much of El Paso's retail business, for example, depends directly upon Mexican visitors. A corollary to a saying understood on both sides goes, *If Mexico sneezes, El Paso gets pneumonia* (Arreola and Curtis 1993; Herzog 1990). If El Paso catches pneumonia, however, so do all other border cities. The U.S. "war against terror" is a case of the flu that has heavily impacted the border economy.

Middle-aged individuals and retired "Anglos," on the other hand, mostly from the northern U.S. states of Ohio, Iowa, Minnesota, Wisconsin, and Illinois, accompanied even by seasonal visitors from Canada, are long-term tourists often referred to as "snowbirds" or "Winter Texans" as well. Their annual migration in campers and RVs to the southernmost region of Texas is cyclically predictable and highly anticipated. This group of once unwelcome individuals (at first seen as invasive) is now viewed as a valuable contribution to the local economy, bringing in millions of dollars annually to both the south Texas and Mexican economies. These "Winter Texans" usually arrive at the first signs of northern chill and return home toward the end of the winter months. In displays of appreciation for the influx of needed revenue, local businesses and franchises meet them with advertisements on billboards saying "Welcome back Winter Texans." Local infrastructure and services are strained with the seasonal onslaught of "Winter Texans" leisurely rolling into the area not just for recreational purposes and to escape winter's wrath, but also to seek comparatively inexpensive medical services such as dental care and pharmaceuticals that are not as stringently regulated in Mexico (Herzog 1990; Lorey 1999). This is by no means a new phenomenon: fifteen years ago, it was noted that more U.S. residents may be using Mexican health services than the reverse. Contrary to provider perceptions and the information on birth certificates, prenatal care is more prevalent than believed. Many more American mothers than reported were receiving early and frequent prenatal care; the problem was, they sought the services in Mexico, and the information was not transmitted back to the United States (Denman and Nichols 1991, 10).

The smaller border communities, such as Ciudad Acuña and Piedras Negras, generally have a public square within a short distance from the international bridge, with currency exchanges, dental and pharmaceutical businesses, tourist shops, various eateries, and bars aligning the square and spilling over onto adjacent streets. Despite these changes and the reality of these communities, many people still believe the border to be unsafe and lawless, especially outside certain areas; therefore, businesses catering to tourists are concentrated in an easily recognizable section of each border city, where most tourist income is derived. Usually within walking distance of the border (many drivers prefer to park on the U.S. side), these concentrated tourist districts provide a sense of security and safety, especially for those apprehensive about being in a foreign country (Arreola and Curtis 1993; Herzog 1990; Timothy 2001).

Tourism and the Binational Economy

Levels of tourism have varied in past years and continue to waver with the strength of the U.S. economy. In the past, when there was money to be spent, border businesses catered to the varying tourist wants as well as needs, leading to an overall negative perception of the borderlands as dirty, crime ridden, and outright dangerous. Then, with the installation of the *Programa Nacional Fronterizo* (PRONAF, a beautification project), Mexican border towns began to clean up their visual attributes and improve their security procedures. The formerly obvious and more centrally located prostitution districts ("boys' towns," or *zonas de tolerancia*) have been relegated to the edges of communities, thus making them less conspicuous. Despite the upgrading of border town tourist centers, a trip beyond the tourist district reveals the effects of rapid growth, in terms of unplanned communities and infrastructure in Mexico along with inadequate social programs and urban services for local inhabitants. Today, *maquiladoras* coexist with local commercial activity, including tourism, in most border cities, but in separate areas of town (Arreola and Curtis 1993).

Ever since the early 1900s, the tourism trade has been a viable source of income for many border communities (Arreola and Curtis 1993). Originally, North Americans frequented border towns to engage in behavior and activities illegal in the United States, patronizing gambling establishments, hiring prostitutes, and imbibing alcohol below the U.S. legal drinking age, especially during the period of U.S. Prohibition (1919–1933). The development of the U.S. transport system allowed accessibility to previously remote border communities. Prior to the enactment of NAFTA, the lure of tourism dollars together with frontier industrial expansion had already enticed interior Mexican nationals to migrate to the border, swelling the populations of once insignificant border towns (Lorey 1999; Martinez 1996).

Tourism and the Border Environment

Ecotourism has been expanded in the interior United States and much of Mexico, but border efforts in ecotourism are quite new, especially in northeast Mexico. Some of the larger protected areas of Mexico are barely outside the border region: in the Mexican states of Nuevo Leon and Tamaulipas there are several spectacular natural areas virtually unknown to U.S. ecotourists, such as Nuevo Leon's Cumbres de Monterrey National Park (Lewis 2004). In Tamaulipas, the El Cielo Biosphere Reserve is internationally important as one of the most biologically diverse sites in the world, yet it is little known in the United States. In El Cielo, women's cooperatives in local villages have been formed to provide services for ecotourism (Lewitsky 2002; Walker 1997). Ecotourism in the border region is currently an underutilized economic development resource.

The perceived threat of terrorists entering the United States through Mexico has recently been added to fears about drug trafficking and undocumented migration as an impediment to tourism. Urbanized stretches of the U.S.-Mexico border (e.g., Ciudad Juarez–El Paso and Tijuana–San Ysidro) are now fortified with steel walls. These barriers will be further hardened by the construction of 670 miles of new "border wall," 370 miles of which had already been constructed by mid-2008. The fence building and later wall building have greatly impacted border cities and often forced undocumented migrants to risk their lives crossing into the United States through barren, waterless regions. Since 1994, almost five thousand of the Mexicans who successfully negotiated the borderline have died in the Sonora desert of southern Arizona (Bridges 2008), more than the total number of deaths at the same point in the Iraq war. New legislation has impacted nontourism as well: a law imposing heavy fines on crossing the shallow Rio Grande/Bravo within Big Bend National Park in Texas to villages on the Mexican side resulted in a significant loss of tourism and ruined the economies of these isolated *pueblitos*. As well, mass media's intense coverage of recent crackdowns on narcotic trafficking and reporting of conflict among Mexico's drug cartels in specific border communities have stigmatized the entire border region as an unsafe place for tourism. Increasing demand for narcotics within the United States is a stated reason for the heightened violence in the Mexican border communities as drug cartels fight for supremacy in such specific gateway communities as Laredo, Texas, whose sister city is Nuevo Laredo, Tamaulipas, which at times has impacted innocent bystanders.

Tourism and Border Urbanization

Within the past two decades, border populations have expanded significantly both in the United States and in Mexico. Land use patterns on both sides reflect the magnitude of in-migration and the difficulties of environmental stewardship. Some previously uninhabited land around border communities is now used for agricultural purposes (especially in the "Valley" of south Texas) or for unregulated settlements established by the growing population.

The southern Rio Grande/Bravo border environment represents several overlapping ecological zones and is in the path of a number of flyways, making it a paradise for birdwatchers. Unfortunately, native and migrating wildlife, dependent on the uniqueness of this area, compete with human economic activities that exploit many of the same natural resources. Discussing the changing face of the border region, Timothy Brown (1997) describes the urban sprawl of Juarez: "Urban sprawl has gobbled up much of the fertile farmland of the lower Rio Grande valley east of Juarez and crawled onto and over all but the highest and most rugged hills and mountains to the city's west. As uncontrolled growth took place and Juarez's industrial base made quantum leaps forward in size and diversity, American maquila firms became more prominent and more visible" (112).

The impacts of people in motion, whether through tourism or undocumented immigration, can be environmentally detrimental. Because reserves and parks comprise only small tracts of land scattered along the border, species that locate themselves in these areas experience considerable human disturbance (Holden 2000). A major form of tourist recreation is wildlife observation, especially of birds, but as a result of recent publicity and tourism marketing, the resulting disturbance is impacting certain species. Undocumented immigrants may add to the ambient level of disturbance by leaving behind exhausted supplies and trash during their long journeys. These unregulated and unmanaged deposits can disrupt the health of the environment as well as the activities of animal species (Adamson 2002). Given that Mexico is a developing country, despite some land being set aside for parks and preserves, financial resources are not as available for wildlife protection; therefore, the state and local government officials who manage the parks and reserves systems in Mexico cannot provide the same degree of vigilance as in the United States (Timothy 2001). The Mexican government also has different and less stringent approaches to zoning and land use policies than the United States, especially in the border region. Environmental mandates affecting air, water, and soil quality are not parallel, and existing laws are poorly enforced on the Mexican side of the border. As wildlife recognizes no political borders, this also affects the health of reserve and park inhabitants on the U.S. side and so calls for cooperation in preservation activities.

THE UNDERBELLY OF NAFTA: COMMERCE AND INDUSTRY

In large part NAFTA (or TLC for Tratado de Libre Comercio), while affecting trade between the interiors of the United States and Mexico, merely formalized what was already happening on the U.S.-Mexico border. After NAFTA, which reduced tariffs on manufactured and agricultural exports and imports, tariffs were imposed on imports to Mexico that were previously duty-free (such as books). NAFTA also failed to provide for a freer flow of people: non-*maquiladora* in-migrants from either country, including professionals, enjoyed no more favorable status than before. One has only to contrast crossing the border from Mexico to the United States with crossing from France to Italy to realize the vast difference between the two kinds of compacts (NAFTA and the European Union): although touted as a "free trade agreement," NAFTA is no such thing.

Further, Mexico was at a disadvantage in NAFTA negotiations. Mexico's relative lack of negotiation experience in international trade resulted from decades of a highly protected import-substitution economy: Mexico, for example, did not join GATT (General Agreement on Tariffs and Trade) until 1986. Under NAFTA the country had to change its economic model from inward-looking quasi-socialism to outward-looking neoliberalism in a very short time. In a macroeconomic sense, Mexican exports to the United States tripled, as imports from the United States doubled during the 1990s; exports to Canada increased by a factor of five and imports by a factor of three (Green 2005). The NAFTA relationship with Mexico was not, and still is not, symmetrical, and this asymmetry is quite evident on the border.

Mexico was until very recently the number two trade partner with the United States (a position now claimed by China), a very close second to Canada, and rapidly moving forward. While Asia has been gaining in importance, the major land-based traffic flow generated by international trade is still north-south rather than east-west: in 2004 economic exchange between Mexico and just one U.S. state, the border state of Texas, amounted to almost 100 *billion* U.S. dollars, and the total Mexico-U.S. trade was over a quarter of a *trillion* dollars (Green 2005; Payan 2006).

NAFTA, Trade, and Transportation

Various factors, NAFTA among them, have markedly increased trade over the past two decades: trade between Mexico and the United States ballooned from about 80 billion dollars in 1993 to, as indicated above, 250 billion in 2001 (Payan 2006). However, trade requires transportation, and one major impact of NAFTA has been upon cross-border traffic, both in trucking (especially through Laredo–Nuevo Laredo) and on rails. As of 2005, it was estimated that as many as five million eighteen-wheel trucks crossed the border annually (Payan 2006): over thirteen thousand a day, or more than five hundred every hour. The congestion is further exacerbated by rail traffic. Rail traffic is projected to increase enormously in the near future, because (1) available highways are becoming overly congested with truck traffic, (2) shipment by rail is cheaper; and, (3) in the near future, considerable U.S. freight traffic crossing the border into Mexico will be destined not for Mexico, but for China (Nel 2008).

All Mexican trucks (including those with Mexican cargo) were, until 2006, denied access into the United States while U.S. trucks are allowed into Mexico (although the waiting lines are very long). On the U.S. side, there has been extremely irregular surveillance of truck loads due to a paucity of inspectors. Few trucks are actually inspected; however, all are delayed, and idling truck engines, adding their exhaust to idling car and bus engines, spew forth enormous amounts of contamination, seriously polluting the air. For example, from the Laredo–Nuevo Laredo crossing, 75 percent of all NAFTA truck and rail traffic proceeds north, clogging U.S. Interstate Highway 35 and making the San Antonio–Dallas portion of that road the most dangerous stretch of interstate highway in the United States.

Here is where necessary porosity of the border clashes with regulatory measures, as the transport issue poses a problem for food inspection, immigration security, and environmental health. U.S. politicians rant against immigration and support the building of a wall to keep people out, but trade is another matter entirely: to talk about raising barriers to cross-border trade would be political suicide. However, trade implies keeping traffic moving, and thus only a very small fraction of shipments into the United States can be inspected. Potentially dangerous individuals, illegal substances, and undocumented immigrants may attempt entrance via truck, bus, or car.

NAFTA and Labor

The North American Free Trade Agreement, according to then-presidential candidate Ross Perot, would result in a "giant sucking sound" as U.S. jobs were siphoned to the other side of the border. Nothing at this scale happened. NAFTA was meant to open borders for purposes of commercial exchange among the three countries of this continent while maintaining political control through tightening borders in other respects, with a further strengthening of the U.S.-Mexico border and the U.S.-Canada border since September 11, 2001 (Stoddard 2002). In spite of an environmental "sidebar," however, NAFTA has done little to halt the environmental devastation introduced by the *maquila* industry.

The operation and proliferation of *maquiladoras* have pulled many southern and central Mexicans to the border for work and damaged relationships between workers in the United States (often through U.S. labor unions) and workers in Mexico. A large body of research on border *maquiladoras* treats both environmental health and labor issues (Fuentes and Ehrenreich 1984; Salzinger 2003; Vila 2003a, 2003b; Wright 2003), including employer preference for female workers with their "nimble fingers," "docility," and "natural patience" versus male workers, perceived as "too restless and impatient to be doing monotonous work with no career value. If displeased they sabotage the machines and even threaten the foremen. But girls, at most they cry a little" (Fuentes and Ehrenreich 1984, 13).

NAFTA, the Border Environment, and Population

Scholars treating environmental health in the literature have failed to include borderland *ecosystems* in their perspectives on the impacts of *maquiladoras*. "Research has largely neglected the intrinsic, underlying biogeographical aspects of environmental degradation in the region" (Peña 1997, 285). While products of formal manufacture have been emphasized, especially parts imported into Mexico and assembled and finished products re-exported to the United States, wastes recovered on the U.S. side and shipped into Mexico are an important part of the border economy. Mexicali, Baja California, is first among North American used-tire cities, for example (Chen 2005). Among the multitude of uses for used tires is fuel for firing bricks, a source of cross-border air pollution.

While NAFTA included labor and environmental concerns only as "sidebars" to the original agreement, it was the first free trade agreement to include environmental provisions at all. The opportunity—and the "hitch"—lay in the enforcement. Out of NAFTA were born environmental initiatives meant to facilitate cooperation in all border areas impacted by the trade agreement. Belausteguigoitia and Guadarrama (1997, 92) describe four main issues that drove environmental concern during the agreement process: "border pollution, pollution havens, common environmental standards, and the impact of trade liberalization on the environment," and out of those concerns were formed the Border Environment Cooperation Commission (BECC), the North American Development Bank (NADBank), and the Integrated Border Environmental Program (IBEP). Prior to the inception of NAFTA, Mexico and the United States forged the International Boundary and Water Commissions (IBWC in the United States, and CILA in Mexico), and the 1983 La Paz Agreement in order to address concerns regarding cross-boundary environmental issues (Belausteguigoitia and Guadarrama 1997).

So-called free trade, however, meant further environmental protection and allaying fears. Increased U.S.-Mexico interactions in business raised serious concerns over potential environmental degradation in border regions, as well as over possible advantages afforded a country whose environmental regulations, while stringent, were weakened by lax enforcement (Tiemann 2000). Vila and Peterson (2003) assert, concerning the Ciudad Juarez–El Paso border area: "Air pollution from automobiles and point sources, including brick kilns and dust from quarries and unpaved roads, has plagued the region" (251). To address these concerns and mitigate negative environmental impacts, BECC and the North American Development Bank were established to fund projects that improve environmental infrastructure, and the IBEP was created in order to facilitate research and investment along the border (Belausteguigoitia and Guadarrama 1997).

BECC focuses its efforts toward projects that enhance environmental infrastructure in the border region including "water supply, wastewater treatment, and solid waste management" (de Mello Lemos and Luna 1999, 44). The commission's composition of binational members as well as local community representatives is designed to elicit trust in its decision-making procedures. Though BECC acts to promote environmental development, it lacks the power to solve specific water concerns; however, there are joint initiatives that deal exclusively with water quantity and quality in the borderlands between Mexico and the United States. The United States Environmental Protection Agency (USEPA) and Mexico's Secretaria del Medio Ambiente, Recursos Naturales y Pesca (SEMARNAP) began negotiations toward "environmental and water resource management on the U.S.-Mexico border" (C. Brown 2003, 555) as early as 1996. This renewed cooperation was meant to be more specific and aggressive in favor of environmental issues than the previous La Paz Agreement (1983) or the Integrated Environmental Plan (IBEP) of 1992.

The USEPA/SEMARNAP Border XXI agreement "focused more directly on issues of importance and established nine bi-national working groups in the areas of natural resources, information resources, environmental health, water, air, hazardous and solid waste, enforcement, pollution prevention, and emergency response" (C. Brown 2003, 556). Border XXI was recently supplanted by Border 2012, and this latest attempt at binational environmental consensus incorporates (to a degree) elements of Border XXI; however, the framework of

Border 2012 emphasizes a more locally participatory approach to decision making (C. Brown 2003).

Population continues to swell, facilitated by increased demand from agribusiness on the U.S. side and the relentless growth of the *maquiladora* industry on the Mexican side (though managers are often from the United States). Infrastructure on both sides of the border is insufficient to support the increasing populations and associated pressures for transportation and other social services. Undeterred, more and more people are migrating to the border area—some permanently and others semipermanently. NAFTA may have further increased population problems on the border by raising false hopes of another Mexican "economic miracle" and then failing to deliver. However, the cementing of North American economic relations was already in progress before NAFTA, and as stated earlier, NAFTA in certain respects merely formalized what was already occurring.

THE U.S.-MEXICAN BORDERLANDS AS A "RISK SOCIETY"

The U.S.-Mexico border is heavily impacted by two aspects of globalization, mentioned in the foregoing: first, a trade/economic flow originating all over the world; second, the need for security against terrorists from outside the area, transnational criminal networks, and undocumented labor. As such it is a *risk society* (Ackleson 2005), which is "a developmental phase of modern society in which the social, political, economic, and individual risks increasingly tend to escape the institutions for monitoring and protection in industrial society . . . [risks are] undesired, unseen, and compulsive within the dynamic of modernization" (Beck 1998, 3–5). To deal with this dynamic, the administration of George W. Bush, enamored of the possibilities posed by the information society, proposed a "Smart Border" Program (Ackleson 2005). As conceived by the Bush administration in the wake of the terrorist attacks of September 11, 2001, the "Smart Border" would pose no obstacle to "legitimate trade and travel" while at the same time "protecting the United States from . . . terrorist attack, illegal immigration, illegal drugs, and other contraband" (U.S. Department of Homeland Security 2002) This involves screening of cargo and individuals and the use of biometrics (Woodward 2001), the latter a technique for automated recognition of people by physical characteristics and such behavioral characteristics as handwriting and voice patterns. A refinement of this approach is the creation of a "virtual" border (Ackleson 2005), which applies border checks not just at the border itself, but in manufacturing plants, along the transport network—and even at governmental agencies and transportation terminals in other countries. With the enactment of a "virtual" frontier, the U.S.-Mexico border will become truly globalized, not just economically but in geographical terms as well.

REFLECTION AND CONTINUATION: NAFTA AND BEYOND

As earlier stated, NAFTA is not analogous to the European Union in the sense that it is not really a "free trade" agreement. It has involved merely the reduction (or, as time has passed, the elimination) of tariffs on certain selected trade items, mainly "big-ticket" items. Others have actually undergone an increase in tariffs. While NAFTA undoubtedly impacts the border region, the major effects of NAFTA may actually be felt deeper in the interior of Mexico (an area for subsequent study, especially with regard to the shifting of populations). The major contributor to economic and population change on the border was not NAFTA but the much earlier Border Industrialization Program, which led to the establishment of *maquiladoras*. The influence of NAFTA has been to spread *maquiladoras* from the border region into the interior of Mexico. Both the Border Industrialization Program and NAFTA (but much more directly the former) have been major agents of globalization on the border and in the interior of Mexico. Binational agreements on labor and the environment have been merely "sidebars" to the original NAFTA agreement. In fact, the most important effect on the border over the twelve years since NAFTA's enactment has not been NAFTA itself but rather the much-publicized "War on Terror." Although NAFTA might have made crossing the border a little easier in the short run, terrorism has made it much harder in the long run. While NAFTA is an economic force that has had political effects, both terrorism and the associated "War on Drugs" are political forces that have had economic effects.

In sum, in the decade after 1994, largely as a result of NAFTA, truck traffic increased faster than efforts to cope with it (e.g., additional bridges), since proportionately more of the increased trade has come by road than by rail (but rail traffic is increasing). Both air pollution and population in border areas have exploded, especially between Tamaulipas/Chihuahua and Texas. While the dollar volume of trade has increased dramatically, overall the incomes of single-proprietor small businesses on the U.S. side have not increased. They may have been hindered by, first, the increased availability of U.S. products in the Mexican interior (a partial result of NAFTA) and, second, the "hardening" of the border due to the twin fears of terrorism and undocumented immigration.

Along the U.S.-Mexican borderlands, where things seem always to be in flux, no conclusion can be drawn. Drug cartels escalate violence in such border towns as Nuevo Laredo and Ciudad Juarez. Even though the victims are primarily Mexican, U.S. tourists have been kidnapped and on rare occasions murdered, resulting in U.S. State Department travel warnings, much to Mexico's consternation. NAFTA traffic, with its associated problems, continues to increase, and the populations of border towns continue to mushroom. Following the breakdown of negotiations on migrant issues after September 11, 2001, increasing undocumented migration became more hazardous as the extension of steel fences in urbanized parts of the border and the Great Wall elsewhere forced migrants to cross through waterless open country. Thus, the measures undertaken to solve problems on the border and in the border region have generated new—but perhaps foreseeable—problems. The U.S.-Mexican borderland continues as a fascinating, vibrant, ever-changing mixture of interpenetrating cultures, perhaps unique in some degrees but typical in others, with gray borderlands resisting efforts to be made black-and-white. The almost two-thousand-mile-long line dividing the United States from Mexico is now a "hyperborder" (Romero 2007), the most active international divide in the world.

PART II

Identities in Transition

CHAPTER SIX

Colonialism or Conviviencia in Frankish Cyprus?

James G. Schryver

A major argument of this book is that borderlands are social processes, products of their contexts and producers of future contexts. In the following chapter I argue that the boundaries that regulate behavior within these borderlands are just as context dependent. These boundaries are not the neat, linear divisions that appear on a map and that we might imagine separating political entities. Instead, they are fluid, porous, and are continually being negotiated and renegotiated between the various communities living in the borderland. They include both zones of mixing and zones of separation on either side (Muldoon 2003, 4).

Thus, an understanding of these boundaries requires careful attention to their various contexts: local, regional, and otherwise. At the same time, our understanding of these contexts both affects and effects the approach used in the interpretation of the boundaries and of the social processes enacted between different groups living within borderlands in general. This chapter acknowledges these challenges to our understanding of borderlands, examines how they have affected our understanding of these issues in the past, and suggests a number of criteria for the proper study of the interactions that occur within them in the future. Each criterion is illuminated through a discussion of its importance to the study of these borderlands and the boundaries formed by the communities living within them. The discussion is organized around the Crusader state that lasted for three centuries on the island of Cyprus (AD 1191–1489). As do other chapters in this volume, this chapter suggests ways in which we might better understand the behavior of different groups living in borderlands who are guided by the boundaries governing their interaction with one another and with members of their own community. Above all, this chapter calls attention to the link between our view of a past society and our understanding of its boundaries and ultimately argues for a more nuanced understanding of borderlands and the interactions that occur within them, both then and now.

As an island, Cyprus plays a strange role in any discussion of borders and borderlands. Contrary to Simons's (1995) claim of homelessness quoted in the introduction to this volume, Cyprus, the island itself a borderland, was "home" to a dynamic and varied population in the late Middle Ages. The most obvious borders are physical and surround both the island and all of the various populations living there. This is true whether one speaks about the current situation where an "open" border still divides the island in two or whether we speak about the situation in the past where the only boundaries were those imposed by geography and topography. From the end of the twelfth to the end of the fifteenth centuries, while the island was united under the rule of the Lusignan dynasty, these physical boundaries—the edges of the island and the two mountain chains that run partially across it—were the only ones that did not really change or evolve. What is more, the different people who inhabited the island brought with them different social and cultural boundaries, both those that were porous and those that were not, as they arrived.

This importation was possible because social and cultural boundaries are in reality the product of a group's customs, habits, and mores—things that do not necessarily change with geographical relocation. However, this does not mean that certain boundaries between these various groups, themselves located within the physical and political boundaries of the kingdom, never changed. On the contrary, they were continually being torn down, rebuilt, and renegotiated. The resulting situation, I believe, was one of spheres of contact where these boundaries crossed or overlapped and instances of interaction in the areas where they did (see also Schryver 2005).

BORDERLANDS AND ARCHAEOLOGY

The Lusignan kingdom of Frankish Cyprus began in 1191 with the conquest of the island by Richard the Lionheart on his way to the Third Crusade. Shortly thereafter, Richard sold Cyprus to the Templars, who retained it for about a year before returning it to Richard, who then sold it to Guy de Lusignan. The island remained in the hands of the Lusignan dynasty until it was annexed by the Venetians in 1489. Throughout this period, the local Greek Orthodox population remained, for the most part, on the island. At the same time, waves of refugees and others from the Crusader mainland (until 1291) mixed with newcomers from both the West and East (see Grivaud 1995; Richard 1979, 1987, 1991; cf. Papacostas 1999, 2006).

One would imagine that this settlement situation presents the perfect setting in which to study violent conflicts as required by the black-and-white model or accommodation and acculturation as posited by the grey model. In fact, studies of the society that formed on the island have generally been divided between two such models. The approach of looking for either/or may seem too one-sided in retrospect, but the field of study of cultural interaction in the Crusader states until recently provided only two choices of models: integration (accommodation and acculturation, or grey) and segregation (conflict, or black-and-white). The second model was developed in reaction to the first, and the two were polar opposites. Yet if one takes into account the whole of the society, attempts to find evidence and examples of either conflict or accommodation/acculturation to the exclusion of evidence and examples of the other are doomed to end in frustration. What is more, including the necessary dimension of time in the analysis only adds to the complexity of the resulting picture. Thus, although at first glance it may seem logical simply to establish which model the evidence shows to be correct and move on, further research shows that each time one is able to identify an example supporting one model, it is also possible to immediately find an example supporting the other. In addition, the more examples one finds of both, the harder it becomes to argue away the evidence for either one, as previous scholars have done. In the end, the evidence seems much more complex than what can be handled within either the buffered, spotty, or layered model.

As an archaeologist, my approach to the borders, borderlands, and boundaries on Frankish Cyprus is grounded in the material culture produced on the island during this period and is guided by two primary concerns that also touch upon the ideas expressed by the other authors of this volume. The first involves locating possible sources of methodology and comparanda in the work of other scholars focused on other periods and other approaches that could help to enlighten my own work. This concern is complicated by the mantra that hangs over those of us who study the past, the warning not to conflate the past and the present. The following quote is one well-expressed example of the ways in which this warning is given: "Although it is an irreplaceable aid to archaeological understanding, one should be aware of the danger of direct transpositions of such data, and particularly of all comparisons, feature by feature, between the modern and the ancient. However attractive the results may sometimes be, the comparison of isolated details errs especially through a lack of security, because it has no way of proving the equivalence of their level of significance in their respective contexts" (Balfet 1965, 172). This sage advice is often taken to the extreme and becomes transformed into a complete prohibition against any use of applications, methods, or theories learned from studies focused on the present. I hope to add to the other examples in this volume that show that the situation is not always so clear-cut and that especially in terms of borders and borderlands, we can indeed learn some important lessons from the past.

The above concern with comparanda and time frame is a direct result of the importance of the second primary concern: context. For archaeologists, the context and provenience of artifacts are key for the understanding of both those artifacts, the site from which they were excavated, the culture that produced them, and their function in that culture. The more we know about these cultures in general, the better we can understand specific stages of their history, the changes that occur between them, and the cultural products (physical, literary, or ideological) that both produced.

From this point of view, borders, like books or buildings, are cultural products that both are affected by change and that effect change in their host cultures. As the introduction to this volume states, they are "dynamic" and "successively responsive." They are therefore phenomena to be studied with appropriate attention given especially to their local contexts (the micro-politics of the borderlands). For example, the rich variety of cultures that crossed paths on Frankish Cyprus during these three hundred years (Armenian, Byzantine, Crusader, French, Islamic, Italian, and Levantine) led to an equally diverse array of expressions in the art and archaeology of the island. In art, these expressions range from the dominance of certain individual styles and elements, such as fourteenth-century French cathedral architecture, to more complete syntheses of various "Western" and "Eastern" artistic elements. As a result, if one approaches these works as products of one coherent society, subject to one rigid set of behavioral rules, whether these rules involve integration of all the various communities, segregation, or instances of both, there are always some pieces of evidence or works of art that do not fit (Schryver 2006b).

From this perspective, it seems that much of the study of borders is concerned with those who are located on the exterior of a culture and their role in separating that exterior and the interior, those on the inside and those on the outside, "us and them." This seems especially true for studies of the frontiers of the Roman Empire, for example, although there have been recent calls for change (for example, Elton 1996). In a similar manner, borderlands are often studied as areas on the exterior of a political, social, or cultural entity, areas referred to as the periphery "where no one ever feels at home."

This view of borders and borderlands is somewhat disconcerting from my particular point of view because the whole area of "the Crusader states" and especially that of Frankish Cyprus is itself a borderland (cf. the views discussed in Ellenblum 2002; 2007, 105–45). As a result, my research focuses on the interior of this entity, and all of the groups I study and all their various interactions occur on the inside. When viewed from the outside, they occur between "them and them." For example, when viewed from outside of the island of Cyprus, they might be seen as occurring between Cypriot and Cypriot. But when viewed from the inside, they occur between "them and us." For example, "Cypriots" might distinguish themselves as belonging to the Greek or Frankish population. This is an important distinction that is often overlooked in more simplistic approaches to the processes occurring within this borderland.

PAST UNDERSTANDINGS OF THE BORDERLANDS

Until the last decade, scholarship concerning the society of the Crusader states mainly centered around the two models of an integrated (grey) and a segregated (black-and-white) society. Although these models were for the most part developed with reference to the Latin East (modern Israel, Jordan, Lebanon, Palestine, and the Syrian Arab Republic), they also affected the scholarship focusing on Frankish Cyprus. They affected and in some ways even determined the ways in which the material culture of these areas, the products of the processes occurring within and across these borders, was understood. They therefore determined the interpretation of the borderlands. For example, evidence fitting the black-and-white model of segregation was taken to imply impermeable borders, while that fitting the grey model of integration was seen as supporting a view of porous boundaries (Schryver 2005, esp. chap. 2).

Ronnie Ellenblum has analyzed the historical debate concerning the interaction of the Franks with the local population in the Latin East (AD 1099–1291) in his book on Frankish rural settlement (1998, 3–38). Ellenblum approaches the issue of impermeable versus porous borders between the various groups living

[138] JAMES G. SCHRYVER

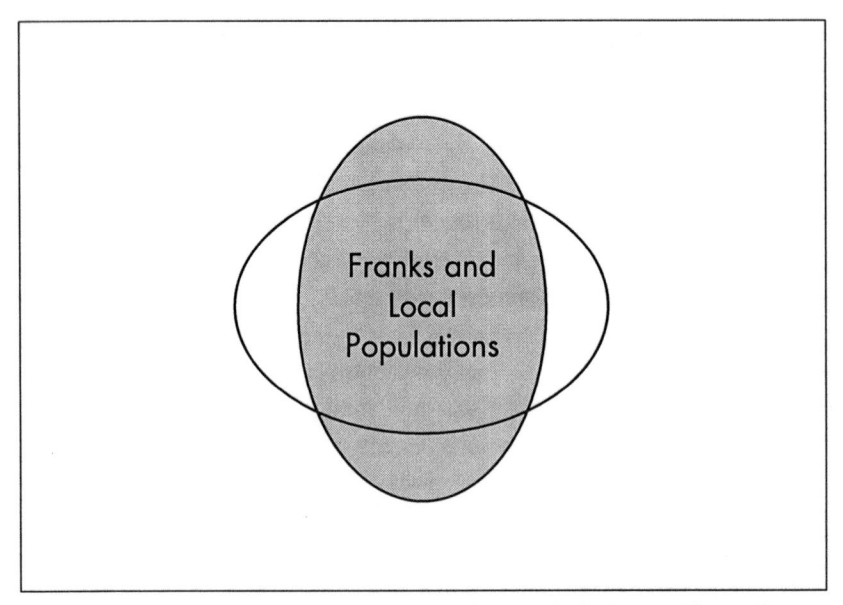

Figure 6.1. A view of the grey model as applied to Frankish Cyprus. The result is an integrated society of Franks and Greeks where the boundaries of both groups are porous. This model is also appropriate for the mainland Crusader states. (Image by author)

there from the point of view of settlement and what it reveals about a segregated versus integrated society in that area. These two views are each linked to the corresponding societal model. His analysis also brings out the major arguments of each side of this debate that have guided the study of society in the Latin East. A similar study focusing on the historiography of the interactions between the Latin and Greek Churches on Cyprus reveals similar trends in the scholarship focusing on the island (Schabel 2001, 36–44). These similarities and their relevance for the study of borders and borderlands today are discussed in more depth below.

A MODEL OF INTEGRATED SOCIETY

Until the 1940s, the generally accepted view of the society of the larger Latin East was one of an integrated society made up of Orientalized Franks and their Arab subjects living together in harmony—the grey model (figure 6.1) (Ellenblum 1998, 3, 10–11; 2007, 43–49). It was a society in which "the Franks had become highly assimilated with the local Oriental communities and resulted in an integrated 'Franco-Syrian society' consisting of the ruling Franks and of their autochthonous subjects" (Ellenblum 1998, 3). The result was a society of tolerance and integration. On Cyprus, this integration would have occurred between the Franks and the local Greek population. In terms of settlement, the proponents of this conception or model of society in the Latin East argued for a situation where there was ubiquitous Frankish settlement in both town and country (for example, Rey 1866, 17). In terms of borderlands, these spread throughout both areas of settlement, and any borders that existed between the two groups were seen as porous.

Proponents of the grey model of an integrated society and thereby porous borders, such as the nineteenth-century French scholar E. G. Rey, focused on the appropriate social processes such as the friendships that sprang up between the Franks and the local populations, including the Muslims; the marriages occurring between members of the different communities; and instances of inter-Christian worship, which included religious and laity from both the Western and various Eastern churches ([1883] 1972, 50, 60–61, 91–92). In addition, Rey and others discussed the many adaptations undergone by the Franks in their new homeland, such as the adoption of local dress and the inclusion of fountains in their homes (4–14; Prutz 1883, 55–72, 508–13). As far as material culture was concerned, these interactions were seen to have created an atmosphere where the Franks could employ local talents to beautify their lodgings. These artisans not only worked in the domestic sphere, but as Rey claimed, they even decorated the Latins' churches ([1883] 1972, 3–9). Yet for many the understanding of this integration was based on exchanges in the other direction, through which the Orientals became French.

These ideas concerning the society of the French colonies in the Latin East were intertwined with the scholarship concerning Frankish Cyprus. In his in-depth discussion of the historiography of the study of Crusader art, Jaroslav Folda calls specific attention to the way in which the extremely visible remains of the Frankish presence on Cyprus affected how the Crusader experience in the Latin East was seen by early French scholars of the subject (1995a, 10). In the nineteenth century, Camille Enlart opened his work on the Gothic and Renaissance art on Cyprus by remarking: "This little kingdom, now vanished forever, lasted for four centuries. It was nothing else but a French colony. Now it is a well-known fact that French colonisation, when it succeeds, produces a complete assimilation, in which it differs from Norman colonization" (1987, 15).

As with other scholars in the later nineteenth and early twentieth centuries, his interpretation of the art matched that of the society produced on the island, one that was for him purely French (1987, 16). In reaching this conclusion, he followed his predecessors, such as Rey and Count Melchoir de Vogüé, writing in the 1860s, and in turn was followed in this interpretation by Paul Descamps, writing in the 1930s (see. De Vogüé 1973, 37–39). The dominant view in the scholarship at this point was one that defined the Latin East as a borderland within which the porous boundaries between the various groups living there allowed the locals to "become French" and to further extend the Eastern borders of that culture.

These scholars saw the proof for their conception of the society of the Latin East in the French architecture that they observed in the Holy Land and on Cyprus. Where the textual historians observed the transplantation of French culture, society, and administration to the Crusader states, the art historians, as can be seen in Enlart's comments above, saw the transportation of the art as well (Enlart 1987, 15–16; De Vogüé 1973, 37–39). Yet their claims for complete assimilation seemed at odds with their claims for an art that did not take many lessons from the Orient, but only gave them, and thus remained for the most part unaffected by any local influences (38–39). Other late nineteenth- and twentieth-century scholars arguing for this integrated or grey view of this society focused on other forms of material culture. For example, they saw the early Frankish coins that copied their Byzantine and Islamic models, and especially those showing the adoption of local dress by Frankish leaders, as supporting their view (Schlumberger 1954, 1:44–45, 2: plate II, no. 7; Prutz 1883, 62, 510; Rey 1871, 9–12, esp. 11; Madelin 1918, 21). However, as is clear in the passage quoted below, for scholars such as Enlart, most of the assimilation across these permeable borders occurred in one direction, making its model a very dark shade of grey indeed.

> The buildings and inscriptions of Cyprus speak our language in all its native purity, just as the history of the Lusignan kingdom bears witness to all the characteristics, good or bad, of our race. The monuments, indeed, like photographs registering passing events, fix and preserve the moving picture of history. It is of course true that French manners, the French language and French art did not take possession of the country so exclusively as to banish Byzantine traditions; but since the French colonists were numerous and intelligent whereas the indigenous population was sparse, not very active and not

6. *Colonialism in Frankish Cyprus?* [141]

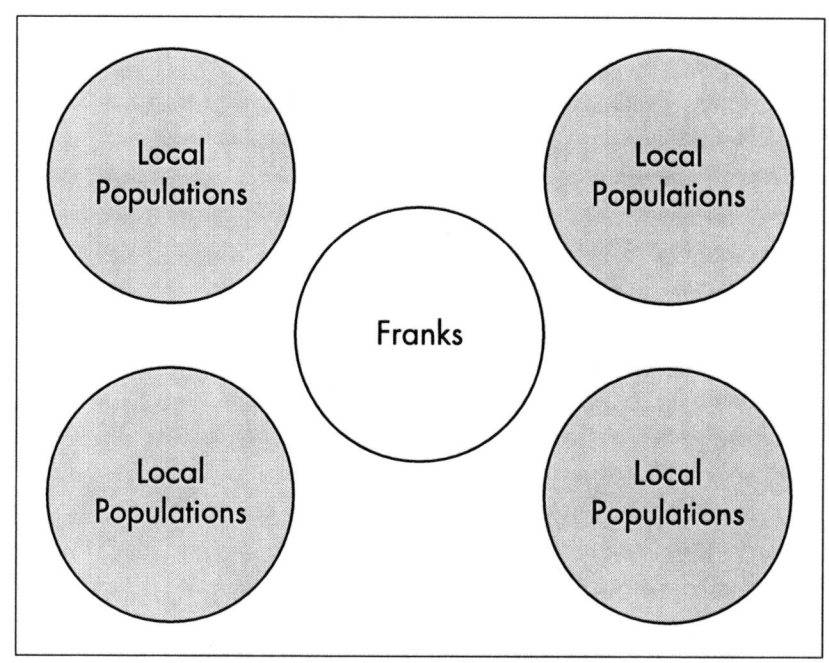

Figure 6.2. A view of the black-and-white model as applied to Frankish Cyprus. The society is segregated and the boundaries of the various groups are impermeable. This model also represents the idea of the minority Franks as being surrounded and put under siege by the more numerous local populations. This model is also appropriate for the mainland Crusader states. (Image by author)

well educated the Greeks to a large extent came under the influence of their conquerors while exercising practically no influence on them. (Enlart 1987, 16)

A MODEL OF SEGREGATED SOCIETY

After World War II, scholars began to criticize this conception of complete integration as an idealized version of events meant to glorify French colonial genius and thereby the right of the French to rule over different peoples. They put forward a new model of the society that emerged in the Crusader states. It envisioned a segregated society based on "constant struggle with the Moslem princes opposed to them" and resulting segregated settlement (Stevenson 1968, 2). The Franks inhabited their castles and various urban contexts while the Muslims inhabited rural ones (Ellenblum 1998, 3, 4–9; 2007, 49–56), and of the Franks, "absolutely no one dared to appear outside the walls" (Smail 1956, 62, my translation; see also William of Tyre 1884, 486, 784). The borders in this black-and-white model were fixed and rigid. The movement across them was limited to violence, essential economic transactions, and superficial adjustments to the climate of the Near East. Scholars such as R. C. Smail and Joshua Prawer were the major proponents of this new model. They saw the interaction and the possibilities for acculturation or assimilation of one group to the other as having been extremely limited (cf. Ellenblum 1998, 3, 5–6; 2007, 49–56).

Although Smail was not the first to develop this conception of a segregated society in the Latin East, he was the first to really contrast the new model with the previous one in a detailed analysis, and his work can thus be seen as the foundation of the new black-and-white model (1956, 63). In his book on Crusader warfare, he contrasted what he saw as two "sharply differing conceptions" of Franco-Syrian society (40; cf. what he says later on 62). In a highly astute observation of the state of the field, he pointed out that the existing scholarship focused either on the evidence for friendly relations between the Franks and the Muslims or on the hostilities between them. He discussed and contrasted these two models, analyzing the evidence in an attempt to see if the two schools of thought could be reconciled, or if a decision could be taken as to which one was more accurate. His main criticism of the previous school of thought concerned what he saw as a lack of critical scrutiny in the use of the sources by its proponents (45). He saw them as having ignored the limitations of the available evidence, something that can still greatly hinder our studies of borderlands (or even foreign centers of power) today. Smail acknowledged the factual truth of much of the evidence put forth by the grey school, arguing for the creation of a new Franco-Syrian nation, but he saw the changes that this evidence referred to as superficial (43–45). In his opinion, the scholars who contended that these changes were anything more were too heavily influenced by the need to prove the special colonial genius of the French, even in the Middle Ages. Above all, he singled out the early twentieth-century French scholar Louis Madelin and his work as the most influential in this regard (41–42). In another parallel between the scholarships of the two areas, similar claims concerning "nominal submission" were also made with reference to the Greek Cypriot vis-à-vis the Latin Church (Schabel 2001, 39, 43).

Later scholars who agreed with Smail's conclusions continued to place these conclusions in opposition to those of the previous school. In addition, they continued Smail's claim that the major difference between the two schools of thought was in the interpretation of the evidence (Prawer 1980, 177, note 49). This is a lesson that modern scholars and policymakers should bear in mind. With the added advantage of hindsight, Ellenblum has observed the following: "Nonetheless it is a fact that more or less the same data led to the creation of two radically opposed interpretations, each of which was supported by the most prominent scholars of the relevant period: the one propounding the integration of the Franks into eastern society and the other, their total segregation" (1998, 5).

One of the pieces of evidence that the proponents of this second model focused on was the Franks' poor treatment of the Greeks in Jerusalem from 1099 onward and the resulting resentment between the two communities (for example, see Smail 1956, 51). Although there was already a long-held tradition in the Cypriot historiography of viewing the contact between the Franks and Greeks on Cyprus as hostile, the new view of the Latin East helped contribute to a focus on similar conflicts by those scholars studying Frankish Cyprus (Schabel 2006). In the second volume of his foundational work on the history of Cyprus, Sir George Hill added to the existing tradition and helped set the tone for at least the next forty years of scholarship: "It has been justly remarked that the picture drawn by many writers of the prosperity and happiness of Cyprus under the Frankish rule is entirely distorted, and that the brilliant surface presented by the Lusignan court or the rich mercantry of Famagusta covered a core of poverty and oppression" (1948, 2:7). Unfortunately, with recent exceptions, this interpretation of the evidence has continued until the present.

As a result, the notion that the Latins and their church completely impoverished and oppressed the Greeks and their church became a factoid in the scholarship on the subject (Schabel 2001, 36–44). In 1985, Costas Kyrris, a leading Cypriot historian, presented an image of Frankish Cyprus where conflicts between the Latin and Greek clergies never ceased, and the Latins were constantly vexing the Greeks (1985, 18–19): "The Lusignan rule was, generally speaking, a period of misfortune, exploitation and oppression for the indigenous Greek population, who had to wage a long, mostly silent struggle for physical, national, religious and cultural survival against the numerically insignificant but politically, socially and militarily powerful new masters" (1985, 212–13). This interpretation was repeated as late as 1987 when Miltiades Efthimiou painted a similar picture in his study of the Latin and Greek Churches on Cyprus (37, 40, 52, 77; cf. Hackett 1901, 136–37). The collection of papers by Benedictos Englezakis that was published in 1995 painted an even bleaker picture (213–20).

However, it appears that as scholars began to look at some of the other many variables that comprise borderland dynamics (one of the lessons of the present volume), this view slowly changed. For example, in the same 1987 work Efthimiou conceded that "the foreigners did not seek to actually and totally dominate the populace" (11; see also Schabel 2001, 41–42). He also sought to understand the particular context of these foreigners within the borderland that Cyprus had become (Efthimiou 1987, 69–77). Still, it has not been until very recently that scholars have begun to reexamine the evidence for the type of relationships that existed between the Latins, Greeks, and their churches, and the processes that occurred in the borderland of Cyprus (Schabel 2001, 36–44).

Thus, it was the older, harsher view of the history of the contact between the Franks and the Greeks that influenced the interpretation of material culture from Frankish Cyprus and the type of borderland that it represented. This was significant in that it also predetermined what types of evidence would receive the most focus and what types would be ignored or left to the wayside. Together with the black-and-white model of segregation and the resulting spotty model of oppression, it strongly affected and to some extent even determined how the material culture produced within this borderland was viewed. In a 1977 article on the ecclesiastical art of Cyprus, T. S. R. Boase stated that "nowhere in the Near East were the Latins so intolerant" (181). It is therefore not surprising that Boase then interpreted the Cathedral of St. George of the Greeks in Famagusta as having been built "to rival the Latin cathedral" (178).

Susan Hatfield Young's study of thirteenth-century painted churches on the island provides another excellent example of this way of thinking (1983). She analyzes and discusses the paintings as products of a society fitting the segregated model proposed by historians where continual struggle between the two churches soured relations between the two populations. Nor can there be any doubt that this model provided the background against which she judged these works: "It is against this rather gloomy background picture that we examine in detail four cycles of Byzantine painting dating from the early period of Frankish rule in Cyprus" (1983, 9). In addition, the Stylianous, authors of the premier book on the painted churches of Cyprus, introduce their work with many of the same sentiments discussed above:

> Cyprus had the same fate as Constantinople [referring to the "merciless destruction and looting"], thirteen years earlier (1191), but it was never again recovered by the Byzantines. The banishment of the Orthodox prelates to the

rural areas brought them closer to their flock, and the resistance of the Orthodox Church of Cyprus against the intruding Latins is reflected in the fine arts. Thus, while the Gothic buildings introduced by the Latins in the main towns influenced the architecture of the later Greek churches, the Byzantine traditions in church painting lived on throughout the Latin period, in the villages and monasteries of the island. *Superficial* Western infiltrations in the sphere of secondary iconographic detail there are, but *in the main* their style remained conservative Byzantine, drawing from the monumental art of the previous centuries. This is evident in the series of frescoes of the first half of the thirteenth century in the church of St. Heracleidius at St. John Lampadistis monastery, and in the church of Panagia tou Moutoulla, dated 1280. (1985, 37; emphasis mine)

Only a few years later, in her study of painting and architecture around the periphery of the Byzantine Empire, Annabel Jane Wharton's reliance on Efthimiou led her to couple her analysis of these media on Cyprus with the idea that "the island was cruelly incorporated into the Crusader territories" (1988, 57; Efthimiou 1975).

CRITICISMS OF THE EXISTING MODELS BASED ON THE PRESENT APPROACH TO BORDERS

The archaeology or material culture left to us by the inhabitants of past borderlands can be extremely important for our study and understanding of them today. As shown above, the proponents of both societal models—grey and black-and-white with spotty (oppressive)—used objects of material culture to illustrate their arguments and make them more convincing. What is perhaps even more important to note for our present attempts to model and understand borderlands it that on the surface, the arguments of both camps seem convincing. For example, if one considers generally the French Gothic cathedrals on Cyprus, or looks at the coinage on the island, the arguments made by the proponents of an integrated society seem well founded. However, as soon as one begins to examine these objects in more detail and to place and then analyze them within their contexts, in other words to acknowledge and examine the many variables that produce a borderland such as Frankish Cyprus, the image of society on the island and the related borders provided by this model starts to unravel. For example, a detailed and thorough investigation of the cathedrals of

Nicosia and Famagusta reveals that they look French in part because they were modeled after French Gothic cathedrals and in part because they were built with the help of artisans from France, many of whom may have worked previously on these same cathedrals. In addition, although the coinage did start out as a copy of the Byzantine coinage, it changed through time as the political message and therefore the designs it carried took new forms.

Of course, just as with the grey model, if one examines only the specific aspects or pieces of the material culture of the Crusader states used to illustrate the conclusions reached by proponents of the combination of the black-and-white model and the spotty (oppressive) model, these conclusions can seem equally convincing. Just as they made use of some of the same texts, these scholars concentrated on some of the same sources of information in the material culture, such as architecture, as did the proponents of the previous model. Proponents of the black-and-white model studying the mainland Crusader states focused on the castles and other works of military architecture built by the Crusaders (for example, see Smail 1956, chap. 7). For them, the outer defense walls embodied the impermeable borders thought to have separated the populations. Scholars studying Frankish Cyprus focused on the differences between the elaborate Gothic cathedrals built in the cities and the mediocre to poor Greek churches built in the countryside. They saw these differences in quality as proof of the oppression and impoverishment of the latter and its relegation to a poverty-stricken countryside by the Latin Church. However, as with the grey model, as soon as one begins to examine these objects in detail, place them in their contexts, and take an interdisciplinary and multifaceted analytical approach, the image of Frankish society created by this model also begins to unravel. For example, the claim that the Greeks were oppressed, impoverished, and reduced to building small and wretched churches in the countryside is belied by the fact that a Greek Orthodox cathedral (St. George of the Greeks) was built in the important port city of Famagusta in the 1370s. One may assume that this also meant that the Greek bishop of Famagusta had been allowed to return from his exile in the countryside to the town (Schabel 2000, 72). More importantly, although the patrons were two rich Greek-Cypriot merchants, the church was built in the French Gothic style of the Latin cathedral (Soulard 2006). It therefore appears that any conception of the two communities as strictly divided along ethno-religious lines is incorrect. In addition, although there were two rebellions in the first two years of Latin rule, after that the various castles on the island saw the most use as the result of attacks or threats by other Westerners, such as Frederick II.

Compounding the problems with the physical evidence just discussed, close scrutiny of the black-and-white model with an eye to the complexity of the situation reveals a number of internal contradictions. It also reminds us, as we are suggesting throughout in this volume, that these borderlands are and were fluid and changing, and it cautions us that we must be careful to recognize that although we may obtain a snapshot view, this view may not be valid for the entire time period with which we are concerned. Once again, I believe that by analyzing the difficulties that past scholars had in grappling with some of these issues, we can improve our ability to do so today. In the least, we may be able to avoid some of the same pitfalls. For example, although Smail stated nobly that his review of the evidence was aimed at *either* a reconciliation of the two schools *or* a selection of one of them as more accurate and thereby correct (1956, 40–41), it seems that he was determined from the outset to show the latter. What is more, it seems that his determination to do this prevented him from seeing, as shown in this study, that the evidence actually supports more of a reconciliation of the two schools. As discussed above, his view of the two conceptions or models of society in the Latin East as polar opposites led him to dismiss the examples of cultural interaction across boundaries and resulting change, which he actually acknowledged, as superficial adaptations that were merely natural given the situation in which the Franks found themselves (1956, 43, 45, 63). Yet had he been just as critical of his own use of the source material, perhaps he would have seen some of the evidence that he ignored in his attempt to demonstrate that warfare was an integral part of life in the Latin East (1956, v, 2).

A careful examination of what Smail proposes reveals some inherent contradictions to the ideal of opposition that he employs when analyzing the model of "la nation franco-syrienne" (see also Folda 1995a, 16n 51). For instance, he twice mentions the fact that the Franks had no choice but to develop a *modus vivendi* with the local populations (Smail 1956, 18, 53). In addition, Smail quotes, as many subsequent (and previous) authors do, the famous sentiment expressed by Fulcher of Chartres:

> Therefore do not marvel when you see signs in the heavens because God works miracles there as he does on earth.... Consider, I pray, and reflect

how in our time God has transformed the Occident into the Orient. For we who were Occidentals have now become Orientals. He who was a Roman or a Frank has in this land been made into a Galilean or a Palestinian. He who was of Rheims or Chartres has now become a citizen of Tyre or Antioch. We have already forgotten the places of our birth; already these are unknown to many of us or not mentioned any more. Some already possess homes or households by inheritance. Some have taken wives not only of their own people but Syrians or Armenians or even Saracens who have obtained the grace of baptism. One has his father-in-law as well as his daughter-in-law living with him, or his own child if not his step-son or step-father. Out here there are grandchildren and great-grandchildren. Some tend vineyards, others till fields. People use the eloquence and idioms of diverse languages in conversing back and forth. Words of different languages have become common property known to each nationality, and mutual faith unites those who are ignorant of their descent. . . . He who was born a stranger is now as one born here; he who was born an alien has become as a native. (Folda 1996, 81–82; Foucher de Chartres 1913, 746–49 [book 3, chap. 37])

Although some scholars have rightly commented that this passage should be viewed with a degree of caution, the changes that Fulcher refers to, are far from the mere superficial changes Smail claims them to be (Folda 1996, 82).

In addition, although Smail acknowledges and even makes use of the evidence provided by contemporary sources, such as the writings of Usamah ibn Munqidh, to support his claims (1956, 44; see also Hitti 1929), he ignores other evidence within these same writings indicating that the local Franks had changed and had become quite different from those who came newly from the West. For example, Usamah relates the story of a trip to Jerusalem and explains that a new arrival to the Latin East kept trying to make him pray facing to the East and eventually had to be ushered away by Usamah's friends among the Templars (Hitti 1929, 163–64). The foreword of Prawer's work on the Latin Kingdom of Jerusalem provides another example. There he explains that he is attempting to "describe and analyzes a mediaeval society transplanted to the Eastern Mediterranean, which created its own social and cultural patterns of existence beyond the physical and cultural boundaries of Europe" (1972). This creation of new patterns of life is hardly something achieved solely through superficial adaptations to local conditions. These examples are extremely important because they illustrate the ways in which ignoring the living, dynamic relations of a borderland can lead to a false understanding.

We must consider another relevant aspect of context regarding the past and present study of borderlands at this point. Just as the proponents of the segregated model pointed out the thinly cloaked praise of France's colonial genius behind the previous model, a number of the scholars who championed the new conflict-focused theories, such as Prawer and Smail, may have projected the conflicts that were part of the contemporary political and social situation in the newly created state of Israel onto the past (Ellenblum 1998, 10; 2007, 55–61). As a result of the lack of an integrated society in this newly born state, it was easy for these scholars to put forward a theory of the Crusader states that was based on a parallel lack of integration. Similar factors were at play in the construction of the spotty model for Frankish Cyprus (Schabel 2001, 37). This observation brings us back to my point about the dangers of conflating past and present. However, as I hope has been made clear so far, we should resist the temptation to set up our own impermeable boundary between the two.

The criticisms discussed above are not the only ones to have been brought forward. Ellenblum, in his analysis, critiques the model or conception of a segregated society in the Latin East based on the errors he sees in each of the arguments put forward by its proponents (1998, chap. 2). First, can it be assumed that the Franks who had lived in both urban and rural contexts in Europe were suddenly urbanized once they arrived in the Holy Land (13–14, 33)? The lack of comprehensive archaeological evidence does not prove the absence of Frankish rural settlement, and details in documents may still have more light to shed on this issue (34–36). Second, the external dangers and threats of warfare that are considered the main reasons that the Franks limited their settlement to cities and their fortresses did not exist (14–19, 32–33). Third, the relationship of Muslims and local Christians with the Franks was too complex to be simplified into one of either total loyalty or total treachery (21–31, 33). Angel Nicolaou-Konnari, Chris Schabel, and others have raised similar concerns regarding the application of the black-and-white model to Frankish Cyprus in their recent respective studies of the historical documents and historical scholarship (Nicolaou-Konnari 1999; Schabel 2001; Nicolaou-Konnari and Schabel 2005). Nicolaou-Konnari has stated that an extensive survey of the historical documents has found no evidence for forced linguistic assimilation of the Greeks by the Franks (1999, 223), and that instances of "oppression" such as the martyrdom of the thirteen Greek Orthodox monks from the monastery of Our Lady of Kantara (Kantariotissa) should not be seen as representative of a general trend, as some have claimed (1999, 293–327, 360; Schabel 2001, 39–40, 58–60).

These criticisms or counterpoints warn against any attempt to understand borderlands that relies too heavily on snapshots of their internal development. They reaffirm, as do other studies in the present volume, that scholars studying these societies and the boundaries that were negotiated within and around them must examine each in the context of various conditions, and any attempt to create models that are meant to be either geographically or chronologically all-inclusive cannot hope to meet with success (cf. Schabel 2001, 44). The implicit understanding that either of the two models apply to the whole period of existence of the Latin East, whether we are talking about the mainland or Cyprus, is one that my present research has shown again and again to be unrealistic. The different societies emerging in the Latin East and Cyprus, not to mention Frankish Greece, were profoundly influenced by local conditions and circumstances (Schryver 2006a). Not one of them was a static or stagnant entity; all were societies that were "successively responsive" and changed over time. Thus, they were far more complex than previous attempts to understand them have imagined them to be (Schryver 2006b, 2008; for Cyprus in this regard). And to continue the comparison outlined in Zartman's introduction, they were certainly not homogeneous entities whose borders, chronological as well as geographical, were like those of the island itself: fixed, easily definable, and therefore impermeable and binding.

Together, all of these criticisms and new evaluations of the evidence cannot fail to cause the student of the society of the Latin East to look for a new conception or model to attempt to understand it. To avoid the pitfalls observed in the previous models, the search for a new model must include a discussion or at least consideration of the following factors, many of them outlined by Zartman in his introduction:

1. The time frame—the length of the period of contact under examination.
2. The number and composition of the components (or communities) in contact.
3. The nature and scope of internal changes or developments that occurred within these communities independently of their contacts.
4. The contextual aspects of the material culture under study, such as audience and function.

6. *Colonialism in Frankish Cyprus?* [151]

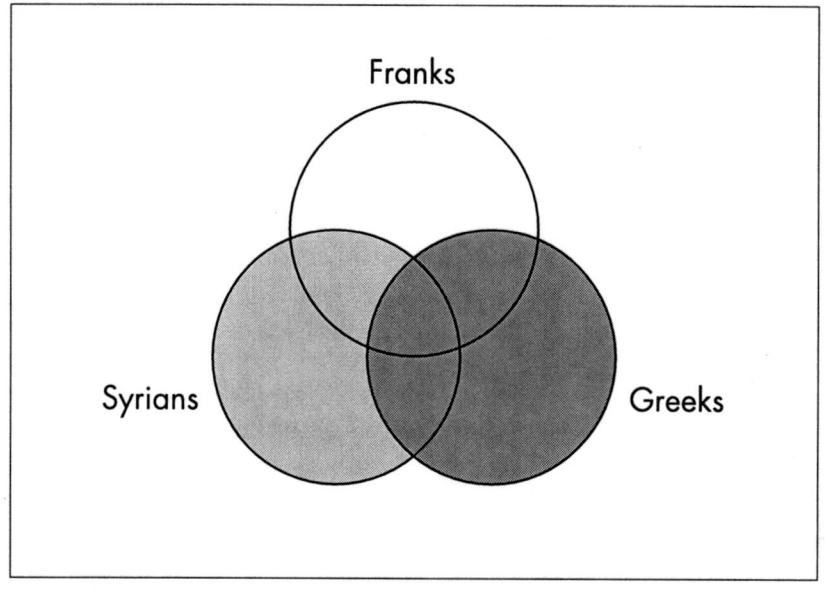

Figure 6.3. A view of the proposed model of society on Frankish Cyprus. The individual groups overlap in certain spheres of life (administration, industry, and religion), and within these overlaps there are possibilities for interaction. However, this does not erase the core identity of the constituent groups, even if the continued interaction does result in change over time. (Image by author)

5. The different views of different audiences inside and outside the contact situation regarding certain objects and monuments.

6. The assumptions that scholars make (consciously and subconsciously) as a result of our own external view of the situation.

TOWARD A NEW MODEL: SPHERES OF CONTACT AND INSTANCES OF INTERACTION

The criticisms of the existing models tend toward the formulation of new conceptions concerning the society of the Crusader states that recognizes its fluidity and ever-changing nature. Both Ellenblum and Nicolaou-Konnari provide the building blocks for a new model of society in the Latin Kingdom of Jerusalem and Frankish Cyprus, respectively. Ellenblum's analysis and criticism of both the evidence and arguments provided by the proponents of a segregated model of society in the Latin East provide another warning about blindly applying our own understandings of things to the past led him to conclude:

> There is no doubt that the Frankish society created in the Levant was not an exact copy of any contemporary European society and that it was influenced by the special conditions of life existing there.... However, the assumption that the Franks abandoned almost completely their rural way of life in favor of an "almost exclusive urban society," while at the same time retaining an appreciable number of the social and political elements which they brought with them from Europe, is difficult to accept without better founded evidence than that produced till now. (1998, 14)

Meanwhile, Nicolaou-Konnari has suggested the following conception of society on Frankish Cyprus: "The cultural encounter will be marked by a conflict between rejection and acceptance of influences aiming at the maintenance of their respective cultural frontiers, on the one hand, and the achievement of conditions of peaceful cohabitation, on the other" (1999, 156). In addition, concerning the importance of the local context to the negotiations of boundaries between these two groups, she states, "The typology of the encounter of the Greek Orthodox and the Frankish Latin cultures in thirteenth-century Cyprus, however, is characterized by particularities that pertain to the social and historical realities of the two ethnic groups involved" (286). A more recent study of other historical sources by Christopher MacEvitt suggests that the Franks and local Christians on the mainland quickly placed each other within their own worldview. For example, to the Armenian rulers living in the area of Odessa, the Franks were just another group of conquerors in a long history of conquerors to come into that area, the newest foreign, political player in a game that had been going on for centuries. The image of Frankish society that emerges from MacEvitt's study is also an image of a society "in which religious and social identities were flexible, and in which violence and tolerance were not exclusive characteristics, but strategies often employed simultaneously" (2008, 14).

There has been an acknowledgment more recently among scholars of the art of Frankish Cyprus that the situation is more complex than previously thought. Annemarie Weyl Carr, for instance, has claimed that the cultural context of these works was one in which there were multiple intercultural penetrations (1995a, 239–56; 1995b, 87–103). She has even called for scholars to set aside the long-held notion of "an Orthodox population ground to artistic muteness by Crusader oppression, and of an artistic geography dominated by the movements of the Crusading armies" (1995b, 98). Folda has also argued for the recognition of the complexity and multiculturalism of this society (1996, 80–91). As early as 1977 he recognized the blend of cultures occurring in the Latin East, "which yielded painting and sculpture unique in style and iconography, a distinctive chapter in the history of medieval art" (1977, 280). In his magnum opus on Crusader art before the Battle of Hattin (1187), Folda remarks that he wishes to study it "as an art seen from the viewpoint of its patrons, clients, and many artists situated in the polyglot multicultural context of the Crusader States" (1995a, 15–16, n. 51).

The new model of the society of Frankish Cyprus that I present here incorporates many of these issues and ideas. It is based on a thorough review of the relevant published material, including those pieces already used by proponents of each of the two models (grey and black-and-white), and a detailed, contextual study of the relevant pieces of material culture. The conclusion most fully supported by this combination is that our view of the society in these areas should change to one in which there was neither total integration nor total segregation. I propose that we imagine a society in which there existed spheres of contact (administration, industry, and religion) between the different communities and instances of interaction within the areas of overlap of each of these spheres (fig. 3). We should also recognize the late twelfth and thirteenth centuries as a period in which similar contact and interaction were already occurring in the mainland Crusader states (regarding religion especially, see Kedar 1998; Dajani-Shakeel, 1990). This explanation may seem to most closely reflect the spotty model, but I would argue that one main lesson to be learned from Frankish Cyprus is that we must keep in mind that the models outlined at the beginning of this book may not work all of the time and in every circumstance. As shown above, an attempt to find the "correct" model will work only if it is the result of the kind of in-depth and interdisciplinary approach proposed in the present volume. And even if a "correct" model is found, it may only be applicable to a brief period of a borderland's history.

TOWARD AN EXPLANATION OF THE BORDERLAND

Why did the borderland that was Frankish Cyprus develop the way it did? As the following twenty-first-century quote shows, the result of neither-nor that is outlined above is not a phenomenon of the Crusader East, nor even of the Middle Ages.

In the matter of immigration, the first of these extreme ideas is that which regards the host country as a blank sheet of paper on which everyone can write whatever he pleases, or, worse, as a wasteland where everyone can set up house with all his own impedimenta without making any changes in his habits or behaviour. The other extreme idea sees the host country as a page already written and printed, a land where the laws, values, beliefs and other human and cultural characteristics have been fixed once and for all, and where all that immigrants can do is conform to them. Both notions strike me as equally unrealistic, sterile and harmful. . . . Some will go on clinging to their own notions, but men of good sense will take a step towards the self-evident common ground: the fact that a host country is neither a *tabula rasa*, nor a *fait accompli*, but a page in the process of being written. (Maalouf 2000, 34)

Franks, Greeks, Westerners, and others each brought with them different worldviews, including experiences from the past and expectations for the future that had to be reconciled. Each group came to the construction of the borders or boundaries between themselves and the other groups with their own needs foremost in mind. This led each group to define its own goals for a negotiation process. As time went on, these goals may have changed due to the evolution of the relevant dynamics both affecting and effecting this borderland. However, the boundaries that resulted and the behaviors that occurred within and across them were still products of this process of reconciliation, responding to the needs of interaction in the administrative, industrial, and religious spheres. Thus, the boundaries were fluid, nuanced, and shifting and were often renegotiated, so that some group boundaries were reinforced while others were made more permeable, in order to keep some borders open and others closed. At the core of the decision as to which boundaries to open was the issue of which boundaries guarded features considered by the group to be important for their self-identification.

When we examine broadly the social and cultural development of Frankish Cyprus, we observe two different, but not mutually exclusive, processes. As discussed above, these processes yield pieces of evidence that in isolation seem alternately to echo a grey or black-and-white model. During the first two centuries of Lusignan rule (1191–1391), there arose a situation in which individual communities on the island began gradually to merge with one another in certain spheres of everyday life, while also continuing to exist as well as develop as separate and distinct entities. In the beginning, the development of the Frankish community on Cyprus was guided by its connections with the Frankish community living in the remaining Crusader settlements on the mainland. The ties that bound these communities to one another had their origins in a shared religious and ethnic identity as well as in a shared sense of destiny regarding the defense of the Holy Land.

These ties were constantly reinforced through the exchange of tangible items such as goods, the exchange of intangible items such as ideas, and by the physical movement of people between the two communities. The similarities between the ceramic record at sites on Cyprus such as the fort of Saranda Kolones and the sugar mills of Kouklia-Stavros, and sites along the coastal Levant indicate that these two Frankish communities traded steadily with one another (Schryver 2005, chap. 3 and append. A). The archaeological evidence indicates that this trade began at least as early as the first decades of the twelfth century (circa twenty years after the first Frankish settlement on the island) and continued until the final demise of the mainland communities almost a century later (Papacostas 1999, 499–500; 2006).

The art historical and historical evidence reveals further details about the contacts between Cyprus and the Crusader mainland. Some of these details relate to the waves of refugees who escaped to the island in the thirteenth century and the nature of the culture they brought with them to Cyprus. Certain works of art, such as an icon of St. Nicholas from the church of St. Nicholas of the Roof in Kakopetria, even allow us to identify some of these refugees. In this particular case, the heraldry shown on the patron's horse in the lower left-hand corner of the icon is thought to be that of the Raven[d]el/[Ravendel] family (Folda 1995b, 218). A range of documents allows us to track the movement of other individuals and groups. Chronicles record Guy de Lusignan's appeal to potential settlers at the end of the twelfth century, and administrative records identify individuals, such as Jean d'Ibelin, and institutions, such as the different religious orders, who owned land in both places (Schryver 2005, chap. 5).

The situation was not limited to only these variables, however, and while the Franks oriented themselves to power centers on the Crusader mainland, the Greeks living on the island were bound to other entities. The murals executed in 1192 in the mountain church of Lagoudera show that the moment of the Franks' arrival did not signal an abrupt end to the influence of Byzantine or Constantinopolitan art or the ties with these power centers. In fact, scholars think that the influence of the latter may have continued up to the sack of that city in 1204 by members of the Fourth Crusade (Schryver 2005, chap. 4). It would seem that the local artists only then turned inward to the Frankish and other populations living on the island for inspiration.

Icons showing a range of influence from these communities were produced on the island throughout the thirteenth century and remind us just how many cultures, identities, and variables may have been at play (Mouriki 1995, 341–43). In a nice echo of the society of this borderland, in 1280 an unknown painter or painters executed the murals of the church in the village of Moutoullas in a style that is called Byzantine by some scholars and Crusader by others, but clearly contains elements of both. The connection with Byzantium was never completely severed, however, as shown by influences from Palaeologan art in the late thirteenth and fourteenth centuries (after the return of the Byzantine court to Constantinople).

At the same time, it appears that the new connections and styles produced within the island's internal artistic community were just as potent and just as dynamic. These new styles, and I would argue that the murals at Moutoullas are a prime example, invite us to rethink our understanding of how the boundaries that were constructed between these various groups function. Are such terms such as *Crusader* and *Byzantine* or *East* and *West* even applicable once the initial contact situation had occurred and a generation or two had passed? What sort of model might we use to represent what was going on? When do the dynamics of a situation or a borderland warrant a change from one model to another? These new (Cypriot?) styles also continued to develop and change along with the composition of the artistic community on the island.

After the first century the situation became more complex and the dynamics that influenced it increased. The society of the island began to focus more inward, and by the end of the fourteenth century we can perhaps begin to speak of a mixed Cypriot identity being formed. Toward the end of the last century of Frankish rule, as the different merchant cities, and especially Venice, began to increase their political influence on Cyprus, we see increased Italian influences in the art produced on the island and the eventual development of what is called an Italo-Byzantine architectural style. The mixing or merging indicated by portions of the material and historical record was coupled with internal developments within each community as well as the renegotiation of more impermeable boundaries between them. At the same time that certain pieces of evidence provide a picture of increasing contact and interaction in the spheres of administration, industry, and religion, other information indicates the continued separation of these communities and also of different communities within them. Part of the separation between certain groups within these two communities is the result of a conscious espousal of a separate identity, whether based in class or ethnicity.

Thus, the picture that emerges is one in which the interaction of groups such as the Franks and Greeks did not result in the "immediate" creation of a new Franco-Greek group but instead gradually increased the tints of one onto the other. In this way, the Franks adopted and adapted elements of the local (and exterior) culture(s) without necessarily giving up their core identity and vice versa (Schryver 2008, for an attempt to model this). Although accurate, the fluid nature of the situation seems almost too rich and too nuanced to be encompassed by a straightforward statement such as, "as new groups entered the borderlands, boundaries were reconstructed to take them into account."

In a lesson for those attempting to identify the parties that make up a borderland, perhaps we should reevaluate our notions of the definitions of terms such as *Frank* and *Greek* during this period. The more we learn about life in the borderland of Cyprus, the more we learn the truth of the statements echoed throughout the present volume. The entities we associate with these terms were never static, never locked to the definition we give them.

As noted, it seems that the two groups followed a course of gradual (although never total) merging. For example, in the fourteenth century there is an increase in the historical evidence for contact between the two populations in the spheres of administration and religion. However, it is important to mention that we simply do not have as many documents from the earlier periods with which to balance these (cf. Beihammer 2006). Nonetheless, the evidence that we do have shows there were certain Greek families who were working their way into the upper levels of Frankish society during this century and the next. Did they consider themselves Frank or Greek? Perhaps the issue for this group was more one of class or status than of "Greekness." In fact, one must wonder if a class-based connection to the Franks affected their cultural identity at all.

If religion was a key marker of identity, then why do we see evidence for so much interaction across boundaries in the sphere of religion? Why do we find an increasing number of complaints concerning the use of private chapels and the attendance at and patronage of ecclesiastical monuments and celebrations of the other's community? These questions and observations lead to the conclusion that any model of this borderland must also incorporate "shifts in and interactions among divisions of classes" while keeping in mind the fact that these divisions did exist and at times were reinforced and protected quite forcefully.

From the point of a view of the artifacts and the art, the archaeologist's primary sources for the study of a borderland, there are a number of important factors that should be taken into account from the beginning when trying to use this evidence to gain an understanding of the borders and boundaries of Frankish Cyprus. These provide useful examples for the study of present borderlands as well: (1) Many of these works provide examples of the complex ways in which both artists and patrons on Frankish Cyprus combined contextual considerations (local, regional, and Mediterranean-wide) in the expressions of their identity through art. (2) The identities of these artists and patrons were multilayered, motivating them to privilege certain aspects over others in any given situation. (3) Just as these individuals had to be able to convey different messages about themselves to different audiences in different contexts, many of these works of art (especially those commissioned by the ruling Lusignan family) had to be able to perform in the same way. (4) When these groups did interact, whether personally or artistically, and even when they began to merge with one another in certain aspects of their identity, this process did not erase other aspects of these same identities (in this case Frankish and Greek) that continued to remain distinct.

If we apply the three-dimensional analysis suggested in the introduction of the present volume, some interesting examples of this last point appear. One way in which the upper class among the Franks tried to remain distinct materialized in the form of a shared concept of what we might refer to today as "fashion sense" or "taste" and "class consciousness." Each of these notions, together with a sense of what was appropriate, would have been enforced at the various social gatherings that the nobles from these communities attended together with those coming from the West. These social gatherings were not the only connection between these communities that was reinforced through the movement of people. Yet, this trend is something that may not be completely visible in the material record. The historical record, however, and specifically the evidence regarding the literature read and produced by the Frankish nobility, indicates that this group was consciously associating themselves with the royal courts of the West and thereby also attempting to distance themselves from the lower classes both at home and abroad. Although it may have been a reaction against their new isolated position, the conscious acts of separation and association through the medium of literature seem to be more closely related to issues of class than of ethnic identity. One of the many tasks for the future will be to further explore this distinction and the construction of these types of internal boundaries.

The image of a Frankish community maintaining its relationships with the French courts in fields such as literature cannot be simplistically reconciled with that of the same Frankish community increasing its interactions with various local populations. Yet, both of these processes occurred. Even as they gradually merged, the various sociocultural groups on the island still considered themselves different from one another in certain aspects. Whether or not people outside of the boundaries of Cyprus considered them all the same is a separate issue. However, it would appear from the multiple layers of interpretation of objects such as the Christian king Hugh IV's "Islamic" brass basin, that at least some of the nobility recognized this fact and sought to (de)emphasize certain aspects of their identities depending on the audience.

Since we do not have evidence for large psychological crises on the island in the fourteenth century, the culture and society of Frankish Cyprus must have developed mechanisms for incorporating these various identities. The society that resulted—if we can even speak of *one* society—was neither static nor monocultural, and the identities within it were just as fluid. Both the individual communities present on Cyprus and the larger culture and society of the island developed over time. It is perhaps at this point, at the beginning of the second half of the fourteenth century, that we can begin to speak of one overarching "Cypriot" society (Schryver 2006b). At the same time, however, we must recognize that our current evidence focuses solely on the nobility and upper class. Another goal for future research is to focus on the identification and exploration of evidence pertaining to other classes living on the island.

To conclude, the model put forth in this chapter proposes a situation in which each community on the island continued to develop within its own boundaries through time and as part of this development came into contact with the other communities on the island. This contact occurred in the spheres of administration, industry, and religion. It is within these areas of contact that instances of interaction across boundaries could occur. These interactions were only allowed to occur or only occurred where they would not threaten other boundaries that each group or subgroup wished to keep impermeable. In turn, the permeability index of these boundaries was dependent upon their relation to the self-identification of each group, their reaction to the present situation, and their preparations for the future.

CHAPTER SEVEN

Constructing National Identity in Ottoman Macedonia

İpek K. Yosmaoğlu

> ... how could a nation resist being found if a nineteenth-century map had predicted it?
> —Thongchai Winichakul, *Siam Mapped*

> Macedonia is the most frightful mix of races ever imagined. Turks, Albanians, Greeks and Bulgarians live there side by side without mingling—and have lived so since the days of St. Paul.
> —John Reed, *The War in Eastern Europe*

If "borderlands are inhabited territories located on the margins of a power center, or between power centers, with *power* understood in the civilizational as well as the politico-economic sense," as the introduction to this book asserts, then Macedonia is a borderland par excellence. Present-day Macedonia is a territory partitioned by four power centers: the eponymous country, which became an independent political entity only recently; Greece, which claims to hold the historical "copyright" to the name *Macedonia*; Bulgaria, the principal contender to Greek claims at the turn of the twentieth century, which now contains the territory known as *Pirin Macedonia*; and Albania, perhaps more because of its historical and demographic association with Macedonia than its possession of the (Macedonian) territory of Mala Prespa and Golo Brodo that flanks the western shores of the Prespa and Ohrid lakes. Macedonia has also been "continually in movement," its borders shifting with each attempt to define it, and its inhabitants continually displaced and uprooted with each attempt to claim it as part of one nation-state or the other.

Macedonia is not a borderland only by virtue of its location between different power centers and shifting definitions. It epitomizes borderlands because it is associated with heterogeneity, complexity, and overlapping identities, qualities that distinguish it from the state's normalizing and centripetal power. It was not a long time ago, however, that Macedonia was none of these things. In fact, it was not very long ago that Macedonia was invented from the ashes of the legendary Kingdom of Macedonia through collective efforts of European ethnographers, geographers, and newly emergent Balkan nation-states. The invention of Macedonia was a process that took place in the nineteenth century, culminating in a violent struggle as the Ottoman Empire's control over these territories gradually diminished.

It is no coincidence that the leading cadre of the Committee of Union and Progress, aka the "Young Turks" that ruled the empire from 1908 until the end of World War I, included many members of Macedonian background among its ranks.[1] It was the first region in Europe to be firmly incorporated into the Ottoman fold—as early as the fourteenth century—and the last that the Ottomans relinquished, in 1912, with the knowledge that it was not simply a territory but the empire itself that they had lost. This was not simply imperial nostalgia: the early Ottoman state had found its embryonic form in medieval Bithynia, but it would not be an unfair assessment to say that Macedonia was the place where it had grown into adulthood and found its own.[2]

For centuries, Macedonia was the heartland of an empire whose early methods of conquest relied more on co-option and inclusion than expulsion and assimilation, and later methods of rule relied on a pragmatic principal of pluralism rather than homogenization.[3] Therefore, the polyglot outlook of Macedonia at the turn of the twentieth century, or its "frightful mix of races," was not an anomaly as some Western Europeans observed, but rather a reflection of the nature of things; and certainly it was not that different from some other parts of the Ottoman Empire—or Austria-Hungary, or Russia, for that matter. In fact, that same "mix of races" must not have found their situation all that frightful since they successfully resisted many attempts to sort them into their proper compartments until their predicament left them no other choice but to become nationalized.[4]

As I. William Zartman points out in his introduction to this volume, we should conceptualize borderlands not as events or even places but as "social processes" because of the ever-shifting dynamics that they represent. This is particularly important in situating Ottoman Macedonia in its proper historical context at the turn of the twentieth century: neither a frontier land in constant flux, nor a stable heartland, but a borderland that best fits this volume's grey model of social relations, where borders are more or less permeable and different groups live within close proximity of one another whether they like it or not. Given this conceptual framework, there are two main issues that I would like to address in this chapter: first, what happens when an abstraction such as a map, which is designed to reflect a static model, is projected onto a set of identities and social relations distinguished by their fluidity; second, and a logical extension of the first, why the imposition of that static abstraction is a necessary (but not sufficient) step toward the creation of the territory to be occupied as the exclusive domain of one particular national group, or its *nation-space* (Öktem 2005). In other words, this chapter is intended to chart the way in which the social reality of a Macedonia partitioned between nation-states was created out of the virtual reality of ethnographic maps printed in the nineteenth and early twentieth centuries.

Before moving onto a discussion of these maps, however, a brief explanation is necessary as to the boundaries of Ottoman Macedonia. Some might argue that the term *Ottoman Macedonia* is an oxymoron since Macedonia did not exist as far as the Ottoman state was concerned, and the Hamidian bureaucracy had excised the term from official correspondence because of its affiliation with the Internal Macedonian Revolutionary Committee. However, one needs to qualify the verb *excise* here: the Ottomans had never referred to this region as Macedonia to begin with. For them, it was part of *Rumeli*, the European territories of the *Memâlik-i Mahrûse-i Şâhâne*, or the protected imperial domains. This practice did not reflect an ideological choice so much as established custom in naming provinces. Moreover, it was only in the mid-nineteenth century that Macedonia was accepted as a current geographic signifier in common European parlance. The Macedonians themselves waited even longer before they knew their homeland as Macedonia rather than, say, Kafadartzi.

The boundaries of Ottoman Macedonia became one of the weightiest issues in the European balance of power following the Russo-Ottoman war of 1877–1878, when the march of the Tsar's army was hardly checked at the Constantinopolitan suburb of Agios Stefanos thanks to the intervention of a Great Power coalition. The terms of the peace treaty that ensued were not only onerous for the Ottomans but posed a potential threat to British and Austro-Hungarian interests by carving out an independent Bulgaria, which would effectively be a Russian client-state of enormous proportions. The Congress of Berlin, convened in June 1878 under the "honest brokership" of Otto von Bismarck, formulated a solution to reestablish the status quo by dividing Bulgaria in three and restoring Ottoman sovereignty in much of what constituted Macedonia on the condition that the Sublime Porte carry out Great Power–sanctioned reforms in the area to improve the lot of the Christian population.

The Berlin arrangement was an uneasy and temporary compromise, however: it failed to assuage the competing ambitions of Balkan states while confirming that the preservation of Ottoman territorial integrity was a dispensable condition for the European balance of power, leaving the door open for an eventual reshuffling of territory. As the Ottoman control over their European dominions became more precarious, the scramble for Macedonia gained momentum. The boundaries of (and within) Macedonia, despite the sanction of internationally recognized treaties, were understood by each party with a stake in the region to be merely tentative, temporary arrangements until replaced by harder lines that conformed to their vision. The Ottomans, on the other hand, clung to their imperial vision even in the face of mounting opposition that chipped away at the fraying edges of their legitimacy. They persistently called the poorly guarded Bulgarian border—practically a highway for the transportation of all kinds of contraband including tobacco, firearms, and people, not *hudûd*, or "frontier," but *hatt-ı imtiyâz*, the "line of concession," not ironically, as those unfamiliar with the region might suspect, but in reference to the legal status of the Bulgarian principality vis-à-vis the Sublime Porte.

There were other, and even more tentative, boundaries in Macedonia that needed to be settled before state borders could be fixed, and these were not drawn on land, but across its inhabitants. The ethnic makeup of the region's population made it a prime target for different Balkan nation-states, each of which had a claim over one (or more) particular community(ies). Not at all collaborating with the wishes of the national propagandist, however, was the geographical distribution of these communities, which, rather than following a conveniently compartmentalized pattern, seemed to blur into one another. This, in addition to historical claims of legitimacy, was the reason why each group had its own definition of the boundaries of Macedonia and concentrated their efforts in areas where they had best chance of success.

The power of maps, and especially ethnographic maps, as a weapon in the struggle for Macedonia was discovered by the Balkan national elite somewhat late in the game, but once discovered, it was adopted with ease and speed. The maps reproduced numerous images of the land and its inhabitants divided into segregated sections, depicting what presumably was the latest statistical evidence about the "racial" composition of the population. True to the conventional visual technique employed in such maps, they were all "chorochromatic" representations of the land. The "choro" that was thus assigned a particular color did not display state boundaries the way they currently were, but the way they ought to be, that is, the exclusive territory of a particular ethnic group.

These maps functioned as an ethnographic grid, constructed on the principle of indivisibility of collective identities—no fractions, as Benedict Anderson said of censuses—separated from one another like the two banks of a border-marking river. The population of Macedonia, on which this grid was imposed, however, was quite far from suited to such divisions. The discrepancy did not only stem from the fact that the overwhelming majority still referenced religion rather than nationality when describing their identity; even in cases where the vernacular of religion had successfully been translated into a nationalist terminology, the differences hardly had a chance to gel simply because of the physical pattern of distribution of different communities across the land, whereby even the most homogenous groupings were interspersed with others. Identities are more fluid than anywhere else in borderlands, and Ottoman Macedonia was not an exception to this general rule—not least because the ultimate victory of the nation-state was still a contingency at the time. Ethnographic maps were the harbingers of that victory, preceded by a bloody struggle in Macedonia. The coagulation of borderland identities into the nation form was a particularly difficult transformation precisely because of the fluidity that formerly characterized them.

The pages that follow first provide a brief overview of Macedonia's "discovery" by European ethnographers and the appropriation of their methods by the Balkan national elites for their own agendas of territorial expansion. I then focus on two specific maps, their authors, and the texts that accompanied them in order to contextualize them within the specific conditions of their production. Finally, I expose the ideological pitfalls inherent in ethnographic mapmaking and the way in which they are tied with the nation-state's constant need to promote the idea of its contents' homogeneity, especially when that homogeneity is most suspect, as in the case of borderlands.

OVERVIEW

Maps of "Turkey in Europe" started to proliferate in prestigious geography journals and atlases published by European scholars from the mid-nineteenth century onward. Many of these maps carried the adjective *ethnographical* in the title and claimed to provide information on the people inhabiting those lands as well as geographic features of the territory. None of these maps, I must note, were depictions of Macedonia in particular—that kind of distinction would only become relevant after the emergence of the "Macedonian Question" and the coinciding foray of the Balkan elites into the art of mapmaking. However, the reinvention of the term *Macedonia* owed much to the same broader trend that resulted in heightened interest in the European dominions of the Ottoman Empire, which were now understood to host an amazing array of peoples with different languages, religions, and customs, living like noble savages untouched by the corrupting influence of modernity. The grand tour, a requisite rite of passage for the polymath gentleman, now went beyond the ruins of Rome into the land of Homer and further north. These early travelers in the area, coming in search of antiquities, first revived the ancient name for these little-known parts of the Ottoman Empire.[5] These explorers were not only writing about geography and the ruins, of course, but the inhabitants of those lands or the "human geography" as well, contributing to a distinct discourse that would have ramifications to this day.[6]

Amie Boué (1854), the first geographer to write extensively on the ethnography of "Turkey in Europe," published an ethnographic map that indicated a large presence of "Bulgarians" in Macedonia, introducing for the first time the notion that Bulgarians constitute the largest "racial" group in the region. Ethnographic studies became more popular during the latter half of the century, and even the "nonspecialist" visitors made sure to note ethnographical peculiarities as they saw fit.

This was also the beginnings of the construction of what we may call a "discourse of pathology" on Macedonia, a place in need of a "lunatic asylum" in the words of G. F. Abbott, an ethnographer and traveler in the region. Even geography seemed to have a purpose; it conspired against logic and order in "European Turkey" and cut it off from more civilized parts of the continent. The French geographer Élisée Reclus, better known as an anarchist, was flummoxed (rather ironically) by the disorder and what he deemed an easterly inclination in the topographical contours of the Ottoman Balkans:

> Their [travelers and geographers] task was by no means an easy one, for the mountain masses and mountain chains of the [Haemus] peninsula do not constitute a regular, well-defined system. There is no central range, with spurs

running out on both sides, and gradually decreasing in height as they approach the plains. Nor is the center of the peninsula its most elevated portion, for the culminating summits are dispersed over the country apparently without order. The mountain ranges run in all directions of the compass, and we can only say, in a general way, that those of Western Turkey run parallel with the Adriatic and Ionian coasts, whilst those in the east meet the coasts of the Black Sea and the Aegean at right angles. The relief of the soil and the water-sheds make it appear *almost as if Turkey turned her back upon continental Europe*. Its highest mountains, its most extensive table-lands, and its most inaccessible forests lie towards the west and the north-west, *as if they were intended to cut it off from the shores of the Adriatic and the plains of Hungary*, whilst all its rivers, whether they run to the north, east, or south, finally find their way into the Black Sea or the Aegean, whose shores face those of Asia. (Reclus 1882, 89; emphasis mine)

The geographical chaos was paralleled with chaos of a different order, Reclus continued, one that had yet to be sorted out:

This irregularity in the distribution of the mountains has its analogue in the distribution of the various races which inhabit the peninsula. The invaders or peaceful colonists, whether they came across the straits from Asia Minor, or along the valley of the Danube from Scythia, soon found themselves scattered in numerous valleys, or stopped by amphitheatres having no outlet. They failed to find their way in this labyrinth of mountains, and members of the most diverse races settled down in proximity to each other, and frequently came into conflict. The most numerous, the most warlike, or the most industrious races gradually extended their power at the expense of their neighbours; and the latter, defeated in the struggle for existence, have been scattered into innumerable fragments, between which there is no longer any cohesion. (89)

Much like the current attitude toward the Balkans that brands it as impossibly complex and utterly simple at once, Macedonian discourse of pathology was also logically inconsistent.[7] The "intermingling of races" made the ethnographer's task impossible, but at the same time everyone except for the inhabitants of Macedonia seemed to be able to assign a nationality to each community— some even assigned nationalities to dogs (M. A. Walker 1864). This seemingly puzzling proximity of different "races" and the preservation of their distinguishing characteristics over centuries made the Ottoman Balkans, including Macedonia, a gold mine for the European ethnographer. In Maria Todorova's words, the region was a veritable "volksmuseum" for Europe (1997, 63). Ethnographic maps were, in a way, explanatory charts for the museum's collections and inevitably reflected the curators' preferences as much as the variety of peoples and cultures they purportedly represented.

H. R. Wilkinson's *Maps and Politics*, published in 1951, provides a complete chronological guide to the ethnographic cartography of Macedonia. The author's analytical methods may seem naive by today's standards that view even the weather map on television with an eye toward discovering the myriad discourses of power hidden within. However, the ethnographic cartography of Macedonia, as even a cursory glance at Wilkinson's compilation will reveal, is so transparently political that any attempt at its iconographic deconstruction is essentially an exercise in stating the obvious. Take a title from 1878, for instance: *Tableau Ethnocratique des pays du sud-est de l'Europe*. The simple replacement of the term *ethnographic* with *ethnocratique* suggests that the author does not even pretend to be presenting a purely "scientific" assessment of data but draws a direct link between the representation of ethnic groups on a map and political claims over a region.

In *The Pen and the Sword*, a classic work of Bulgarian historiography, James F. Clarke wrote of the "cartographical misfortune" of Bulgarians, caused by "the persistence of classical cartographic conventions—the dead hand of Ptolemy—together with the *terra incognita* nature of the Turkish Balkans which prevailed up to the second half of the nineteenth century." This meant that the Bulgarians "in addition to re-educating themselves . . . had the task of educating Europe" 1988, 34). The "cartographic misfortune" of Bulgarians was evidently overturned, because the period from 1842 to 1877 witnessed the publication of several maps of "Turkey in Europe," all of which depicted large Slav settlements, designated as "Bulgarian."

After 1877–1878, however, the preponderance of "Bulgarians" on ethnographic maps came to be challenged. New criteria were introduced in determining the ethnic makeup of the population, propaganda met counter-propaganda, and, more importantly, the "Bulgarianness" of Macedonian Slavs, which had been accepted as more or less self-evident, came to be questioned. While maps favoring one particular group continued to be the norm, there appeared a few exceptions that questioned the representation of homogenous distributions, and factors such as school enrollment were introduced as more reliable measures of national consciousness. This was also the period during which the Balkan elite got increasingly involved in the production of these maps, ending the monopoly of European scholars on the subject.

After the publication, in 1889, of Spiridon Gopčević's pro-Serbian map of Macedonia, more maps that focused specifically on Macedonia rather than the conventional "Turkey in Europe" charts, started to appear.[8] An interesting addition to the spread were maps showing the distribution of schools, or ethnographic distribution based on school data. This trend was largely the invention of Greek nationalists who were despairing at the notion, gaining firmer ground in Western Europe, that Macedonia was largely inhabited by a Slav population.[9] The school statistics were relatively easy to compile, and their authenticity was hard to challenge. They also happened to favor Greek schools, which, despite the relatively recent rivalry of Bulgarian and (to a lesser extent) Serbian schools, benefited from the authority of the Patriarchate as well as the material and human support of the Greek state and the Greek bourgeoisie. More importantly, the criterion of school attendance combined consciousness and culture as the main determinants of national identity rather than racial or linguistic factors, thereby emphasizing the element of free will and invoking the charisma for European public opinion of Greek culture and its classical heritage. The most significant example to this trend is the "Carte des Écoles Chrétiennes de la Macédoine" published in Paris in 1905.[10] The Bulgarian camp produced their rebuttal in Brancoff's (aka Mishev) statistics of Christian schools, complete with tables, map, and explanatory note, which claimed that Greek schools were protected by the Ottoman government, whereas Bulgarians could not even get a permit to open up a school in areas where the population had joined the Exarchate, but given sufficient time, Bulgarian schools would prevail because they offered better education (Brancoff 1905, 77–79).

CARTOGRAPHIC AUTHORITY AND THE CREATION OF NATION-SPACE

Maps are visual aids that we tend to take for granted; they help us find our way along the interstate, locate a museum in an unfamiliar city, imagine lands we have yet to visit, and locate ones we have visited in relation to one another in our memory. They are practical cognitive tools that help us organize complex spatial relations in a readable format. I would argue that it is precisely this feature of the map medium to translate complexity into two dimensions that lends it so easily to ideological manipulation, and nowhere is this manipulation more consequential than on ethnographic maps. Ethnographic maps, through the dictum that national will is the ultimate principle of political legitimacy, reflect the nation-space, its reach and its boundaries, which may or may not coincide with actual political boundaries. The important point here is that these maps are drawn not only to reflect but also to will that space into existence.[11]

Ethnographic maps, by their nature, "flatten and enclose" the space inhabited by people and their everyday existence primarily by depicting borders in two dimensions as clear demarcation lines. Boundaries are never blurred and transitions are never gradual. They are snapshots of one moment, defined or chosen by the mapmaker, and not images of continuity and movement. As such, they are utterly unsuited for the depiction of something that is inherently mutable, such as ethnic identity, and even more so in borderlands, where the only constant seems to be resilience of hybridity. This makes the stakes even higher for ethnographic maps of borderlands, the perfect examples of why these maps show not what is but what should be—they are the areas where the reach of the nation-state or its purported homogeneity is most precarious and therefore should be reclaimed all the more vehemently.

This point was not at all lost on the Balkan national elites, especially in Greece, toward the end of the nineteenth century. The publications of European geographers that literally put the southern Slavs—and mostly Bulgarians—on the map of Southeastern Europe as the dominant ethnicity triggered off a retaliating series of maps that aimed to undo that perception by the Greek side. I would like to focus here on two of these maps, published within a year of one another, because the conditions under which they were drawn and disseminated provide useful clues as to how ethnographic cartography was increasingly understood to be a tool of territorial hegemony.

These are the "Stanford Map" published in 1877 (figure 7.1), and Kiepert's *Tableau Ethnocratique* from 1878 (figure 7.2). It was commonly assumed that the credit for the former belonged to Edward Stanford, the publisher, but in fact the anonymous author was Ioannis Gennadius, a diplomat and bibliophile who was the chargé d'affaires of the Greek Embassy in London at the time and who later served as the minister to London and to The Hague.[12] In the pamphlet that accompanied the map, Gennadius argued that "the different nations

Figure 7.1. *Ethnological Map of European Turkey and Greece with Introductory Remarks on the Distribution of Races in the Illyrian Peninsula and Statistical Tables of Population* (London: Edward Stanford, 1877 [Ioannis Gennadius]).

and races inhabiting European Turkey and the western portion of Asia Minor" could not really be classified according to clearly defined categories; therefore, in his words, it was "an abortive, not to say an impossible, undertaking to establish in a graphic representation the distribution and intermixture of race, language, and creed in Turkey." Instead, Gennadius suggested that "a practically useful ethnological map" would "explain and represent the actual relations in which those nations stand toward one another" (*Ethnological Map of European Turkey* 1877, 2). In the resulting figure, "the actual relations" appear to favor the Greeks, whose color covered most of the peninsula.

Figure 7.2. Heinrich Kiepert. *Tableau Ethnocratique des pays du sud-est de l'Europe* (Berlin: Imprimerie de Kerskes & Hohmann, 1878 [K. Paparrigopoulos]).

Gennadius insisted that the area north of the Balkans was characterized by long-time Bulgarian settlement, whereas the south had remained purely Greek, and even the so-called Bulgarians of northern Macedonia and Thrace were Greek. In his own words:

> During a period of darkness, internal convulsions and administrative prostration, the mixed Greek and Bulgarian populations of those regions were gradually merged into a new and common body, neither purely Bulgarian, nor purely Greek, but appertaining to both races. This mixed people may be appropriately designated as "Bulgarophone Greeks," for it is easily proved that Greek is the prevalent element in its constitution. The outward features of this race differ considerably from those of the Bulgarians north of the Balkans; the latter are clearly of the Mongolian type, whereas South of the Balkans we find the Caucasian, and very frequently the purely Greek type. Their dress is identical with that of the Greeks whereas a Bulgarian is always distinguished by the unavoidable pootoor—breeches large and full to the knee and tight around the leg to the ankle—and the characteristic cylindrical-shaped cap, or calpak of black sheep skin. Their language is not only more smooth and much softer than that of the Northern Bulgarians, but it contains an immense admixture of Greek words, wholly incomprehensible to a pure Bulgarian.... In their churches, their schools, and their correspondence they always use the Greek language, which they understand and study. (*Ethnological Map of European Turkey* 1877, 13)

One of the most striking characteristics of this excerpt is the way Gennadius presents costume as a distinguishing feature of the Bulgarian "race." This is not as surprising as one might think, given that the term *race* had not yet gained the strictly biological sense—especially one deriving from the color of skin—as it would during the first decades of the twentieth century, and language, customs, habits, and religious beliefs were counted among the "mental" factors that distinguished one group from another (see, e.g., *Illustrations of the Principal Varieties of the Human Race* [1850], 2). It is also worth noting that the "race" Gennadius associated Bulgars with was not Slavs, a group recently discovered by a sympathetic European audience, but Tartaric hordes descending upon Eastern Europe.[13]

The "non-aryan" roots of Bulgars were a favorite topic especially of authors who wanted to give credence to Greek claims in the Balkan Peninsula. For instance, according to Driault, they were "not pure Slavs, they seem to be Slavicized Tartars" (1912, 286). The implication was that the Bulgarians were racially inferior. The "non-aryan" Bulgar roots constituted such a problematic issue that even advocates of the Bulgarian side in the Struggle for Macedonia, such as H. N. Brailsford, had to come up with apologetic explanations as to the racial purity of Macedonian Slavs:

> They [Macedonian Slavs] are not Serbs, for their blood can hardly be purely Slavonic. There must be in it some admixture of Bulgarian and other non-Aryan stock.... On the other hand, they can hardly be Bulgarians, for quite clearly the Servian immigrations and conquests must have left much Servian blood in their veins, and the admixture of non-Aryan blood can scarcely be so considerable as it is in Bulgaria. They are probably very much what they were before either a Bulgarian and or a Servian Empire existed—a Slav people derived from rather various stocks, who invaded the peninsula at different periods. (1906, 101)[14]

Gennadius, by invoking the dominant rhetoric about racial hierarchy and depicting it on a map, gave the Greek elite a powerful weapon to fight against the claims of romantic Slavophiles: the weapon of cultural and racial superiority. Ioanna Stephanopoli, in a pamphlet on the populations of Macedonia, would echo Gennadius's words when she argued that "Bulgarians are not Macedonians, and Macedonians are not Bulgarians." And, she added, "if they are proud of belonging to the Family of Aristotle, of Alexander, of the Diadochoi, they [the inhabitants of Macedonia] would find it demeaning in their own eyes to be confused with the 'peoples without glory' who have not added even the smallest stone to the edifice of civilization that humanity has been erecting for centuries" (1903b, 7). It is interesting to note that the rhetoric of racial and cultural superiority was not exclusively used by the European-educated Greek national elite by the beginning of the twentieth century. The same sense of civilizational distinction could be detected in the discourse of Greek Orthodox notables in Macedonia when they pleaded with Ottoman authorities for protection against Bulgarian encroachments on their community. For instance, when the Greek notables of Salonika and the city's bishop petitioned the Ottoman governor in March 1904 demanding that Bulgarian insurgents be punished more severely, they made extensive use of allusions to the superiority of Rumlar (Greeks), who "have acquired an exalted place in international opinion as well that of the Ottoman state thanks to their accomplishments in civilization and learning from time immemorial" and to the inferiority of the Bulgarians, who were "a 'nation' that has not benefited from the grace of civilization and learning."[15] Complaints about Bulgarian bands' transgressions emphasized the attacks on teachers and schools, underscoring the point that precisely this progress in "education and civilization" was targeted.

The second example, a map published by Heinrich Kiepert in 1878, is an even more impressive example in terms of demonstrating how a race's "fitness to rule" could be articulated and depicted through the use of ethnographic geography. Heinrich Kiepert, a professor of geography at the University of Berlin, was considered by many in Europe, including Bismarck, to be the best cartographer of the times (Colocotronis 1919, 484; Wilkinson 1951, 67). Kiepert's second map, published only two years after the appearance of the cartographer's well-known *Ethnographsiche Übersichtskarte*, displayed an image that was almost the exact negative of its predecessor (Kiepert 1876, 1878b).

In the map shown in figure 7.2, Kiepert had allocated most of the region of Macedonia to the Bulgarian "race." Thrace was shown as half Turkish and half Greek; further north a more or less similar proportion was observed between Turks and Bulgars. This map had received such a good reception in Europe that it had been used as a reference at the Congress of Berlin—clear praise for its perceived objectivity.[16] Kiepert's second map was accompanied with a *Notice explicative sur la carte ethnocratique des pays helléniques, slaves, albanais, et roumains*, which essentially argued that it was a mistake to base political boundaries on ethnographic maps. To correct this mistake, a new style called *ethnocratique* was introduced. The new method entailed "the separation of South-Eastern Europe according to divisions or groups of race, and, to the possible extent, *natural* frontiers, historical requirements, traditional affinities, and to assign to each division or group a single color. This color would not claim rigidly that the constituent parts of each section are occupied exclusively by a single race, it would only indicate the race that would be preponderant" (1878a, 5; emphasis mine). Was Kiepert really espousing this new and rather odd method that would presumably project a reliable picture of Macedonia based on the principal of ethnic "preponderance"? Could Kiepert be making this bold move for the sake of publicity? As it turns out, his motives were of a different order and, as revealed by his lengthy correspondence with a certain Konstantinos Paparrigopoulos during the time he was preparing it for publication, were highly questionable in terms of the author's professional integrity.[17]

Rarely recognized by Anglophone academia, Konstantinos Paparrigopoulos (1815–1891) was one of the greatest names of Greek national historiography.[18] At the time of his correspondence with Kiepert, he was among the members of Sullogos pros Diadosin tōn Ellinēkōn Grammatōn (Society for the Dissemination of Greek Letters), which took an active interest in ethnographical maps of "European Turkey" (Dimara 1986, 336; Svolopoulos 1992, 358). Feeling the need to counter the alarming prestige Bulgarians seemed to have with ethnographic cartographers—confirmed by the recent recruitment of Europe's best, Kiepert, to their side—Paparrigopoulos took it upon himself to persuade Kiepert to draw a new, and remarkably different, map sponsored by the Society (Dimara 1986, 343 [based on Alexander Rizos Rangavis's memoirs]). The historian left for Berlin in July 1877 with this goal.

During his stay in Berlin, Paparrigopoulos apparently convinced Kiepert to draw a map of the regions comprising the Peloponnese, Thessaly, Epirus, Macedonia, Thrace, and Eastern Rumelia. During their first meeting, he provided specific requirements concerning the borders of the map and how it should be "colored." During the year that passed between this meeting and the publication of the final version of the map, Kiepert and Paparrigopoulos maintained a correspondence, over the course of which the famous cartographer changed his earlier depiction of the region almost entirely, in line with Greek claims, despite his initial reservations concerning the coloring of certain regions and the name(s) to be printed on the map.

In one of his letters Kiepert asked to be informed of any alterations to the borders that he had proposed, in which case, he further demanded, Paparrigopoulos's or another committee member's name be cited as the "coloring author" of the map. It is possible to infer from Kiepert's letter dated October 9, 1877, from Naples that Paparrigopoulos did not accept the proposed modifications. Kiepert was surprisingly accommodating in his response, when he stated that he "perfectly appreciated the reasons and the facts" presented by Paparrigopoulos to prove that the southern part of Macedonia was more than half Greek. Concerning a revised version of the map, he wrote that it was impossible to draw an exact line from memory and suggested to Paparrigopoulos to send a "sample of the entire map" colored according to his corrections.

However, even the flexibility that Paparrigopoulos seems to have magically cultivated in Kiepert had its limits, and the name proposed by Paparrigopoulos for the map, "Chart of Greek Lands," obviously transgressed them, for the cartographer retorted: "I have nothing to object to Pinax *tōn Ellēnikōn Chōrōn* [Chart of Greek lands], except for the fact that at least half of the area represented on the map includes lands that were never either Hellenic or Hellenized, like Serbia, Wallachia, Danubian Bulgaria, Montenegro, Northern Albania" (Dimara 1986, 366).

Paparrigopoulos's letter to Kiepert dated February 16, 1878, from Athens reveals that the letter and the latest color proof of the map sent by the cartographer had not settled the differences concerning the limits of Greek dominance in the regions of Thrace, Macedonia, and Epirus. Paparrigopoulos was also not very happy about Kiepert's objection to the title of the map and pointed out that it was enough to take a look at Kiepert's own proof to see that "these lands [Hellenic or Hellenized] fill up more than three quarters of the whole map" (Dimara 1986, 368). The title of the final and published version of the map suggests that this became the only compromise Kiepert could obtain from Paparrigopoulos. Moreover, the cartographer had repeated his demand about placing the authorship for coloring under someone else's name, and despite their previous conversations, the Kingdom of Greece had been given "a color different than other Hellenic lands." This last "mistake" seemed to be the straw that broke the camel's back. Paparrigopoulos was indignant:

> As you see, Professor, your last work is far from corresponding to the first arrangements, to which you had kindly given your complete consent. It goes without saying that it is impossible to accept these modifications. We cannot but attribute them to a simple misunderstanding; we also have the firm hope that after the considerations we hereby presented to you, you will kindly give M. Reimer the necessary instructions in order to place the different colors conforming to the basis established by you, and that we hastened to accept. We have sent a telegram to M. Reimer in order to stop all further work on the map, until an agreement can be reached between us. (Dimara 1986, 369)

The bluff evidently had the desired effect, because Kiepert's final letter dated February 25, 1878, from Berlin was almost apologetic in its acceptance of the terms suggested by Paparrigopoulos:

> I did not, in any manner want to anticipate by this temporary sketch (which, as M. Reimer told me should not represent anything other than a sample of the style of coloring) the definitive decision about the frontier lines to adopt.

I had thought instead with M. Reimer that the printing of the map (the corrections of which are at the moment on lithography stones) should be deferred for a short term, from what it seems, when it will be possible to present in it the new frontiers of Bulgaria, Serbia, and Montenegro established by the peace [Treaty of San Stefano].... However, if you absolutely want to be in possession of a certain number of samples of the map, intended for the needs of the moment, we can print and color them, according to the instructions and corrections that you would like to send." (Dimara 1986, 370)

In the same letter Kiepert implored, yet again, that another name along with his be published as the coloring author, afraid that he would be found accountable by critics who would not know, in his words, to "distinguish between the very different trends of this map, and the ethnographic maps" that he had published earlier. In the end, it was Paparrigopoulos who prevailed, even though it seems to have taken another three to four months for him to persuade the geographer with his persistence and what no doubt must have been compelling (dis)incentives—unfortunately not documented. We do learn from a letter by Paparrigopoulos to his protégé Argiropoulos that the final agreement was reached around June. In the same letter, it is hard to miss a certain element of irony in Paparrigopoulos's style when he uses the title "the eminent geographer" [ο επιφανής γεωγράφος] repeatedly when referring to Kiepert: "The eminent geographer (who nowadays is busy with the translation of his Russian maps of Asian borders into French for the conference [of Berlin] on Bismarck's commission), the eminent, well, geographer was persuaded to color our chart the way we wanted it to be from the beginning; and even better, *under his name.*"[19]

The letters clearly show Paparrigopoulos's determination to get a geographer who was named "Europe's best" by none other than Bismarck to publish a map supporting Greek claims. It was not good enough to obtain a map simply *drawn* by Kiepert; it also had to have his seal of authority—and so the key issues that surfaced many times in the correspondence were "coloring" and "authorship," which brought the project to a standstill at least twice because of Kiepert's understandable reluctance to paint a huge chunk of Southeastern Europe in Greek colors. But the disagreements were ultimately resolved by Paparrigopoulos's persuasion tactics, covering a wide range from flattery to bribery and from criticism to outright bluffing.

Paparrigopoulos's talent in manipulating ethnographic maps surpassed that of Gennadius because he did not only deploy that map as an apparatus of power, a visual tool with which the Greek nation's rights over an expanse of territory was asserted. He also highlighted the subjectivity of the whole process and questioned the *authority* of ethnographical maps in principle. The literal issue of authorship was the most important symbolic element of the map, communicating to the public the *scientific authority* embodied in the geographer's name. Gennadius had claimed that authority by remaining anonymous and giving the impression that the map was prepared by a British author.[20] By contrast, Paparrigopoulos usurped the already existing and unquestionable authority of Kiepert by making sure that his name was the only one to be printed on the map and the text that accompanied it (written, however, by Paparrigopoulos himself), deliberately misleading the reader. The result was so convincing that even the otherwise meticulous and thorough Wilkinson did not doubt its authenticity when he wrote: "In the explanation accompanying the map Kiepert outlined the difficulties inherent in the production of an ethnographic map and he maintained that the use of such maps for drawing up political boundaries was a malpractice which no geographer ought to countenance" (1951, 75).

It is difficult to gauge the exact magnitude of the impact that the Kiepert-Paparrigopoulos map had in Western Europe. It is likely that it remained somewhat obscure in comparison to Kiepert's previous work, but Paparrigopoulos's persistent efforts helped him kill two birds with one stone.[21] Paradoxical as it may sound, the first of these was demonstrating that ethnography was not an exact science. He did this by disclosing his correspondence with Kiepert to representatives of European powers in Athens, months before he had guaranteed the publication of the map under his terms.[22] To the letters he had attached a memo, in which he argued that while no one would dispute the merits of Kiepert's geographical work, the same certainty could not be sustained for its ethnographical component, because Kiepert himself was "far from believing in the absolute value of the data we have on the population of the diverse races of the Orient" (Svolopoulos 1992, 361). Questioning the criteria whereby the "ethnographic component" of a map was determined meant that one could introduce alternative methods that would result in different outlooks. This did not detract from the power of maps, however. To the contrary, it underscored their importance in visualizing a political objective without naming it as such and making it available in its simplest form to the observers, which was the second, and more conventional, use of Paparrigopoulos's map. The map thus conceived was not intended for an audience among the geographers of Europe, for whom it was probably too crude, but for circulation in classrooms in Macedonia at schools that the *Syllogos* provided with textbooks, teachers, and, apparently, maps. In a way, Paparrigopoulos gave the Greek public a means to transform the faith they had in their stakes in Macedonia and the much needed assurance that if maps were to be drawn in order to "display the races of the Orient," the heritage of Greek civilization was a more justifiable principle than sheer numbers in determining their colors.[23]

MAPS AND TERRITORIALITY

According to Robert David Sack, a theoretical geographer, territoriality signifies something more complicated than simple spatial relationships. It is, above all, "the key geographical component in understanding how society and space are interconnected" (1986, 3). A given delimited area is not "territory" in and of itself; it becomes so "only when its boundaries are used to affect behavior by controlling access" (19). Territoriality has three aspects that define it as such: it must involve "some form of classification by area"; it must "contain a form of communication"; and "each instance of territoriality must involve an attempt at enforcing control over access to the area and to things within it, or to things outside of it by restraining those within" (21–22). Sack's theory is not necessarily restricted to territoriality of nations, states, and nation-states, but its applicability in these contexts is clear. Maps of Ottoman Europe—be they drawn and disseminated by European scholars or local national elites; be they hung up on walls of diplomatic residences in London or military schools in Istanbul—represented rivaling territorialities. In other words, cartography, as the primary apparatus of territoriality, was another front in the battle to establish hegemony over the disputed lands of the Ottoman Empire.

More pertinent to the "conceptual characteristics of the human condition in borderlands" is cartography's unique power to create the spatial definition of a nation, normalized and anchored to a physical shape. In *Siam Mapped*, a seminal work that combined Sack's definition of territoriality as applied to the specific context of nationhood and Benedict Anderson's theorization of the nation as an imagined community, Thongchai Winichakul made a case for the creation of Thai nationhood, where he persuasively argued that maps did not follow the social reality of a nation dispersed across delimited domains; they were not depictions of something that already existed, but predictions of it. He presented the process through which Thai nationhood was articulated as a confrontation between indigenous definitions of the realm and its modern geographical interpretations and called the resulting novel concept of the nation's territoriality its "geo-body [...] merely an effect of modern geographical discourse whose prime technology is a map" (1994, 17). Even though the geo-body of a nation "appears to be concrete to the eyes as if its existence does not depend on any act of imagining" (17) it was a fully imagined concept, just like the nation itself. In Winichakul's explanation of the genesis of nationhood, maps replaced the role of print capitalism and language from Anderson's model.[24]

I find this model to be a useful tool for understanding the maps presented here even though their production processes do not parallel each other perfectly. At the basis of Winichakul's methodology is an engagement with the tensions arising from the collusion of premodern and modern discourses of geography, which our present examples cannot simulate. There is a similar tension, however, between maps intended for international and national consumption, which we cannot overlook. Moreover, Winichakul's identification of the order in which maps and national boundaries are engendered, whereby the imagined precedes the real, holds for maps of Ottoman Macedonia as well.

One final point concerns the way in which the boundaries of the nation's "geo-body" were imagined and articulated. A theme that was often stressed in notes accompanying maps of Macedonia was "natural boundaries." For instance, explaining the ethnocratique method, Paparrigopoulos (posing as Kiepert) wrote that "natural frontiers" were followed to the possible extent in his new map of Southeastern Europe. Even though there was nothing natural about the way the population of a certain area was identified, measured, and captured in color on a map depending on the "scientific criteria" applied by the author, the assumption was that natural boundaries did exist. This basic assumption was not challenged by the fact that the "social reality" rarely fit within the confines of those natural boundaries. The real challenge was to ensure that those delimitations were enforced in such a way that the natural boundaries—however defined—were respected. Drawing a map that respected those boundaries was the first step in that process.

Another example is the observations of H. N. Brailsford,[25] in his book *Macedonia, Its Races and Their Future*: "Macedonia lies confounded within three *vilayets* (i.e., provinces), which correspond to no *natural* division either racial

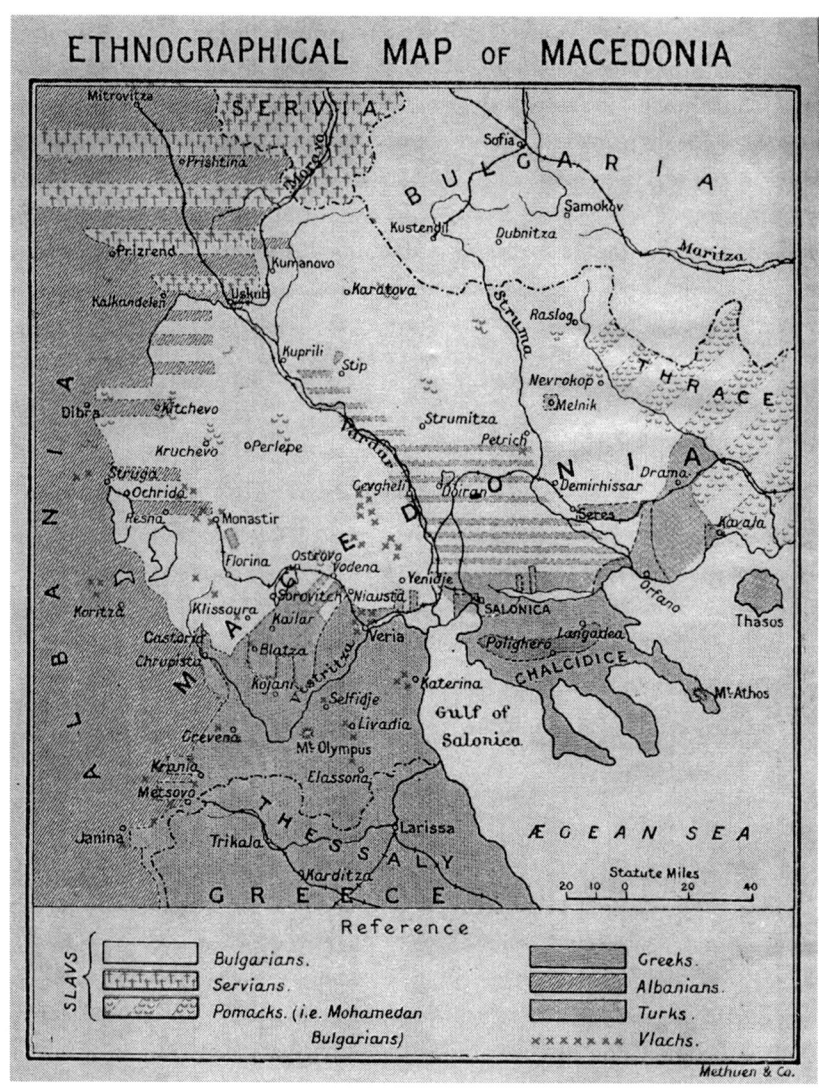

Figure 7.3. H. N Brailsford. *Macedonia, Its Races and Their Future* (London: Methuen, ca. 1905).

or geographical. [. . .] The result is that no race attains a predominance, and no province acquires a national character. The *natural* arrangement would have been to place Greeks, Servians, and Albanians in compartments of their own, leaving the Bulgarians to occupy the center and the East" (1906, 7). In fact, the obligatory ethnographical map that Brailsford appended to his book did just that. What he called "Bulgarians" occupied the center and east of the peninsula, while Chalkidiki was marked as Greek territory. Other ethnic groups recognized by the author were assigned symbols rather than colors. Not counting the random disturbances on the map, it more or less conformed to what Brailsford would argue was the "natural" arrangement of races.

Natural frontiers, or more precisely, the lack thereof, in Ottoman Macedonia was an important theme in another, earlier publication written in response to the British Blue Book of 1889. Its anonymous author criticized the British Consul in Salonica in his failure to acknowledge their existence:

> Mr. Blunt [the consul] ought to have admitted that the administrative division of Turkey is not scientific, that is to say, it has not as a basis *natural boundaries*, nor is it stable, and at the same time to have recorded one at least of the many arbitrary changes in the boundaries, such as that of the department of Velisso, which eight years ago did not belong to the Vilayet of Salonica, and was annexed to it later on upon the demand of the Russian Embassy in Constantinople, in order to fictitiously strengthen the Bulgarian element in the vilayet of Salonica, which would in consequence thus acquire different geographical boundaries and another ethnological character.

This author then presented an alternative, more "scientific" approach to the boundary problem:

> I confine myself to the following remarks 1) that it is both just and practicable to give to these three Macedonian vilayets such geographical boundaries as to be separated from each other by lines, parallel to the Macedonian coast on the Aegean 2) that the delimitation of the geographical boundaries of the vilayet of Salonica on such a scientific basis would include about as much Christian population as Mr. Blunt records in treating of the present vilayet of Macedonia 3) that the principal and most heroic method for the attainment of tranquility in Macedonia, in which Mr. Blunt is interested, and, moreover, for the removal of the intricacies of the Macedonian question, for which Lord Salisbury is justly concerned, would be the scientific administrative division of Macedonia upon the basis of its natural boundaries.[26]

It is difficult to imagine how and why "parallel lines" would be any more "natural" than the existing boundaries of the Macedonian provinces. A glance at a topographical map of Macedonia makes one realize that there are no unyielding mountain chains, unsurpassable rivers, or impossibly isolated plains in its geography. Assuming geographical formations would determine demarcation lines, or "natural boundaries," it is extremely difficult to argue in favor of one division as opposed to the other. But topography was not even the issue here; these "natural boundaries" in effect amounted to what we could today call "ethnic gerrymandering." It was a way of imagining the geo-body of a nation on paper, sterilized and not obfuscated by blurry visions of ethnic ambiguity.

The subjectivity of such divisions may seem self-evident, but at the time the problem with ethnographic maps was attributed more to the quality of scholarship and accuracy of projections than the principle that endorsed the drawing of these maps. That principle was none other than the "principle of nationalities," which dictated that national (thus natural) boundaries, *socially* manifested, ought to precipitate the political ones finally drawn on a map. In an article published in the *Bulletin of the American Geographical Society* in 1913, W. L. G. Joerg compared the recent political map of the Balkans following the conclusion of the second Balkan War with an ethnographic map drawn by the famous geographer Jovan Cvijić. According to Joerg, "despite minor discrepancies," this comparison showed that "at last the guiding principle of European history since the beginning of the nineteenth century, the establishment of coincident racial and political boundaries, has made itself felt in Balkan affairs." The celebratory tone of the article and hopeful words for the future of the Balkan peoples ring hollow, and nowhere more poignant than in Joerg's conclusion that "the reapportionment of Balkan territory on broad lines *does* satisfy the requirements of the principle of nationalities. In this lies the significance of the recent conflicts; in this, too, lies the hope of the future. Given the opportunity to work out their own destinies, the Balkan peoples, we may hope, will enter upon a new era of progress and development" (1913, 829–30; emphasis in original).

The fiction that conflict is permanently resolved once the demarcation lines between people coincide with their respective political entities is held in high esteem to this day, and at the root of it lies the assumption that those demarcation lines are reflected in patterns that can be translated into, and inform political boundaries on, a map. This fiction surfaces time and again in commentaries on conflict situations in those strangely heterogeneous zones of the world, such as contemporary Macedonia. During the late 1990s when the (Western) world observed the mounting tension in the Republic with anxiety, the two authors of an op-ed piece in the *New York Times*, "Redraw the Map,

Stop the Killing," argued that violence was "inevitable" given the reluctance of Slavs to work with Albanians. They proposed a plebiscite that would determine whether Albanians wanted to stay or leave, and then they would "partition" Macedonia.

CONCLUSIONS

I have tried, in this chapter, to emphasize the potential of the map medium to create, predict, and enforce the territoriality of a nation. I should finally note an important feature of cartography that contributes to this enterprise through its disinvestment of moral concerns, thereby rendering the map a completely benign exercise to the observer. It is what J. B. Harley has called the "socially empty space" depicted on a map, or its "abstract quality" that "lessens the burden of conscience about people in the landscape" (1988, 303). Drawing maps, especially ethnographic maps, involves decisions that go well beyond mere technical issues. Colorful blocks on an ethnographical map, as Gennadius suggested, did not only demonstrate how different ethnic groups "stand with respect to one another," but they also made a powerful statement about their discontents, or people who did not fit the scale. This statement was not as loud and clear as that voiced by the guerrillas carrying out the legwork and preparing the ground for the ideal of the nation-state to become reality. It did, however, serve the same ideal of homogeneity within the nation's (imagined) boundaries.

Smadar Lavie and Ted Swedenburg, in their introduction to *Displacement, Diaspora, and Geographies of Identity*, refer to the Chicana poet Gloria Anzaldúa's analogy of the border as an "open wound ... where the Third World grates against the First and bleeds" (1987, 14–15). This is a chilling, powerful image that we could also transfer to the borderlands of the Ottoman Empire, in this case Macedonia, at the beginning of the twentieth century. Instead of two worlds determined and set apart by economic development (as well as cultural difference, real or perceived), what we have here is a border zone where a new world order with the nation-state on the ascendant grates against a decaying empire. The movements across the border—and through people—of liberation fighters, brigands, and soldiers help to create that new order that sharpens the vertical line that is the border and homogenizes the horizontal area that is the frontier. Hybridity survives in memory and, to a more limited extent, in practice. This image may even have the advantage of offering us a new frame of analysis that could allow us to question the nation-state without glorifying the empire that preceded it.

Notes

1. The founding members of the Young Turk movement were overwhelmingly "ethnic Turks" principally from the Balkans and the Caucasus and also from Arab and Kurdish areas, rather than Ottoman Muslims from central Anatolia. Erik Jan Zürcher is well justified in proposing that we call them "Children of the Borderlands" (2003, 275–86).

2. A recent study that offers new insights into the early period of Ottoman rule, or *tourkokratia*, in the Balkans is Heath Lowry's *Shaping of the Ottoman Balkans, 1350–1550* (2008).

3. On early methods of Ottoman conquest see Halil İnalcık's seminal article "Ottoman Methods of Conquest" (1954). On the administration of different religious communities of the Ottoman Empire see Braude and Lewis (1982).

4. I have argued elsewhere (Yosmaoğlu 2006) that it was not only the actions of the warring parties but also the classificatory practices of the Ottoman state such as the implementation of a census that emboldened narrow sectarian differences into a basis for national identity and conflict.

5. The "reinvention" of Macedonia by nineteenth-century travelers and geographers is not something identified by deconstructionist historians in the late twentieth century. In 1920, Ivanoff wrote, for instance: "Cet ardent désir des Balkaniques de ressusciter le nom de Macédoine est stimulé par les publications des Européens sur la péninsule balkanique, surtout depuis le commencement du XIXe s. Nous ne citerons que les noms des explorateurs les plus en vue: Félis de Beaujour, Couisinéry, Pouqueville, Urquhart, Viquesnel, Boué, Grisebach, Grigorovitch, etc. Dans leurs études sur les Balkans, ils considèrent la Macédoine comme une unité géographique" (1920, 5).

6. One of the most influential explorers in the region was E. M. Couisinéry (1831).

7. The parallels with Orientalism are clear here. On this issue, in addition to Todorova (1997), see Fleming (2004, 1218).

8. Strictly speaking, Gopčević was not the first pro-Serbian cartographer of the region, but it seems that he earned this reputation because his work became widely available to European scholars after its publication in *Petermann's Mittheilungen*. His most important predecessors were M. S. Miloyevitch (1873), Colonel Dragashevitch (1885), and M. Veselinovitch (1886) (Cvijić 1906, 29).

9. Even in a mainstream source of general information such as *Encyclopædia Britannica* (1910), the population of Macedonia was described as follows: "The greater part of Macedonia is inhabited by a Slavonic population, mainly Bulgarian in its characteristics; the coast-line and the southern districts west of the Gulf of Salonica by Greeks, while Turkish, Vlach and Albanian settlements exist sporadically, or in groups, in many parts of the country."

10. According to Cvijić, "there is nothing which represents better than this chart the gigantic efforts of the Greeks to Hellenise these two vilayets" (1906, 32). School statistics

in favor of Greeks were initially published in the form of statistical tables, but the visual impact of a map was certainly stronger. For statistics see *The Population of Macedonia* (1905) and Stephanopoli (1903a).

11. A telling example of how these maps can be used to popularize the idea of border changes are depictions of conflict zones, such as Kosovo or now, more relevantly, Iraq in wide-readership magazines such as the *Atlantic Monthly* or *Vanity Fair*, which have published alternatives to the current map of Iraq with no self-conscious examination of this kind of exercise's inextricable links to colonialism.

12. It seems that even Kiepert was not able to figure out the identity of the author, his inquiries having been answered by only the information that he was Greek. See letter from Kiepert to Paparrigopoulos published in Svolopoulos (1992, 366). In 1906, Cvijić disclosed Gennadius's name as the author (1906, 22), but the knowledge must have remained obscure since Wilkinson listed the map as anonymous (1951, 71).

13. More specifically he described them as "a mixed people formed by the fusion of Mongolian and Hunnish tribes, with much Tartaric blood in their veins [...] It is true that owing to a close contact with Slav races the Bulgarians, during their descent upon the Balkan peninsula, absorbed into a widely different dialect a large proportion of Slavonic words. But the Bulgarian language contains also a considerable Turkish element; and by a similar process the Slavs of Turkey have adopted many Bulgarian words, the roots of which are not to be found in Slavonic" (*Ethnological Map of European Turkey* 1877, 11). The Bulgarians had been classified among the Southern Slavs by A. Balbi in 1828 in his *Atlas Ethnographique du Globe ou classification des Peuples Anciens et Modernes d'après leurs langues* (cited by Wilkinson 1951, 29), and this classification was more or less the norm especially among ethnographers who gave precedence to linguistic affiliation.

14. Another example of attempts to "rectify" the racial stock of Bulgarians is Tozer's explanation of their "Slavization": "The Bulgarians, who form the largest element in the Christian population from Salonica to the confines of Albania, are a very interesting people, and are highly spoken of for industry and honesty. They are the most numerous of all the nationalities inhabiting European Turkey, and are estimated between five and six millions. There can be no doubt that the original Bulgarians were of Turanian descent, and near relations, if not actual descendants, of Attila's Huns; but after they became so intermingled with the Slavonian inhabitants of that country that they adopted their language. A large number of them seem to have emigrated into Western Macedonia before the ninth century, and there, in all probability, received a further infusion of Slavonic blood. The traces of this are very evident in the present appearance of the people; for the Tartar type of face, which generally is remarkable for its permanence, has here for the most part disappeared. Notwithstanding this, you will not often find a people with such well-marked characteristics. They have straight noses,

high cheekbones, flat cheeks, and very commonly light eyes; their complexions are frequently almost swarthy from exposure to the sun, but the children are generally fair" (Tozer 1869, 176).

15. Prime Ministry, Ottoman State Archives, TFR.I.SL 33/3228, March 6, 1904, Greek Community of Selânik to Rumeli Vilayeti. The Ottoman word used is *kavm* (from the Arabic *qaum*), which may mean both "nation" and "race."

16. Wilkinson notes Bismarck's high regard for Kiepert and mentions that his map was used at the Congress of Berlin and "was regarded as part of Bismarck's 'honest brokerage'" (1951, 67–68). It must be noted, however, that Kiepert's maps used at the Congress of Berlin were prepared under Russian sponsorship (see Karpat 1985, 26), were first published in Russian, and, according to Paparrigopoulos, were translated into French after Bismarck's orders to be used at the Congress (see Paparrigopoulos's correspondence with P. Argiropoulo in Dimara 1986, 348).

17. France, Ministère des Affaires Etrangères, A.A.E; C.P, Grèce, 106: Tissot (Athènes) à Waddington, 6 Mars 1878; 25 Mars 1878, Annexe à la Dépêche Politique d'Athènes, No 35 du 25 Mars 1878, published in K. Svolopoulos, pp. 361–70.

18. The only biography of Paparrigopoulos written in English, to my knowledge, is the unpublished Ph.D. dissertation of Demosthenes Kontos (1986). A well-researched and extensive biography in Greek is Dimara's *Kōnstantinos Paparrēgopoulos* (1986). According to Antonis Liakos, Paparrigopoulos's magnum opus *History of the Greek Nation (1860–1874)*, was the definitive "grand narrative and introduced a new style to national historiography" by replacing the third person hitherto favored by Greek historians with a pronounced use of "we" and, even more significantly, by introducing a continuity into the Greek nation's genealogy that incorporated the Byzantine past and "turned the national identity into a native-produced one" (Liakos 2001, 33).

19. Emphasis mine. Paparrigopoulos's letter to Argiropoulo, p. 348. Colocotronis also made a sarcastic remark about the geographer's willingness to publish a map negating his previous work: "Certainly M. Kiepert did not want to disappoint anyone" (Colocotronis 1919, 484).

20. The confusion created was enough that Dimara, as recently as 1986, cited "the famous English Edward Stanford" as the author of the map (Dimara 1986, 343).

21. Cvijić does not mention the original, but he does refer to Nicolaides's rendering of it (1899) and notes that he was "astonished to see Kiepert's name on this map" (Cvijić 1906, 32).

22. This is why we do not know how exactly he convinced Kiepert to publish the map under his name (see Svolopoulos 1992, 360).

23. N. Kasasis, president of the University of Athens and the society "Hellénisme," wrote: "Mais ce n'est pas par l'importance numérique que les Grecs maintiennent leur supériorite incontestable sur les autres races; c'est encore par l'influence de leur culture

intellectuelle, de leur activité commerciale et économique, en un mot par le triple privilège de l'ancienneté, de l'intelligence et de l'argent" (1903, 63–64).

24. Anderson himself picked up this thread and named maps, census, and museums as the three significant institutions of nationhood in colonial contexts in a chapter he amended to the *Imagined Communities* (1991).

25. Henry Noel Brailsford was a journalist who participated in the British Relief effort in Macedonia after the Ilinden Uprising of 1903; he was also one of the authors of the "Carnegie Report" on the Balkan wars.

26. *The English Blue Book Regarding Macedonia*, comments by A.K., Athens, 1891, pp. 7, 9 (Blue Book No. 3 1889, Turkey, Official Correspondence on Eastern Affairs).

CHAPTER EIGHT

Pioneers and Refugees
Arabs and Jews in the Jordan River Valley

Rachel S. Havrelock

This chapter deals with the Jordan River or Jordan Rift Valley. The valley stretches from the Sea of Galilee/Kinneret in the north to the Dead Sea in the south and forms a border both natural and political that distinguishes the East (Transjordan) and West Banks (Cisjordan) as well as the Hashemite Kingdom of Jordan and the state of Israel. It is the site of a fluctuating borderland. Although the river's northern course from sources in Lebanon, Syria, and Israel into the Sea of Galilee is of interest as the western demarcation of the disputed Golan Heights, a borderland experience exists only in regard to Druze communities, whose members are Israeli citizens at the same time that they maintain cultural, familial, and social contacts in Syria. Similarly the dry wadi south of the Dead Sea, the Arava, functions as a border between Israel and Jordan and has been a site of bold and dangerous Israeli border crossings but does not host a borderland dynamic (Havrelock 2007a).

The Jordan River Valley can be identified as a borderland in the Deuteronomistic writings of the Hebrew Bible (books of Deuteronomy, Joshua, Judges, Samuel, and Kings) where Israelite tribes straddled the border, intermixed with other ethno-national groups and maintained a marginal position vis-à-vis the power centers at Shiloh and later Jerusalem. Because the dating of the Deuteronomistic writings is constantly debated by biblical scholars, one cannot take the biblical representations as indicative of the times that they purport to portray. In other words, the texts could reflect a manner of lived reality around the ninth to sixth centuries BCE or the memories and values of communities living in Babylonian exile or in Judea in the Persian period. What can be ascertained with more certainty is the degree of influence that such biblical texts exerted on transhistorical Jewish and Christian communities and, as we will see, the degree to which these texts influenced the border-making activities of the British during their Mandate in Palestine as well as those of early Zionist leaders. In the long, long stretch between even the latest biblical writings and the twentieth century, the Jordan River sometimes differentiated between the administrative zones of empire but always suggested a dramatic symbolic divide for Jewish and Christian pilgrims and thinkers. The focus here rests on the valley as a borderland from the time of the British Mandate, through the wars between Israel and the Arab States and into the early twenty-first century.

The borderland case is here argued based on evidence from Palestinian and Israeli national myths. The myths were gathered from written and archival sources as well as from interviews conducted with narrators in Jordan, the Palestinian West Bank, Israel, and the Palestinian and Israeli Diasporas. The working premise is that the symbolic borders of nation are drawn in national mythology and that such borders work to outline national identity and draw contrasts with neighboring groups. Such myths accrue particular force when two or more groups share a spatial location. In the absence of defining territorial boundaries, such groups become acutely invested in abstracted representations of such boundaries. The attachment to such borders ironically is greater in cases of muted or disputed dividing lines. The nation exists first as a mythic idea that is then advocated and fought for in material spheres. The mythic idea proliferates in several forms. It is the basis for the identity of those who belong to the nation, and because it is present in the sphere of individual imagination, the mythic idea can be referenced in partial as well as complete forms. Following the anthropologist Bronislaw Malinowski (1948, 114–17), myth is here treated as the map of social organization. The social order, justified and chartered in mythic accounts of origin and formation, becomes inscribed on landscapes and bodies as a seemingly indelible reality.

Borders are first asserted in national mythology, but how does this pertain to the experience of borderlands? It is argued that while asserting a social order and justifying hierarchies, national myths also betray ambivalence about the clarity of distinction and the definitiveness of borders. So at the same time that a border is constructed, concessions will be made to the fact that it is porous. We will see how the very national myths that construct the Jordan River as the defining border of Israel in some cases and Palestine in others also reveal the borderland characteristics of the Jordan River Valley. On one level the stories propose the irreconcilability of the two national formations, but on another they point to a simultaneous although divergent process of aspiring to the hermetic amid a situation of contact. In the lived experience reflected and justified by the national myths, the Jordan River Valley conforms to such borderland characteristics as the presence of identifiable differences between borderlanders and other residents of the same state and the existence of constant flux and movement that resolves certain tensions while engendering others. However, it is potentially unique or paradigmatic of a borderland where the inhabitants do not have common experiences or interactions that give rise to social or political mediation. Instead a profound sense of ethno-national distinction results from events in the Jordan River Valley. The irony is that a shared symbol—the Jordan River—operates in at least two distinct, diametric contexts with the effect of promoting discord.

The sense of distinction in turn moves inward toward the center where it helps to constitute national identity. Three broadly defined groups are at play in the River Valley: Jordanian citizens on the east side of the river, Israeli citizens to the west, and Palestinians residing on both banks of the river. These categories can be muted somewhat by the recognition that Palestinians are also citizens of Jordan although they are distinguished in political, social, and economic terms from other Jordanians and that Jordanian as well as Israeli residents of the Jordan River Valley (the Valley itself as opposed to the larger East and West Banks) work largely in agriculture or tourism.

The Jordanian government is the player most at ease with the notion of the valley as a borderland. The West Bank and its Palestinian population belonged to Jordan between 1948 and 1967, during which time a sizable number of Palestinian refugees were absorbed largely in the Jordan and Zarqa River Valleys. When Israel conquered the West Bank in 1967, Jordan again absorbed Palestinian refugees. Since the 1994 Israel-Jordan peace treaty, a boundary line has been drawn in the middle of the Jordan River. In Israeli and Palestinian contexts the Jordan River is evoked as an immutable signifier of the national collective. Events that transpire at the Jordan are enshrined in the national lore of Palestinians and Israelis, borderland figures are commemorated as heroes, and sharply distinct identities are formulated at the Jordan and then transmitted to the centers as national norms.

BORDERLAND FLUX

Two processes characterize the changes that have transpired in the Jordan River Valley over the past one hundred years. On one hand, borders and the entities that they delimit have varied significantly, and on the other hand, the populations residing in the Jordan River Valley have increased and shifted. Both of these dynamics have symbolic reflexes that in turn exert influence on the formation of national character. The reality of borders that morph and remain uncertain elicits attachment to a utopian mapping of the land with stable and clear partitions. The ideal map in both Palestinian and Israeli contexts stretches from the Mediterranean Sea to the Jordan River. The map is perpetuated in Israeli society as a factual artifact found in government representations, history books, and tourist materials at the same time that the West Bank is recognized and referred to as "the territories." In Palestinian society the map exists in official contexts such as government offices, school and university classrooms, and representations that circulate throughout the Arab world while it also proliferates on quotidian items such as jewelry, clothing, posters, graffiti, and tattoos.

The Jordan River assumed authority as the periphery of national territory by way of the Bible and the British. As indicated above, the Jordan operates as a de facto boundary in Deuteronomistic narratives and is a declared boundary in Numbers 34:12 and Ezekiel 47:18, biblical texts attributed to priestly sources. The Jordan, however, is not the only eastern boundary of ancient Israel to appear in biblical sources. In fact, the Euphrates River appears more frequently in this role (Havrelock 2007b). These biblical delimitations were relevant to British cartographers and administrators once the British Empire found itself in possession of the territory between the Mediterranean and beyond the Euphrates. The Palestine of their making could potentially conform to either model. The Bible's relevance to the imperial project was assumed as natural since the territory was valuable largely as the place where biblical events transpired. At the Anglo-French boundary convention of March 1923, the Jordan River was established as the boundary of Palestine and Transjordan. To some degree the boundary was artificial since the British effectively controlled both sides, and the Hijaz Railway east of the Jordan was perceived as more of a delimiting factor by the Jordan Valley's residents. Politically speaking, a difference was palpable insofar as the Hashemite Abdullah had jurisdiction over Transjordan; however, the Jordan proved a porous and easily crossed border. From 1923 to

1947 a borderland dynamic can be traced in which movements and migrations in the name of trade, grazing, economic opportunity, and religious freedom were common. A perceived dichotomy between the agriculturalists on the West Bank and the Bedouin on the East Bank is remembered in documents of the time, while there is also evidence that commerce and exchange characterized the relationship between residents on the two riverbanks.

Despite the fact that the Jordan was not a very deep border in this period, its designation as such exerted tremendous influence on Jewish and Palestinian nationalists. As long as the British authorities were uncertain of where exactly the borders of Palestine fell (during 1917–1923), Palestinian and Jewish nationalists advocated a range of proposals. For example, at the 1919 Paris Peace Conference, Zionist representatives from Histadrut (labor union) proposed a Jewish homeland spanning from Aqaba in the south to Sidon in the north and from the Mediterranean to a line just east of the Hijaz Railway that ran from Damascus to Amman and then south in a straight line (Gil-Har 1979). The Zionist proposal of a Jewish National Home spanning the banks of the Jordan was effectively crushed in 1922 when Winston Churchill's White Paper detached Transjordan from the territory of Mandate Palestine.[1] Arab nationalists imagined an independent Syria spanning the Mediterranean to at least the Euphrates and perhaps to the Persian Gulf. Arab national aspirations of this sort were dispelled when the French gained control of Lebanon and Syria and the British of Palestine and Iraq. Once the British conception of Palestine stabilized in 1923, Arab and Jewish nationalists alike became certain of the terrain to which they aspired. This meant that although the conditions in the Jordan Valley were characteristic of a borderland, Arab and Jewish nationalists understood events that transpired at the Jordan as relating to national struggle and advocacy. The Jordan River Valley became a place where it was important to assert a boundary.

Boundary-making activities took two interrelated forms. Nationalists placed themselves, as in the Jewish case, or highlighted their presence, as in the Arab, in the Jordan Valley. Such presence assumed symbolic import for the collective as it became enshrined in national mythology as stories about representative pioneers and refugees. The stories in question pertain to the borderland scenario during the time in which they transpire as well the desire for differentiation rather than interconnection in the multiple contexts of their recitation. The population shifts in the Jordan Valley are typified in stories of heroic pioneers and refugees that circulate and are recited at symbolic times and sites.

MY HOME IS OVER JORDAN

Over the past one hundred years, the Jordan River Valley has been characterized by transit and migration, voluntary and forced. Because of the symbolic import of movement across the river, accounts of Jordan River crossings are remembered and transmitted as the respective national legacies of Israelis and Palestinians. While the myths constitute the very act of claiming the land and thereby discount the ownership of the other group, Palestinian and Israeli Jordan River crossing stories also share common elements. The stories of both groups conceive of the East Bank as a site of danger and the West Bank a place of safety and portray the Jordan as the gateway to a homeland definitively located on the West Bank. The East Bank, in turn, figures as an ambivalent landscape associated with exile and danger, evident in the Hebrew designation of the eastern shore as "the other side of the Jordan" and the British title "Transjordan."

It should come as no surprise to find pioneers and refugees populating tales about border crossing since borderlands are "liminal zones in which residents, wayfarers and the state are continually contesting their roles and their natures" (Donnan and Wilson 1999, 64). Borderland inhabitants experience identity in constant motion and occupy a different position and relation to power based on the side of the line where they find themselves. Thus Palestinians can be either pioneers or refugees depending upon whether they are west or east of the Jordan. In the Israeli context, the elite pioneers of the state lived beside the Jordan River and reversed the long-held Jewish paradigm of exile as that place beyond the river. While the Palestinian and Israeli Jordan River stories share geographic conceptions and the same boundary between home and exile, there is also an evident asymmetry between the narrative traditions. Taken as a whole, the Israeli stories speak to the collective transformation from refugees to pioneers, and the Palestinian accounts track how the collective slipped from pioneers to refugees. The Israeli stories record the building of a state, heavily coded as the fulfillment of the ancient Jewish mandate of return to an ancestral land, and the Palestinian stories speak to the devastating loss of land and way of life and perpetuate an acute desire for return to the original habitations of earlier generations.

Pioneer and refugee are the poles of identity for the inhabitants of the Jordan Rift Valley. The two types of migrants metonymically point to larger trends in Jewish and Palestinian nationalism and bequeath a kind of authenticity to their descendants based on primacy and initiative in the case of the pioneers and loss and suffering in the case of the refugees.[2] The genetic and ethnic descendants of pioneers are by implication the rightful inheritors of territory developed through the labor of their forerunners. Descendants of refugees inherit displacement as well as a bond with a point of origin sustained through memory and memorial practices. Memory in such cases serves as the map of the way back home (Khalili 2005). In many ways, the refugee and the pioneer are two sides of the same coin since settlement more often than not involves someone else's displacement.

PIONEERS

Archaeology as well as broader historical questions about antiquity has acute political import in the Israeli-Palestinian conflict (Zerubavel 1995, 26; Abu El-Haj 2001, 81; Attias and Benbassa 2003, 159). As perhaps the central example among many, the Jewish claim to the land based on biblical reports of God's territorial promises to the People of Israel is both absorbed and countered by the Palestinian claims of Canaanite origins. Although antiquity has a manner of unsurpassed authority, more recent accounts of brave progenitors also find a place in the national lore of Palestinians and Israelis. The West Bank city of Ramallah, for example, is not associated with any kind of biblical or religious importance like the cities of Bethlehem or Nablus, but rather with the intrepid spirit of founding families. This founding story involves the distinction mentioned above in which the East Bank figures as a place of threat and the West Bank as a place of refuge while at once acknowledging the banks of the Jordan as a borderland where Christian and Muslim clans inevitability lived together and had daily contact. Despite the centrality of Intifada tales in current Palestinian cultures and the power of these tales to legitimate and grant status to the teller no matter his or her age or social status, the founding story of Ramallah is influential (Kanaana 1993).

As it extols their ancestors and explains their interconnection, the story is a staple of Palestinian Christian culture. As Palestinian society becomes increasingly Islamic and the elevated class status of Christian Palestinians eroded as a result, the stories of Christian pioneers affirm contemporary Christian inclusion in Palestinian society and maintain Christian class privilege by iterating their role as forerunners. The importance of such narratives, however, is not restricted to Christians since the pioneering migrations across the Jordan open accounts of Ramallah's history as narrated in monographs and websites

(Ramallahonline, Ramallah.com, Wikipedia, and various Palestine blogs). Palestinians from Ramallah as well as from other regions cherish the origin of a purely Palestinian Arab city whose rise predates the colonial reinvention of the Middle East and, in certain instances, marshal it as a counterclaim to the Israeli pioneer myth.

One version of Ramallah's beginning was told to me by a Ramallah native in his fifties who explained that the founding family named the Haddadin consisted of seven brothers. The division into seven clans continues to define the social structure of Christian Ramallah. Familial unity is expressed in the collective decision to emigrate when one family member was threatened. A sense of unity among the Christians and indeed the people of Ramallah is in turn a plausible result of contemporary tellings of the tale.

> How did Ramallah begin? It began hundreds of years ago, when we left Jordan and crossed the river. Before Ramallah, we lived in Shobak where the seven brothers were born. One brother had a small girl. From the time she was born, his neighbor came over to say, "Mabrouk."[3] This neighbor was Muslim.
>
> When he came from his house to his neighbor's house, he told the father: "Your daughter is going to marry my son."
>
> It is very hard to do this. The father told him, "She's still a baby."
>
> He told him, "Yes, I know that she's still a baby, but in ten or fifteen years, this girl is for my son." He didn't take it seriously. He thought that it was just a joke because, no way, Christians and Muslims. When the girl reached fifteen years of age, the neighbor came by and wanted to meet the girl.
>
> All of the seven brothers stuck together and said, "No way." To their neighbor they said, "Let us think about it and we'll tell you in one month." That same night they all took their children and their people and came to Palestine. They crossed the river and then put cut scraps of metal all over the river. When the Muslim neighbor and his people followed them on horseback, the legs of the horses got cut up in the river because no one could see the metal scraps at the bottom of the water. When all of the horses started to fall down, they turned back because they couldn't cross the river. When the brothers came to Palestine, one grew vegetables, one made windows and one brother had to cut down the trees of Ramallah. Ramallah is not like El-Bireh, which is level, it is hilly and filled with trees. All of the seven brothers lived in Ramallah and all Christians in Ramallah are descended from the seven broth-

ers. I'm from Dar Yusef. My father told me this story and so did my grandfather. When we were little, our great-grandmother told all the children, "we are from so and so."[4]

Printed versions more invested in establishing historical precedent date the migration to the Ottoman rule of the sixteenth century. All versions mention the Transjordanian town of Shobak, and some speak of Kerak as an additional point of origin. On one level the story employs the Jordan as a symbol of separation between Christians and Muslims: the Christian clan flees the prospect of intermarriage by traversing the river, and their Muslim pursuers are able to follow them into Palestine. On another level it points to the difficulty of maintaining a discrete religious community in a borderland atmosphere. Since Christian and Muslim families are neighbors, the notion of joining the families through marriage seems, at least to the Muslim neighbor, a logical next step. The threat of intermarriage, of course, prompts the flight, and Ramallah is depicted in contrast as a pristine and empty landscape where the Haddadins make their imprint.

The different versions of the Haddadin story air the complexity of the relationship between Palestinian Christians and Muslims. One story begins on the uneasy note that the Haddadins are encircled by the Bedouins and lorded over by a despotic prince; instability results from the fact that the lines of distinction are not clearly drawn (Abu Rayya 1980, 12–13). The story does not end on a note of religious distance or spatial separation, but rather by pointing toward the potential peace between Christians and Muslims in a city established by Christians who fled persecution. In Khalil Abu Rayya's printed version, Rashid Haddadin, the father of the girl, has a strong alliance with his Muslim neighbor, Husayn Banawiyah. As Husayn likewise feels oppressed by the local prince's tyranny, the two organize their families and flee together. In Naseeb Shaheen's printed version, the wronged party is Rashid's brother, Sabra, who eventually returns eastward and reconciles with the Muslim prince. Rather than religious separation enacted by a geographical border, a portrait emerges of the Jordan River Valley as the site of intermingled religious groups who nonetheless maintain their own traditions. The migrations are remembered at least in part as founding moments in which Palestinian pioneers found refuge west of the Jordan and displayed pluck and ingenuity in developing the land. Palestinian pioneer tales show the double dynamic of employing the Jordan River as a symbol of Christian/Muslim difference while also attesting to a borderland scenario in which both groups migrate across the River in the name of economic opportunity.

A parallel dynamic defines the efforts of Jewish pioneers along the banks of the Jordan River during the pre-state formation known as the *Yishuv*. In their writings as well as in the stories about them that continue to circulate in Israeli society, the effort and ultimate triumph of securing the Jordan as a border of the Jewish homeland coexists with records of interaction with local Arab populations. Such interactions were not necessarily unique to the Jordan River Valley, but the position of the Jewish communities at the very-wished-for margin of the future state meant that survival itself was of prime concern to them. On the theme of pioneers, we focus here on the founding members of Kibbutz Degania Alef, the first successful Jewish experimental farming collective established in Mandate Palestine in 1908 just east of the Jordan River. The founding members were young Jews from Eastern Europe who fled pogroms and increasingly restricted societies and arrived in Palestine with utopian visions. While the early immigrants to Palestine/Israel are called "pioneers" in common parlance, the founders of Degania are the pioneers' pioneers whose labors established the first kibbutz (Troen 2003, 5). *Halutz*, the Hebrew word for "pioneer," is a biblical term used in reference to the military vanguard that crosses the Jordan ahead of the other tribes (Joshua 1:14, 4:12–13) and serves as the infantry in the battle of Jericho (Joshua 6:7). The first kibbutzniks on what would later be called Degania recreated themselves on the model of the biblical pioneers and staked a claim on the east side of the Jordan alongside a small Arab tenant farming community called Um-Juni owned by a Persian Bahai landholder.

The Deganians perceived themselves as working in some degree of tandem with the neighboring residents of Um-Juni with whom they lived during their first year by the Jordan (Kibbutz Degania Alef 1962, 19). Not only did the Degania pioneers learn most of their farming, dairy, and food practices from the people of Um-Juni, but they also provided one another with labor during the harvest and invited the other group to holidays and celebrations. It must be noted, however, that the residents of Um-Juni as well as those in other neighboring villages like Samakh were no longer neighbors by the end of the 1948 Arab-Israeli war and that the Degania pioneers were those in the business of farming and not acquiring the future land of Israel.

The land on the banks of the Jordan was purchased by the Jewish National Fund with the intention of staking a frontier of farmland. Like the Haddadin of Ramallah who felled trees, the Degania pioneers are remembered as spending their initial days on the land moving rocks in order to clear arable soil. The location of Degania on the eastern shore of the Jordan River generated a multi-

8. *Pioneers and Refugees* [199]

valent symbolism. To begin, a national-religious sentiment underlay the act of settling on the banks of the Jordan River, the paradigmatic locale of Jewish freedom. Lacking familiarity or knowledge about the homeland to which they returned, the immigrants viewed the land through a biblical lens. The Degania memory book records a nostalgic dialogue between a pioneer and the Jordan during which he addresses the river by asking "did we not dream of you from the moment that we learned to read holy texts" (Kibbutz Degania Alef 1962, 206). While the Degania founders were secular, socialist Jews with a traditional Jewish background and education, crossing, living, and planting beside the Jordan were ritualized acts of collective liberation. Although the reality of establishing the community and learning farming techniques suitable for the region involved interaction with Arab neighbors on every front, the enterprise was conceived of through the temporal lens of Jewish history rather than the spatial reality of an Arab borderland.

The perception of a difference between West and East Banks becomes apparent in the founders' accounts of their troubles with Bedouin bandits and thieves who find sanctuary in the mountains east of the Jordan River Valley following raids of their fields. The accounts present a picture in which peril lurks to the unknown east, and the Jordan serves as a line between danger and safety. Lives as well as property were lost during the raids of bandits from the east.[5] Moshe Barsky was killed by Bedouins while crossing the river from east to west on his way to get medical supplies from the village of Menahamieh. Moshe's toughness is extolled in the account of how he sent his horse back to Degania to preserve the community's precious commodity and fought his attackers with the intent of changing the image of the Jew in Bedouin eyes as soft and easily killed "Children of Death." Although he protected the horse, he lost his gun. "It wasn't until late that night that we found him, lying with a stick and a pair of shoes on his head: this was a sign of vengeance, it meant that in the fighting he had killed or wounded someone" (Baratz 1957, 80).

Steadily the pioneers adjust to frontier law, setting up a night watch over fields and property and smuggling weapons of their own. Confronted with the indifference of the Ottoman authorities after the murder of Yosef Zaltzman and the theft of two mules, the members of the community decide to "take matters into their own hands." Degania member Tanhum Tanfilov finds an Arabic-speaking companion from a neighboring community and travels to the city of Salt in Transjordan. Received hospitably and fed generously by Bedouin hosts and local villagers alike, they are unable to learn anything about Zaltzman's murderers. Once they arrive in Salt, they covertly discover their animals in dire condition and repossess them. Unable to determine a target for vengeance, they leave the increasingly menacing city and return home (Tanfilov 2001, 16). Yosef Fine, Degania's Zionist cowboy, becomes famous in the region for his stealth missions to Syria in order to acquire weapons. On one journey, he hid guns beneath the carriage seats of an unsuspecting woman and group of children from Degania, and after another journey, Fine's mother resolved to transport weapons in a secret pouch stitched into a wide skirt (Kibbutz Degania Alef 1962, 31). Fine's purchase of weapons in Syria eerily foreshadows the approach of a massive front of tanks, armored cars, and cannons from Syria on Degania in the 1948 war.

Where Transjordan figures as the Haddadin point of origin as well as a place of impending peril from which they must flee in the Palestinian frontier stories, it appears in the Degania stories as both a locale of anti-civilization, associated with the danger of marauding thieves and hostile inhabitants as well as one of advanced civilization hosting the well-developed cities of Damascus, Amman, and Irbid and the possibility of trade and commerce. The Transjordan is a place of exposure where someone from the west side is likely to get killed. In this sense, the river or at least the river valley serves as a boundary between life and death, and the story sounds a warning that crossings to the "other side" should not be undertaken without significant purpose. The story enforces a sense of limit; while the Degania pioneers continue to farm and live east of the Jordan, they come to consider the lands just beyond their fields as the terrain of danger.

Another risk that the pioneers faced is that Degania would be excluded from the future Jewish homeland if the British set the boundary of Mandate Palestine precisely at the Jordan. From 1917 Zionists leaders were absorbed with the question of Mandate borders since they imagined that these boundaries would be inherited by an eventual state of Israel. In 1919 Degania members encountered British officers from the Frontier Commission inspecting the Jordan where they planned to fix the border. During a guided tour of Degania, the pioneers convinced the officers to include the community in Mandate Palestine and to fix the border south of the Sea of Galilee at the Yarmuk River rather than the Jordan. When the question of the Jordan as a border was next taken up by the British, Degania members persuaded Chaim Weizmann to advocate on their behalf. Another British delegation led by Colonial Emery visited Degania, and due to the persuasion of another tour, the Yarmuk remained the boundary.

Despite the border-drawing efforts of the British, Zionist efforts to shore up future borders through development, and Arab resistance to the influx of Jewish immigrants, the Jordan River Valley displayed resilience as a borderland throughout the period of the British Mandate. This is evident at several social levels. For Bedouin tribes, the river presented no obstacle to seasonal migration, economic contact, and banditry. On the West Bank, the increasingly tense relationships between Arabs and Jews and the ethic of employing only Jewish labor in building Jewish communities and infrastructure did not prevent the exchange of goods and trade. In terms of Arab-Jewish contact on the East Bank, British policies of delimiting Zionist endeavors ultimately proved an insurmountable obstacle. Yet contacts between Zionist leaders, Transjordan Bedouin Sheikhs, and likely the Emir Abdullah point to interaction about the Jordan River Valley on the highest political levels. With the exception of Degania and Naharaim, the location of the first hydroelectric plant, there were no Jewish colonies built east of the Jordan River despite the efforts of the early Zionist leaders to secure such lands through diplomatic means and purchase (Ilan 1984, 2–3, 10).

Despite the fact that prior to 1948 the Zionist leadership saw the Hijaz train line as the reasonable eastern border for the state of Israel and did not recognize the Jordan River as a limit, in the end they surrendered the claim to the East Bank and relinquished the vision of Jewish communities on both sides of the River.[6] The fact is particularly surprising in light of the fact that some Arab landowners in Transjordan as well as the Emir Abdullah, at certain points, publicly expressed the desire that Jews purchase or lease these lands and that Transjordanian agriculture and economy be jointly developed by Jewish and Arab efforts. No such arrangement came to pass due to insufficient Jewish funds allotted to the Transjordanian project, growing Arab resistance to the influx of Jewish immigrants, and the opposition of the British. In his meticulous study of Jewish attempts to settle Transjordan, Zvi Ilan (1984, 63) expresses bafflement at the failure of the Zionist leadership to acquire significant holdings east of the Jordan prior to the Arab rebellion of 1936 and the subsequent polarization of Arab and Jewish communities. The key, in my estimation, is to emphasize the degree to which early Zionist thought and practice related to the land through the Bible and felt more ambivalent about contested biblical land than they did about the territory definitively within biblical borders.

While representatives of Jews and Transjordanians alike tried to persuade the British to remove the blocks to economic partnership, debates raged in the respective camps about whether to focus Zionist efforts on both banks of the Jordan or exclusively on the western side and whether a Jewish presence in Transjordan would impede Arab national ambitions. The Jordan River Valley during the period of the British Mandate was politically contested as well as internally contested within the leadership of the British, the Zionists, and the Transjordanians. While several leaders of Zionist organizations were actively engaged in trying to acquire East Bank land holdings, there were also discussions about an eventual transfer of Arab Palestinians from future politically recognized Jewish territory to the east side of the Jordan (C. Simons 1988). This plan, partially enacted during the 1948 and 1967 wars, reveals a dichotomy in the Zionist imagination between the potential homeland west of the Jordan and the wilderness east of the Jordan.

Interestingly the one Zionist project given the green light by Mandate authorities on the east side of the Jordan led to a vision of an integrated Jewish-Arab community. In 1926 a Russian-born engineer named Pinchas Rutenberg was granted the concession by Mandate authorities to harness the waters of the Jordan in order to generate electricity. The manifestation of his efforts was the Naharaim (Two Rivers) hydroelectric plant at the confluence of the Jordan and Yarmuk Rivers (opened officially in 1933) for which Emir Abdullah pledged six thousand dunams of Transjordanian land in exchange for access to electricity. Rutenberg worked closely with Emir Abdullah and other Transjordanian leaders on the deal and ultimately provided electricity to both banks of the Jordan. During the course of these negotiations, Rutenberg saw the power of collective Arab-Jewish enterprise. Later in his life, Rutenberg became influenced by the figures of Brit Shalom, a group of intellectual binationalists based largely in Jerusalem, and began to draw up plans to develop a utopian community along the shores of the Zarqa River, a Jordan tributary south of Amman. Rutenberg imagined the river separating a Jewish and an Arab community so that each group could maintain its customs and traditions with a massive hydroelectric plant on the river serving as an economic bridge. Management and labor at the plant would be entirely integrated so that both Jews and Arabs were bosses and workers with an equal stake in development. Rutenberg moved the plan beyond conception by entering into serious negotiations with Transjordanian tribal leaders and raising money among Jewish donors. Rutenberg's Zarqa plan was ultimately thwarted by British authorities, and Zionist designs on Transjordan halted. The vision is striking, however, particularly in light of the fact that Zarqa later became a city of Palestinian exiles and a Hamas stronghold. It illustrates in the language of development and economic planning how a bifurcating river can also be a unifying force.

REFUGEES

A critical number of the early Jewish pioneers were refugees who fled the restrictions and pogroms of Europe hoping to "cross the Jordan" to safety. "Just as the First Aliya (1882–1904) formed part of a wave of Jewish migration sparked off by a series of pogroms in Eastern Europe, so the Second Aliya was a proximate result of the persecution to which Russian Jews were subjected between 1903 and 1907" (Near 1992, 11). Degania's Joseph Baratz (1957, 6) traces his commitment to Zionism to the pogrom that rocked his village in the Pale of Settlement: "In 1903 the quarter of the town in which we lived was sacked. We escaped unhurt but afterwards I saw the wounded and went to the funeral of those who were killed. Perhaps it was this that turned my thoughts seriously towards Zionism." As they correctly perceived, the climate in Europe was becoming increasingly menacing, and a different scenario needed to be created in order for Ashkenazi Jews to stay alive. The Israeli pioneer rhetoric is replete with imagery of vitality and rebirth. The rebirth, understood to be collective, entailed the rescue and resuscitation of waves of Jewish refugees.

In the process of absorbing their refugees by the millions, the Jewish pioneers created the Palestinian refugees. The Jewish immigrants from Europe brought with them the notion that "war refugees seldom returned to their former places of residence if the victorious enemy had occupied their homes," and they resettled their refugees in deserted Arab towns and on confiscated Arab lands (Gelber 2001, 8). To a certain degree, flight and the transplant of identity represented a level of normalcy to Jews and not the worst thing that could be done to a people. Refusing to recognize the claim of Palestinian refugees, Israel barred their return. The abandoned villages and lands surrounding Degania were quickly adapted as temporary absorption centers for new Jewish immigrants and then transformed into permanent Jewish communities (Kibbutz Degania Alef 1962, 311). Following the evacuation of neighboring Arab towns, the Degania pioneers had a sudden seniority that entailed participation in the project of absorbing and settling Jews. It should be noted that while the plight of refugees is a shared mode of justifying Jewish and Palestinian nationalism, both kinds of refugees have been mistreated in the national context. Many Holocaust survivors who immigrated to Israel were rebuked for not having stood up to the forces of fascism and for marching "like sheep to the slaughter" (Segev 1986). Among West Bankers, Palestinian refugees were viewed with "a mixture of pity and contempt" stemming from "the sense that the refugees were 'defeated,' 'losers,'... complicit in their degradation" (Bisharat 1997, 214).

The members of Degania had a new sense of their role following the decimation of their relatives in the Holocaust. Realizing that there was no Old World for them to go back to and perceiving that they were the only vital force in world Jewry, their position became intractable; the commitment to self-defense brought about a new readiness to take up arms and to settle as many refugees as possible. As a result, the relationship between the Deganians and their Arab neighbors worsened. This was the trend in the Jordan River Valley as well as almost every other region where Jews and Arabs had contact. The Arab disposition toward the Jews became acrimonious as the numbers of Jewish immigrants increased and larger tracts of land were purchased and settled. The Arab Revolt of 1936 had heightened the distrust on both sides.

While all conflicts surrounding the withdrawal of the British and the partition plan can be seen as struggles over dividing lines, the Jordan served as a primary military front for Arab armies and assumed strategic importance as the eastern point of entry to Jewish communities and settlements. Thus as the Israelis fought in the name of their new homeland at the Jordan front, a dramatic percentage of Palestinians lost theirs through an eastward crossing. The year 1948 is synonymous with the *Nakba,* the great disaster that befell the Palestinians; the collective expulsion from the Galilee and other regions is termed the *Nuzuh,* the "Exodus" from Palestine. The cataclysmic loss involved with the Exodus is a primordial event in Palestinian identity narratives (Sayigh, 1998, 42–58) and brands the Jordan "as *the* border: the closest one spiritually, the one traveled across most painfully, the one that most fully characterizes the displacement and the proximity of its cause" (Said, 1994, 8). In the Palestinian imagination, the Jordan bifurcates the eras of pre-1948 and post-1948 and stands for the distancing impediments that prevent a collective return.

The Palestinian Exodus had several waves beginning with the mass flight prior to May 15, 1948, and continuing with assumedly temporary emigrations combined with intimidation, expulsion, and deportation at the hands of the Israeli Haganah forces. At the beginning of the hostilities, buses went daily to Transjordan brimming with those eager to escape military engagement; eventually the price of travel became so expensive that this mode of transit was available only to the wealthy. King Abdullah's Arab Legion Army opened fords over the river for those who could not find the money to travel by bus. As the war continued, Jewish military groups expelled Palestinians and forced the inhabitants of the Jordan Valley as well as other regions across the bridges and fords of the river. This was the case, for example, with the town of Beisan, close to the Sheikh Hussein Bridge, from which many inhabitants departed prior to the expiration of the British Mandate, and those who remained were ultimately transported either to Nazareth or across the River by the Israeli troops.[7]

As Israel and the Arab States continued the war and negotiated a cease-fire, about 100,000 Palestinians found themselves as refugees in Transjordan.[8] Despite the fact that the refugees had lost their homes and property and definitively dwelled in the terrain of exile, they fared better than their counterparts in the Transjordanian-controlled West Bank where the displaced huddled in orchards and lacked food and water. After arriving, the East Bank refugees lived in tents and received food rations and small quantities of money from the authorities and then moved to International Red Cross camps built outside of Amman, Zarqa, Salt, and Irbid. They would eventually be granted citizenship. However, when the news traveled of the superior conditions east of the Jordan, the Transjordanian government labored to distribute food to the refugees in Jericho and to prevent their movement across the River. Again the Jordan served as the border between uncertainty and stability, although in this case greater stability was to be found on the East Bank. When the West Bank was under Jordanian control, patterns of economic development and policy encouraged the migration, particularly of the wealthy and educated, to the East Bank (Nevo 1998, 4). However, from the point of view of the Palestinian refugees, their Exodus would find no end until they returned en masse to their point of origin west of the river.

When Israel conquered the West Bank from Jordan in the 1967 war, the victory was significant not only for the strategic and territorial gains, but also because it fulfilled the biblical prophecy of the Jordan as the eastern border of the Land of Israel. Although Jordan lost the West Bank, those who lost most were the West Bank Palestinians, some of whom lost their homes for the second time since 1948. At least 150,000 Palestinians were exiled to the East Bank of the Jordan and barred from crossing westward. For these Palestinians as well as for the larger global community of Palestinian refugees, the Jordan River came to symbolize the border between home and exile. To cross the Jordan from West to East was to descend into a shadowland of loss and negation, and to imagine a westward crossing was to dream of the redemption of coming home. (Although the terrain east of the Jordan epitomizes exile for the Palestinians, the Hashemite Kingdom of Jordan is, in fact, the only country where as citizens they are legally at home.) This valuation of the East and West Banks parallels precisely that of the first Israelis who described ending their exile through immigration to Israel as "crossing the Jordan River."

During the Six-Day War of 1967, known to Palestinians as *al-Naksa*—the Setback—large numbers of Palestinians were transferred from the West Bank to Jordan. Some fled the war, but others were bused to the Allenby Bridge by Israeli troops and others driven out by force (Masalha 1999). A significant number of Palestinians found themselves in a state of exile with tenuous refuge on the Jordanian East Bank.[9] The Palestinians who crossed the Jordan in 1967 lost their homes, businesses, and belongings and became refugees dependent upon UN aid and alms.[10] In Jordanian society, they were politically integrated at the same time that they were discriminated against and blamed for forfeiting their land to the Jews (Mishal 1978, 111–20). Even the landscape of their resettlement proved a bleak shadow of West Bank terrain: "Those who fled from the West Bank left behind them fertile areas for the semi-desert plains of the East Bank" (Dodd and Barakat 1969, 6). These tremendous losses and the transformation of Palestinian life, status, and communal structure are articulated in accounts of the traumatic banishment across the river. By the time the 1967 refugees reached the other side, all previous social structures were inverted or overturned. Although other borders were crossed by Palestinians during and after the 1967 war, the crossing of the Jordan came to symbolize Palestinian dispersion (Slyomovics 1998, 188). Home was left behind on the West Bank in what became the occupied West Bank and reconstructed through rituals of memory, including storytelling. "Because Palestinian culture is largely oral, Palestinian refugees often express their experiences and sentiments through folklore" (Siddiq 1995, 88).

The alternate ways in which Palestinians in the Diaspora recall the difference between the East and West Banks became apparent to me while conducting interviews at a San Francisco market that served as a gathering place for Palestinian men.[11] An older Palestinian who immigrated to the United States in 1971 told me of the youthful adventure when he and his friend swam across the Jordan following the 1948 war and found that "the other side was so beautiful, but life was the same." It was not until the Israelis came, in his estimation, that everything was "divided between Israelis, Palestinians, and Jordanians." A younger man interrupted the story saying, "I don't think that it was so beautiful on the other side." His story of flight from Jerusalem to a refugee camp in Zarqa recounts the collapse of the family structure and the humiliation of the refugee.

> We left because my father's oldest son scared him by saying, "Let's go, let's go, they're going to kill us." My father put all of us in the car and because he lost everything, he became blind. My sister was kicked from behind. We walked across the bridge. Other people walked under the bridge or swam through the water. The hardest part wasn't leaving, it was coming to Jordan. After we crossed the border to Jordan, they treated us like gypsies. After that, my brothers and I never went to school again. I'm mad about this to this day. I'm forty-four now and I tell my son that he has to go to school. Don't think that the Arabs like Palestinians. I've lived in Saudi Arabia, Kuwait, Iraq, Syria and Lebanon, and no one likes the Palestinians. They say: You sold your land.
>
> In Jordan, they threw us in large camp where we lived in a tent. The United Nations gave us some food and opened schools, stuff like that, but when the PLO started, the FBI started behind us. The Jordanians treated us like gypsies and put us in different schools. The PLO later opened a school for the children. When I crossed, I crossed with a lot of people, and the Israelis walked with us and fired their guns. We crossed the King Hussein Bridge. My father went blind when he lost everything. It was a terrible life. I was nine years old when they kicked us out, that's all.[12]

The account begins and ends with the image of the blind father, a symbol of the emasculated patriarch and the refugee's loss of power and self-determination. In this interview, the narrator accounts for his father's blindness as a result of his losing everything, but in a later interview, he told me that it was a result of "the black water" in the refugee camp of Zarqa. The family's honor is eroded by the father's loss of vision as well as the sister's loss of honor when she is kicked "from behind," presumably by Israeli soldiers. The degrading gesture not only shames her but also disgraces her male relatives, who find themselves in the position of being unable to defend her or their honor. In this case, the Jordan delineates antithetical experiences: residence with property and status in Jerusalem and homeless dependence and scorn on the East Bank. The act of crossing the Jordan is an experience of loss, an experience that ushers the Palestinians of 1967 into a state of instability, and an experience of international scrutiny and suspicion. Although the border is definitive, the refugees persist in the limbo of displacement in the borderland zone of a Jordan River Valley refugee camp.

The family is part of a mass flight that the narrator recalls as a chaotic attempt to find sanctuary across the river. The sanctuary turns out to be of the most rudimentary kind in that they are given a tent and small amounts of food. The sense of loss and disempowerment is emphasized in Jordan, where they are treated like gypsies and provided with only the most basic of needs. The only people who help the refugees are United Nations relief workers whose handouts are perceived as colonial merchandise (Schulz 2003, 50; Schiff 1995, 72). After his family's flight from Jerusalem, the narrator confronts the inevitable instability of every situation: the Israelis bar a return, the Jordanians discriminate against him, the Arabs in other countries blame him for his status as a refugee, and the aid organizations appear as an imperial tool. Again the Jordan River is the border between stability and instability as the East Bank proves to be a location of negation and as the first stop in a long series of temporary "homes" in exile.

It can be said that since 1967, the Jordan River has gained depth and political force as a border. The reinforcement of this border through demarcation, military surveillance, and eventually the Israel-Jordan peace treaty has had the effect of restricting borderland contacts. The relevant models for understanding the scenario include the black-and-white, the grey, and a hybrid spotty-layered model. A black-and-white model characterizes the way in which the Jordan River separates the state of Israel and the Hashemite Kingdom of Jordan; despite the terms of the 1994 peace treaty, there is little contact and much hostility in transborder relations. From 1994 to the beginning of the Second Intifada in 2000, Israelis did travel in significant numbers to Jordan particularly to visit Petra. During this period some trade alliances and business contacts did result, although several fizzled during the height of the Intifada. A grey borderland model approximates the scenario in which Palestinians live on both the East and the West Banks with different political status while affiliating primarily as Palestinians. At this point, Palestinians in Jordan can be three or four generations removed from 1948 and well integrated in Jordanian society, yet a sense of connection or common cause persists with West Bank counterparts. As stated in the introduction, Jewish settler communities in the West Bank form "a spotty-layered model" in which settlements are walled off from Palestinian environs and accessed through special roadways. Contacts between settlers and West Bank Palestinians are negligible and often violent with the exception that Palestinian workers often have construction jobs within the settlements. The models are further complicated by the "spotty" existence of populous Palestinian refugee camps on both sides of the Jordan and by the fact that some Palestinian towns and cities fall under the political jurisdiction of the Palestinian Authority. Such towns and cities, however, are by no means autonomous.

Since 1967 and the two Palestinian Intifadas, the images of the pioneer and refugee as well as the specific narratives discussed above have been used to shore up Palestinian and Israeli national claims and to justify the militarism of both cultures. In other words, the national myths have maintained an intractable hold on the notion of the Jordan River as the signifying border of the nation. A borderland dynamic, however, has persisted against the odds among Palestinians. Crossing the Jordan border is common in the name of visiting relatives and celebrating family events, and Palestinians often travel to Jordan to seek medical care or to fly internationally from the Amman airport. During my crossings of the Jordan River, I noticed that it was common for Palestinians living in Jordan to bring produce back from the West Bank. I was informed that this was a means of maintaining a mnemonic link to ancestral lands. Once again people and goods travel across the Jordan River amid a divisive political scenario. In this way the resilience of the Jordan River Valley as a borderland becomes apparent.

The tropes of pioneer and refugee were merged rhetorically and mobilized to stoke revolutionary impulses among Palestinian exiles on the East Bank. The rhetoric of the Palestinian guerrilla movement in the late 1960s and early 1970s was that Palestinians needed to transform their refugee status by acting as "pioneers" who infiltrate, attack, and cause maximum damage to Jewish communities west of the Jordan. The *fida'iyin* (guerrilla) movement contested the borders, and with them the legitimacy, of Israel through perpetration, sabotage, and the establishment of quasi-state apparatuses in exile while promoting a vigorous national identity that defied perceptions perpetuated by Israel and the Arab states. Resistance brought the new avatar of Palestinian identity into relief, and the Jordan River became a prime target as the resource that sustained Israeli communities and enabled immigration as well as the demarcation line beyond which Palestinians had been driven. In addition, operating independently in border zones leveraged the Palestinian position within Arab states by creating an intermediary space for the formation of Palestinian institutions, asserting an identity distinct from pan-Arab or other Arab national formations, and "political(ly) outbidding" other commitments to Palestine through persistent presence and attack (Sayigh 1997, 174). Since not only had the Arab regular armies met with defeat in the 1967 war, but the Arab regimes, to varying degrees, had also immobilized the refugees through prohibitions, the rise of a distinctly Palestinian resistance was an assertion of self-determination amid the state of statelessness.

While several clandestine groups focused on Palestinian restoration via Israeli destruction formed around the post-1967 peripheries, it was ultimately Fatah operating in the Jordan River Valley that seized the reins of the Palestinian Liberation Organization (PLO) and assumed leadership of the national movement. Through devotion to territorially focused guerrilla tactics and the creation of a victory narrative that countered historical circumstances, the Fatah leadership aligned the definitions of *warrior* and *Palestinian*. Training camps were established just east of the Jordan, the longest continuous border with Israel, to offer rebel-minded Palestinians an alternative to the stasis and despair of UN refugee camps. Similar to the way in which the Degania founders sought to reverse the image of the weak and humbled Jew at the Jordan, the early Fatah recruits endeavored to shift the image of the Palestinian from a dependent refugee to an impassioned revolutionary worthy of emulation by the whole Arab world. In both cases, image reversal required resistance, and resistance easily morphed into provocation.

Counter to the formation of the Palestinian guerrilla fighter, the pioneer trope persisted in reference to kibbutz founders at the same time that it authorized the culture of Israeli settlements. Within Israeli society, the founders and first generation of kibbutz members secured enormous class privilege and economic exception. Although the Jewish National Fund purchased the land for communities like Degania, the kibbutz members and their descendants emerged as its owners. After the establishment of the state of Israel, the kibbutzim continued to receive substantial government subsidies and support. Kibbutz members constituted a political elite associated with the Labor Party. The continued transmission of the pioneer myth through school trips to pioneer sites, museums, and interactive exhibits (Katriel 1997, 169), and the establishment of retreat centers and guesthouses that offer urban visitors contact with the natural environment and accomplishments of the kibbutzim, operate to secure the privileged status of kibbutz members despite the fact that the kibbutzim have largely privatized. Thus the myth of the kibbutz has outlived the institution of the kibbutz.

As other movements and new values have taken hold in Israel, the pioneer myth has been reformulated, co-opted, and even satirized. While the myth has lost ground among secularists and liberals due to increased national cynicism in the wake of the Palestinian uprising, the birth of new historicism, and the privatization of the kibbutzim, it maintains a presence in Israeli national consciousness. It is most active among settler communities in the West Bank. The settlers see a direct line of continuity between the pioneers who established communities at contested borders and brought the national reality in line with their will rather than capitulating to imperial regulation and their walled communities in the Occupied Territories. The fact that the kibbutz members formed militias that ultimately morphed into military units is seen to provide further warrant for the manner of vigilante justice practiced by the settlers. The settlers, like the pioneers, have state sanction for their communities and similarly receive government subsidies for the act of living in the borderland. "These new settlers regarded themselves as disciples of the early Zionist pioneers. And like their role models, many of them chose to farm the new land: agriculture was seen not merely as a way of life, but as a moral and patriotic calling" (Segev 2006). Descriptions of Israeli settlers as the new pioneers persuade many Israelis not affiliated with the movement of the territorial rights of settlers but work more powerfully to justify an ethos by any means necessary. This is most true among settler communities in the central West Bank since the settlements along the Green Line serve largely as more affordable bedroom communities for Israeli cities, and those along the Dead Sea are more oriented toward tourism and ecology than ideology. The settlements in the heart of the West Bank close to sites where biblical events transpired host an extreme form of religious nationalism. In this sense, the subtle religious motivation that underlay the founding of secular socialist Jewish communities is amplified to an apocalyptic pitch.

Palestinian novels like Sahar Khalifeh's (2000) *Wild Thorns* fashion Palestinians crossing from Jordan to the West Bank as pioneers in search of home in an altered homeland.[13] *Wild Thorns* opens as Usama, the young hero, crosses the Jordan border after a sojourn in "the oil states" (Khalifeh 2000, 8) in order to be reunited with his widowed mother and seek employment in Nablus. As he undergoes interrogation by Israeli officers and then gazes out at the barren landscape from a shared Mercedes taxi, he is haunted by a vision of "idyllic green meadows, the clear waterfall tumbling over the bottles of soft drinks in the green valley, the bags of almonds piled up in front of the waterfall, beneath the towering walnut trees" to which he expected to return (19). While the very unfamiliarity of his homeland makes him into a pioneer in a strange land, he confronts security zones, barriers, and overcrowding rather than the vast tracts of land usually associated with pioneers. "Yes, heaven was here beneath his feet and before his eyes. But he was now a prisoner in the genie's bottle." The restrictions he faces on his mobility and autonomy result in his development as a kind of anti-pioneer who is allowed no freedom to settle, work, and celebrate the passage of time, and so he affiliates with a paramilitary resistance group that transforms his every impulse into acts of warfare.

Amid the divisive rhetoric and the militarized clashes, the West Bank maintains borderland characteristics. What and whose it is remains uncertain and in flux. Gideon Levy (1999), a journalist for the left-leaning Israeli newspaper *Ha'aretz*, characterized the Jordan River border as a study in multiple national illusions:

> If you want to see a brilliant trompe l'oeil, a dazzling apparition, the ultimate phantasmagoria—the place to visit is Allenby Bridge on the Jordan River. . . . Dozens of Palestinians of all ages are standing in line and waiting to go through passport control, just as people do in any other country. But which country are they entering? Israel? Then what in the world are all these Palestinian policemen doing here? Palestine? Then what in the world are all these Israeli police doing here? A joint terminal? Then who in the world is the sovereign power here?

Jordanian, Palestinian, and Israeli rhetorical claims to the Jordan River are matched by symbols and guards positioned at the border. Palestinians whose families and affiliations crisscross the border undergo the greatest scrutiny. Since they are the ones who cross the Allenby Bridge, it is upon them that the border is imposed. Gideon Levy's 1999 account of the Jordan River border brings another characteristic of the borderland into relief: at the same time that borders are sites of national assertion, they are also those places where sovereignty claims overlap and unravel. The uncertainty of Israeli and Palestinian national claims and the collective anxiety regarding the next territorial manifestation of such claims contributes to the severity of the occupation and intractability of the resistance.

CONCLUSION

The moral of this comparative story is that a symbol shared by two ethnic groups but diametrically interpreted leads to more strife than two distinct symbolic systems. This study of the Jordan River contributes to the literature of *multilocality*, "the multiplicity of meanings ascribed by human actors to space" (Douglas 1998, 90) by showing the common components of competing narratives. As noted by William Douglass, "we . . . find borderlands to be particularly rich contexts within which to discern such overlapping, yet competing, views of the physical (and social) landscape" (90). A deep rift results when two groups delimit their identity along the same coordinates, and the contest over space becomes a clash of self-definition. Because borders symbolize a collective whole, the overdetermination of a single border exerts a ripple effect of contentious engagement on other fronts. A borderland is a space where distinct conceptions of group identity come into contact, producing either the celebrated hybrids of postmodern thought or essentialist identities reinforced through encounter with the Other.

The fact that Israelis and Palestinians both identify the Jordan as the western border of their homelands means that they claim precisely the same place through similarly structured narratives. The border lore is perpetuated whether a new generation grows up on the land of their ancestors or distant from it in a proximate or far-flung Diaspora. The insistence on a native land with circumscribed borders is perpetuated in order to carve out Israeli and Palestinian national identities, and therefore the revision of such images is taken as an attack on legitimacy. The collective identities of Palestinians and Israelis are forged by the dissemination of particular stories about the land and the respective group's relationship to specific places. The Jordan borderland is a case that exhibits how the crossing of borders and existence of populations that transcend them can confer strong identification with a border as a symbol of the national polity. Equally constructed, the Israel and the Palestine imagined as bucolic landscapes populated solely by one's kinspeople never existed and never will, as the land in question has always been the crossroads of empires and Semitic peoples. Perhaps because the homeland has no precise territorial corollary, the tales of its founding and loss are perpetuated as part of the utopian dimension of nationalism. As evident in the violent history of Israeli-Palestinian engagement, the more utopian the national vision, the more likely it is to foster militarism and breed fanaticism.

The intransigence of the national positions that arise from homeland lore must be contended with prior to the negotiation of political borders. Should a political leader deliver a reduced nation to the public prior to the modification of ancestral and religious claims, he would likely fall as a martyr. The symbolic weight of places like the Jordan influences the tenacity of struggle as well as the unwillingness to make concessions. For example, a state of Palestine can only be envisioned as west of the Jordan, despite a Palestinian population that straddles the river, because of the deep association of the East Bank with Palestinian exile. The notion of retreating from the Jordan in order to make way for such a Palestinian state is considered a sharply painful concession for most Israelis who associate the Jordan with transhistoric Jewish freedom and believe that the 1967 war secured the rightful borders of the Jewish state.

Prior to the redrawing of borders between Israelis and Palestinians, a comprehensive, comparative study of the borders' multiple meanings should be undertaken. Such a study, reviewed by both negotiation teams as well as the outside councils, would acknowledge the veracity of both claims and make clear to all what is at stake for both parties. Since Palestinians and Israelis are largely unaware of the other's geographic traditions, the recognition of shared elements could serve as a vehicle of mutual recognition. If, in presenting the negotiated borders of two distinct states to the public, religious and national concerns are addressed, then the Palestinian as well as the Israeli public may accept the borders as national progress rather than the relinquishing of the dream of a Greater Palestine/Israel.

Amid the migration and the dispute, the Jordan remains a sad, storied river that is soon to dry and leave its pioneers and refugees to either side without the most needed resource for the sustenance of human life (Turner, Nassar, and Khateeb 2005). As the Jordan River gradually disappears, it becomes more vivid in the national imaginations of Israelis and Palestinians and functions like the pioneers and refugees as a reiteration of the undeniable and absolute claim to the land. In a recently published concept document, Jordanian, Palestinian, and Israeli environmentalists stress the necessity of a multinational collaboration in order to manage and rehabilitate the Jordan River Valley as an ecosystem. The competition over the Jordan as a border and as a water source has led the governments of Syria, Jordan, and Israel to divert as much water as they can from the Jordan without acknowledging the threat to its continued existence. According to the "Crossing the Jordan" document, recognition of the shared value of the Jordan as a vital resource and symbol offers Jordanians, Palestinians, and Israelis a historic opportunity to work together in order to protect ecological resources no matter where the eventual borders will fall.

Notes

1. "Since Churchill's temporary decision *not* to encourage—or even allow—the building of a Jewish National Home in eastern Palestine ran counter to the provisions of the Mandate, he decided to change the terms of the Mandate, which was redrafted to provide that Britain was not obliged to pursue the Balfour Declaration policy east of the Jordan river" (Fromkin 1989, 513).

2. For the suffering of ancestors as a mode of land claim, see Boyarin (1996, 8).

3. *Mabrouk,* meaning "congratulations," functions here as a blessing for the birth of the daughter as well as the formula through which the Muslim neighbor enacts the marriage contract. "'Mabrouk,' meaning congratulations is an oral formula that enacts the deed that will be congratulated" (Muhawi and Kanaana 1989, 236).

4. Interview, San Francisco, April 17, 2001. The story is reproduced in the idiomatic English of the speaker. Arabic is his mother tongue.

5. "For several years, Lower Galilee had been subject to the incursions of tribes of Bedouins from across the Jordan, particularly at times of harvest. In November and December 1913, three Jewish settlers were killed, one in Degania, one in Kinneret, and one in Sejera, and guard duty became part of the regular life of the *kvutza* (community)" (Near 1992).

6. Ze'ev Jabontinsky separated himself from the mainstream Zionist movement over the abandonment of the project to purchase and settle the East Bank. The Revisionists never surrendered the aspiration for a Jewish State on both banks and maintained the slogan "Two banks to the Jordan: One is ours and the other too."

7. Beisan fell on May 12, 1948. Most of the villages in the Jordan Valley as well as Tiberias were not abandoned due to military raids, but because of the fear of Jewish forces and orders from Arab leadership (see Benvenisti 2000, 131–32). After the surrender of Beisan, the Golani Brigade ordered its inhabitants to evacuate (see Morris 1999, 213, and Nazzal 1978, 17).

8. The number of 1948 refugees in Transjordan is hard to determine. Some estimates put it at 160,000 and others at 60,000. The 1950 United Nations Economic Mission to the Middle East reported 100,905 refugees in the East Bank. The total number of 1947–1949 refugees is also disputed. Benny Morris shows how difficult it is to arrive at a precise number. In light of estimates by the British Foreign Office in 1949, he sets the number between 600,000 and 760,000 (1987, 298).

9. The numbers are disputed. The Jordanian government claimed that 361,000 people were displaced from the West Bank, UNRWA reported 162,000, and a 1993 study by the Israeli Institute for Applied Economic Policy Review enumerated 100,000 displaced persons in Jordan.

10. Within the Jordanian definition, the 1967 Palestinians are not classified as refu-

gees "since they were living in Jordan up to 1967 and are currently 'displaced persons' rather than refugees who have crossed an international frontier" (Weighill 1968, 16).

11. The problems with applying the term *Diaspora* to the Palestinian experience are considered by Helena Lindholm Schulz (2003) and Smadar Lavie and Ted Swedenburg (1996).

12. Interview with Palestinian man conducted on April 13, 2001.

13. In his study of possible migration waves following the granting of the Palestinian right to return, Sari Hanafi identifies "an initial pioneer group" that would return to Israel or a liberated Palestine from the Diaspora (2005, 79).

CHAPTER NINE

Who's Who across the U.S.-Mexico Border
Identities in Transition

Harriett Romo and Raquel R. Márquez

The U.S.-Mexico border has many dimensions and a multitude of effects on the lives of those living in its borderlands. In its most basic capacity a borderline serves to divide two countries, as in the case of the United States and Mexico, where the border simply functions to delineate where one nation-state ends and the other begins. The intensity of transnational migration from Mexico to the United States also challenges the defining power of the nation-states. Michael Kearney reminds us that "members of transnational communities similarly escape the power of the nation-state to inform their sense of collective identity" (1998, 126).

The arbitrariness and shifting nature of a border can be attested to by border changes in the aftermath of wars between nation-states. The annexation of Mexican territories by the United States through the Treaty of Guadalupe Hidalgo ending the U.S.-Mexico War in 1848 is the result of a negotiation that brought about half of Mexico's territory into the United States and incorporated the 75,000 to 86,000 Mexicans living in that territory as U.S. citizens in the process (Montejano 1987; Martinez 1975). The 3,200-kilometer boundary line was completed through U.S. acquisition of the Gadsden Purchase in 1853. Subsequent boundary adjustments have been few (e.g., El Chamisal). Yet the divisive objective behind a borderline has very real consequences for individuals who live within a border region.

Boundaries signify who belongs and who does not, and to a large extent they also help shape the identifying characteristics of those who belong (Suarez-

Orozco 2001). In moving beyond viewing a border region as merely a geographical territory to viewing it as an area that encompasses the meeting of peoples, the relationships among people and institutions in their respective nation states, multiple languages, and two social and political systems, the richness of the borderlands begins to emerge. Moreover, as noted in the introductory chapter, the dynamic nature of a borderland community requires us to view the borderlands beyond "places or even events, but as social processes." By focusing on the social processes, we can begin to see the important role migration plays within borderland communities.

The relationship of migration and border communities remains intricately woven together and undoubtedly complex. The movement of Mexican migrants as they search for work often leads them to the border, and while many migrate further north, others settle in the borderlands. Scholarly research has long addressed the complexity of migration dynamics, but the dominant theoretical frameworks previously viewed migration as a linear process between sending communities and receiving communities (Bustamante 1973; Bach 1978; Cornelius 1976; Portes and Bach 1985). Today, migration scholars recognize that migration processes often do not follow such a linear trajectory. Increasingly researchers are documenting how individuals live transnational lives that allow for intricate and ongoing linkages across communities (Massey 1987; Massey, Goldring, and Durand 1994; Basch, Glick Schiller, and Szanton Blanc 1994; Levitt 2001; Levitt and Waters 2002; Romo 2008; Márquez 2008).

This chapter addresses the complexity of identity construction for individuals living transnational lives along the U.S.-Mexico border in the cities of San Antonio and Laredo, Texas, and Monterrey in the state of Nuevo Leon, Mexico. The large majority of Latinos living in these urban areas are the products of the intermixing of Africans, Indians, Spaniards, and Anglos who have lived in these regions. Although race has commonly been associated with physical characteristics, our understanding of race is based on the view that race is socially constructed (Omi and Winant 1994). The U.S. Census does not treat Latinos/Hispanics as a racial group, but as an ethnic group. As a result, Latinos are free to identify as "white," "other," or "multiracial," or, in the case of a small proportion, "black" (Saenz 2004). The variations noted by census reports of the Latino population suggest that U.S.- and foreign-born Latinos have different notions of the concept of *race*. Many foreign-born Latinos in the United States were not members of minority groups in their home countries and view racial identity with considerable fluidity (Saenz 2004; Stephen 2007). Similarly, Latinos may shift their racial or ethnic identification in varying contexts and situations.

The manner in which a person identifies reflects, in part, a person's level of assimilation and the extent to which that individual has incorporated into mainstream American society (Gordon 1964; Alba and Nee 2003). Identifying as "white" is associated with assimilation, whereas identifying as "other" or "multiracial" is associated with ethnic retention. Newly arrived immigrants constantly fashion identities somewhere on a continuum between their home community's identities and the new possibilities in the United States, resulting in a complex construction of identity (Alba 1990). For *mexicanos*, identity construction may also be a factor of time of migration (i.e., migration before 1970 or migration in the 1980s or 1990s). Other factors such as English fluency, U.S. citizenship status, socioeconomic level, labor force participation, occupation, time in the United States, gender, generation, family networks remaining in Mexico, and previous experiences in the United States also influence how individuals view themselves and others. Alejandro Portes points out that immigrants struggle with these factors as they integrate into their new communities. Immigrant parents must further struggle with how their second-generation children acculturate into American society. They must grapple with generational effects such as whether their children will hold on to their ethnic identity, language, cultural values, and other markers of identity (Portes and Rumbaut 2006). We argue that the complexity of identity construction increases within a transnational context as individuals are confronted with the fluidity of transnational processes.

The identity of Mexican-origin population in the United States is also affected by the increasing number of recently arrived immigrants from Mexico, the large number of Mexican Americans concentrated in the U.S. Southwest, and the increasing Latino population in general. The Latino population in the United States expanded from 22.4 million in 1990 to 35.3 million in 2000, a growth rate of 58 percent, and it continues to grow at a rate greater than six times that of the non-Latino population in the country (U.S. Census 2000; Saenz 2004). According to a Census Bureau press release (U.S. Census, May 1, 2008), the number of Hispanics in the United States represents an increase of 1.4 million since July 2007, making this group the fastest growing of all ethnic or racial groups in the United States and meaning that Hispanics remain the largest minority group in the nation. Approximately 64 percent of Latinos living in the United States are of Mexican origin. In addition to growth in numbers,

Latinos are increasing their social and political influence in the United States. Thus, it is important to understand how Latinos reflect on these changes and what contributes to American and Latino identities. As U.S.-Mexico relationships become increasingly important in a global economy and as the United States overemphasizes border enforcement instead of border crossings, it is important to understand the complex interplay among household needs, border conditions, and work, and how people carry personal experiences. The need for income, family ideologies, and generational differences also factor into the complex border spaces.

FIELDWORK AND RESEARCH BACKGROUND

The data in this chapter present the collaborative efforts of two research projects. The first, located in San Antonio, Texas, a major urban U.S. city with a Hispanic majority population, explored transnational identities in the extended border cities of San Antonio and Monterrey, Nuevo Leon, Mexico. The second research project, situated in Laredo, Texas, a smaller Hispanic majority community located directly on the border, provided a sample of women border residents whose families extend across borders. The interview questions guiding the San Antonio study were adapted to capture the nuances of Laredo's identity as a cross-border community, San Antonio as a U.S. extended border city, and Monterrey as a northern Mexican extended border city.

The overall qualitative design included in-depth, extensive tape-recorded interviews ranging from three to six hours in length. The San Antonio sample included 250 interviews of Mexican immigrants and Mexican Americans representing high school students and adults from different socioeconomic levels with transnational experiences. The smaller Laredo sample consisted of 20 interviews with women, all of whom were of Mexican origin. To include Mexican perspectives, we traveled further inland 150 miles to Monterrey, collecting an additional 22 interviews with *mexicanos* who had transnational connections to San Antonio or Laredo.

Our rationale for choosing these three cities is that they are linked historically, economically, and culturally. For example, five international bridges connect the sister cities of Laredo and Nuevo Laredo. These linkages facilitate the movement of people, goods, and binational trade and are the lifelines for the many families whose strong familial ties extend across the border. Critical to Laredo's development during its 250-year history has been its placement along a U.S.-Mexico trade corridor ultimately solidifying markets in both directions (Arreola 2002). This strategic position has helped shape the movement of goods and people within this border community and the formulation of transnational relationships among San Antonio, Laredo, Nuevo Laredo, and Monterrey. The data from Monterrey in northern Mexico and Laredo right at the borderline combined with our fieldwork in San Antonio support the literature in identifying individuals who live in large transnational communities and who are often connected to one or more transnational sites rather than to just one place. For example, a 2002 Mexican Consulate Office report on the place of origin of legal Mexican immigrants in San Antonio showed that no single Mexican state represented the majority of Mexican immigrants in the city. In fact, it was found that a number of northern Mexican states as well as interior states send migrants to San Antonio.

To capture such complexities, we used qualitative software, Atlas TI, to create a database to facilitate the management of large amounts of qualitative data. Coding the transcribed interviews in this manner allowed us to focus on theory as a connected network of links among entities (Denzin and Lincoln 1994). The interviews addressed issues of parental background, neighborhood, immigration status, transnational contacts and social networks, language use, family and child raising practices, school and work experiences, political involvement, stereotypes, and perceptions of success. A wide range of questions about identity were incorporated throughout each interview. The following sequence of questions reflects the main identity questions asked:

- What would you consider your race to be?
- What about your ethnicity?
- When you refer to yourself, what do you call yourself?
- Are you or anyone in your family of multiethnic background? If yes, explain.
- Do you ever identify as Latino or Hispanic? In what context?
- Do you ever identify as a Mexican or Mexican American? In what context?
- Which is more common for you to say, Mexican/*mexicano*, Chicano or Mexican American, or American? What do these terms mean to you?
- Do you ever use the term Anglo or White? In what context?
- Do you feel more or less Mexican now?
- What does it mean to be an American?

While these questions specifically addressed the concept of identity, issues of identity often emerged throughout the course of the interview, particularly in questions about language, citizenship, transnational relationships, and family and served to validate previously obtained information.

One of the goals in this collaboration was to examine the transnational links that bind families across the cities of San Antonio, Laredo, and Monterrey—three cities with long historical ties strengthened by mission settlements, merchant routes, wars, treaties, migration streams, culture, language, and, most of all, families.

SAN ANTONIO AS A TRANSNATIONAL COMMUNITY

San Antonio plays an important role in understanding the Latino population of the Southwest. San Antonio is the tenth largest city in the United States, with a population of over 1.5 million. More than 59 percent of the city's residents are Hispanic (the majority of whom are of Mexican origin). Census predications estimate the number of persons of Hispanic origin to grow to over 1.2 million Hispanics by 2040 (Census 2000). As a result of decreasing birth rates, the non-Hispanic white population in the city continues to decrease. While there are concentrations of other ethnic groups in San Antonio, such as the 6 percent African American population, and very small percentages of other ethnic groups such as Chinese and Lebanese, there are no large cultural groups competing with the Mexican-origin population (Census 2000).

We argue that San Antonio can be viewed as an extension of the U.S.-Mexico border for a significant number of reasons, especially when viewed through a transnational lens. Mexican migration has left a legacy of rooted Mexican cultural beliefs and practices in the essence of San Antonio. A place becomes a "transnational social field," as argued by Peggy Levitt (2001) in *The Transnational Villagers*, when space is created by the continuous interchanges between sending and receiving communities, a space that enables individuals to actively function in both places simultaneously. Many Mexican family members regularly travel between San Antonio and various Mexican communities, but particularly Laredo, Texas, and Monterrey, Mexico. San Antonio also has a large population of multigenerational residents who do not travel to Mexico, and yet their lives also encompass strong Mexican cultural beliefs, values, foods, and the Spanish language—all elements of a transnational social field (Basch, Glick Schiller, and Szanton Blanc 1994; Levitt and Waters 2002). Included in this social field are a wide range of formal and informal institutions that support a way of Mexican life and perpetuate transnational identities and transnational experiences in San Antonio. For example, San Antonio has a large Mexican Consulate Office with a consul who very actively promotes and protects the welfare of Mexican nationals living in the city. Additionally, San Antonio has a permanent extension campus for the Universidad Nacional Autonoma de Mexico that recently celebrated its sixty-year anniversary in San Antonio. The city's Instituto Cultural de Mexico is one of only four such institutions funded by the Mexican government to promote cultural activities, art exhibits, and other forms of Mexican identity and cultural life. San Antonio also supports very active regional *clubes*, such as Club de Nuevo Leon and El Club de Coahuila, organizations that actively sponsor social and cultural activities linking the residents in San Antonio to their communities of origin.

As a result of these connections, we find large neighborhoods in San Antonio that are populated with a high concentration of Mexican residents that also include multigenerational San Antonians and recently arrived immigrants. For example, the West Side of San Antonio has a population of 133,464 residents. Ninety-three percent of the population of the West Side identified in the 2000 census as Hispanic (with the majority of Mexican origin), of which 18 percent are foreign born (Making Connections 2002). The West Side functions as one of several large areas within the city where a person's life can center completely within a Mexican transnational field using traditional markers such as foods of preference, the use of Spanish, culturally related business transactions, and the Mexican or Mexican American self-identify (Rosales 2000; Márquez, Mendoza, and Blanchard 2007).

Another marker of the nature of San Antonio's transnational environment is the continued use of Spanish throughout the city and a pride in maintaining oral and literacy skills in both English and Spanish. Unlike California, Texas has not outlawed the provision of bilingual education, and the San Antonio community readily embraces this educational tool to enhance bilingualism. Bilingual educational programs are implemented in various school districts throughout San Antonio, including one of the wealthiest, upper-class Anglo neighborhoods in the area. Spanish is commonly heard in major shopping malls, businesses, restaurants, banks, and neighborhood supermarkets.

San Antonio's transnationalism is further fostered by the art community. The San Antonio Museum of Art (SAMA), for example, embraces the art history of Mexico and the artistic contributions of Mexican culture. The museum's holdings include one of the largest Mexican folk art collections in the United States and extensive works by Mexican and Mexican American artists.

SAMA hosted the opening of a major Mexican exhibit in 1990, a major Mexican American show in 2002, and a collection from a wealthy Monterrey family in 2003, and it continues to host other cultural events on a regular basis. El Instituto Cultural de Mexico, funded and operated by the Mexican government, additionally offers San Antonio residents a continuous presentation of Mexican cultural events and exhibits. The latest element to broaden San Antonio's Mexican artistic identity is the construction of the Alameda Museum, a Mexican cultural museum built in partnership with the Smithsonian Institution in Washington, D.C.

Along with this transnational cultural component, San Antonio plays a strong economic role in banking and commercial industries that travel back and forth between San Antonio and various Mexican communities. Today, it is common for large banking and investment companies to maintain offices in both San Antonio and Monterrey. With the location of the NAFTA trade alliance offices in San Antonio, Laredo and San Antonio have become major economic centers for U.S.-Mexico trade and commerce. We argue that all of these factors contribute to San Antonio's "transnational social fields" and support the premise of San Antonio as a transnational community. The dynamic quality of institutions and relationships within these extended borderlands emphasizes that these borders are not places or events but social processes.

THE SAN ANTONIO EXPERIENCE

The San Antonio interviews illuminated identity issues related to social class, generational transmission by families, stereotypes, neighborhood context, the role of historical legacy, and the significance of the Spanish language. Equally important, the interviews illustrate the ways in which the continuous influx of new migrants to San Antonio works to renew and reinforce the Mexican identity of the city. In another example of the impact of time in the borderlands, younger respondents discussed the notion of becoming more conscious of their American identity because of the process of constantly comparing themselves to "the other," the newly arrived Mexican immigrant. Older immigrants explained that they felt "more Mexican" as they tried to maintain their Mexican cultural roots amid the pressures of assimilation.

Labels of self-identify can relate directly to the historical period in which an individual grew up as well as to the current time period. Cultural repertoires and ethnic identity boundaries, like structural conditions, change over time

(Lamont 2000). In the 1940s and 1950s during the era of Jim Crow, discrimination against persons of Mexican background was intense (Montejano 1987). Throughout the Southwestern United States, the dramatic surge in Mexican population has strengthened anti-Mexican or anti-immigrant boundaries (Vila 2003a).

Attitudes toward a particular ethnic group and anti-immigrant sentiments during different historical times can influence the ways members of the groups see themselves. A Mexican American U.S. citizen interviewed in San Antonio explained how the terms he used to identify himself had changed over time and in response to attitudes toward Mexicans. He stated: "I am a *mestizo*. God only knows how many blends there are. But I'm mainly probably Indian. But I would say I am an Apache. And then I am to some extent Spanish and maybe a little Italian. God only knows what the mixtures were in Mexico." When asked what his ethnicity was, he responded, "I'm a Mexican American." When asked if he had ever identified as a Latino or Hispanic, he then responded:

> Well, we were identified as everything. At one time, and I was growing up in the thirties, we were the *Mexicans*. Then, came the forties with the *Latinos*. Or *Latins*. *Latin Americans*. In those days, the police used that, which I hate. Latin. What the hell is Latin? . . . We're not from Panama or Colombia. Of course to the gringos, we were the *greasers* and, you know, *Mescans*. And then, we became the *Mexican Americans* in the 1950s. Then came the sixties, and we became the *Chicanos*. And now we are, the newest name, *Hispanic Americans* . . . Or *Latino* . . . At one time, they used to put, "C," *Caucasian*.

Responses indicated the continued racial hierarchies present in the borderlands and the identity categories into which people from Mexico are often cast. This man had experienced the changing relations of Mexican-origin people and Anglo-Americans as they evolved over time in the U.S. Southwest. He remembered the use of disparaging terms such as *Mescans* and *greasers* and a reluctance to even use the term *Mexican* in the 1930s and 1940s. Then he identified with the terms created in the Mexican Civil Rights Movement, such as *Chicano*, (Acuna 1988), and he acknowledged that today he is considered part of the more inclusive group *Hispanics* and *Latinos*. He also noted in earlier time periods a confusion existed about racial identification in his reference to the official recording of *Caucasian* as a racial designation on government agency records for Mexican-origin people on the basis that they were not Negro or Black. This man's experience was similar to that of many others who struggle to maintain their ethnic identity under challenges from other groups or in changing situations (Barth 1969).

In the San Antonio sample, few of the high school students self-identified using the term *Chicano*. Adolescents particularly did not choose to use the term *Chicano* because they identified the term with "old people who sat on the corners" or "people in California." One young high school girl explained that she only used the term *Latina* when she wanted to be assertive, but for the most part used the terms *Mexican American* or *Hispanic*. Students and adults chose ethnic identity terms according to the context and the groups with which they were interacting, and they generally accepted terms of the time. These examples support our view of identity as constructed and flexible as opposed to fixed. The choices of preferred terms illustrate that personal and group identity is defined in opposition to other meanings against which they take on their own significance. The identities preferred by these respondents are multiple, self-reflexive, and plural. They are tied to the spatial context, social conditions, and time periods in which the subjects live.

Mixed and complex ancestry, the hybridity of border residents, membership in second and subsequent generations, and uncertainty about one's ethnic background all reduce the probability of identifying with one ethnicity and influence the intensity and meaning of ethnic identity. One young woman identified herself as *Chicana* because her mother wanted her to identify in that way. Her parents came to California as young undocumented immigrants but now have gained citizenship status. Born in California, the daughter has lived in San Antonio for seven years. When asked what she considered her race to be, she replied, "Chicana. My mom wants me to say 'Chicana' because I'm from California." She then went on to explain that she also used the term *Latina* when she wrote papers in school, and had used the terms *Mexican* or *Mexican American* "when I'm signing forms or stuff." She drew on the terms *Mexican* or *Mexicana* when she was around her uncles, who are undocumented immigrants. This young woman demonstrates that some patterns of self-identity and boundaries are more likely in particular contexts than in others. She further identified as *Mexican* or *Mexican American* when she was required to sign official documents and as *Latina* or *Mexican American* to please her teacher, but around her Mexican relatives she demonstrated a unity with them and their condition as undocumented workers by using her *mexicana* identity. Her mother was active in the civil rights movement in California and wanted to transmit that heritage to her daughter. But while the daughter acknowledged that she was born in California, she did not have the cultural roots and experience tied to inequality that would allow her to share that collective identity with the Chicano movement. The individualism at the heart of ethnic identity constrains parents' transmission of their ethnicity to their children, but given the massive contact across borders, the U.S.-Mexico border region has the potential of reinforcing the younger generation's Mexican heritage identity.

Similarly, the historical experience of ethnic groups in the United States has little meaning for young Mexican recent immigrants coming into the country. For example, when an eighteen-year-old high school student who was born in Mexico and who has lived in San Antonio for several years was asked questions about race, he indicated he did not understand the concept of racial groups as they are constructed in the U.S. He explained: "Soy mexicano, pero creo que no pertenezco a ninguna . . . porque ya me hice una combinación de todos." (I am Mexican, but I don't think any of the terms apply to me . . . because now I am a combination of all.) He identified his ethnic group as *mexicanos* but explained, "Yo soy quien soy. . . . A veces me preguntan quien eres, no pues soy Hispano, a veces digo soy mexicano, realmente soy uno en todos." (I am who I am. At times they ask me, "Who are you?" No, well, I am Hispanic. Sometimes I say I am *mexicano*. Really, I am all in one.) Our interviews indicate that foreign-born Mexicans are likely to have different notions about race than U.S.-born Mexican Americans. The young man quoted above was not a member of a minority group in Mexico and does not feel like a minority in the United States—he is just who he is. He, like many others in the San Antonio sample, defined his ethnic group by place of birth—Mexican if one were born in Mexico, and Mexican American or Hispanic if one were born in the United States. In actuality, he identified with both countries. Thus, while the political borders may place some constraints on identity, nation-state borders may or may not correspond to the "social boundaries" of membership and exclusion.

The majority of the respondents interviewed in San Antonio chose the terms *Hispanic* or *Mexican American* rather than *Chicano* or *Latino*. Perhaps, because San Antonio is a major urban city with a Hispanic majority, Mexican Americans feel a part of that larger population. Ethnic identity is complicated by the arrival of new immigrants whose presence reinforces the view that recent arrivals are *mexicanos* and those born in the U.S. are "Mexican Americans" or "Hispanics." However, ethnic solidarity and a self-conscious recognition of ethnic origin as a social bond become stronger under certain conditions, such as living among concentrations of the ethnic group, belonging to ethnic organizations, and having friends of the same ethnic group (Alba and Nee 2003). San Antonio is a place where individuals who grow up in ethnic neighborhoods can continue to reside in majority ethnic social spheres, such as in the West Side. Because Mexican-origin residents are the ethnic majority in those communities, residents there are more likely to have families that are not of mixed ancestry and are likely to speak the Spanish language. Many Hispanic youth in the city have similar experiences in all Mexican school environments. Most attend schools where Mexican-origin students are the majority. The confusion that existed over race and ethnicity in the interviews in San Antonio suggests that the categories of race and ethnicity may have blended together. This malleability is partly due to the complexity of ancestry for many Latinos or Hispanics. This blending may be a result of an increasing reality that overt expressions of ethnic background and cultural identity are of less significance for young people who live in a majority Hispanic city, attend majority Hispanic schools, and have experienced little overt racial or ethnic discrimination.

THE LAREDO EXPERIENCE

As we move the discussion directly to the borderline, it is important to note that proximity to the border does not act as a prerequisite for transnationalism; in fact, many border residents never cross the international boundary. Nevertheless, the Laredo data indicate that transnationalism was a part of the lives of women involved in this study, and transnational processes actively shaped their lives and those of their families. For many who live in this city, the border is an artificial, man-made, political line transcended by family and cultural dynamics. As Zartman points out in the introduction to this volume, the social aspects of border communities often spill over regardless of the official political boundary between neighboring states.

Laredo, Texas, is a community originally settled by Spaniards in 1755. Today, Laredo, with a population of nearly 200,000, represents the second-fastest growing city in Texas and one of the fastest-growing communities in the United States (Arreola 2002). Laredo's early history as a Spanish settlement established its position along the north/south U.S.-Mexico corridor along which trade, goods, and people moved freely between Mexico and the United States (Arreola 2002). The implications of these early linkages have been far reaching as today an annual average of seventeen million north- and southbound vehicles and nearly nine million north and southbound pedestrians cross the five bridges at the Laredo/Nuevo Laredo border (Laredo Development Foundation 2002).

At present, Laredo, like all Texas border communities, has a high concentration (94 percent) of Mexican-origin population (Census 2000). Uniquely, Laredo represents the largest of twenty-five existing "continuous" Hispanic communities in the country, meaning it is a community where Hispanics have maintained a majority presence during the city's entire existence. The distinction of being the fastest-growing city in Texas places Laredo into the national ranks of the country's fastest-growing cities. Interestingly, the extremely high Mexican concentration spared Laredo residents from the more common racial segregation experienced in racially mixed communities throughout the Southwest (Arreola 2002). The segregation in Laredo is based on class differences largely due to the presence of *colonias*, small, unincorporated communities developed outside city boundaries that receive limited services and lack access to water, electricity, paved roads, and indoor plumbing (Márquez 1998, 2008).

Situated directly across the border from Laredo is the major northern Mexico border city of Nuevo Laredo, Tamaulipas. Nuevo Laredo reports a population of over 500,000, thus increasing the neighboring border cities' total population threefold to 693,000 (Laredo Development Foundation 2002). From an aerial view, the Laredo–Nuevo Laredo area appears as one large metropolitan city. In this border region, the divisive capacity of a national border and a borderline loses its power. The Laredo–Nuevo Laredo area is representative of the grey area ideal type described by Zartman in the introduction to this volume. It is an area where the different populations fully intermingle, producing an intermediate population and culture composed of a combination of traits and people from the two sides of the border. Yet this borderland has been characterized by movement in time (from its Spanish roots to its Mexican identity) and in space (by the shifting of the physical border of the Rio Grande) and by the nature of the transnational interactions of families. It is at the cultural, social, and familial level where the interconnectedness between Laredo and Nuevo Laredo appear (Arreola 2002). All twenty women interviewed in this project spoke of strong familial ties extending across the borderline and of family responsibilities that rippled fluidly across the Rio Grande River, a river that functions as a natural barrier along the Texas-Mexico border.

Border dynamics in these cities are commonly viewed through a transborder lens, rather than a transnational lens, since it is easy to discern how proximity to a border facilitates transborder activity. We argue that the application of a transnational lens accentuates those processes that allow border residents to maintain intricate linkages across both communities without relinquishing allegiance to either country (Márquez 2008). Transnational connections in this study often appeared in the women's family relationships but additionally were expressed in terms of identity, place, and space.

For example, Serena, a forty-year-old mother of three children, conceptualized her family as a transborder family, but she also identified her family household as a household that transcends a divisive border. Selena stated, "My parents still live in Nuevo Laredo as well as one sister, and I do have my two brothers who live on the American side. Here in Laredo, they are all within a mile or two. I have a lot of cousins and relatives that live in Laredo as well as in Nuevo Laredo. . . . I had friends from this side, so going back and forth is no big deal. We're one big community. We are just separated by the river. . . . But life was always on both sides." Selena further described how her extended family in Mexico maintained the family's transnational linkages. The distances were real for her and all of her relatives as they moved about Mexico and the United States, but the ties were firmly woven into one family unit. One can see the importance of the family's movement back and forth as she described her family relations: "I have family in Monterrey, Mexico, and in Mexico City, and I don't see them as often as I would like to, but maybe on the average of twice a year they come to Laredo to visit the family. My mother's sister lives in Monterrey, and they come shopping to Laredo, Texas. She will come to see her sisters [in Texas]. My aunt in Mexico City has children living here in Laredo, and she comes a lot [to Texas]." Similar to the situation for Selena's family, distance does not weaken the ties in Elena's family. On the contrary, Elena's family moves easily between the direct border and Monterrey, which lies approximately 150 miles in northern Mexico. Elena's family linkages strongly revolve around holidays and celebrations. "My cousins in Monterrey, they can't wait until Thanksgiving [which is not celebrated in Mexico]. They are always here. For my son's birthday my cousin from Monterrey was here and we had a *carne asada* [barbeque or cookout]. . . . New Year is when we get together with them, or they come here [to Laredo] to celebrate."

That families acted as transnational units became clear in the interviews, but, in addition, the women identified in a very transnational sense. At times they were conflicted, and other times they described the naturally shifting nature of their identity. Mexican heritage was central to their identity, and their cultural expressions emitted pride and loyalties not necessarily tied to birthright.

Valeria, a professional woman born in the United States who has previously lived away from the border, maintained a strong Mexican identity and represents the fluidity that a transnational identity offers a person. She described herself:

> I guess my more personal side is Mexican. I like being over there. I like the food and I like the people. I like the houses, but I guess I have to make a living, so I play the part. I mean. I'm here. But probably, it is very conflicting for me. I don't know. I don't even know how to answer this question. It's weird. I don't think I can define my ties to Mexico. I don't think I can define it. I mean, not with words.... We have like double identities. I mean, I have, half of my papers are Mexican. Half of the other ones are American. And there's two different addresses and two different everything.

Another Laredo woman, Paloma, age forty-four, was born in Mexico, lives in Laredo, and has dual citizenship. She views herself as Mexican but expressed fewer personal conflicts than Elena. She stated, "I think I feel more of a Mexican. I stand more for the things that I brought with me. For some reason, they become stronger in you once you are here, even though you have to deal with other ways of being, beliefs, and values. I believe I kept my traditions and culture pretty much."

In Lorena's case, a distinction exists between how she perceived herself, or her ethnic identity, and her birthright status as an American. Lorena, a twenty-two-year-old adult who is attending college, explains, "I feel that I am Mexican, but I'm not really from there because I was born in the United States. But then I don't completely belong here because I don't speak English.... Sometimes I feel that I don't belong no where." For Lorena, her identity resides somewhere in between the two cultures.

Alicia, who at forty-one years old is a teacher and a long-time resident of Laredo, identified strongly with her Mexican heritage. She described herself: "I don't feel that I have ties in the United States, to tell you the truth. I take advantage of the things you have here, the opportunities. But I think that my mind and everything is over there [in Mexico]. But I don't know, it has been such a long time [since she lived in Mexico] that I don't know if it's only my memories and how I feel about it and then growing and feeling completely different from here." Alicia's transnational background is as fascinating as it is complex in that she self-identifies as a *Chilanga*, a Mexico City native, and lives on the border with dual citizenship. As a Jewish woman, her language fluency includes Yiddish and Hebrew, Spanish and English. Alicia's circumstances and experiences have given her a wide range of identity choices and possibilities for describing her racial and ethnic identity. She can describe herself as Jewish, as a Mexican American, as a Mexican national, or as an American. She can identify with her regional roots in Mexico City or with her borderlands identity in Laredo. Whatever identity she chooses, it will be socially constructed and situational. It will also depend on who asks and who defines the labels. The transnational lives of these women living in the Laredo and Nuevo Laredo borderlands illustrate the penetrating effects of transnational actions, relationships, and identity processes.

THE MONTERREY EXPERIENCE

As we coded the Monterrey, Nuevo Leon, interviews, one interview particularly illustrated the complexity of identity construction within transnational communities as it occurs on the Mexican side of the continuum. We interviewed Professor Muñoz at the Mexican university in Monterrey where he teaches. He maintains a home in Monterrey, where he grew up, and commutes to San Antonio, Texas. His workweek Monday through Friday is in Monterrey; on Friday he travels to his second home in San Antonio where his wife lives. In describing who he is and his relationship to both countries, he stated: "[My ties are] [h]alf and half because I was born here, because I'm Mexican, because I have a place where I can work and do sometimes think that is worthwhile. I feel very attached [to Mexico], but at the same time I feel very attached to the U.S. because of all my years that I spend there and my American life. So it's very close to half and half." When explaining what home represents to him, his articulate response clearly describes the transnational state of his life and the impact transnationalism has on how he sees himself:

> I hate to say, but when I'm in the U.S. I say, "O.K., I'm going to go home now [to Mexico]." When I am here [in Mexico], "I am going home to visit my wife," so both are home, in that sense. That's how I feel, and that's the truth. Once I'm in San Antonio, I have to bring out my American driver's license. For example, I had a driver's license when I got there for thirteen years. I still renew it because I have an address there. When I'm here I feel like I have two personalities in that sense.... I have two wallets.... I have an American wallet and a Mexican wallet. So basically I end up playing [a new role] when I change wallets. That's like changing personalities.... I dominate it very well

and I manage too. It's an adjustment. It's not like I'm two different people. It's the same person, only two situations and two different cultures. I feel like I am the same person, but behaving differently depending on the situation. . . . I think that I have adjusted very well to being in two cultures and being equally involved in both of them. If I could vote over there I would vote.

In describing his ethnic identity, the complexity of his transnational identity stood out: "I am Mexican by birth but a citizen of the world, by choice. I don't like being branded from one part of the world or the other. I know it is a political necessity, but I don't see myself as fully Mexican, but I don't see myself as American either. . . . I don't pretend to be anybody else. I describe myself as an American. I've been living there for thirteen years and I lived over there anyway." Yet, when asked: If somebody were to ask you, "¿De dónde eres?" Dr. Muñoz replied, "I'd say from Monterrey, Mexico." In a way, Dr. Muñoz is both embracing his Mexican identity and opposing it; he is Mexican but he does not see himself as fully Mexican. We find, at present, the American racial identification system pushes residents to be either one or the other and makes it difficult to be both Mexican and American. With increasing border security, the transnational lifestyle embodied in Dr. Muñoz's choice to be a citizen of the world may become more difficult.

CONCLUSION

In Laredo, we found that transnational processes allowed the respondents to maintain cultural linkages enabling family ties to remain intact across bordering nation-state boundaries. The shifts in identity depending on context and the relationships maintained across borders clearly illustrate the constant movement and human processes evident in the U.S.-Mexican borderlands. Moreover, with these transnational linkages the women in Laredo maintained their family's social networks in new forms of space and place that facilitated their movements within a transnational corridor. Included within this movement are identities that encompass both sides of their border life.

The dynamics of the U.S.-Mexico border allow the persistence of borderland identities in extended metroplexes such as San Antonio, Texas, and Monterrey in northern Mexico. In San Antonio, the interviews we conducted with persons living transnational lives indicate a similar complexity to the lives of people in Laredo. San Antonio is a community with strong historical, political, and social linkages to Mexico. Today Mexican nationals can become American citizens without giving up their Mexican national identity. San Antonio maintains a close relationship to Mexico, assuring that large numbers of children will be born in the United States to Mexican parents or in Mexico to American citizens. The people interviewed in this study do not think of racial stratification in terms of black and white (Stephen 2007; Vila 2003a). When asked to identify their race, they unanimously use an ethnic term that is a reflection of the borderlands, such as *Mexican American, Mexican,* or *Hispanic.* Increasingly complex identities of second- and third-generation Mexican Americans require that the categorical distinctions that members of society are recognizing constantly change and expand. These dynamics in borderlands transnational identities reflect self-identities and interrelations across physical borders that have changed over time as the sociopolitical situations of Mexicans and Mexican Americans have changed over time. The U.S.-Mexican borderlands provide an ideal type for studying the resilient nature of boundary dynamics and identities. Boundaries are affected by social and cultural differences, by social class and residential differences, by immigration status, and by generation. In contemporary communities like San Antonio, transnationalism, pride in racialized neighborhood enclaves, such as the West Side, and the increasingly important economic and political relations with Mexico provide reinvigorated incentives for families to maintain Mexican ethnic affiliations (Márquez, Mendoza, and Blanchard 2007).

Multiple identities combine in interesting ways through social class, gender, and power relations, making the U.S.-Mexican borderland a more nuanced, complex, and even contradictory space than most literature portrays. Not all borders are as unequal economically and politically as the U.S.-Mexico border. Not all borders have a history of conflict and territorial acquisition that has resulted in a hybridization of people and space like the U.S.-Mexican borderland. The complexity of border identities peculiar to the U.S.-Mexico border may not be transferred easily to theories or empirical studies of other borderlands (Heyman and Campbell 2004). However, as we continue to examine the history and evolution of borders through the work, family, and community lives of people who live in these borderlands, we find new cultural dynamics, emerging subcultures, multiple identities, and a new understanding of transnational boundaries. As we explore issues of citizenship, nationality, and ethnicity—especially in the personal trajectories and worldviews of border residents—we will gain a deeper understanding of border processes and the people who cross borders.

CHAPTER TEN

Looking across the Horizon

Shelley Feldman

Borders, boundaries, frontiers, and margins are important tropes in contemporary research. Each suggests particular relations between place, space, and people and generates creative opportunities and innovative ways to think about state rule, state formation and interstate relations, nationalism, community, and, significantly, identity and belonging. Importantly, each trope generates distinct bodies of literature and new and exciting empirical foci. Frontiers, for example, as the formalization of the boundaries of empire, are sites of analysis that challenge the naturalization of national space to reveal the cartographic imagination of rulers and kings, of mapmaking as a social and political project, and of the production of place as an ongoing political and cultural activity. Frontiers, in other words, are to be understood neither as open space to be conquered nor as physical territories that exist beyond the national state, but rather are to be examined pace Henri Lefebvre (1991) as social and cultural productions. As such, frontiers may separate politically established states and be recognized as "zones of contact" (Pratt 1992), but they must nonetheless be examined as historical configurations, interpreted as constituting and constructing what has come to be understood as the other's otherness and the colonizer's own identity (Gupta and Ferguson 1997).

In contrast to debates on spatio-territorial fixity, as in research that treats frontiers as outside of the national state and configuring its border, discussions of margins often are understood relationally, where social, political, and cultural differences collide, (e)merge, and create new spaces of identity, border making, and (be)longing, what Anzaldúa (1987) refers to as hybrid spaces. Marginals, as Victor Turner (1974, 232–33) reminds us, are "simultaneously (by ascription, cooptation, self-definition, or achievement) of two or more groups whose social definitions and cultural norms are distinct from, and often even opposed to, one another." Marginals, he continues, "often look to their group of origin, the so-called inferior group, for communitas, and to the more prestigious group in which they mainly live and in which they aspire to higher status as their structural reference group." In these explorations, the referent is often, but not always, an already given state system.[1]

Margins also are recognized as places of particular vision offering their inhabitants a view of inside and outside, the included and excluded, the powerful and the powerless (hooks 1984; Das and Poole 2004). As Veena Das and Deborah Poole (2004, 4) suggest, those living on the margins offer "a unique perspective [for] understanding ... the state, not because it captures exotic practices, but because it suggests that such margins are a necessary entailment of the state, much as the exception is a necessary component of the rule."

Concepts that generally presume spatial fixidity—refugees, exiles, migrants—are found to be salient either for the period of the Westphalian nation-state or, if used, are ahistorically applied, in reified fashion, across time and place. Today, however, the spatial turn in the social sciences has stimulated creative thinking and innovative exploration that are especially suggestive for the study of borderlands since they reveal the complex and myriad expressions and multifaceted character of borderland life, fixed as well as mobile, de- as well as reterritorialized, stable and ambiguous. Borderlands are increasingly understood to be "present wherever two or more cultures edge each other, where people of different races occupy the same territory, where under, lower, middle and upper classes touch, where the space between two individuals shrinks with intimacy" (Anzaldúa 1987, preface). As such, borderlands offer opportunities to ask the following kinds of questions: How are communities and relations of rule constituted in particular places and times? If states are not always and already constituted, how are they forged in relation to different community and class interests? As collectivities (states) are partitioned or when communities live in different relation to centers of power, how do they constitute senses of collective (national) belonging and selfhood? How do we understand national belonging when nations are now understood to cross state boundaries and where citizenship is now recognized as plural rather than singular? As Das and Poole (2004) might frame it, how do political legitimacy and identities emerge as a function of boundary making and as effects of state practice?

Particularly exciting about the literature addressing these spatio-temporal themes is its interdisciplinary character incorporating the disciplines of anthropology to sociology and history to literature. The result is analyses that offer robust interpretations of the processes and relations of power, inequality, and rule that characterize borderland community life. And whereas many studies and collections tend to accept the view that borders and national frontiers are self-evident, spatially discrete units of analysis, this volume unsettles such assumptions to offer instead cross-disciplinary, historical, and comparative studies of the processes and relations that characterize borderlands as socially constituted spaces of lived experience and social imaginings. In different ways, the cases in this volume situate these processes in the shadow of a political border and recognize the specificity of what Timothy Mitchell (1999) and Michel-Rolph Trouillot (2001) identify as "state effects." Borderlands are products and relations of these effects, producing boundaries and jurisdiction where legibility and control are often less stable and marked than in the centers of power.[2]

These case studies also make an important contribution to discussions of borderlands because they recognize the changing and continuous reconfigurations of population flows and movements. While some of the contributors (Gavrilis, Stea, Zech, and Gray; Márquez and Romo) appreciate the particularity of the current, post-Soviet period of neoliberal reform as shaping borderland relations, especially in relation to the global demand for labor, commodities, and rights, other contributions highlight relations of mobility and sedentarization during various regimes of power (Bárta; Schryver). Consequently, whereas some collected volumes focus solely on the contemporary moment or a single site (Vila 2003a), the contributions in this volume appreciate that population movements and flows reflect long-term and ongoing expressions of community and state formation and examine borderland relations before the instantiation of the current nation-state system as well as during the period of formal colonialization. The language of colonial state space, for example, acknowledges an official narrative of colonial rule and border formation that, as in the case of India, represented only one borderland configuration—an undivided India—one that transformed a precolonial period of princely states and different borderland identities and configurations and established the context for the sovereign territorial states of India, Pakistan, and Bangladesh. Each of these moments reflects different negotiations of identity, belonging, and security that help to shape territoriality and changing forms of rule.

Recent interest in place and state-making has turned attention to the contested character and structuring of national space, processes that are made evident and elaborated in Timothy Mitchell's (1991, 2002) magisterial account of the making of colonial Egypt. In James Scott's (1998) imaginative interpretation, *Seeing like a State,* he explores sedentarization and legibility as social and political processes of state building and social control, while struggles over citizenship, rights, and political authority unsettle the fixity of state forms. These themes are especially suggestive for analyses of the Israeli-Palestinian crisis, the crises of once undivided Yugoslavia, Korea, or Vietnam, or in what we understand to be the independent states of Ireland, Bangladesh, India, and Pakistan. Such studies make two critical contributions. First, they query state building as solely a response to external pressures, demands, or threats that assume a state form and an imperative for administrative control (Gavrilis, Blumi, this volume). Second, they draw attention to the human condition in the shadow of the border and, by doing so, recognize how experience changes across both time and place (Stea, Zech and Gray, this volume).

In these cases, the borderland—the Israeli or Cypriot Green Lines, Ottoman Albania and Yemen, the Korean DMZ, the Kashmiri LOC, or the U.S.-Mexico border—constitutes communities that shape people's relation to state boundaries, to their kin across the border, and to the communities located more proximate to centers of state power and authority.[3] Such borderland communities often are characterized by varied relations of mobility and include the securing of employment, maintaining relations with distant kin, and recent migrations in search of what are presumed to be robust networks and markets of opportunity. To some extent, demographic analyses have begun to capture some of these dynamic relations, but their focus is often on the determinants and effects of population mobility on social integration, assimilation, and security rather than on the negotiations and human conditions that such mobility entails. Likewise, while demographic concern with assimilation and the coexistence of ethnic communities in plural contexts is an important research focus, the field has been less attentive to the structural relations that constitute states and national formations and to questions of hybridization and multiple identities as aspects of identity formation and as relations of exclusion and inclusion. Moreover, the historical specificity of these relations as sites of contestation and negotiation have been far from adequately explored by those working within the disciplinary bounds of demography.

Yet, the study of borderland relations, as William Zartman (this volume) makes evident, has increasing salience in a dramatically transforming global economy. Struggles over political boundaries and questions of sovereignty, violence and resistance among marginalized communities over recognition of rights and citizenship, and tensions and dilemmas over identity and belonging in the context of an increasingly nomadic life remain critical issues for analysis. Our nomadic, crossings-over lifestyle is revealed, for instance, in Arjun Appadurai's (1996) focus on translocalities and Edward Said's (1984, 1994) apprehension of exile as the normative condition of the present, a metaphor of modernity. As Georgio Agamben (1998, 127) similarly emphasizes, it is recognition of our refugee status whereby the "[d]eclarations of rights represent the originary figure of the inscription of natural life in the juridico-political order of the nation-state." Here Said and Agamben echo Hannah Arendt's brilliant postwar critique of the relationship between nation-states and human rights,[4] where displaced populations are marked by a particular national identity that cannot be readily substituted. As Arendt (1994, 267) makes explicit, "Once [people] had left their homeland they remained homeless, once they had left their state they became stateless, once they had been deprived of their human rights they were rightless, the scum of the earth."

This insightful reflection anticipates many of the themes explored in this volume, even if this framing fails to unsettle the a priori assumption of states as given and of the contested valence of homeland in a globalizing world economy. Arendt's insight also opens a space to explore the meanings attendant to neoliberalism, a discourse that may capture, but often fails to elaborate, the contradictory consequences of free markets with its support for the open flow of capital and commodities coupled with its constraints on legal labor mobility. Important for understanding displacements and borderlands associated with global transformation is growing insecurity as the "free market" devalues labor by challenging "local" wage rates and relations and nationally constituted environmental and labor laws in ways that place economically vulnerable populations on the edge of legal protections and secure rights. It also establishes the conditions for legal and illegal migration among people in search of work, particularly among those living on the borders of states where the costs of reproduction, labor markets, and wage rates differ "on the other side."

The partition of once shared collective or state spaces—Greece, India, Yugoslavia—also means that people are now required to redefine as well as struggle for the rights and resources they assumed accompanied their membership within a community. People living along border areas, especially those who might regularly cross a state border for home or work or who may live temporarily on either side of a border, are obliged to continually negotiate with "their" new and established communities in order to build and maintain connections and senses of belonging. Here, Turner's (1974) foresight is worthy of recall. In these contexts people negotiate their marginality as they struggle to secure rights and representation with communities in which they are either marginal from centers of power and state authority or excluded from equitable participation because of their status as illegal or temporary residents; they are not citizens. As David Stea, Jamie Zech, and Melissa Gray (this volume) show, marginal populations often negotiate with policies and practices of social exclusion for rights and protections. Importantly, such negotiations between marginal populations and state authorities on each side of a "national" border are constrained by the political interests and economic desires of those in power. Harriet Romo and Raquel R. Márquez (this volume) also show, in their exploration of prohibitions on border crossing, that such negotiations are framed by continually changing U.S. economic and political interests.

Changes in the way borders are monitored to exclude transgressions or facilitate permeability or porous movements also correspond to shifting political and economic interests. But, however understood, border crossings are creatively manipulated by those forced to observe their rules, where decisions to cross a border illegally, or engage in activities that can be sanctioned, are often carried out at great personal cost. The variability of border behavior and control is well illustrated by the Bracero Program in the United States, when cheap wage labor from Mexico was invited into the country to labor in the agricultural fields in California. The success of the program depended on limited controls of the border. With changes in labor demand, border controls were tightened and people who had established work and kin relations in the United States were forced to reimagine the meaning of belonging, citizenship, and rights and to establish new modes of labor exchange and family life. Similarly, Blumi (this volume) shows, in her comparison of experiences under British and Ottoman rule, how territorialization "had the unanticipated consequence of dividing vibrant cultural and economic districts into competing zones of political and economic interests." These new modes of cultural and economic exchange, including illegal border crossing and the increased policing of the frontier, engage the creative manipulation of people to sustain relations across a legal divide about which they have little control and for which transgressions are usually criminalized and carry severe sanction. Today, these complex and changing relations demand more coherent and just policy proscriptions and their enforcement as the movement of people accompany the movement of money and commodities.

In addition to the movements of people across established borders, borders represent sites for the illegal transfer of goods that, as our authors remind us, constitute complex relations among communities. Smuggling, like illegal population flows, is as much a challenge to state authority and legitimacy as it is about the illegal transfer of particular commodities. As Isa Blumi (this volume) reveals, the Işkodra trading families helped create a thriving smuggling network wherein the Montenegrin state actively encouraged smuggling even as it sought to cleanse its territories of the very Albanians who conducted this trade. George Gavrilis (this volume) and Rachel Havrelock (this volume), also highlight the significance of smuggling among borderland communities, whether such illegal behavior is carried out to secure resources or to gather weapons in self-defense. These studies use the border as a point of departure for exploring how lines of enclosure and exclusion structure people's daily lives.

Importantly, borders are not merely physical demarcations that separate one political entity from another; they are, rather, sets of social relations organized and systematized through legal and normative institutions to reproduce these relations as sites of control. The meanings attendant to borders, however, are neither fixed for any particular community nor necessarily shared across communities but instead are relations in constant negotiation. Borderland relations constitute and are constituted by the changing meanings that attend to what usually are assumed to be natural boundaries between states within a world system of nation-states. To be sure, communities living proximate to a national border construct their meanings in ways that may differ from other spatial locales living either closer to centers of power or in places less directly monitored by state authorities. This suggests that there is much to learn from borderland communities, not only because they provide a window on processes of community and identity formation, relations of exclusion, and the social practices associated with struggles for recognition, security, and rights, but also because they offer critical insights into communities in flux; they provide a site where collectivities are not defined primarily by spatio-territorial categorization. As such, borderland communities exceed easy categorization and legibility by constituting relations of belonging and identity as hybrid, multiple, and complex, or what, in other contexts, is viewed as transnational. The case studies in this volume do not underestimate the significance of territorial categorization in shaping collective formations but extend understanding of such formations in ways that are not overdetermined by structural and spatial relations and by the assumed giveness of the nation-state.

Frederik Barth's (1969) work, almost a half-century ago, reveals the complicated relations that characterize people's lives in regions split by state sovereignty. Barth's focus was not on the line of separation per se, or the political history that shaped how particular borders were constituted. Rather, his concern was the region surrounding the border, the kin relations that were forged or fractured by political decisions that treated place as space, as uninhabited territory that ignored the social and cultural life of those who make their homes and populate its landscape. The borderline in this context was the referent that would come to constitute the lives of those who dwelt in its shadow. Others, to be sure, have attended to how the space defined by the line becomes a site of contested belonging, exclusion, and political struggle. Joya Chatterji (1999), for example, examines the role of Cyril Radcliffe in defining the partition lines of South Asia under British colonial rule, while others show how the British Mandate of Palestine, a Middle East territory that once included modern-day Israel, Jordan, the West Bank, and Gaza, became separate sovereign states. These sites and others have been, and continue to be, sites of ongoing contestation.

What differentiates Barth's contribution from the studies in this volume, however, was his focus on newly divided communities that were forced to negotiate new relations of family and kin across a political divide. This emphasis on political change rather than on continuous movement does not sufficiently account for the ways that political divisions are accompanied by new rules of belonging and longing—an emergent symbolic world—as well as new opportunities enabled or denied by the policies that shape each border community along the divide. To reiterate Thomas Wilson and Hastings Donnan's (1998, 5) refrain, "most studies have focused on how social relations, defined in part by the state, transcend the physical limits of the state and, in so doing, transform the structure of the state at home and its relations with its neighbours."

The contributors in this volume extend these offerings by incorporating two important foci. The first is recognition that while historical analyses of states crucially depend on the specificities of place and community making, political communities predate the instantiation of the Westphalian nation-state system and thus make the notion of borderlands a far more complicated concept than studies limited to cross-national border crossing. Surely a focus on states as emblematic of borderlands offers an important focus for interpreting how communities sustain their kin relations and develop new relations and identities in the wake of constraints imposed by political division. A focus on interstate relations also contributes to how we understand relations of assimilation and marginalization in the context of linguistic, ethnic, religious, and class divisions of transborder communities. But, by framing analyses in fixed territorial categories, such studies treat state and nation formation as a single process. What the case studies here suggest is that communities are constituted not only as new political sovereigns in response to a particular state authority but also through other relations of belonging that do not necessarily overlap with state forms. While nationalism represents a particular form of identification,[5] it is suggestive to imagine a distinction between states and nations where the latter is not confined to the legal border of the state and where, for example, ethnic communities do not correspond to territorially based identities but exceed them.

Second, while ethnographic accounts are central to how we apprehend community and identity formation and negotiations for rights and recognition, another trace on borderland communities is offered through the archives. The papers in this volume show how archival materials provide suggestive insights for understanding the experiences of everyday life in borderland communities, including, but not limited to, the contemporary moment. Bárta's (this volume) creative use of Egyptological evidence reveals both the historical suggestiveness of the study of borderlands beyond the contemporary moment and the rich resources that are available in what seem like unorthodox evidentiary materials.

Importantly, too, as Ann Stoler (2002, 87–90) reminds us, inquiries into the archive ought not be concerned solely with its content but also with "its particular and sometimes peculiar form." Here, Stoler is concerned with not taking categories for granted. As she expands, we must attend to knowledge production as a social process where archives are to be thought of as "monuments of states as well as sites of state ethnography." The case studies herein begin to implode the taken-for-grantedness of received categorization and evidence and elaborate its residues as contributing to understanding processes of boundary formation and social exclusion.

Stoler's insights also are suggestive in explanations of difference where borders convey a social imaginary of exclusion. As she notes in her collaboration with Frederick Cooper (1997, 4) a "grammar of difference" is accomplished through technologies of rule that map territories socially and geographically and that, under colonialism, "helped define moral superiority and maintain cultural differences... [of legitimacy and] violence. Such relations of difference, the logic of border exclusions, undergird "notions of citizenship, sovereignty, and participation," arenas of conflict and negotiation characteristic of borderlands and central to the offerings in this volume.

In sum, this multidisciplinary collection offers both contemporary comparisons and historical reimaginings of borderland communities. Engaging key concepts that animate analyses of borderlands—state, nation, community, identity, and subjectivity—each contribution reveals the complex transactions that are embodied in state and national formations, communities, and other social collectivities and identities. Substantively, the chapters offer historical and contemporary readings of the borderland, highlighting boundary formation in ways that anticipate the nation-state system and that we take as self-evident; the complex terrain of imperial negotiations and the often contradictory sets of generational desires that are forged or left unmet over processes of negotiation; the tensions and contradictions that accompany financial, commodity, and population movements; and identity formations among displaced and mobile populations. This choice of temporal and substantive diversity constitutes the core of the collection's overall argument: that borderlines and borderlands are both the background and the field of evolving processes of community making and identify formation, processes that characterize all social life framed by relations of power.

Notes

1. Here one might think of communities differentiated by class, gender, ethnicity, sexuality, and the like, collectivities not dependent on a nation-state system.

2. Challenges to boundary maintenance and control may be most forcibly punished in these areas because control is contradictorily enacted in and on the borderland. While populations living on the border may be least legible and controllable by centers of power, their transgressions often are among the most threatening to national order, boundary maintenance, and state sovereignty. See also Tilly 2004.

3. To be sure, connections with and across the border are not delimited to those living proximate to it, but in important ways border communities likely differ from those more centrally located within the nation-state. It is on their distinctiveness that our attention is focused.

4. Agamben (1998: 126–34) offers a challenging engagement with Arendt by engaging the tensions between *homme* and *citoyen*.

5. Such a claim need not ignore or fail to appreciate the rich literature on nationalism, but as we have learned over the past few decades, the building of national identity and the routine (Billing 1997) as well as more orthodox interpretations of nationalism recognize it as a political project attendant to the power and interests that constitute state formation. The literature and debate are voluminous, but a few key sources include Benedict Anderson 1983; Chatterjee 1993; Eley and Suny 1996; Gellner 1983; Hutchinson and Smith 1994; Kohn 1955; and Winichakul 1994.

CONCLUSION
Borderland Policy
Keeping Up with Change

I. William Zartman

The two theses of this work—that movement rather than any particular model is the central characteristic of borderlands, and that in this characteristic movement borderlands always prepare for the next move at the same time as they respond to the last one—pose both problems and bases for a policy-relevant understanding of appropriate ways to deal with the borderland condition. It would be easier to handle borderlands if they would only hold still and if there were just one appropriate policy to deal with them once and for all, two conditions that stand at the opposite of the defining characteristics of borderlands. Yet policymakers have to deal with the situation in their borderlands at any particular time, resolving its problems and handling its challenges. Whether in Pharaonic Egypt, the Ottoman Balkans, contemporary South Asia, Israel-Palestine, or the U.S. Southwest, policies have to be devised to meet the challenges of the moment. But this needs to be done within a recognition that the situation reflects characteristics of fluidity and direction, that solutions have their consequences, and that policy needs to look ahead as well as behind.

An understanding of borderlands as dynamic social processes (both active and passive) has policy relevance, for human organisms and power centers alike will have to deal with the moving phenomenon and need to have a full appreciation of it to participate in it and react to it appropriately. The prime lesson for policy is to appreciate the changing nature of borderlands rather than trying to conceive of them or impose on them a fixed reality. Sharp impositions create their own reactions, making impositions even more difficult and starting new dynamics.

POLICIES

Given these characteristics, previous millennia and present dilemmas do not indicate specific policies but rather afford general insights that can serve as a context for policymakers dealing with the problems of the moment. Many of these insights simply emphasize the importance of paying attention to borderlands in their own right, as a subject of policy; other refer to more defined characteristics of the regions.

1. Borderlands have as much sociopolitical meaning as borders. Political attempts to end a state at its geographical limits create a transborder socioeconomic area or borderland whose nature has to be examined and understood if the boundary is to be maintained. The fact that there is so much literature on boundaries and so little on borderlands can easily mislead policymakers into thinking that it is the line rather than the space that matters and that the line can be defended without consideration of the space on either side. Although the preceding chapters focused on borderlands as their topic, their discussion makes it clear that the line had an impact on the region and the region gave meaning to the line. Whether the policy of the state is to impose a hard line (a black-and-white model) or a soft zone (a grey model) or some mixture in between, it meets the reaction of the borderlands, and the ensuing dynamics determine whether the border "works" or not.

Regardless of the central or national view of things, the borderland will continue to pursue its ways and reassert itself, like water seeping under the door. It is generally better for the state to give such local tendencies some room, lest they turn directly subversive to the policies that try to inhibit them. Sometimes, it is important for the states to simply "let go" and let the local-level administrators and border guards have autonomy and flexibility in border affairs. They know the area better than imported officials, and given leeway, they can also then be coopted to be better agents for the state. Centralization of border guards tends to encourage escalation of events rather than giving cross-border conflict resolution a chance. Borderland control of borderland affairs undermines the simplistic understandings of ethnicity and political participation and contributes to a more sophisticated understanding of the overt and subtle meanings of ethnicity and nation. Relationships between ethnicity, nationalism, imperial systems and local cultures, and statecraft and state capacity are complex anywhere, but arguably more so in borderland regions.

2. The second lesson is that policy needs to anticipate the consequent reac-

tions and not just address the present situation, whatever it is. Borderland policy needs to think ahead, dealing with the current challenge but also anticipating the impact of the policy and the changes that ensue. While it may be true of any policy, it is more strongly characteristic of borderlands that problem-solving solutions are also problem-creating solutions. The nature of the region, more or less artificially divided between two (or more) evolving power centers, bears a continual evolution from one stage to another. Faced with a hostile neighbor, are the two sides sharply divided? Commercial and other transactions will leak across the divide, challenge it, and create a group or class of middlemen. Faced with traditional transborder movement, is the separating line made an open door? The richer or stronger side will become saturated or subverted and will feel a need to close the door. Faced with local life and identity far away, does the center hold the periphery loosely, keeping control by allowing local identities and transactions to flourish in the borderland? When the center weakens, the borderland will spawn pressures to become its own center. Faced with assertions of borderland identity, does the center occupy the borderland and hold it tight? The guards may make common cause with the periphery, or the periphery may move to the center and take it over.

Policymakers cannot be expected to avoid such policies because of possible later consequences, or else they would be able to make no policy at all. But they should be aware of likely consequences down the road where dealing with one situation creates a new one that needs to be dealt with, keeping an eye out for signs of the appearance of consequences, and should lighten the weight of the present solution so as not to provoke the anticipated backlash. The land of the Jordan River is unfortunately rich with examples. Israeli policies toward the Palestinian-occupied borderlands in the 1970s and 1980s after the June War of 1967 consisted of carrots or employment opportunities for cooperative Palestinians and sticks or imprisonment for rebellious others; but by 1987 employed Palestinians saw the disparity with employed Israelis and the unchanged distance to their goal of liberation and so erupted into the first *intifada* in 1987, a foreseeable reaction of relative deprivation in an improved but stymied evolution. One borderland policy had created an unanticipated reaction that the initial policy had sought to deter. Policies must be flexible enough to change with the changing (as we say, fluid) boundaries that they affect and effect. That these boundaries are changed by these policies is also an eventuality that they must consider.

3. The third lesson is that demarcation and permeability are the two requirements for an effective border, what Thomas Friedman (2006) has called "high

fences, big gates." People on both sides of the border need to know with certainty where the line is, and they need to be able to cross it. If not, they will make their own way, and the process will take on a life outside of the proscribed policy. States need to create a border that balances security with openness. The two are not obvious complements, but they need not be mutually exclusive. Uncertain, contested, and undemarcated boundaries constitute the largest single cause of interstate wars, and they play havoc with the already fluid dynamics of their borderlands. But impenetrable boundaries sharpen the artificial nature of the lines that separate neighbors; borderlands need to breathe, outside the political restraints of the line of sovereignty. If undemarcated boundaries cause wars, impenetrable boundaries cause incidents. People will risk their lives to cross them, and the borderlands become a bastion of refuge. Obviously the pressure is one-sided: Americans do not cross the desert to get to Mexico, and Spaniards do not scale accordion wire fences to get into Morocco. But there is traffic going both ways—south to spend money, north to earn it—and that traffic links the borderlands on both sides in their heterogeneity.

While demarcation and permeability are undisputed values, they also pose their own contradictions. Pursuit of both in the extreme can cause incoherence and undercutting. As the Romo-Márquez chapter points out, U.S. policy at the Mexican border seeks to encourage, or at least facilitate, traditional as well as touristic movement between the two countries, while at the same time tightening border controls against smuggling of people and goods. In the end, because one policy demands active measures over the other's passive measures, the U.S. overemphasizes border enforcement at the expense of border crossing. The smuggling is an unintended consequence of the free flow; the hardening of the border creates new and larger tensions in U.S.-Mexican relations that the two friendly capitals do not seek, but it can lead to a backlash creating a new situation to be resolved. A four-pronged policy measure of enforcement, a guest worker program, closer cooperation with Mexico, and improved efficiencies for legal transit was repeatedly introduced in Congress in the 1990s and early 2000s but still awaits adoption. Similar analyses can be made of the other borderlands studied, and many more.

CHANGE

Globalization reaffirms and changes all this. Borderlands will continue to exist, as they have since the Early Kingdoms, showing the same characteristics as before and evoking the same sort of policy responses and recommendations. But they will also be leapfrogged, so that in important ways the centers will be "borderlandified" while at the same time keeping their distinctiveness and relationship with their peripheries.

Since borderlands are sociopolitical or socioeconomic phenomena, they are essentially local reactions to past and present stimuli, and their memories are long. Traces of the Marches between the Dukedoms of Normandy and Brittany in France or of the Border States between North and South in the United States can still be found, on the ground and in people's behaviors, even though the causes and power relations that formed them are long gone. Some borderland behaviors may be outmoded in some places—it is unlikely that borderlands will break away from the center in many parts of the world, notably Europe and the Americas—but that is not the only eventuality for borderlands, and it still remains a possibility among others in some areas—notably Southern Sudan, Casamance, Nagaland, Tamil Eelam, among others. As remarkable a measure as the Schengen Agreement, the 1985 European Union convention that moved customs and immigration to the outer limits of the EU for twelve countries, certainly weakened the importance of some borderlands within its boundaries but did not eliminate them, and it merely moved full-force boundaries to the EU's rim, pushing out borderlands along with it. NAFTA has certainly not eliminated the Tex-Mex borderlands, to the contrary, and NAFTA is not the EU, as the Stea, Zech, and Grey chapter emphasizes.

On the other hand, globalization makes borderlanders of us all, as it pokes through sovereignty, leaps over boundaries, implants peripherarians in the center and centralities in the peripheries. The global South struggles not to become simply a borderland of the North, as the North outsources many of its basic functions—manufacturing, services, peacekeeping—to economic, communications, and military mercenaries. The South repays the Northern invasions under the colonial era with a reverse flow that moves North African and Anatolian borderlands to the suburbs of Paris, Brussels, Berlin, and Vienna, just as the Mexican borderlands have moved to sections of Washington and New York.

Globalization means interpenetration but not homogenization (not yet and probably never). It makes for a lumpy stew, and some of these lumps are borderlands. Some are along borders, as noted, where they always were, as far back as the Middle Kingdoms of Egypt. Others have broken loose and floated to the center, where they anchor themselves on the outskirts or even on the inside of the city, with all the characteristics of social organization, identity, commerce, functional differentiation, and outpost occupation that they had when they were borderlands. It is here that the first policy lesson reaffirms itself, that borderlands, wherever they may be located, need to be understood in their complexity. Exclusively treating the floating borderland in the globalizing world as merely an ethnic enclave or a class ghetto or a homeland extension or any other of the many elements in its nature is to ignore the lesson of Lusignan Cyprus, Ottoman Moldovia, or migrant Kashmiris that borderland populations are many things. Rather than a simplistic understanding of ethnicity and political participation, a more sophisticated understanding of the overt and subtle meanings of ethnicity and nation and of the relationships between ethnicity, nationalism, imperial systems and local cultures, and state craft and state capacity is necessary for dealing with the challenging phenomenon of globalized borderlands.

In that situation, the same sources of dynamics—evolution of power centers, imposition of new boundaries, shifts in horizontal and vertical social divisions—operate on the borderlands people, wherever they are. The analysis has not been outmoded but extended. In this situation, the borderlands effect still acts in relation to power centers, situated in neighborhoods around cities rather than being contained in territories around states. Like the townships on the edges of apartheid South African cities or the Palestinian ghettos on the edge of Israel, they act as borderlands affected by shifts in power, boundaries, and social divisions.

REFERENCES

Abbott, Andrew. 1995. "Things of Boundaries." *Social Research* 64 (4): 857–82.
Abu El-Haj, Nadia. 2001. *Facts on the Ground: Archaeological Practice and Territorial Self-Fashioning in Israeli Society.* Chicago: University of Chicago Press.
Abu Rayya, Khalil. 1980. *Ramallah: Ancient and Modern.* Ramallah: American Federation of Ramallah.
Ackleson, Jason. 2004. "Unpacking Borders—Review." *International Studies Review* 6 (2): 324–26.
———. 2005. "Border Security in Risk Society." *Journal of Borderlands Studies* 20 (1): 1–22.
Acuna, Rodolfo. 1988. *Occupied America: A History of Chicanos.* New York: HarperCollins.
Adamson, Joni. 2002. "Encounter with a Mexican Jaguar." In *Globalization on the Line: Culture, Capital, and Citizenship at U.S. Borders,* edited by Claudia Sadowski-Smith, 221–40. New York: Palgrave.
Agamben, Georgio. 1998. *Homo Sacer: Sovereign Power and Bare Life.* Stanford: Stanford University Press.
Ahituv, S. 1984. *Canaanite Toponyms in Ancient Egyptian Documents.* Jerusalem: Magnes Press.
Alba, Richard D. 1990. *Ethnic Identity: The Transformation of White America.* New Haven: Yale University Press.
Alba, Richard D., and Victor Nee. 2003. *Remaking the American Mainstream: Assimilation and Contemporary Immigration.* Cambridge, Mass.: Harvard University Press.
Amiran, R., I. Beit Arieh, and J. Glass. 197. "The Interrelationship between Arad and Sites in Southern Sinai in the Early Bronze Age." *Israel Exploration Journal* 23 (4): 193–97.
Anderson, Benedict. 1983. *Imagined Communities: Reflections on the Origin and Spread of Nationalism.* London: Verso.
———. 1991. *Imagined Communities: Reflections on the Origin and Spread of Nationalism.* Rev. ed. London: Verso.
———. 1998. *The Specter of Comparisons: Nationalism, South-East Asia, and the World.* New York: Verso.
Anderson, M. S. 1966. *The Eastern Question, 1774–1923: A Study in International Relations.* London: Macmillan.

Andreas, Peter. 2000. *Border Games: Policing the U.S.-Mexico Divide*. Ithaca: Cornell University Press.

———. 2003. "A Tale of Two Borders: The U.S.-Mexico and U.S.-Canada Lines after 9-11." Center for U.S.-Mexican Studies, University of California, San Diego. http://repositories.cdlib.org/usmex/andreas, accessed April 13, 2009.

Anzaldúa, Gloria. 1987. *Borderlands–La Frontera: The New Mestiza*. San Francisco: Aunt Lute Books.

Appadurai, Arjun. 1996. "Sovereignty without Territory: Notes for a Postnational Geography." In *The Geography of Identity*, edited by Patricia Yaeger. Ann Arbor: University of Michigan Press.

Arendt, Hannah. 1994 [1966]. *The Origins of Totalitarianism*. New York: Harcourt Brace.

Arnold, Do., F. Arnold, and S. Allen. 1995. "Canaanite Imports at Lisht, the Middle Kingdom Capital of Egypt." *Egypt and the Levant* 5:13–32.

Arreola, Daniel D., and James R. Curtis. 1993. *The Mexican Border Cities: Landscape Anatomy and Place Personality*. Tucson: University of Arizona Press.

Asiwaju, Anthony Ijaola. 1985. "Partitioned Culture Areas: A Checklist." In *Partitioned Africans: Ethnic Relations across Africa's International Boundaries, 1884–1984*, edited by A. I. Asiwaju, 252–59. London: Christopher Hurst; Lagos: University of Lagos Press.

———. 1996. "Borderlands in Africa: A Comparative Research Perspective with Particular Reference to Western Europe." In *African Boundaries, Barriers, Conduits and Opportunities*, edited by Paul Nugent and A. I. Asiwaju, 253–65. London: Pinter.

———. 2000. "Fragmentation or Integration: What Future for African Boundaries?" In *Borderlands under Stress*, edited by Martin Pratt and Janet Allison Brown. International Boundary Studies Series. The Hague: Kluwer Law International.

Atif Pasha, *Yemen Tarihi*. 1908 [1326]. Darsaadet: Manzume-i Efkar Matbaası.

Attias, Jean-Christophe, and Esther Benbassa. 2003. *Israel, the Impossible Land*. Translated by Susan Emanuel. Stanford: Stanford University Press.

Bach, Robert L. 1978. "Mexican Immigration and the American State." *International Migration Review* 12 (Winter): 536–58.

Baines, J., and J. Málek 1980. *Atlas of Ancient Egypt*. New York: Facts on File.

Baines, J., and N. Yoffee. 1998. "Order, Legitimacy, and Wealth in Ancient Egypt and Mesopotamia." In *Archaic States*, edited by G. M. Feinman and J. Marcus, 199–260. Santa Fe, N.M.: School of American Research Press.

Balfet, Helene. 1965. "Ethnographical Observations in North Africa and Archaeological Interpretation: The Pottery of the Maghreb." In *Ceramics and Man*, edited by Frederick R. Matson, 161–77. Chicago: Aldine.

Baratz, Joseph. 1957. *A Village by the Jordan*. New York: Sharon Books.

Bard, K. A. 2008. *An Introduction to the Archaeology of Ancient Egypt*. Oxford: Blackwell.
Barkey, Karen. 1994. *Bandits and Bureaucrats: The Ottoman Route to State Centralization*. Ithaca: Cornell University Press.
———. 2008. *Empire of Difference: The Ottomans in Comparative Perspective*. New York: Cambridge University Press.
Bárta, M. 2001. "The Interactions of Egypt, Sinai and Southern Palestine during the Late Old and the Middle Kingdom (EB IV–MB IIA)." *ASOR Newsletter* 51 (3/Fall): 12–14.
———. 2003. *Sinuhe, the Bible, and the Patriarchs*. Prague: Set Out.
Barth, Frederik. 1964. "Competition and Symbiosis in North East Baluchistan." *Folk* 6 (1).
———, ed. *Ethnic Groups and Boundaries: The Social Organization of Culture Difference*. Boston: Little, Brown.
Bar-Yossef, et al. 1986. "Nawamis and Habitation Sites near Gebel Gunna, Southern Sinai." *Israel Exploration Journal* 36 (3–4):121–67.
Basch, Linda D., Nina Glick Schiller, and Cristina Szanton Blanc, eds. 1994. *Nations Unbound: Transnational Projects, Global Predicaments and Deterriorialized Nation-States*. New York: Gordon and Breach.
Baud, Michiel, and Willem van Schendel. 1997. "Toward a Comparative History of Borderlands." *Journal of World History* 8 (2): 211–42.
Bayart, Jean-François. 1996. *The State in Africa: The Politics of the Belly*. London: Longman.
Beck, Ulrich. 1998. "Politics of Risk Society." In *The Politics of Risk Society*, edited by Jane E. Franklin. Cambridge, Mass.: Polity.
Beihammer, Alexander. 2006. "Byzantine Chancery Traditions in Frankish Cyprus: The Case of the Vatican *MS Palatinus Graecus 367*." In *Identités Croisées en un Milieu Méditerranéen: Le cas de Chypre*, edited by Sabine Fourrier and Gilles Grivaud, 301–15. Mont-Saint-Aignan Cedex: Publications des Universités de Rouen et du Havre.
Beith Arieh, I. 1974. "An Early Bronze Age II Site at Nabi Salah in Southern Sinai." *Tel Aviv* 1: 144–56.
———. 1981. "An Early Bronze Age II Site Near Sheikh ʿAwad in Southern Sinai." *Tel Aviv* 8: 95–127.
Belausteguigoitia, Juan Carlos, and Luis F. Guadarrama. 1997. "United States Mexico Relations: Environmental issues." In *Coming Together? Mexico-U.S. Relations*, edited by Barry P. Bosworth, Susan M. Collins, and Nora Claudia Lustig. Washington, D.C.: Brookings.
Bennafla, Karine. 1999. "La fin des territoires nationaux? État et commerce frontalier en Afrique centrale." *Politique Africaine*, no. 73: 25–49.
Ben-Tor, A. 1991. "New Light on the Relations between Egypt and Southern Palestine during the Early Bronze Age." *Bulletin of the American Schools of Oriental Research* 281: 3–10.

———, ed. 1992. *The Archaeology of Ancient Israel*. New Haven: Yale University Press and Open University of Israel.
Benvenisti, Meron. 2000. *Sacred Landscape: The Buried History of the Holy Land since 1948*. Berkeley: University of California Press.
Biggs, Michael. 1999. "Putting the State on the Map: Cartography, Territory, and European State Formation." *Comparative Studies in Society and History* 41 (2/April): 374–405.
Billing, Michael. 1997. *Banal Nationalism*. London: Sage.
Bisharat, George E. 1997. "Exile to Compatriot: Transformations in the Social Identity of Palestinian Refugees in the West Bank." In *Culture, Power, Place: Explorations in Critical Anthropology*, edited by Akhil Gupta and James Ferguson. Durham, N.C.: Duke University Press.
Black, Jeremy. 1997. *Maps and History: Constructing Images of the Past*. New Haven: Yale University Press.
Blumi, Isa. 2000. "Looking beyond the Tribe: Abandoning Paradigms to Write Social History in Yemen during World War I." *New Perspectives on Turkey* 22 (Summer): 117–45.
———. 2003. "Thwarting the Ottoman Empire: Smuggling through the Empire's New Frontiers in Ottoman Yemen and Albania, 1878–1910." *International Journal of Turkish Studies* 9 (September): 251–70.
———. 2004. "Reconsidering the Social History of Ottoman Yemen, 1872–1918." In *Counter Narratives: History, Contemporary Society and Politics in Saudi Arabia and Yemen*, edited by Madawi al-Rasheet and Robert Vitalis, 103–19. New York: Palgrave, 2004.
———. 2007. "Seeing Beyond the River Drin: Sarajevo, Ottoman Albanians and Imperial Rivalry in the Balkans after 1878," *Kakanien* (2007): 1–9.
———. 2008. *Redefining Balkan Nationalism: Albanian Identities at the End of the Ottoman Era*. London: I. B. Tauris.
Boase, T. S. R. 1977. "The Arts in Cyprus: An Ecclesiastical Art." In *A History of the Crusades*, edited by Kenneth M. Setton. Vol. 4. *The Art and Architecture of the Crusader States*, edited by Harry W. Hazard, 165–95. Madison: University of Wisconsin Press.
Boggs, S. Whittemore. 1940. *International Boundaries*. New York: Columbia University Press.
Boué, Amie. 1840. *La Turquie d'Europe, ou observations sur la géographie, la géologie, l'histoire naturelle, la statistique, les moeurs, les coutumes, l'archéologie, l'agriculture, l'industrie, le commerce, les gouvernements divers, le clergé, l'histoire, et l'état politique de cet empire*. 4 vols. Paris.
———. 1854. *Recueil d'itinéraires dans la Turquie d'Europe, détails géographiques, topographiques, et statistiques sur cet empire*. Vienne: Libraire de L'Académie Impériale des Sciences.

Bourriau, J. 1990. "Canaanite Jars from New Kingdom Deposits at Memphis, Kom el-Rabia." *Eretz-Israel* 21: 18–26.

Boyarin, Jonathan. 1996. *Palestine and Jewish History: Criticism at the Borders of Ethnography*. Minneapolis: University of Minnesota Press.

Brailsford, H. N. 1906. *Macedonia, Its Races and Their Future*. London: Methuen.

Brancoff, [Dimitar Mishev]. 1905. *La Macédoine et sa population chrétienne*. Paris.

Brandl, B. 1992. "Evidence for Egyptian Colonisation in the Southern Coastal Plain and Lowlands of Canaan during the EB I Period." In *The Nile Delta in Transition: 4th-3rd Millennium B.C.*, edited by E. C. M. van den Brink, 441–76. Tel Aviv: Israel Exploration Society.

Bratton, Michael, and Nicolas van de Walle. 1997. *Democratic Experiments in Africa: Regime Transitions in Comparative Perspective*. Cambridge: Cambridge University Press.

Braude, Benjamin, and Bernard Lewis, eds. 1982. *Christians and Jews in the Ottoman Empire: The Functioning of a Plural Society*. New York: Holmes and Meier.

Brett, E. A. 2006. "State Failure and Success in Uganda and Zimbabwe: The Logic of Political Decay and Reconstruction in Africa." CSRC working paper no. 78. London: Crisis States Research Centre.

Bridges, Levi. 2008. "Border Walkabout." *Inside Mexico* 18 (June): 12–17.

Brink, Edwin C. M. van den, and Thomas E. Levy, eds. 2002. *Egypt and the Levant: Interrelations from the 4th through the Early 3rd Millennium BCE*, London: Leicester University Press.

Brown, Christopher. 2003. "New Directions in Binational Water Resource Management in the U.S.-Mexico Borderlands." *Social Science Journal* 40: 555–72.

Brown, Timothy C. 1997. "The Fourth Member of NAFTA: The U.S.-Mexico Border." *Annals of the American Academy of Political and Social Science* 550: 105–21.

Brownlie, Ian. 1979. *African Boundaries*. Berkeley: University of California Press.

Bury, G. Wyman. 1911. *The Land of Uz*. London: Macmillan.

Bustamante, Jorge A. 1973. "The Historical Context of Undocumented Mexican Immigration to the United States." *Aztlan* 3: 257–81.

Cadırcı, Musa. 1988. "Renovations in the Ottoman Army, 1792–1869." *Revue Internationale d'Histoire Militaire* 67: 87–102.

———. 1997. *Tanzimat Döneminde Anadolu Kentleri'nin Sosyal ve Ekonomik Yapısı*. Ankara: Türk Tarih Kurumu.

Calva, Jose Luis. 2003. NAFTA and Peasant Protests. *Voices of Mexico*, no. 63: 50–53.

Campbell, Howard. 2005. "A Tale of Two Families: The Mutual Construction of 'Anglo' and Mexican Ethnicities along the U.S.-Mexico Border." *Bulletin of Latin American Research* 24 (1): 23–43.

Carter, Paul. 1987. *The Road to Botany Bay: Exploration in Landscape and History*. Chicago: University of Chicago Press.

Chabal, Patrick, and Jean-Pascal Daloz. 1999. *Africa Works: Disorder as Political Instrument*. Oxford: James Currey; Bloomington: Indiana University Press.

Chandler, Andrea. 1998. *Institutions of Isolation: Border Controls in the Soviet Union and Its Successor States, 1917–1993*. Montreal: McGill-Queens University Press.

Chatterjee, Partha. 1993. *The Nation and Its Fragments: Colonial and Postcolonial Histories*. Princeton: Princeton University Press.

Chatterji, Joya. 1999. "The Fashioning of a Frontier: The Radcliffe Line and Bengal's Border Landscape." *Modern Asian Studies* 33: 185–242.

Chen, Xiangming. 2005. *As Borders Bend: Transnational Spaces on the Pacific Rim*. Lanham, Md.: Rowman and Littlefield.

Clarke, James Franklin. 1988. *Pen and the Sword: Studies in Bulgarian History*. Ed. Dennis P. Hupchick. Boulder: East European Monographs.

Collins, David. 1985. "Partitioned Culture Areas and Smuggling: The Hausa and the Groundnut Trade across the Nigeria-Niger Border from the Mid-1930s to the Mid-1970s." In *Partitioned Africans: Ethnic Relations across Africa's International Boundaries 1884–1984*, edited by A. I. Asiwaju, 195–221. London: C. Hurst; Lagos: University of Lagos Press.

Colocotronis, V. 1919. *La Macédoine et l'Hellenisme, étude historique et ethnologique*. Paris: Berger-Levraut.

Cornelius, Wayne. 1976. "Mexican Migration to the United States: The View from Rural Sending Communities." Working paper: Center for International Studies, M.I.T.

Couisinéry, E. M. 1831. *Voyage dans la Macédoine, contenant les recherches sur l'histoire, la géographie et les antiquités de ce pays*. Paris: Imprimerie Royale.

Cvijić, J. 1906. *Remarks on the Ethnography of the Macedonian Slavs*. London: Horace Cox.

Czerny, E. 1999. *Tell el-Dabba IX. Eine Plansiedlung des frühen Mitleren Reiches*. Denkschriften der Österreichischen Akademie der Wissenschaften 16. Vienna: Österreichische Akademie der Wissenschaften.

Dajani-Shakeel, H. 1990. "Natives and Franks in Palestine: Perceptions and Interaction." In *Conversion and Continuity: Indigenous Christians in Islamic Lands, Eighth to Eighteenth Centuries*, edited by M. Gervers and R. J. Bikhazi, 161–84. Papers in Medieval Studies 9. Toronto: Pontifical Institute of Medieval Studies.

Dakin, Douglas. 1972. *The Unification of Greece, 1770–1923*. New York: St. Martin's Press.

Das, Veena, and Deborah Poole. 2004. "The State and Its Margins." In *Anthropology in the Margins of the State*. edited by Veena Das and Deborah Poole. Santa Fe, N.M.: School of American Research Press.

Davison, Roderic H. 1983. "The Ottoman-Greek Frontier Question, 1876–1882, from Ottoman Records." In *Nineteenth Century Ottoman Diplomacy and Reforms*, edited by Roderic H. Davison.

---. 1999. "The Ottoman Empire and the Congress of Berlin." In *Nineteenth Century Ottoman Diplomacy and Reforms*, edited by Roderic H. Davison. Istanbul: Isis Press.

Dawisha, Karen, and Bruce Parrott, eds. 1997. *The End of Empire?* London: Sharpe.

de Mello Lemos, Maria Carmen, and Antonio Luna. 1999. Public Participation in the BECC: Lessons from the Acaferico Project, Nogales, Sonora. *Journal of Borderland Studies* 14 (1): 43-46.

Denman, Catalina A., and Andrew W. Nichols. 1991. Crossing the Border for Bargain Medicine: Findings of the Primary Health Care Review in Ambos Nogales. *Carnegie Quarterly* 36 (1-4): 8-10.

Denzin, Norman K., and Yvonna S. Lincoln, eds. 1994. *Handbook of Qualitative Research*. Thousand Oaks, Calif.: Sage.

Dever, W. G. 1985a. "Village Planning at Be'er Resisim and Socio-Economic Structures in EB IV Palestine." *Eretz-Israel* 18: 18-28.

---. 1985b. "From the End of the Early Bronze Age to the Beginning of the Middle Bronze Age." In *Biblical Archaeology Today*, edited by J. Aviram et al., 113-35. Jerusalem: Israel Exploration Society.

De Vogüé, Melchior. 1973. *Les églises de la Terre Sainte*. Toronto: Presses de l'Université de Toronto.

Dimara, K. Th. 1986. *Kōnstantinos Paparrēgopoulos, ē epochē tou, ē Zōē tou, to ergo tou*. Athens: Morfotiko Idryma Ethnikis Trapezis.

Dodd, Peter, and Halim Barakat. 1969. *Rivers without Bridges. A Study of the 1967 Palestinian Arab Refugees*. Beirut: Institute for Palestine Studies.

Donnan, Hastings, and Thomas Wilson, eds., 1994. *Border Approaches: Anthropological Perspectives on Frontiers*. Lanham, Md.: University Press of America.

---. 1999. *Borders: Frontiers of Identity, Nation and State*. Oxford: Berg.

Doolittle, W. 1998. "Challenging Regional Stereotypes: The Case of Northern Mexico." *Southwest Geographer* 2: 15-39.

Douglass, William. 1998. "A Western Perspective on an Eastern Interpretation of Where North Meets South: Pyrenean Borderland Cultures." In *Border Identities: Nation and State at International Frontiers*, edited by Thomas M. Wilson and Hastings Donnan. Cambridge: Cambridge University Press.

---. 2002. Foreword to *Possible Paradises: Emigration to the Americas*, edited by José Manuel Azcona Pastor. Reno: University of Nevada Press.

Driault, Edouard. 1921. *La question d'Orient depuis ses origines jusqu'à la paix de Sèvres*. Paris: Librairie Félix Alcan.

Driault, Edouard, and Michel Lheriter. 1925. *Histoire diplomatique de la Grèce de 1821 à nos jours*. Vols. 1-3. Paris: Les Presses Universitaires de France.

Efthimiou, Miltiades B. 1975. "Greeks and Latins of Thirteenth Century Cyprus." *Greek Orthodox Theological Review* 20: 35-52.

———. 1987. *Greeks and Latins on Cyprus in the Thirteenth Century*. Brookline, Mass: Hellenic College Press.
Ellenblum, Ronnie. 1998. *Frankish Rural Settlement in the Latin Kingdom of Jerusalem*. Cambridge: Cambridge University Press.
———. 2002. "Were There Borders and Borderlines in the Middle Ages? The Example of the Latin Kingdom of Jerusalem." In *Medieval Frontiers: Concepts and Practices*, edited by David Abulafia and Nora Berend, 105–19. Aldershot, Hampshire, U.K.: Ashgate.
———. 2007. *Crusader Castles and Modern Histories*. Cambridge: Cambridge University Press, 2007.
Elton, Hugh. 1996. *Frontiers of the Roman Empire*. Bloomington: Indiana University Press.
Eley, Geoff, and Ronald Suny. 1996. *Becoming National: A Reader*. Oxford: Oxford University Press.
Encyclopædia Britannica. 1910. "Macedonia." Vol. 17. 11th ed., p. 216.
Englebert, Pierre, Stacy Tarango, and Matthew Carter. 2002. "Dismemberment and Suffocation: A Contribution to the Debate on African Boundaries." *Comparative Political Studies* 35 (10): 1093–118.
Englezakis, Benedict. 1995. "Cyprus as a Stepping Stone between East and West in the Age of the Crusades: The Two Churches." In *Studies in the History of the Church of Cyprus, 4th–20th Centuries*, vol. 11, edited by Silovan and Misael Ioannou, translated by Norman Russell, 213–20. Aldershot, Hampshire, U.K.: Variorum.
Enlart, Camille. 1987. *Gothic Art and the Renaissance in Cyprus*. Translated by David Hunt. London: Trigraph in association with the A. G. Leventis Foundation.
Esse, D. L. 1989. "Secondary State Formation and Collapse in Early Bronze Age Palestine." In *l'Urbanisation de la Palestine à l'âge du Bronze ancien: Bilan et perspectives des recherches actuelles*, edited by P. de Miroschedji, 81–107. British Archaeological Reports, International Series 527. Oxford: Hadrian Books.
Ethnographische Übersichtskarte des Europäischen Orients. 1876. Berlin: D. Reimer.
Ethnological Map of European Turkey and Greece with Introductory Remarks on the Distribution of Races in the Illyrian Peninsula and Statistical Tables of Population. 1877. London: Edward Stanford. (Attributed to Ioannis Gennadius.)
Fischer, H. G. 1959. "A Scribe of the Army in a Saqqara Mastaba of the Early Fifth Dynasty." *Journal of Near Eastern Studies* 18 (4): 260–65.
———. 1963. "Varia Aegyptiaca." *Journal of the American Research Center in Egypt* 2: 17–52.
Fleming, K. E. 2004. "*Orientalism*, the Balkans and Balkan Historiography." *American Historical Review* 105.
Flynn, Donna K. 1997. "We Are the Border: Identity, Exchange, and the State along the Benin-Nigeria Border." *American Ethnologist* 24 (2): 311–30.

Folda, Jaroslav. 1977. "Painting and Sculpture in the Latin Kingdom of Jerusalem, 1099–1291." In *A History of the Crusades*, edited by Kenneth M. Setton. Vol. 4: *The Art and Architecture of the Crusader States*, edited by Harry W. Hazard, 251–80. Madison: University of Wisconsin Press.

———. 1995a. *The Art of the Crusaders in the Holy Land*. Cambridge: Cambridge University Press.

———. 1995b. "Crusader Art in the Kingdom of Cyprus, c. 1275–1291: Reflections on the State of the Questions." In *Cyprus and the Crusades: Papers Given at the International Conference "Cyprus and the Crusades," Nicosia, 6–9 September, 1994*, edited by N. Coureas and Jonathan Riley-Smith, 209–37. Nicosia: Society for the Study of the Crusades and the Latin East and the Cyprus Research Centre.

———. 1996. "Crusader Art in the Twelfth Century: Reflections on Christian Multiculturalism in the Levant." In *Intercultural Contacts in the Medieval Mediterranean*, edited by Benjamin Arbel, 80–91. London: Frank Cass.

Forster, Craig B. 2005. "Overview of the Border+20 System Model Prototype: The Paso del Norte region." In *The U.S.-Mexican Border Environment: Dynamics of Human-Environment Interactions*, edited by Edward Sadalla. San Diego: San Diego State University Press.

Foucher de Chartres. 1913. *Fulcheri Carnotensis Historia Hierosolymitana (1095–1127)*. Edited by Heinrich Hagenmeyer. Heidelberg: C. Winter.

Friedman, Thomas, 2006. "High Fences, Big Gates." *International Herald Tribune*, April 6, p. 7.

Fromkin, David. 1989. *A Peace to End All Peace: Creating the Modern Middle East, 1914–1922*. New York: Henry Holt.

Fuentes, Annette, and Barbara Ehrenreich. 1984. *Women in the Global Factory*. Boston: South End Press.

Fund for Peace. 2007. *Failed States Index 2006*. Washington, D.C.: Fund for Peace. http://www.fundforpeace.org/web/index.php?option=com_content&task=view&id=104&Itemid=324, accessed April 20, 2009.

Galán, José M. 1995. *Victory and Border: Terminology Related to Egyptian Imperialism in the XVIIIth Dynasty*. Hildesheim: Gerstenberg Verlag.

Ganster, Paul. 2000. *The U.S.-Mexico Border Environment: A Road Map to a Sustainable 2020*. San Diego: San Diego State University Press.

Garcia, John. 2005. Conference presentation, University of Arizona.

Gardiner, A. H., T. E. Peet, and J. Černý. 1952. *The Inscriptions of Sinai*. London: Egypt Exploration Society.

Gavin, Ray J. 1975. *Aden under British Rule, 1839–1967*. London: C. Hurst.

Gavrilis, George. 2008. *The Dynamics of Interstate Boundaries*. New York: Cambridge University Press.

Gelber, Yoav. 2001. *Palestine 1948: War, Escape and the Emergence of the Palestinian Refugee Problem*. Brighton, U.K.: Sussex Academic Press.

Gellner, Ernest. 1983. *Nations and Nationalism*. Ithaca: Cornell University Press.

Georges, Giorgos. 1996. *He Prote Makrochronia Hellenotourkike Dienekse: To Zetema tes Ethnikotetas, 1830–1869*. Athens: Ekdoseis Kastaniote.

Gerber, James. 2007. "Border States: California, Texas, and Relations with Mexico." In) *El TLCAN y la Frontera Mexico–Estados Unidos: Aspectos Economicos*, edited by Jorge Eduardo Mendoza Cota. Mexico, D.F.: Porrua.

Gil-Har, Yitzhak. 1979. "The Separation of the East Bank from the Land of Israel." *Katedra* 12: 47–69 (Hebrew).

Gophna, R., and J. Portugali. 1988. "Settlement and Demographic Processes in Israel's Coastal Plain from the Chalcolithic to the Middle Bronze Age." *Bulletin of the American Schools of Oriental Research* 269: 11–28.

Gordon, Milton. 1964. *Assimilation in American life: The Role of Race, Religion, and National Origins*. New York: Oxford University Press.

Green, Rosario. 2005. "Address," University of Texas Campus Club, September 20.

Greenhut, Z. 1995. "EB IV Tombs and Burials in Palestine." *Tel Aviv* 22: 3–46.

Gregory, Derek. 1994. *Geographical Imaginations*. Oxford: Blackwell.

Griffiths, Ieuan. 1996. "Permeable Boundaries in Africa." In *African Boundaries: Barriers, Conduits and Opportunities*, edited by Paul Nugent and A. I. Asiwaju, 68–83. London: Pinter.

Grivaud, Gilles. 1995. "Éveil de la Nation *Chypriote* (XIIe–XVe siècles)." *Sources Travaux Historiques* 43–44: 105–16.

Gupta, Akhil, and James Ferguson. 1997. "Culture, Power, Place: Ethnography at the End of an Era." In *Culture, Power, Place: Explorations in Critical Anthropology*, edited by Akhil Gupta and James Ferguson, 1–29. Durham, N.C.: Duke University Press.

Haaland, Gunner. 1969. "Economic Determinants in Ethnic Processes." In *Ethnic Groups and Boundaries: The Social Organization of Culture Difference*, edited by Fredrik Barth. Boston: Little, Brown.

Hackett, John. 1901. *A History of the Orthodox Church of Cyprus from the Coming of the Apostles Paul and Barnabas to the Commencement of the British Occupation (A.D. 45–A.D. 1878) together with some Account of the Latin and Other Churches Existing in the Island*. London: Methuen.

Haiman, M. 1996. "Early Bronze Age IV Settlement Pattern of the Negev and Sinai Deserts: View from Small Marginal Temporary Sites." *Bulletin of the American Schools of Oriental Research* 303: 1–32.

Hall, Colin Michael. 1994. *Tourism and Politics: Policy, Power, and Place*. West Sussex, U.K.: John Wiley.

Hall, Colin Michael, and V. O'Sullivan. 1996. "Tourism, Political Stability and Violence."

In *Tourism, Crime and International Security Issues*, edited by Abraham Pizam and Yoel Mansfeld. Chichester, U.K.: Wiley.

Hanafi, Sari. 2005. "Social Capital and Refugee Repatriation: A Study of Economic and Social Transnational Kinship Networks in Palestine/Israel." In *Exile and Return: Predicaments of Palestinians and Jews*, edited by Ann M. Lesch and Ian S. Lustick. Philadelphia: University of Pennsylvania Press.

Hannig, R. 2003. *Lexica 4: Egyptian Dictionary I: Old Kingdom and First Intermediate Period.* Mainz am Rhein: Philipp von Zabern.

Hansen, Niles. 1981. *The Border Economy: Regional Development in the Southwest.* Austin: University of Texas Press.

Harley, J. B. 1988. "Maps, Knowledge, and Power." In *The Iconography of Landscape: Essays on the Symbolic Representation, Design and Use of Past Environments*," edited by Denis Cosgrove and Stephen Daniels. Cambridge: Cambridge University Press. 277–312.

Hartung, U., L. J. Exner, N. Porat, and Y. Goren 2001. *Umm el-Qaab II: Importkeramik aus dem Friedhof U in Abydos (Umm el-Qaab) und die Beziehungen ägyptens zu Vorderasien im 4. Jahrtausend v. Chr.* Mainz am Rhein: Philip von Zabern.

Hatfield Young, Susan. 1983. "Byzantine Painting in Cyprus during the Early Lusignan Period." PhD diss., Pennsylvania State University.

Havrelock, Rachel 2007a. "My Home Is over Jordan: River as Border in Israeli and Palestinian National Mythology." *National Identities* 9 (2): 114–16.

———. 2007b. "The Two Maps of Israel's Land." *Journal of Biblical Literature* 126 (6): 649–67.

Helck, W. 1962. *Die Beziehungen Ägyptens zu Vorderasien im 3. und 2. Jahrtausend v. Chr. Ägyptologische Abhandlungen 5.* Wiesbaden: Harrassowitz.

———. 1977. "Grenze, Grenzesicherung." In *Lexikon der Ägyptologie*, edited by W. Helck and W. Westendorf. Vol. 2: 896–97. Wiesbaden: Harrassowitz.

Herbst, Jeffrey. 2000. *States and Power in Africa: Comparative Lessons in Authority and Control.* Princeton: Princeton University Press.

Herzog, Lawrence A. 1990. *Where North Meets South: Cities, Space, and Politics on the U.S.-Mexican Border.* Austin: Center for Mexican American Studies, University of Texas.

Heyman, Josiah, and Howard Campbell. 2004. "Recent Research on the U.S.-Mexico Border." *Latin American Research Review* 39 (3): 205–20.

Hill, George. 1948. *A History of Cyprus.* Vol. 2: *The Frankish Period, 1192–1432.* Cambridge: Cambridge University Press.

Hirschman, Albert O. 1978. "Exit, Voice, and the State." *World Politics* 31 (1/October): 90–107.

Hitti, Phillip K., ed. and trans. 1929. *An Arab-Syrian Gentleman and Warrior in the*

Period of the Crusades: Memoirs of Usāmah ibn-Munqidh. New York: Columbia University Press.
Hoffman, M. A. 1979. *Egypt before the Pharaohs*. New York: Knopf.
Holden, Andrew. 2000. *Environment and Tourism*. New York: Routledge.
hooks, bell. 1984. *Feminist Theory: From Margin to Center*. Boston: South End Press.
Hopmann, P. Terrence. 2001. "Disintegrating States: Separating without Violence." In *Preventive Negotiation: Avoiding Conflict Escalation*, edited by I. William Zartman. Lanham, Md.: Rowman and Littlefield.
Hutchinson, John, and Anthony D. Smith, eds. 1994. *Nationalism*. Oxford: Oxford University Press.
Ilan, Zvi. 1984. *Attempts at Jewish Settlement in Trans-Jordan, 1871–1947*. Jerusalem: Yitzhak Ben-Zvi (Hebrew).
Illustrations of the Principal Varieties of the Human Race. [1850]. Arranged according to the system of Dr. Latham, with descriptive notes by Ernest Ravenstein, London: James Reynolds.
İnalcık, Halil. 1954. "Ottoman Methods of Conquest." *Studia Islamica* 2 (1954): 103–19.
———. 1973. "Application of the Tanzimat and Its Social Effects." *Archivum Ottomanicum* 5.
Ingrams, Harold. 1938. "The Exploration of the Aden Protectorate." *Geographical Review* 27 (4): 634–39.
International Boundary and Water Commission (IBWC), U.S. Section/Texas Clean Rivers Program. 2003. *2003 Regional Assessment of Water Quality in the Rio Grande Basin*. El Paso, Texas: IBWC.
Ivanoff, J. 1920. *La Question Macédonienne au point de vue historique, ethnographique et statistique*. Paris, Librairie J. Gamber.
Jacob, Harold. 1915. *Perfumes of Araby: Silhouettes of Al Yemen*. London: Martin Secker.
Jelavich, Charles, and Barbara Jelavich. 1993. *The Establishment of the Balkan National States, 1804–1920*. Seattle: University of Washington Press.
Joerg, W. L. G. 1913. "The New Boundaries of the Balkan States and Their Significance." *Bulletin of the American Geographical Society* 45: 829–30.
Johnston, Barbara R., and Gregory Button. 1994. "Human Environmental Rights Issues and the Multinational Corporation: Industrial Development in the Free Trade Zone." In *Who Pays the Price? The Sociocultural Context of Environmental Crisis*, edited by Barbara R. Johnston. Washington, D.C.: Island Press.
Jones, Dilwyn. 2000. *An Index of Ancient Egyptian Titles, Epithets and Phrases of the Old Kingdom*, Vols. 1–2, British Archaeological Reports, International Series 866 (1–2). Oxford, U.K.: Hadrian Books.
Joseph, Richard. 2003. "Africa: States in Crisis." *Journal of Democracy* 14 (3): 159–70.

Kadel, Elisabeth. 2002. "Contamination: Crossing Social Borders." *Qualitative Studies in Education* 15 (1): 33–42.

Kahler, Miles, and Barbara F. Walter, eds. 2006. *Territoriality and Conflict in an Era of Globalization*. New York: Cambridge University Press.

Kanaana, Sharif. 1993. "The Role of Women in Intifadah Legends." *Contemporary Legend* 3: 37–61.

Kanawati, N., and A. McFarlane. 1993. *Deshasha: The Tombs of Inti, Shedu and Others*. Australian Centre for Egyptology Reports no. 5. Oxford, U.K.: Aris and Phillips.

Karpat, Kemal H. 1985. *Ottoman Population, 1830–1914: Demographic and Social Characteristics*. Madison: University of Wisconsin Press.

Karpat, Kemal H., and Robert W. Zens. 2003. *Ottoman Borderlands: Issues, Personalities, and Political Changes*. Madison: University of Wisconsin Press.

Kasaba, Reşat. 1989. *The Ottoman Empire and the World Economy: The Nineteenth Century*. Albany: State University of New York Press.

Kasasis, N. 1903. *L'Hellénisme et la Macédoine*. Paris: Imprimerie de la Renaissance Latine.

Katriel, Tamar. 1997. "Remaking Place: Cultural Production in Israeli Pioneer Settlement Museum." In *Grasping Land: Space and Place in Contemporary Israeli Discourse and Experience*, edited by E. Ben-Ari and Y. Bilu, 147–75. Albany: State University of New York Press.

Kayaoğlu, Turan. 2007. "The Extension of Westphalian Sovereignty: State Building and the Abolition of Extraterritoriality." *International Studies Quarterly* 51 (3): 649–57.

Kearney, Michael. 1998. "Transnationalism in California and Mexico at the End of Empire." In *Border Identities: Nation and State at International Frontiers*, edited by Thomas W. Wilson and Hastings Connan, 117–41. Cambridge: Cambridge University Press.

Kedar, B. Z. 1998. "Latins and Oriental Christians in the Frankish Levant, 1099–1291." In *Sharing the Sacred: Religious Contacts and Conflicts in the Holy Land, First to Fifteenth Centuries CE*, edited by Arieh Kofsky and Guy G. Stroumsa, 209–22. Jerusalem: Yad Izhak Ben Zvi.

Khalifeh, Sahar. 2000. *Wild Thorns*. Translated by Trevor LeGassick and Elizabeth Fernea. New York: Interlink Books.

Khalili, Laleh. 2005. "Commemorating Contested Lands." In *Exile and Return: Predicaments of Palestinians and Jews*, edited by Ann Lesch and Ian Lustick. Philadelphia: University of Pennsylvania Press.

Kibbutz Degania Alef. 1962. *Degania through the Years: Stories of the Fifty Years of the Collective*. Tel Aviv: Devar (Hebrew).

Kofos, Evangelos. 1975. *Greece and the Eastern Crisis, 1875–1878*. Thessaloniki: Institute for Balkan Studies.

Kohn, Hans. 1955. *Nationalism, Its Meaning and History*. Princeton: Princeton University Press.

Koliopoulos, Giannes. 1987. *Brigands with a Cause: Brigandage and Irredentism in Modern-Greece, 1821–1912*. Oxford, U.K.: Clarendon Press.

Köksal, Yonca. 2002. "Local Intermediaries and Ottoman State Centralization: The Tanzimat Reforms in the Provinces of Edirne and Ankara." PhD diss., Sociology Department, Columbia University.

Kontos, Demosthenes. 1986. "Konstantinos Paparrigopoulos and the Emergence of the Idea of a Greek Nation." PhD diss., University of Cincinnati.

Kratochwil, Friedrich. 1986. "Of Systems, Boundaries and Territoriality: An Inquiry into the Formation of the State System." *World Politics* 39 (1): 27–52.

Kyrris, Costas. 1985. *History of Cyprus*. Nicosia: Nicocles.

Lamont, Michele. 2000. *The Dignity of Working Men: Morality and the Boundaries of Race, Class, and Immigration*. New York: Russell Sage Foundation; Cambridge, Mass.: Harvard University Press.

Laredo Development Foundation. 2002. *Location and Population*. Laredo, Texas: Laredo Development Foundation.

Larémont, Ricardo René. 2005. "Borders, States, and Nationalism." In *Borders, Nationalism, and the African State*, edited by Ricardo René Larémont. Boulder, Colo.: Lynne Rienner.

Lavie, Smadar, and Ted Swedenborg, eds. 1996. *Displacement, Diaspora and Geographies of Identity*. Durham, N.C.: Duke University Press.

Lefebvre, Henri. 1991. *The Production of Space*. Malden, Mass.: Blackwell.

Levitt, Peggy. 2001. *The Transnational Villagers*. Berkeley: University of California Press.

Levitt, Peggy, and Mary C. Waters, eds. 2002. *The Changing Face of Home: The Transnational Lives of the Second Generation*. New York: Russell Sage Foundation.

Levy, Gideon. 1999. "More Than Meets the Eye." *Ha'aretz* online newspaper, September 3.

Levy, T. E., et al. 1997. "Egyptian-Canaanite Interaction at Nahal Tillah, Israel (ca. 4500–3000 B.C.): An Interim Report on the 1994–1995 Excavations." *Bulletin of the American Schools of Oriental Research* 307 (August):1–51.

Lewis, Gerald Shane. 2004. "Prospects for Expanded Alternative Tourism in Los Cumbres de Monterrey National Park Region, Nuevo Leon and Coahuila, Mexico." Master's thesis, Texas State University, 2004.

Lewitsky, Miranda. 2002. "Characteristics of a Successful Community Cooperative: A Case Studying the Community of Alta Cimas, El Cielo Biosphere, Tamaulipas, Mexico." Master's thesis, Southwest Texas State University.

Liakos, Antonis. 2001. "The Construction of National Time: The Making of the Modern Greek Historical Imagination." *Mediterranean Historical Review* 16: 27–42.

Lorey, David E. 1999. *The U.S.-Mexican Border in the Twentieth Century*. Wilmington, Del.: Scholarly Resources.

Lowry, Heath. 2008. *Shaping of the Ottoman Balkans, 1350–1550*. Istanbul: Bahçeşehir University Publications.

Luhman, Niklas. 1982. "Territorial Borders as System Boundaries." In *Cooperation and Conflict in Border Areas*, edited by Raimondo Strassoldo and Giovanni Delli Zotti. Milan: Franco Angeli Editore.

Maalouf, A. 2000. *On Identity*. Translated by Barbara Bray. London: Harvill Press.

MacEvitt, Christopher Hatch. 2008. *The Crusades and the Christian World of the East: Rough Tolerance*. Middle Ages Series. Philadelphia: University of Pennsylvania Press.

Macfie, A. L. 1996. *The Eastern Question, 1774–1923*. London: Longman.

MacGaffey, Janet, and Rémy Bazenguissa-Ganga. 1999. "Personal Networks and Trans-Frontier Trade: Zairean and Congolese Migrants." In *Regionalisation in Africa: Integration and Disintegration*, edited by Daniel C. Bach, 179–87. Oxford: James Currey; Bloomington: Indiana University Press.

Madelin, Louis. 1918. *L'Expansion française de la Syrie au Rhin*. Paris: Plon-Nourrit.

Malinowski, Bronislaw. 1948. "Myth in Primitive Psychology." In *Magic, Science and Religion, and Other Essays*, selected by Robert Redfield. Prospect Heights, Ill.: Waveland Press.

Making Connections—San Antonio. 2002. Westside Survey. http://www.mc-sa.org/research/reports/default.asp, accessed May 8, 2009.

Marcus, E. S. 1998. "Maritime Trade in the Southern Levant from Earliest Times through the Middle Bronze IIA Period." Unpublished diss., Oxford University.

Márquez, Raquel. 1998. "Migration Processes: Impoverished Women Immigrants along the Texas/Mexico Border." PhD diss., University of Texas at Austin.

———. 2008. "Transborder Interactions and Transnational Processes in a Border Community, Laredo, Texas." In *Transformations of La Familia on the U.S.-Mexico Border*, edited by Raquel R. Márquez and Harriett D. Romo. Notre Dame, Ind.: University of Notre Dame Press.

Márquez, Raquel, Louis Mendoza, and Steve Blanchard. 2007. "Neighborhood Formation on the West Side of San Antonio, Texas." *Latino Studies* 5 (3): 288–316.

Martinez, Oscar J. 1975. "On the Size of the Chicano Population: New Estimates 1850–1900." Axtlan 6 (1): 43–67.

———. 1994. "The Dynamics of Border Interaction: New Approaches to Border Analysis." In *Global Boundaries*, edited by Clive H. Schofeld. Vol. 1 of *World Boundaries*. London: Routledge.

———, ed. 1996. *U.S.-Mexico Borderlands: Historical and Contemporary Perspectives*. Wilmington, Del.: Scholarly Resources.

Masalha, Nur-eldeen. 1999. "The 1967 Palestinian Exodus." In *The Palestinian Exodus*,

1948–1998, edited by Ghada Karmi and Eugene Cotran. New York: Ithaca Press, 63–109.

Massey, Douglas S. 1987. *Return to Aztlan: The Social Process of International Migration from Western Mexico*. Berkeley: University of California Press.

Massey, Douglas S., Luin Goldring, and Jorge Durand. 1994. "Continuities in Transnational Migration: An Analysis of Nineteen Mexican Communities." *American Journal of Sociology* 99 (May): 6.

McDermott Hughes, David. 1999. "Refugees and Squatters: Immigration and the Politics of Territory on the Zimbabwe-Mozambique Border." *Journal of Southern African Studies*, 25 (4): 533–52.

McFarlane, A. 2003. *Mastabas at Saqqara: Kaiemheset, Kaipunesut, Kaiemsenu, Sehetepu and Others*. Australian Centre for Egyptology Reports no. 20. Oxford: Aris and Phillips.

Mearsheimer, John. 2001. "The Impossible Partition." *New York Times*, January 11.

Mearsheimer, John J., and Stephen Van Evera. "Redraw the Map, Stop the Killing." *New York Times*, April 19, 1999.

Medlicott, William N. 1938. *The Congress of Berlin and After*. London: Methuen.

Mendoza, Sylvia Paola. 2008. "Has Corn Inclusion into the NAFTA Agreement Exacerbated Poverty and Inequality in Mexico?" Unpublished master's thesis, Fletcher School, Tufts University.

Merkx, Jozef. 2002. "Refugee Identities and Relief in an African Borderland: A Study of Northern Uganda and Southern Sudan." *Refugee Survey Quarterly* 21 (1/2): 113–46.

Migdal, Joel S. 1988. *Strong Societies and Weak States: State-Society Relations and State Capabilities in the Third World*. Princeton: Princeton University Press.

———. 2001. *State in Society: Studying How States and Societies Transform and Constitute One Another*. Cambridge: Cambridge University Press.

Miles, William F. S. 2005. "Development, Not Division: Local versus External Perceptions of the Niger-Nigerian Boundary." *Journal of Modern African Studies* 43 (2): 297–320.

Milliken, Jennifer, and Keith Krause. 2002. "State Failure, State Collapse and State Reconstruction: Concepts, Lessons and Strategies." *Development and Change* 23 (5): 753–74.

Mishal, Shaul. 1978. "Coexistence in Protracted Conflict." In *West Bank/East Bank: The Palestinians in Jordan, 1949–1967*, 111–20. New Haven: Yale University Press.

Mitchell, Timothy. 1991. *Colonizing Egypt*. Berkeley: University of California Press.

———. 1999. "Society, Economy, and the State Effect." In *State/Culture: State-Formation after the Cultural Turn*, edited by George Steinmetz, 76–97. Ithaca: Cornell University Press.

———. 2002. *Rule of Experts: Egypt, Techno-politics, Modernity*. Berkeley: University of California Press.

Montejano, David. 1987. *Anglos and Mexicans in the Making of Texas, 1836–1986*. Austin: University of Texas Press.

Morris, Benny. 1987. *The Birth of the Palestinian Refugee Problem, 1947–1949*. Cambridge: Cambridge University Press.

———. 1999. *Righteous Victims: A History of the Zionist-Arab Conflict*. New York: Random House.

Morris, E. F. 2005. *The Architecture of Imperialism: Military Bases and the Evolution of Foreign Policy in Egypt's New Kingdom*. Leiden: Brill.

Morris, Stephen D. 2005. *Gringolandia: Mexican Identity and Perceptions of the United States*. New York: Rowman and Littlefield.

Mouriki, Doula. 1995. "Thirteenth Century Icon Painting in Cyprus." *Studies in Late Byzantine Painting*, 341–443. London: Pindar.

Muhawi, Ibrahim, and Sharif Kanaana. 1989. *Speak Bird, Speak Again: Palestinian Arab Folktales*. Berkeley: University of California Press.

Muldoon, James. 2003. *Identity on the Medieval Irish Frontier: Degenerate Englishmen, Wild Irishmen, Middle Nations*. Gainesville: University Press of Florida.

Mumford, Gregory. 1999. "Wadi Maghara." In *Encyclopedia of the Archaeology of Ancient Egypt*, edited by Kathryn A. Bard, 875–78. London: Routledge.

———. 2006. "Tell Ras Budran (Site 345): Defining Egypt's Eastern Frontier and Mining Operations in South Sinai during the Late Old Kingdom (Early EB IV/MB I)." *Bulletin of the American Schools of Oriental Research* 342: 13–67.

Mumford, Gregory, and S. Parcak. 2004. "Pharaonic Ventures into South Sinai: El-Markha Plain Site 346." *Journal of Egyptian Archaeology* 89: 83–116.

Napolitano, Janet. 2009. Keynote address presented at the conference "Toward a Better Border: The United States and Canada." Brookings Institute, Washington, D.C., March 25.

Nazzal, Nafez. 1978. *The Palestinian Exodus from Galilee*. Beirut: Institute for Palestine Studies, 1978.

Near, Henry. 1992. *The Kibbutz Movement: A History: Origins and Growth, 1909–1939*. Oxford: Oxford University Press.

Nel, Pierre. 2008. "Railroads—Farewell to San Miguel?" Unpublished manuscript.

Nevo, Joseph. 1998. "The Jordanian, Palestinian and the Jordanian-Palestinian Identities." Paper presented at the Fourth Nordic Conference on Middle Eastern Studies, "The Middle East in a Globalizing World." Oslo, August 13–16.

Newberry, Percy E. 1893. *Beni Hasan, Part I*. London: Egypt Exploration Fund.

Newman, David. 2006. "The Resilience of Border Conflict in an Era of Globalization." In *Territoriality and Conflict in an Era of Globalization*, edited by Miles Kahler and Barbara F. Walter, 85–110. New York: Cambridge University Press.

Nicolaou-Konnari, Angel. 1999. "The Encounter of Greeks and Franks in Cyprus in the Late Twelfth and Thirteenth Centuries Phenomena of Acculturation and Ethnic Awareness." PhD diss., University of Wales, Cardiff.

Nicolaou-Konnari, Angel, and Chris Schabel, eds. 2005. *Cyprus: Society and Culture, 1191–1374.* The Medieval Mediterranean, vol. 58. Leiden: Brill.

Nugent, Paul. 1996. "Arbitrary Lines and the People's Minds: A Dissenting View on Colonial Boundaries in West Africa." In *African Boundaries: Barriers, Conduits and Opportunities*, edited by Paul Nugent and A. I. Asiwaju, 35–67. London: Pinter.

———. 2002. *Smugglers, Secessionists and Loyal Citizens on the Ghana-Togo Frontier: The Lie of the Borderlands since 1914.* Oxford, U.K.: James Currey; Athens: Ohio University Press; Legon: Sub-Saharan.

Ohlson, Thomas, and Mimmi Söderberg. 2002. *From Intra-State War to Democratic Peace in Weak States.* Uppsala Peace Research Papers no. 5. Department of Peace and Conflict Research, Uppsala Universitet, Uppsala, Sweden.

Öktem, Kerem. 2005. "Reconstructing Geographies of Nationalism: Nation, Space and Discourse in Twentieth Century Turkey." PhD thesis, St. Antony's College, Oxford University.

Omi, Michael, and Howard Winant. 1994. *Racial Formation in the United States: From the 1960s to the 1990s.* New York: Routledge.

Oren, Eliezer D. 1987. "The 'Ways of Horus' in North Sinai." In *Egypt, Israel, Sinai: Archaeological and Historical Relationships in the Biblical Period*, edited by A. F. Rainey, 69–119. Tel Aviv: Tel Aviv University.

———. 1997. "The 'Kingdom of Sharuhen' and the Hyksos Kingdom." In *The Hyksos: New Historical and Archaeological Perspectives*, edited by Eliezer D. Oren, 253–83. Philadelphia: University Museum, University of Pennsylvania.

Oren, Eliezer D., and I. Gilead. 1981. "Chalcolitic Sites in Northeastern Sinai." *Tel Aviv* 8: 25–44.

Orhonlu, Cengiz. 1990. *Osmanlı İmperatorluğunda Derbend Teskilatı.* Istanbul: Istanbul Universitesi Edebiyat Fakültesi Yayınları.

Ortaylı, İlber. 1985. *Tanzimat'tan Cumhuriyet'e Yerel Yönetim Geleneği* İstanbul: Hil Yayın.

Ottaway, Marina, and Stefan Mair. 2004. "States at Risk and Failed States: Putting Security First." Carnegie Endowment for International Peace, Democracy and Rule of Law Project, Policy Outlook. Washington, D.C.: Carnegie Endowment for International Peace.

Paganele, Spuridonos K. 1882. *Odoiporikai Semeioseis: B', He stratiotike katalepsis Artes kai Thessalias.* Athens: Enoseos.

Papacostas, Tassos. 1999. "Secular Landholdings and Venetians in 12th-Century Cyprus." *Byzantinische Zeitschrift* 92 (2): 479–501.

———. 2006. "Architecture et communautés étrangères à Chypre aux XIe et XIIe siècles." In *Identités Croisées en un Milieu Méditerranéen: Le cas de Chypre*, edited by Sabine Fourrier and Giles Grivaud, 223–40. Mont-Saint-Aignan Cedex: Publications des Universités de Rouen et du Havre.

Papajani, Adrian. 2001. "Veprimtaria Ekonomike e Firmave Tregtare Çoba dhe Bianki." *Arkivi Shqiptar* 2: 19–28.

Payan, Tony. 2006. *The Three U.S.-Mexico Border Wars: Drugs, Immigration, and Homeland Security*. Westport, Conn.: Praeger.

Peach, James. 2005. "Modeling the Demographic Characteristics of the Paso del Norte Region." In *The U.S.-Mexican Border Environment: Dynamics of Human-Environment Interactions*, edited by Edward Sadalla. San Diego: San Diego State University Press.

Peckham, Robert Shannan. 2001. *National Histories, Natural States: Nationalism and the Politics of Place in Greece*. London: I. B. Tauris.

Peña, Devon G. 1997. *The Terror of the Machine: Technology, Work, Gender, and Ecology on the U.S.-Mexico Border*. Austin: Center for Mexican American Studies Books, University of Texas Press.

Peña, Sergio, and Cesar Fuentes. 2005. "Modelado del marco institucional gobernando el uso del suelo y los derechos del agua en la region fronteriza Mexico-Estados Unidos." In *The U.S.-Mexican Border Environment: Dynamics of Human-Environment Interactions*, edited by Edward Sadalla. San Diego: San Diego State University Press.

Pick, James B., Nanda Viswanathan, and James Hettrick. 2001. The U.S.-Mexican Borderlands Region: A Binational Spatial Analysis. *Social Science Journal* 38: 567–95.

The Population of Macedonia: Evidence of the Christian Schools. 1905. London: Ede, Allon and Townsend.

Portes, Alejandro, and Robert L. Bach. 1985. *Latin Journey: Cuban and Mexican Immigrants in the United States*. Berkeley: University of California Press.

Portes, Alejandro, and Ruben Rumbaut. 2006. *Immigrant America*. Berkeley: University of California Press.

Pratt, Mary Louise. 1992. *Imperial Eyes: Travel Writing and Transculturation*. London: Routledge.

Prawer, Joshua. 1972. *The Latin Kingdom of Jerusalem*. New York: Praeger.

———. 1980. *Crusader Institutions*. Oxford: Clarendon Press.

Prenkaj, Marjan. 1998. *Prizreni dhe Rrethina në Shekullin XIX dhe në Fillim te Shekullit XX*. Prishtinë: Instituti i Historisë.

Prutz, Hans. 1883. *Kulturgeschichte der kreuzzüge*. Berlin: E. S. Mittler und Sohn.

Pyenson, Lewis. 1993. *Civilizing Mission: Exact Sciences and French Overseas Expansion, 1830–1940*. Baltimore: Johns Hopkins University Press.

Quintero Nunez, Margarito, and Craig Forster. 2005. "Paso del Norte Air Quality." In

The U.S.-Mexican Border Environment: Dynamics of Human-Environment Interactions, edited by Edward Sadalla. San Diego: San Diego State University Press.

Raşid, Ahmed. 1874 [1291]. *Tarih-i Yemen ve San'a'*. 2 vols. Istanbul: Basiret Matbassı.

Reclus, Elisée. 1882. *The Earth and Its Inhabitants*. Edited by E. G. Ravenstein. Vol. 1 (Greece, Turkey in Europe, Rumania, Serbia, Montenegro, Italy, Spain, and Portugal). New York: D. Appleton.

Redford, Donald B., editor in chief. 2001. *The Oxford Encyclopedia of Ancient Egypt*. Oxford: Oxford University Press.

Reed, John. 1916. *The War in Eastern Europe*. London: Scribners.

Rey, Emmanuel Guillaume. 1866. *Essai sur la domination française en Syrie durant le moyen âge*. Paris: Impr. par E. Thunot et cie.

———. 1871. *Etude sur les monuments de l'architecture militaire des croisés en Syrie et dans l'île de Chypre*. Collection de documents inédits sur l'histoire de France. Paris: Impr. nationale.

———. 1972. *Les colonies franques de Syrie aux XIIème et XIIIème siècles*. New York: AMS Press.

Richard, Jean. 1979. "Le peuplement latin et syrien en Chypre au XIIIe siècle." *Byzantinische Forschungen* 7: 157–73.

———. 1987. "Culture franque et culture grecque: Le royaume de Chypre au XVème siècle." *Byzantinische Forschungen* 11: 399–415.

———. 1991. "Culture franque, culture grecque, culture arabe, dans le royaume de Chypre au XIIIème et au début du XIVème siècle." *Hawliyat Far' al-Adab al-'Arabiyah (Annales du Département des Lettres Arabes)* 6 (B): 235–45.

Richard, S. 1987. "Question of Nomadic Incursions at the End of the 3rd Millennium BC." In *Studies in the History and Archaeology of Jordan*, vol. 3, edited by A. Hadidi. Amman: Department of Antiquities.

Richards, Paul. 1996. "The Sierra Leone-Liberia Boundary Wilderness: Rain Forests, Diamonds and War." In *African Boundaries: Barriers, Conduits and Opportunities*, edited by Paul Nugent and A. I. Asiwaju, 205–21. London: Pinter.

Richardson, Chad. 1999. *Batos, Bolillos, Pochoss, and Pelados: Class and Culture on the South Texas Border*. Austin: University of Texas Press.

Rizkana, Ibrahim, and Jürgen Seeher. 1989. *Maadi 3: The Non-Lithic Small Finds and the Structural Remains of the Predynastic Settlement*. Mainz: Philip von Zabern.

Rogan, Eugene L. 1999. *Frontiers of the State in the Late Ottoman Empire: Transjordan, 1850–1921*. Cambridge: Cambridge University Press.

Roitman, Janet. 2001. "New Sovereigns? Regulatory Authority in the Chad Basin." In *Intervention and Transnationalism in Africa: Global-Local Networks of Power*, edited by Thomas M. Callaghy, Ronald Kassimir, and Robert Latham, 240–66. Cambridge: Cambridge University Press.

Romero, Francisco. 2007. *Hyperborder: The Contemporary U.S.-Mexico Border and Its Future*. New York: Princeton Architectural Press.

Romo, Harriett D. 2008. "The Extended Border: A Case Study of San Antonio as a Transnational City." In *Transnational Families on the Southwest Borderlands*, edited by Raquel R. Márquez and Harriett D. Romo. Notre Dame, Ind.: University of Notre Dame Press.

Rosales, Rodolfo. 2000. *The Illusion of Inclusion: the Untold Political Story of San Antonio*. Austin: University of Texas Press.

Rosenau, James N. 1993. "Coherent Connection of Commonplace Contiguity? Theorizing about the California-Mexico Overlap." In *The California-Mexico Connection*, edited by Abraham F. Lowenthal and Katrina Burgess. Stanford: Stanford University Press.

Rotberg, Robert I. 2003. "Failed States, Collapsed States, Weak States: Causes and Indicators." In *State Failure and State Weakness in a Time of Terror*, edited by Robert Rotberg. Washington, D.C.: Brookings.

Rubio, Blanca. 2003. "The Mexican Countryside and NAFTA". *Voices of Mexico* 63: 55–58.

Sack, Robert David. *Human Territoriality: Its Theory and History*. Cambridge: Cambridge University Press, 1986.

Sadowski-Smith, Claudia, ed. 2002. *Globalization on the Line: Culture, Capital and Citizenship at U.S. Borders*. New York: Palgrave.

Saenz, Rogelio. 2004. *Latinos and the Changing Face of America*. The American People: Census 2000 series. New York: Russell Sage Foundation; Washington, D.C.: Population Reference Bureau.

Sahlins, Peter. 1988. *Boundaries: The Making of France and Spain in the Pyrenees*. Berkeley: University of California Press.

Said, Edward *Orientalism*. New York: Vintage, 1979.

———. 1984. "Reflections on Exile." *GRANTA* 13: 159–72.

———. 1994. *Culture and Imperialism*. New York: Vintage Books.

Salzinger, Leslie. 2003. "Re-forming the 'Traditional Mexican Woman': Making Subjects in a Border Factory." In *Ethnography at the Border*, edited by Pablo Vila, 46–72. Minneapolis: University of Minnesota Press.

Samatar, Said S. 1985. "The Somali Dilemma: Nation in Search of a State." In *Partitioned Africans: Ethnic Relations across Africa's International Boundaries, 1884–1984*, edited by A. I. Asiwaju, 155–93. London: C. Hurst; Lagos: University of Lagos Press.

Sayigh, Rosemary. 1998. "Palestinian Women as Tellers of History." *Journal of Palestine Studies* 27 (2): 42–58.

Schabel, Chris. 2000. "Archbishop Elias and the Synodicum Nicosiense." *Annuarium Historiae Conciliorum* 32 (1): 72.

———. 2001. *The Synodicum Nicosiense and Other Documents of the Latin Church of Cyprus, 1196–1373*. Nicosia: Cyprus Research Center.

———. 2006. "The Myth of Queen Alice and the Subjugation of the Greek Clergy on Cyprus." In *Identités Croisées en un Milieu Méditerranéen: Le cas de Chypre*, edited by Sabine Fourrier and Gilles Grivaud, 257–77. Mont-Saint-Aignan Cedex: Publications des Universités de Rouen et du Havre.

Schiff, Benjamin. 1995. *Refugees unto the Third Generation: UN Aid to the Palestinians*. Syracuse, N.Y.: Syracuse University Press.

Schlumberger, Gustave Leon. 1954. *Numismatique de l'Orient latin*. Graz, Austria: Akademische Druck-u. Verlagsanstalt.

Schmidt, Heike. 1996. "Love and Healing in Forced Communities: Borderlands in Zimbabwe's War of Liberation." In *African Boundaries: Barriers, Conduits and Opportunities*, edited by Paul Nugent and A. I. Asiwaju, 183–204. London: Pinter.

Schneckener, Ulrich, ed. 2004. States at Risk: Fragile Staaten als Sicherheits- und Entwicklungsproblem. SWP-Studie. Berlin: Stiftung Wissenschaft und Politik.

Schryver, James G. 2005. "Spheres of Contact and Instances of Interaction in the Art and Archaeology of Frankish Cyprus, 1191–1359." PhD diss., Cornell University.

———. 2006a. "Is There ONE Crusader Archaeology?" In *SOMA 2004: Symposium on Mediterranean Archaeology: Proceedings of the Eighth Annual Meeting of Postgraduate Researchers*, edited by Jo Day et al. BAR international series, 1514. Oxford: Archaeopress.

———. 2006b. "Monuments of Identity: Latin, Greek, Frank and Cypriot?" In *Identités Croisées en un Milieu Méditerranéen: Le cas de Chypre*, edited by Sabine Fourrier and Giles Grivaud, 385–405. Mont-Saint-Aignan Cedex: Publications des Universités de Rouen et du Havre.

———. 2008. "Cyprus at the Crossroads: Understanding the Paths Taken in the Art and Architecture of Frankish Cyprus." In *POCA 2005: Postgraduate Cypriot Archaeology: Proceedings of the Fifth Annual Meeting of Young Researchers on Cypriot Archaeology, Department of Classics, Trinity College, Dublin, 21–22 October 2005*, edited by Giorgos Papantoniou, Aoife Fitzgerald, and Siobhán Hargis. BAR International Series, 1803. Oxford: Archaeopress.

Schulz, Helena Lindholm, with Juliane Hammer, 2003. *The Palestinian Diaspora: Formation of Identities and Politics of Homeland*. London: Routledge.

Schulz, R., and M. Seidel, eds. 1998. *Egypt: The World of the Pharaohs*, Cologne: Könneman.

Scott, James. 1998. *Seeing like a State: How Certain Schemes to Improve the Human Condition Have Failed*. New Haven: Yale University Press.

Segev, Tom. 1986. *1949: The First Israelis*. New York: Henry Holt.

Sergeant, Lewis. 1897. *Greece in the Nineteenth Century: A Record of Hellenic Emancipation and Progress: 1821–1897*. London: T. Fisher Unwin.

Sfeka-Theodosiou, Aggelike. 1989. "He prosartese tes Thessalias: He prote fase sten ensomatose mias Hellenikes eparchias sto Helleniko kratos (1881–85)." PhD thesis, Aristoteleion University, Thessalonike.

Shaw, Ian, ed. 2000. *The Oxford History of Ancient Egypt*, Oxford: Oxford University Press.

Siddiq, Muhammad 1995. "On the Ropes of Memory: Narrating the Palestinian Refugees." In *Mistrusting Refugees*, edited by E. Valentine Daniel and John Chr. Knudsen. Berkeley: University of California Press.

Simon, Joel. 1997. *Endangered Mexico: An Environment on the Edge*. San Francisco: Sierra Club Books.

Simons, Chaim. 1988. *International Proposals to Transfer Arabs from Palestine, 1895–1947: A Historical Survey*. Hoboken, N.J.: Ktav.

Slyomovics, Susan. 1998. *The Object of Memory: Arab and Jew Narrate the Palestinian Village*. Philadelphia: University of Pennsylvania Press.

Smail, R. C. 1956. *Crusading Warfare, 1097–1193*. Cambridge Studies in Medieval Life and Thought, new ser., vol. 3. Cambridge: Cambridge University Press.

Soulard, Thierry. 2006. "L'architecture gothique grecque du royaume des Lusignan: Les cathédrales de Famagouste et Nicosia." In *Identités Croisées en un Milieu Méditerranéen: Le cas de Chypre*, edited by Sabine Fourrier and Giles Grivaud, 355–84. Mont-Saint-Aignan Cedex: Publications des Universités de Rouen et du Havre.

Southall, Aidan. 1985. "Partitioned Alur." In *Partitioned Africans: Ethnic Relations across Africa's International Boundaries 1884–1984*, edited by A. I. Asiwaju, 87–103. London: C. Hurst; Lagos: University of Lagos Press.

Stary, Bruno. 1999. "Cross-Border Trade in West Africa: The Ghana-Côte d'Ivoire Frontier." In *Regionalisation in Africa: Integration and Disintegration*, edited by Daniel C. Bach, 169–77. Oxford: James Currey; Bloomington: Indiana University Press.

Stavans, Ilan. 2003. *Spanglish: The Making of a New American Language*. New York: HarperCollins.

Stea, David. 2000. "El 'Cordon' y la 'Region Beige': Un Panorama." *Sociotam* 10 (1).

Stea, David, Silvia Elguea, and Camilo Perez Bustillo. 1997. "Environment, Development, and Indigenous Revolution in Chiapas.," In *Life and Death Matters: Human Rights and the Environment at the End of the Millennium*, edited by Barbara Rose Johnston, 213–37. Walnut Creek, Calif.: Altamira Press.

Stephanopoli, I. Z. 1903a. *Grecs et Bulgares en Macédoine*. Athens: Imprimerie Anestis Constantinidis.

———. 1903b. *Macédoine et Macédoniens*. Athens: Imprimerie Anestis Constantinidis.

Stephen, Lynn. 2007. *Transborder Lives: Indigenous Oaxacans in Mexico, California, and Oregon*. Durham, N.C.: Duke University Press.

Stevenson, William Barron. 1968. *The Crusaders in the East: A Brief History of the Wars of Islam with the Latins in Syria during the Twelfth and Thirteenth Centuries*. Beirut: Lebanon Bookshop.

Stoddard, Ellwyn R. 2001. *U.S.-Mexico Borderland Issues: The Bi-national Boundary, Immigration and Economic Policies*. Vol. 1 of the Borderlands Trilogy. El Paso, Texas: Promontory.

———. 2002. *U.S.-Mexico Borderlands Studies: Multidisciplinary Perspectives and Concepts*. El Paso, Texas: Promontory.

Stoler, Ann Laura. 2002. "Colonial Archives and the Arts of Governance." *Archival Science* 2 (1–2): 87–109.

Stoler, Ann Laura, and Frederick Cooper. 1997. "Between Metropole and Colony." In *Tensions of Empire: Colonial Cultures in a Bourgeois World*, edited by Frederick Cooper and Ann Laura Stoler, 1–55. Berkeley: University of California Press.

Strassaldo, R. 1989. "Border Studies: The State of the Art in Europe." In *Borderlands in Africa*, edited by Anthony I. Asiwaju and P. O. Adeniyi. Lagos: University of Lagos Press.

Strong, Frederick. 1842. *Greece as a Kingdom; or, A Statistical Description of That Country*. London: Longman, Brown, Green and Longmans.

Strudwick, Nigel. 2005. *Texts from the Pyramid Age*. Leiden: Brill.

Stylianou, Andreas, and Judith A. Stylianou. 1964. *The Painted Churches of Cyprus*. Stourbridge: Mark & Moody.

Suarez-Orozco, Carola, and Marcelo M. Suarez-Orozco. 2001. *Children of Immigration*. Cambridge, Mass: Harvard University Press.

Svolopoulos, K. 1992. "O Kōnstantinos Paparrēgopoulos kai ē Chartografēsē tēn Chersonēsou tou Aimou apo ton Heinrich Kiepert." In *Afierōma eis ton Kōnstantinon Vavouskon*. Thessaloniki: Ekdoseis Sakkoula.

Tableau Ethnocratique des pays du sud-est de l'Europe par Heinrich Kiepert. 1878. Berlin: Imprimerie de Kerskes and Hohmann.

Tanfilov, Tanhum. 2001. *Stories of Tanhum*. Edited by Yona Ben-Yaakov and Miriam Shion. Tel Aviv: Degania Alef.

Tatsios, Theodore George. 1984. *The Megali Idea and the Greek-Turkish War of 1897: The Impact of the Cretan Problem on Greek Irredentism, 1866–1897*. Boulder, Colo.: East European Monographs.

Tiemann, Mary. 2000. *NAFTA: Related Environmental Issues and Initiatives*. U.S. Department of State. http://fpc.state.gov/fpc/6143.htm, accessed January 1, 2005.

Tilly, Charles. 1992. *Coercion, Capital, and European States, AD 990–1992*. Cambridge, Mass.: Blackwell.

———. 1999. "Survey Article: Power—Top Down and Bottom Up." *Journal of Political Philosophy* 7 (3): 330–52.

———. 2004. "Social Boundary Mechanisms," *Philosophy of the Social Sciences* 24: 211–36.

———. 2005. *Identity, Boundaries and Social Ties*. Boulder, Colo.: Paradigm.

Timothy, Dallen J. 2001. *Tourism and Political Boundaries*. New York: Routledge.

Todorova, Maria. 1997. *Imagining the Balkans*. New York: Oxford University Press.

Tozer, Henry Fanshawe. 1869. *Researches in the Highlands of Turkey*. London: John Murray.

Troen, S. Ilan. 2003. *Imagining Zion: Dreams, Designs, and Realities in a Century of Jewish Settlement*. New Haven: Yale University Press.

Tronvoll, Kjetil. 1999. "Borders of Violence—Boundaries of Identity: Demarcating the Eritrean Nation-state." *Ethnic and Racial Studies* 22 (6/November): 1037–60.

Trouillot, Michel-Rolph. 2001. "The Anthropology of the State in the Age of Globalization." *Current Anthropology* 42: 125–38.

Tuan, Yi-Fu. 1977. *Space and Place: The Perspective of Experience*. Minneapolis: University of Minnesota Press.

Turner, Charles D. 2000. "Water Issues along the Rio Grande Elephant Butte Reservoir: A Water Quality and Quantity Assessment." In *The U.S.-Mexican Border Environment: Water Issues along the U.S.-Mexican Border*, edited by Paul Westerhoff, 9–20. San Diego: San Diego State University Press.

Turner, Michael, Khaled Nassar, and Nader Khateeb. 2005. *Crossing the Jordan: Concept Document to Rehabilitate, Promote Prosperity and Help Bring Peace to the Lower Jordan River Valley*. Edited by Gidon Bromberg. Amman: EcoPeace/Friends of the Earth Middle East.

Turner, Victor. 1974. *Dramas, Fields, and Metaphors: Symbolic Action in Human Society*. Ithaca, N.Y.: Cornell University Press.

Ülkekul, Cevat. 1998. *Cumhuriyet Dönemi Türk Haritacılık Tarihi*. Istanbul: Dönence.

U.S. Census Bureau. 2000. http://www.census.gov/, accessed April 13, 2009.

———. 2008. U.S. Hispanic Population Surpasses 45 Million; Now 15 Percent of Total. Washington, D.C.: U.S. Census Bureau.

U.S. Department of Homeland Security. 2002. "Securing America's Borders Fact Sheet: Border Security. January 25." http://www.dhs.gov/xnews/releases/press_release_0052.shtm, accessed April 13, 2009.

U.S.-Mexico Border Health Commission. 2009. *Border Region*. http://borderhealth.org/border_region.php, accessed April 13, 2009.

Van Schoik, Rick. 2004. "Conservation Biology in the U.S.-Mexican Border Region." *World Watch* 17 (6): 36–39.

Vasquez, John. 1993. *The War Puzzle*. Cambridge: Cambridge University Press.

Veremis, Thanos. 1990. "From the National State to the Stateless Nation, 1821–1910." In *Modern Greece: Nationalism and Nationality*, edited by Martin Blinkhorn and Thanos Veremis. Athens: Sage-Eliamep.

Vila, Pablo, ed. 2003a. "The Polysemy of the Label 'Mexican.'" In *Ethnography at the Border*, edited by Pablo Vila, 105–40. Minneapolis: University of Minnesota Press.

———. 2003b. "Processes of Identification on the U.S.-Mexico Border." *Social Science Journal* 40: 607–25.

Vila, Pablo, and John A. Peterson. 2003. "Environmental Problems in Ciudad Juàrez-El Paso: A Social Constructionist Approach." In *Ethnography at the Border*, edited by Pablo Vila, 251–78. Minneapolis: University of Minnesota Press.

Vincent, Joan. 1990. *Anthropology and Politics: Visions, Traditions, and Trends.* Tucson: University of Arizona Press.

Vogel, C. 2004. *Ägyptische Festungen und Garnisonen bis zum Ende des Mittleren Reiches.* Hildesheim: Gerstenberg Verlag.

Walker, Mary Adelaide. 1864. *Through Macedonia to the Albanian Lakes.* London: Chapman and Hall.

Walker, Scott. 1997. "Ecotourism Demand and Supply in El Cielo Biosphere Reserve, Tamaulipas, Mexico." Master's thesis, Southwest Texas State University.

Ward, Peter. 1999. *Colonias and Public Policy in Texas and Mexico: Urbanization by Stealth.* Austin: University of Texas Press.

Warnock, John. 1995. *The Other Mexico: The North American Triangle Completed.* New York: Black Rose Books.

Weighill, Marie-Louise. 1968. "Palestinians in Exile: Legal, Geographical and Statistical." In Rivers without Bridges: A Study of the Exodus of the 1967 Palestinian Arab Refugees, edited by Peter Dodd and Halim Barakat. Beirut: Institute for Palestine Studies.

Weiner, Myron 1996. "Bad Neighbors, Bad Neighborhoods: An Enquiry into the Causes of Refugee Flows." *International Security* 21 (1): 5–42.

Westerhoff, Paul. 2000. *The U.S.-Mexican Border Environment: Water Issues along the U.S.-Mexican Border.* San Diego: San Diego State University Press.

Weyl Carr, Annemarie. 1995a. "Art in the Court of the Lusignan Kings." In *Cyprus and the Crusades: Papers Given at the International Conference "Cyprus and the Crusades," Nicosia, 6–9 September, 1994*, edited by N. Coureas and J. Riley-Smith, 239–74. Nicosia: Society for the Study of the Crusades and the Latin East and the Cyprus Research Centre.

———. 1995b. "Images of Medieval Cyprus." In *Visitors, Immigrants and Invaders in Cyprus*, edited by Paul W. Wallace, 87–103. Albany, N.Y.: Institute of Cypriot Studies, University at Albany, State University of New York.

Wharton, Annabel Jane. 1988. *Art of Empire: Painting and Architecture of the Byzantine Periphery: A Comparative Study of Four Provinces.* University Park: Pennsylvania State University Press.

Wilkinson, Henry Robert. 1951. *Maps and Politics: A Review of the Ethnographic Cartography of Macedonia.* Liverpool: Liverpool University Press.

William of Tyre. 1884. *Historia Rerum in Partibus Transmarinis Gestarum*. In *Recueil des Historiens des Croisades, Historiens Occidentaux*. Vol. 1. Paris: Imprimerie Royale.

Wilson, Thomas, and Hastings Donnan, eds. 1998. *Border Identities: Nation and State and International Frontiers*. New York: Cambridge University Press.

Winichakul, Thongchai. 1994. *Siam Mapped: A History of the Geo-Body of a Nation*. Honolulu: University of Hawai'i Press.

Woodward, John D., Jr. 2001. *Biometrics: Facing up to Terrorism*. Santa Monica, Calif.: Rand Corporation.

Wright, Melissas W. 2003. "The Politics of Relocation: Gender, Nationality, and Value in a Mexican Maquiladora." In *Ethnography at the Border*, edited by Pablo Vila, 23–45. Minneapolis: University of Minnesota Press.

Yasamee, F. A. K. 1996. *Ottoman Diplomacy: Abdulhamid and the Great Powers, 1878–1888*. Istanbul: Isis Press.

Yekutieli, Y. 1998. "The Early Bronze Age I of North Sinai: Social, Economic, and Spatial Aspects." PhD diss. Beer-Sheva: Ben Gurion University of the Negev.

Yıldız, Hakkı Dursun. 1992. *150. Yılında Tanzimat*. Ankara: Türk Tarih Kurumu.

Yosmaoğlu, I. K. 2006. "Counting Bodies, Shaping Souls: The 1903 Census and National Identity in Ottoman Macedonia." *International Journal of Middle East Studies* 38: 55–77.

Zartman, I. William. 1992. "Internationalization of Communal Strife: Temptations and Opportunities." In *The Internationalization of Communal Strife*, edited by Manus Midlarsky. New York: Routledge.

———, ed. 1995. *Collapsed States: The Disintegration and Restoration of Legitimate Authority*. Boulder, Colo.: L. Rienner.

Zerubavel, Yael. 1995. *Recovered Roots: Collective Memory and the Making of Israeli National Tradition*. Chicago: University of Chicago Press.

Zürcher, Erik Jan. 2003. "The Young Turks: Children of the Borderlands?" In *Ottoman Borderlands: Issues, Personalities and Political Changes*, edited by Kemal Karpat and Robert W. Zens. Madison: University of Wisconsin Press. 275–86.

CONTRIBUTORS

MIROSLAV BÁRTA, Czech Institute of Egyptology, Charles University, Egyptologist working in Egypt since 1991. His recent publications include *Sinuhe, the Bible and the Patriarchs* (Prague 2004) and *Abusir XIII: Tomb Complex of the Vizier Qar* (Prague 2009).

ISA BLUMI, New School for Social Research (MA) and New York University's joint History and Middle Eastern/Islamic Studies program (PhD, 2005). He teaches modern Middle Eastern and Balkan history at Georgia State University.

SHELLEY FELDMAN is director of Feminist, Gender and Sexuality Studies and professor of development sociology at Cornell University, and a visiting professor in Sociology at the Fernand Braudel Center at Binghamton University. Her ongoing research includes projects on moral regulation, social and spatial restructuring, state formation, and militarization. She is presently collaborating on a project to theorize militarism as a routine of everyday life with consequences for sovereignty, rights, and social relations. She co-edited the *International Social Science Journal* special issue "Moving Targets: Displacement, Impoverishment, and Development," which included her article "Bengali State and Nation Making: Partition and Displacement Revisited." Other contributions include "Social Regulation in the Time of War: Constituting the Current Crisis"; "Metaphor and Myth: Gender and Islam in Bangladesh"; and "Intersecting and Contesting Positions: World Systems, Postcolonial, and Feminist Theory."

GEORGE GAVRILIS is the author of *The Dynamics of Interstate Boundaries* (Cambridge University Press, 2008). He teaches in the Department of Government at the University of Texas at Austin.

MELISSA GRAY is completing her doctoral studies in Environmental Geography at Texas State University–San Marcos and is currently working as a geography instructor at the University of Wisconsin–Parkside.

[280] CONTRIBUTORS

RACHEL S. HAVRELOCK is assistant professor of Jewish Studies and English at the University of Illinois at Chicago.

RAQUEL R. MÁRQUEZ is an associate professor at the University of Texas at San Antonio. Her most recent publications are, with coeditor Harriett Romo, *Transformations of La Familia on the U.S.-Mexico Border* (University of Notre Dame Press, 2008) and, with coauthors Louis Mendoza and Steve Blanchard, "Neighborhood Formation on the West Side of San Antonio" in *Latino Studies* (2007).

HARRIETT ROMO is a professor in the Department of Sociology at the University of Texas at San Antonio. She is the coeditor, with Raquel R. Márquez, of the recent book *Transformations of La Familia on the U.S.-Mexico Border* (University of Notre Dame Press, 2008) and author of the review essay "Immigrants, Guest Workers, and Policy Issues: Perspectives on Mexican Transnationalism" in *Latin American Politics and Society* (2009). She teaches courses on border studies, immigration and race, and ethnic relations.

JAMES G. SCHRYVER is an assistant professor of art history at the University of Minnesota, Morris. In addition to his work on Cyprus, recent publications include the results of excavations in Petra, Jordan, and at the proposed site of Horace's Villa in Licenza, Italy.

DAVID STEA is a research associate at the Center for Global Justice, Mexico, and professor emeritus at Texas State University–San Marcos. His background is in psychology, engineering, and architecture, and his publications include the books *Image and Environment*, *Maps in Minds*, and *Environmental Mapping*, and 150 articles, monographs, and book chapters in several languages.

JUDITH VORRATH is a PhD student at the Center for Security Studies (CSS) at ETH Zurich and is working at the Swiss National Centre of Competence in Research (NCCR), "Challenges to Democracy in the 21st Century." She focuses on issues of conflict and democratization in the African Great Lakes region and has recently published "From Refugee Crisis to Reintegration Crisis? The Consequences of Repatriation to (Post-)Transition Burundi" in *L'Annuaire de l'Afrique des Grands Lacs 2007–2008*.

İPEK K. YOSMAOĞLU is assistant professor of Ottoman history at the University of Wisconsin–Madison. She is currently working on a book manuscript on religion, violence, and political culture in Ottoman Macedonia at the turn of the twentieth century.

I. WILLIAM ZARTMAN is Jacob Blaustein Professor Emeritus of International Organization and Conflict Resolution, former director of the Conflict Management Program at the Johns Hopkins University School of Advanced International Studies in Washington, D.C., and vice-president of the Council of American Overseas Research Centers (CAORC). He is the author or editor of many books and articles including *Imbalance of Power* (Lynne Rienner, 2009); *Negotiation and Conflict Management: Essays on Theory and Practice* (Routledge, 2008); *Peacemaking in International Conflict: Methods and Techniques* (United States Institute of Peace 2007); and *Cowardly Lions: Missed Opportunities to Prevent Deadly Conflict and State Collapse* (Lynne Rienner, 2008).

JAMIE ZECH is a doctoral student of environmental geography at Texas State University–San Marcos. Her research focuses include the social dimensions of the human-environment relationship, the dynamics of urban gentrification, and the geography of environmental movements.

INDEX

'Abdali, 77
Abdülhamid II, 59, 63
Abdullah, Emir, 192, 201, 202
Abishay, 34
Abydos, 25–26
Acuña, 112, 120
Aden, 74, 75, 76–77, 79
Ader, 32
Adriatic Sea, 68, 70, 80, 166
Aegean Islands, 68–69
Aegean Sea 46, 166, 182
African Americans: in segregated America, 8; on U.S.-Mexico border, 108, 222
African borderlands, 85–104; and double triangle of power relations, 85–86, 87; economic activities in, 94–96; identities in, 93–94; neo-patrimonial approach to, 88–89, 90, 99, 102–4; and scope of study, 90–92; and smuggling, 95–96; state presence in, 96; violence in, 99–100
Agios Stefanos, 162
Albania, 58–73, 79–80, 238; creation of borderland in, 58–60; Northern, 62–63; Ottoman economic policies in, 68–70; relation of, to Macedonia, 160, 176, 181, 184; and smuggling, 69, 70–73
Algeria, 14
Aliyas, 203

Alsace, 7
Amenemhat II, 35
Amenemhat III, 35, 36
Amman, 193, 200, 202, 205, 209
Anaki, 37
Andorra, 12
Angola-Zambia border, 100
Anglo-French boundary convention of 1923, 192
Antivari/Bar, 69
Apartheid, 6, 8, 250
Aqaba, 193
Arab-Israeli War of 1948, 198, 200, 206
Arab-Israeli War of 1967, 191, 202, 205, 206, 209–10, 247
Arab Legion Army, 204–5
Arab Revolt of 1936, 204
Arad, 28, 35
Arava, 189
Arizona, 108, 110, 112, 122
Arkata, 37
Armatolobryse, 44
Aroer, 32
Arta, 48, 54
Arta, Gulf of, 43
Ashkelon, 37
Asiatics. See Bedouin
'Asir, 74, 75
Assab, 79
Austria-Hungary, 59, 161

Bab ed-Dhra, 31, 32
Baja California, 110, 112, 126
Balkans: and Berlin Congress, 163–64; and ethnography, 167–69, 172, 183; in nineteenth century, 7, 161; and Ottoman Empire (*see* Albania)
Baltic states, 14
Bangladesh, 237, 238
Barsky, Moshe, 199
Bedouin: and Egypt, 21, 27, 31–36, 38–39; and Jordan Valley, 193, 197, 199, 201
Beer Resisim, 31
Belgium, nineteenth-century, 12
Beni Hassan, 34–35
Benin-Nigeria border, 95, 97, 98, 99
Berlin Conference of 1884–1885, 88
Berlin Congress of 1878: and Albania and Yemen, 54, 60, 62, 63–67, 68, 71, 75; and Berlin Treaty, 63; and legitimacy of boundaries, 12; and Ottoman Macedonia, 162–63, 174
Berlin Group, 36–37
Bethlehem, 195
Biafra, 14
Bianki, 68
Bismarck, Otto von, 163, 174, 177
Bithynia, 161
Black-and-white model, 7
Bojana River, 69, 70
Border Environment Cooperation Commission (BECC), 126–27
Border Industrialization Program, 129
Borderlands: anthropological studies of, 4; change in, 248–50; definitions of, 1–2, 236; and dimensions of analysis, 9–10; dynamics in, 11–14; global economy of, 238–39; models of, 6, 7–8, 246; policy formation in, 246–48; political science studies of, 4; spatio-territorial themes of, 235–38
Borderlands Interdisciplinary Project (BLIP), xi, 5
Borders: characteristics of, 6; definitions of, 5–6, 85; movement across, 240–41
Bosnia and Herzegovina, 60
Brazil-Venezuela border, 109
Brit Shalom, 202
Brittany, 246
Buffered model, 7–8
Buhari military regime, 99
Bulgaria, 160, 162–63, 173, 176–77, 182
Bulgarians, 165, 167–68, 169, 172–74, 175, 181
Byblos, 27, 28, 30, 35, 37
Byzantines, 140, 144, 145, 146, 155, 156

Cairo, 24
Canaan. *See* Egypt: contacts of, with Canaan
Cartography, 49–50, 63–64, 167, 179–84
Casamance, 249
Catalonia, 9, 14; Catalonians, 1; Cerdanya Valley, 9
Center for Environmental Management (CERM), 117
Chad Basin, 98
Chihuahua, 110, 113, 129
Cis-Jordan. *See* West Bank
Ciudad Acuña, 112, 120
Ciudad Juarez, 111, 114, 117, 123
Coahuila, 110, 112, 116
Çoba, 68
Colonias, 109–10, 112, 116, 229
Colorado, 113
Committee of Union and Progress, 161
Congo, 12, 86

Congress of Berlin. *See* Berlin Congress of 1878
Constantinople, 144, 156
Convention on the Suppression of Brigandage in 1856, 49, 51, 54
Côte d'Ivoire–Ghana border, 95, 97
Council of American Overseas Research Centers (CAORC), 5
Croatia, 14
Crusader states, 135–37, 140, 141, 146, 149, 151–53
Crusades: Third, 134; Fourth, 155
Cumbres de Monterrey, 116, 121
Cyprus: application of borderland models to, 135, 137–39, 142, 145–50, 154; Frankish (Lusignan), 8, 133–59, 250; Greek Orthodox population of, 134–35, 152–53; Green Line in, 6, 13, 238; integration of Franks and Greeks on, 139–41; modern day, 7, 9; Orthodox Church of, 145

Damascus, 193, 200
Darfur, 14
Dayton Conference of 1993, 12
Dead Sea, 26, 28, 32, 189, 211
Degania. *See* Kibbutz Degania Alef
Deming, 110
Den, 26
"Denkschrift über Albanien" (Lippich) 65
derbents, 44–45, 46
Deshasheh, 29
Deutoronomistic writings, 189, 192
d'Ibelin, Jean, 155
Djoser, 26, 27
Draç, 70
Drustvo Svetgo Save, 66
Dulcino. *See* Ulqin

Eagle Pass, 110
East Bank. *See* Transjordan
Egypt: ancient geographic borders of, 23, 38–39; application of borderland models to, 38; contacts of, with Canaan, 24–32, 35–37; contacts of, with Sinai, 24, 26–33, 35–36; Egyptology, 21–22; Middle Kingdom of, 22, 33, 34, 35, 36, 37, 38; nineteenth-century, 12; Old Kingdom of, 23, 27, 28, 30, 31, 37, 38; third millennium contacts of, with Levant, 21–39
Eilat, 28
El-Arish, 27, 31
El Cielo Biosphere Reserve, 121
Elephant Butte Dam, 113
El Paso, 111, 114, 117, 119
Emery, Colonial, 200
En Besor, 24, 25
English Channel, 109
En Ziq, 32
Epirus, 48, 175, 176
Ethiopia-Somalia-Kenya border, 100
Euphrates River, 193
European Union, 124, 129, 249
Evia, 43
Execration texts, 36–37

Famagusta, 143, 144, 146
Fatah, 210
Fida'iyin movement, 209
Fine, Yosef, 200
France: and cartography of Ottoman Empire, 49–50; colonial systems of, 94, 139, 142; influence of, in Cyprus, 136, 139, 145–46, 159; influence of, in Red Sea, 68, 75, 78–79
Franglais, 109
Frederick II, 147

Front Line States, 6
Fulcher of Chartres, 147–48

Gadsden Purchase, 217
Galilee, Sea of, 189, 200
Gaza, 27, 31, 242
Gebel Gunna, 24
Gebel Qaaqir, 31
General Agreement on Tariffs and Trade (GATT), 124
General Allotment Act of the 1880s, 107
Gennadius, Ioannis, 169–74, 178, 184
Ghana–Côte d'Ivoire border, 95, 97
Golan Heights, 189
Golo Brodo, 160
Great Britain: British Blue Book of 1889, 182; and colonialism, 94, 110, 242; influence of, in Aden, 74–78, 79; influence of, on Ottoman-Greek relations, 43, 48–49, 54; Mandate in Palestine (*see* Palestine)
Greece, 239; border of, with Ottoman-Empire (*see* Ottoman-Greek border); Greek Kingdom, 43, 176; and Macedonia, 160, 168–70, 172–79, 181–82; population of, in Cyprus, 137, 139, 143–44, 149, 155, 157; rapprochement of, in relations with Ottoman Empire, 52
Grey model, 7
Gruda, 72

Haci Zeynel, 68
Haddadin family, 196–97, 198, 200
Hamas, 202
Har Yaroham, 32
Har Zayyad, 32
Hausa, 93–94
Hawshabi, 76
Hebron Hills, 31

Hekenhenenu, 38
Hidalgo, 112
Hijaz, 74
Hijaz Railway, 192, 193, 201
Histadrut, 193
Hoti, 72
Hugh IV, 159

Ida, 29
Iktanu, 32
Imeni, 36
India, 237, 238, 239
Inshas, 36
Integrated Border Environmental Program (IBER), 126–27
Internal Macedonian Revolutionary Committee, 162
International Boundary and Water Commission (IBWC), 113, 126
International Red Cross, 205
Intifadas, 195, 208, 209, 247
Iraq, 193
Irbid, 200, 205
Ireland, 238
Iron Curtain, 6, 7, 13
Irredentism, 48, 54, 99
Isa Boletini, 68
İşkodra, 63, 65, 68–70, 71, 72, 241
İşkodra, Lake, 70
Israel: borderlands in (*see* Jordan River Valley); Green Line of, 6, 12, 211, 238; Jordan River border of (*see* Jordan River); national myths of, 194–95, 198, 203–4; and settlements in Palestine, 8, 208, 210–11; and Zionists/Zionism, 190, 193, 200–202, 203, 211
Israel-Jordan Peace Treaty of 1994, 191, 208
Italy, 59, 70, 72, 75, 78–79, 124
İzmir, 46

Jericho, 198, 205
Jerusalem, 143, 148, 189, 202, 207–8
Jerusalem, Latin Kingdom of, 148, 151
Jewish ghettos, 8
Jewish National Fund, 198, 210
Jim Crow era, 225
Jordan, Hashemite Kingdom of, 9, 189, 191, 205, 206, 208–9
Jordan River: and Allenby Bridge, 206, 212; and Bedouins, 32; as border, 190–91, 201–2; national myths of, 189, 192, 194, 198–99, 209, 211–14; and Sheikh Hussein Bridge, 205, 207; symbolism of, to refugees, 203–6, 208
Jordan River Valley: application of borderland models to, 208; pioneers of, 195–203; population and border shifts in, 192–93; refugees in, 203–12; symbolism of, 194–95
Joual, 109
Juarez, 111, 114, 117, 123

Kaaper, 28–29, 38
Kakopetria, 155
Karitza, 52
Kashmiri Line of Control (LOC), 6, 13, 238
Katang, 14
Kelmendi, 72
Kenya-Ethiopia-Somalia border, 100
Kerak, 197
Khakheperra, King, 34
Khaled Iskander, 31
Khebded, 36
Kheti, 34
Kheti III, 33, 38
Khirbet Iskander, 32
Khnumhotep II, 34
Kibbutz Degania Alef, 198–200, 201, 203, 204, 210

Kiepert, Heinrich, 171, 174–78
Kinneret (Sea of Galilee), 189, 200
Kivu, 14
Kom el-Rabia, 36
Korea, 238; DMZ of, 6, 238; 38th Parallel of, 13
Kosova, 58, 61, 63, 66, 71, 72
Kouklia-Stavros, 155
Krajina, 8
Kurdistan, 14

Lahj, 77
Lahj, Sultan of (Fadl b. Muhsin), 76–77, 78
Lahun, 26
La Paz Agreement of 1983, 126, 127
Laredo, 110, 114, 218, 220–24, 229; identity in, 228–32, 234; Laredo-Nuevo Laredo crossing, 124, 125
Latin Church, 142, 146
Latin East, 127–38, 147, 150; as integrated society, 138–41; as segregated society, 141–45, 152
Layered model, 7, 8
Lebanon, 65, 189, 193
Liberia–Sierra Leone border, 100
Lippich, Fredlich, 65–66
Lisht, 36
Lusignan, Guy de, 134, 155

Maadi, 24
Macedonia: ethnographic maps of, 162, 164, 168, 169–79; as Kafadartzi, 162; Kingdom of, 161; Ottoman, 162–84; Pirin, 160; in present day, 160
Maghrib, 8
Mala Prespa, 160
Malesia e Madhe, 61, 65
Malesore, 62, 66, 67
Malta, 68, 69

Manifest Destiny, 113
Mashabbe Sade, 32
Massawa, 78, 79
Mediterranean Sea, 23, 192, 193
Medua, 70
Memâlik-i Mahrûse-i Şâhâne, 162
Memphis, 36
Merikare, King, 33, 37
Mexicali, 126
Mexican Civil Rights Movement, 225, 226
Mexican Revolution, 106, 111, 112
Mexican-U.S. border. *See* U.S.-Mexican border
Mexico, Gulf of, 114
Mirgissa, 36–37
Models: application of, to policies, 246; black-and-white, 7; buffered, 7–8; grey, 7; layered, 7, 8; mixtures of, 7; spotty, 7, 8
Moldova (Moldovia), 9, 250
Molocha, 44
Montenegro, 58, 60–61, 63, 67–68, 69–70, 71–72
Monterrey, 218, 220, 221, 222; identity in, 232–33
Moutoullas, 156
Mozambique-Zimbabwe border, 94, 98
Mugar, 37
Muhsin, Fadl b., 76–77, 78
Mukha, 76, 79
Muqbil, Muhammad Nasir, 76

Nablus, 195, 211
Nagaland, 246
Naharaim hydroelectric plant, 201, 202
Nakba, 204
Naksa, al-. *See* Arab-Israeli War of 1967
Naqada, 24
Narda (Arta), 48, 54
Nationalism, 3, 14, 93–94, 235, 243, 245; Jewish, 194, 203, 213; Palestinian, 194, 203, 213; religious, 211
Nawamis, 24
Nazareth, 205
Neferhetep, 34
Negev, 24, 25, 30, 31, 32
New Mexico, 110, 113
Nicosia, 146
Nigeria-Benin border, 95, 97, 98, 99
Nigerian-Niger border, 93, 94, 95, 98
Niger-Nigerian border, 93, 94, 95, 98
Nikola, Prince, 68, 70
Nile Delta, 25, 27, 32, 35, 36, 38; Eastern Delta, 24, 28, 29, 32
Nile Valley, 23, 38
Normandy, 249
North American Development Bank (NADBank), 126–27
North American Free Trade Agreement (NAFTA): and border environment, 112–15; and border population, 111–12; and commerce and industry, 123–28; effects of, on U.S.-Mexican border, 16, 105–30, 224, 249; perceptions of, 115–16
Northern Ireland, 14
Nubia, 35, 36, 38
Nuevo Laredo, 114, 122, 130, 220, 221
Nuevo Leon, 112, 121, 218
Nuzuh, 204

Ocampo, 112
Odessa, 152
Ohrid Lake, 160
Oranais, 14
Ottoman Empire: and Albania (*see* Albania); border of, with Greece (*see* Ottoman-Greek border); conflict of, with Russia, 48; control of, over

Macedonia, 161; facing expansionist threats, 59; rapprochement of, in relations with Greece, 52; and Yemen (*see* Yemen)
Ottoman-Greek border, 40–56, 102; application of borderland models to, 41–43, 48, 54–55; banditry and smuggling along, 42, 46, 47–48, 53–54; cooperation of border guards on, 41–42; creation of, 43; customs extraction at, 47; increased investment on, 49–50; militarization of, 42; state building on, 45–46

Pakistan, 237, 238
Palestine: and ancient Egypt, 30, 35, 37, 38; and British Mandate, 190, 192–93, 200–201, 205, 242; and Christians, 195–96; national myths of, 190–91, 194, 195–97, 204–7; and refugees, 203–12
Palestinian Liberation Organization (PLO), 207, 210
Papago (Tohono O'Otam), 107–8
Paparrigopoulos, Konstantinos, 174–79
Paris Peace Conference of 1919, 193
Paşa, Haci Hüseyin, 46
Pecos River, 114
Peloponnese, 175
Petra, 208
Phanariots, 14
Piedras Negras, 120
Pirin Macedonia, 160
Pocho, 109
Portunol, 109
Prespa Lake, 160
Prizren, 73
Programa Nacional Fronterizo (PRONAF), 121

Prohibition, 112, 121
Punta, 43

Qaa, 26

Ramallah, 195, 196–97
Ravendel family, 155
Red Cross, International, 205
Red Sea, 68, 74, 75, 78, 79, 80
Richard the Lionheart, 134
Rio Bravo. *See* Rio Grande
Rio Conchos, 112, 114
Rio Grande: Big Bend, 114, 116, 122; as border, 108, 110, 112, 113; Republic of, 107; Rio Grande Compact Commission, 113; Valley, 107, 114, 123; water allocation from, 113–14
Roman Empire, 3, 14, 137
Rumeli, 162
Russo-Turkish War of 1877 (Russo-Ottoman War), 54, 162
Rutenberg, Pinchas, 202

Sabil, Abdallah Bey, 77
Salt, 199–200, 205
Samakh, 198
San Antonio, 110, 116, 125, 218, 220–22; identity in, 224–28, 232, 233–34; and Instituto Cultural de Mexico, 223; museums of, 223–24; regional *clubes* in, 223; transnational community of, 222–24; and Universidad Nacional Autonoma de Mexico, 221
San Diego, 110
Sandinistas, 117
San Luis Potosi, 119
Sapa, 37
Saqqara, 26, 29
Saqqara/Brussels group, 36–37

Saranda Kolones, 155
Schengen Agreement, 249
Schleswig-Holstein, 7
Sekhemkhet, 26
Senegambian Confederation, 96
Senusret I, 35
Senusret II, 34
Senusret III, 35, 36
September 11, 2001, 108, 117, 119, 125, 128, 130
Serbia, 60, 63, 68, 71, 176–77
Serer, 29
Shabe, 98
Shephelal, 25
Shiloh, 189
Shkoder/Scutari, 70
Shkoder, Lake, 72
Shobak, 196, 197
Sicily, 68, 69
Sidon, 193
Sierra Leone–Liberia border, 100
Sinai. *See* Egypt: contacts of, with Sinai
Sinuhe, 21, 22, 34
Slavs, 68–69, 167, 172–73, 184
Slovenia, 14
"Smart Border" Program, 128–29
Somalia-Kenya-Ethiopia border, 100
Sonora, 108, 110, 116
South Africa–Front Line States border, 6
Spanglish, 109
Spotty model, 7, 8
Stanford Map, 169–74
Sudan, 249; border with Uganda, 100
Sullogos pros Diadosin tōn Ellinēkōn Grammatōn, 175
Syria, 189, 193, 200, 214

Tableau Ethnocratique des pays du sud-est de l'Europe, 167, 169, 171
Ta'izz, 74, 75, 77
Tamaulipas, 110, 121, 129
Tamil Eelam, 249
Tanfilov, Tanhum, 199–200
Tanzimat reforms, 45, 58–59, 63
Tarkhan, 26
Tartars, 172–73
Tel Arad, 24
Tell el-Dabba, 35–36
Tell el-Farain, 28
Tell el-Hayat, 32
Tell el-Yahudia, 36
Tell Ibrahim el-Awad, 28
Tell Um Hammad, 32
Tel Sakan, 24
Templars, 134, 148
Tepa, 29
Texas, 107, 110, 112–14, 115, 120; nineteenth-century, 12; Texas State University, 107; trade of, with Mexico, 124; University of Texas–Brownsville, 107
Thessaly. *See* Tirhala
Thrace, 172, 174, 175, 176
Tihama, 75
Tirhala, 46, 48, 54, 175
TLCAN. *See* North American Free Trade Agreement
Tohono O'Otam, 107–8
Transjordan: detachment of, from Mandate Palestine, 193; Egyptian influence in, 30, 31, 37; geography of, 189, 192; pioneers in, 197, 199–202; refugees in, 204–5
Transnistria, 9
Treaty of Guadalupe Hidalgo, 217
Trikkala. *See* Tirhala
Tucson, 110
Tunisia, 68
Tuz, 72

Uganda-Sudan border, 100
Uj, 25
Ulazza, 37
Ulqin, 67, 68, 69, 70
Um-Juni, 198
United Nations, 207, 208, 210
U.S. Border Patrol, 111
U.S.-Canada border, 6, 117–18, 125; Quebec–New England border, 109
USEPA/SEMARNAP Border XXI Agreement, 127–28
U.S.-Mexican border: application of borderland models to, 106; Arizona-Sonora border, 106; border crossings at, 118–19; and *Bracero* Program, 111–12, 240; California–Baja California border, 106, 110; and *chorizo*, 107, 114; Ciudad Juarez–El Paso border, 122, 127, 130; Great Wall and "hardening" of, 107–8; identity along, 108–10; and *maquiladora* program, 111–12; and NAFTA (*see* North American Free Trade Agreement); Texas-Mexico border, 7, 108, 110, 116, 229; Tijuana–San Ysidro border, 122; tourism along, 119–23; and transnational identity research, 220–22
U.S.-Mexico War of 1848, 217

Venetians, 134, 156
Venezuela-Brazil border, 109
Vietnam, 238

Wadi Digla, 24
Wadi Faynan, 32
Wadi Maghara, 24, 26, 29, 36
Wadi Riqita, 28
Wadi Tumilat, 36

Wallachia, 14, 176
War on Drugs, 108, 129
War on Terror, 108, 118, 119, 129
Ways of Horus, 24, 28–29, 35–36
Weizmann, Chaim, 200
Wenet, 29
Weni, 29
West African colonial systems, 94
West Bank, 8, 9, 242; geography of, 189; modern history of, 191; pioneers in, 195, 201; refugees in, 204–6, 208–9, 211–12
Westphalian system, 3, 236, 242
White Paper of 1922, 193
World Bank governance indicators, 87–88
World War I: lead-up to, 79, 161; post-, 111, 141

Yarmuk River, 200, 202
Yemen, 58–62, 73–80, 238; creation of borderland in, 58–60; Italian interference in, 78–79; new opportunities and changing politics in, 75–78; smuggling and Ottoman economic policies in, 73–75
Yishuv, 198
Young Turks (Committee of Union and Progress), 161
Yugoslavia, 238, 239
Yuma, 112

Zahorov, Konstantin, 74
Zaltzman, Yosef, 199–200
Zambia-Angola border, 100
Zarqa, 202, 205, 207
Zarqa River, 202
Zarqa River Valley, 191
Zimbabwe-Mozambique border, 94, 98

LaVergne, TN USA
06 December 2009

166134LV00003B/6/P